Child Abuse

Child Abuse

AN EVIDENCE BASE FOR CONFIDENT PRACTICE

Fifth edition

David Wilkins, David Shemmings and Claire Pascoe

Open University Press

Open University Press
McGraw-Hill Education
8th Floor, 338 Euston Road
London
England
NW1 3BH

and Two Penn Plaza, New York, NY 10121-2289, USA

First published 1993
Second edition 2000
Third edition 2006
Fourth edition 2012
First published in this fifth edition 2019

Commissioning Editor: Vivien Antwi
Editorial Assistant: Karen Harris
Content Product Manager: Ali Davis

A catalogue record of this book is available from the British Library

ISBN-13: 9780335248087
ISBN-10: 033524808X
eISBN: 9780335248094

Library of Congress Cataloging-in-Publication Data
CIP data applied for

Typeset by Transforma Pvt. Ltd., Chennai, India

Fictitious names of companies, products, people, characters and/or data that may be used herein (in case studies or in examples) are not intended to represent any real individual, company, product or event.

Printed in Great Britain by Bell and Bain Ltd, Glasgow

Praise for this book

"This is an important addition to the child abuse and child protection literature. Drawing from a variety of current research carried out by professionals and academics from a range of disciplines, this book will be an excellent companion for students, academics and practitioners working in this challenging but important area of work."

Dr Elena Martellozzo, Online child protection expert.
Middlesex University, UK

"This is a comprehensive text which explores the legislative, cultural and historic context in which today's child protection has been shaped. Building on previous editions, it provides a valuable and up-to-date insight into contemporary child protection practice. The book presents theoretical concepts and studies in an accessible way and will enable readers to develop an evidence-based approach and understanding of a range of issues facing child protection professionals".

Rebecca Avery, Education Safeguarding
Advisor (Online Protection), The Education People

"How did we get to where we are in our response to child abuse – and what might the future hold? This book provides a timely, comprehensive and thoughtful response to this question; demonstrating the importance of understanding our journey to present day practices if we are to improve the protection of children in the future. Integrating historical, sociological, psychological and biological perspectives, and grappling with the ethical as well as practical challenges of child abuse responses, the authors provide us with an overview upon which we must learn from past successes, as well as tragedies, as we utilise and further build an evidence base for confident social work practices around the world."

Dr Carlene Firmin, Principal Research Fellow in
Contextual Safeguarding, University of Bedfordshire, UK

Dedicated to the memory of the late Brian Corby and to the thousands of child protection professionals committed to keeping children safe.

Acknowledgements

We would like to thank the following people for their contributions and their help, without which this book would not have been written: Hayley Wilkins, Yvonne Shemmings, and Shirley Pascoe for their remarkable patience and unwavering support; Vivien Antwi (Commissioning Editor), Ali Davis (Content Product Manager) and Karen Harris (Editorial Assistant) from McGraw-Hill, for their skilled and expert guidance through the writing process, and for overseeing the production of this book.

Contents

List of tables

Introduction

The late Brian Corby

The first three editions of this book were written by Brian Corby (1946–2007), one of the best-known and most respected experts in the field of child protection. In this, the fifth edition, we would again like to pay tribute to his work and contribution.

Providing a practitioner knowledge base

It was noted in the Introduction to the first edition of this book that it 'is important that practitioners are fully conversant with what is known about child abuse and that they are able to weigh up the strengths and weaknesses of that knowledge'. This remains the case with this fifth edition. None of the editions of the book to date have attempted to provide a 'how to' guide to child protection and this again remains the case with this edition. Rather, the target audience is that of the relatively autonomous practitioner developing her/his judgement about child abuse based on knowledge derived not only from academic research and evaluation of practice interventions but also from studies on the history, politics and social construction of the subject.

So what has changed since the last edition?

Central government policy and child protection

We stated in the previous edition that 'Since 1993 the task of protecting children has become more and more determined by central government policy and guidelines.' This is arguably still the case. This trend was also in evidence at the time of the second and third editions of this book, published in 2000 and 2006 respectively. The 1990s witnessed a considerable shift in thinking about how best to organise for and respond to child protection concerns. First, serious child abuse was seen to be a relatively rare occurrence among all the referrals made about child care concerns, and, second, by placing all its focus on such serious abuse, state intervention to support families with children in need was being neglected. A third issue was that the intrusive style and nature of child protection interventions were leading to an alienation of families and, therefore, to less trust on their part in state services to provide support and help. These findings and concerns led to considerable policy changes and a shift in emphasis towards the idea of 'safeguarding' children by focusing on needs-led work with children and their families. The comprehensive assessment framework, introduced in 2000, set out how this could be achieved (Department of Health 2000).

The publication of this framework was followed by the Every Child Matters (DoH, 2003) agenda and later by Professor Eileen Munro's report on the state of CP in England. These sources all sought to highlight in different ways the importance of early, effective help being given to children who may otherwise require a more expensive and more intrusive form of intervention later on.

Since the last edition we have witnessed a significant period of austerity in the UK caused partly by the global financial crisis of 2008 and we have seen a significant reduction in preventive services across the country. Coupled with a sometimes hostile response to child deaths from parts of the media which castigates child protection professionals, especially social workers, we have a perfect storm which, arguably, has taken child protection policy and practice back years, to a more punitive configuration based upon blame.

Victoria Climbié, Peter Connelly and other tragic child deaths

In the Introduction to the third edition, the death of 8-year-old Victoria Climbié was discussed. Following Victoria's death at the hands of her great-aunt and her partner, the Laming Report (2003) emphasised the failings of the whole child protection system. As a consequence, Laming's main recommendations – closer management of professionals who work directly with families, greater accountability throughout all agencies with child protection responsibilities and the strengthening of inter-agency recording and information-sharing by electronic technology – were mostly concerned with establishing procedures and protocols rather than with developing the expertise of practitioners. Laming's findings were incorporated into legislation via the 2004 Children Act.

In 2007, 17-month-old Peter Connelly ('Baby P') died. In the intense public scrutiny that followed, one could not help but notice similarities with the death of Victoria. They both died at the hands of adults who were meant to be caring for them and they were both known to professionals and services tasked with protecting children. Following Peter's death, a number of inquiries took place, including a further report by Lord Laming (2009) and a review of child protection in England by Professor Eileen Munro (see below). The second Laming Report argued that the necessary reforms were already in place and that child protection practitioners simply needed to 'get on with it'. However, Laming also found that child protection services were underfunded, too focused on process and targets at the expense of keeping children safe, that progress was being hindered by the lack of a nationwide computer system and that an over-complicated assessment process encouraged practitioners to complete tasks while losing sight of the child's overall experience.

Since the previous edition there have been other deaths of children that were extensively covered in the British media. Each serious case review into the tragedy found failings in the system which again confirm Munro's findings.

Progress on *The Munro Review of Child Protection*

The Munro Review of Child Protection (Munro 2010, 2011a, 2011b) sought to understand why previous reviews and inquiries had failed to produce the much sought-after improvements in practice. Munro argued that to understand what happens in child protection, especially how and why things go wrong, we need to understand what motivates the behaviour of professionals as well as how the systems in place to protect children often result in unintended consequences. The review set out a thorough and analytical overview of the state of child protection in England. Munro was careful to say that previous reviews and inquiries had been well meaning but also noted that the processes and procedures which developed as a result and over time had reduced significantly the amount of contact professionals were able to have with children. Some will argue that progress on implementing the recommendations of her report has been slow but one of the key changes has been the establishment of a post of Chief Social Worker and the Department of Education's Innovation Fund, established to encourage teams to experiment with new ways of working with families, by getting out of the office and away from the computer screen and doing more direct work with children and families. Some £300m has already been allocated to this.

Knowledge and procedures

Whatever progress is eventually made on the Munro Report, it remains the case that, even in circumstances where professionals have increased autonomy, this does not entirely remove the need for procedures to guide practice. A study of the implementation of the child assessment framework shows how social workers can use their knowledge, skills and understanding to good effect even when required to follow procedures (Millar and Corby 2006). As Brian Corby argued in the third edition, it is important for professionals who work directly with families to have a sound knowledge base when working within systems and protocols, because of the dangers of assuming that systems can replace, rather than enhance, judgement. However, we also feel strongly that it is no less important for practitioners who work directly with families to have a good knowledge base when, as envisaged by the Munro Report, they are to be asked to take on even more responsibility for exercising professional judgements regarding children who may be at risk of harm.

Aims and objectives

We will focus on a broad range of sources of knowledge about the mistreatment of children, drawing on a variety of research and thinking carried out in different professional and academic disciplines: social work, medicine, history, sociology, philosophy, social policy and psychology. We intend to achieve this by presenting up-to-date research-based knowledge in a critical way, evaluating its strengths and weaknesses, and giving particular attention to how the values and beliefs of researchers influence their findings.

The changing knowledge base

The scope of child protection work has increased and developed dramatically since the publication of the first edition of this book in 1993. At that time the main concerns were with intra-familial neglect and abuse and the main forms of abuse were physical, sexual and emotional. The early 1990s saw increased concern about organised abuse and a rise and fall in concerns about ritual abuse. Throughout the 1990s and into the new millennium, the abuse of children in institutional settings was a constant concern. Bullying of children has been another issue that has come onto the agenda, as has their commercial sexual exploitation. Concerns about the effects on children of parental drug and alcohol misuse, parental mental health and domestic violence have also become more central and in the late twentieth and early twenty-first centuries there have been major questions raised about paedophiles. In general terms, there was a shift in emphasis onto extra-familial abuse during this period and away from intra-familial abuse. Arguably, there has subsequently been an increase again in concerns about intra-familial abuse but without necessarily a reduction in concern about extra-familial abuse. Other emerging concerns – such as child abuse and neglect in an international context, the treatment of child asylum seekers in Britain, abuse of children on the internet and Fabricated or Induced Illness (FII) (previously known as Munchausen's syndrome by proxy) – are discussed further and with a view to developing a more international feel to this edition. Since the last edition – which, it is worth bearing in mind, was only six years ago – we have seen new challenges. There has been a series of scandals in the Catholic and Anglican communities in the USA and the UK about the abuse of children by priests. We have also seen the exposure of paedophiles working as high-profile celebrities in the media, including, in the UK, Jimmy Savile, Rolf Harris, Paul Gadd (aka Gary Glitter) . . . and the list goes on. We have also witnessed the spectre of organised gangs that have sexually exploited children and young people and there are far more concerns now compared to six years ago about abuse connected with the internet, for example, sexting, bullying through the uploading of pornographic and illegal images, the infiltration by paedophiles into gaming and social media by posing as children. And these challenges have been made worse as a result of child trafficking and 'modern-day' slavery, which have both increased significantly. Finally, we have seen over the past few years a general raising of awareness about female genital mutilation (FGM) and what is now known as 'faith-based' abuse, i.e. practices aimed at identifying children thought to have been inhabited by 'demons' or 'evil spirits' (and some of these forms of abuse can be horrific and sometimes fatal).

The field of study of child abuse and neglect is such a diverse and fast-changing one that it is not easy to maintain coherence. In order to do this, however, we have decided to adhere to the format of previous editions as far as possible and to incorporate new information and topics within that format. However, as a guide to this, it should be noted that material from key British and international journals for 1999 to 2018 has been researched together with relevant British and American books and government reports and publications. Material adding new or strengthening information has been included. Some older references have been discarded where their findings have been replicated by newer studies. Where appropriate, government statistics used have been replaced by the latest figures.

The extent of child abuse and neglect

Estimates of the prevalence and incidence of child maltreatment may not have direct relevance for fieldwork but they are crucial in the wider allocation of resources and in the development of policy. This information also gives a sense of the size of the problem and of how numbers of children felt to be at risk have changed over time. There are two main sources of statistical knowledge. The first, drawn largely from government departments, measures the incidence of child abuse as reported, recorded or registered by official agencies. The second, deriving from a broader research base, measures the incidence and prevalence of abuse in a given sample of people.[1] As a result, official statistics tell us more about the way in which child abuse is defined in practice and responded to over time, whereas research studies tell us more about the 'hidden' problem, about abuse that does not come to the attention of official authorities.

In previous editions we included at this point a number of tables containing various data purporting to offer a snapshot of the level of different types of abuse at the time of writing. We decided this time to resist that temptation, for the simple reason that definitions vary so much between – and even within – countries and cultures. This problem is further compounded by the well-known differences between the 'incidence' of abuse, i.e. the number of known cases, and the prevalence of abuse, i.e. estimates of the actual *level* of abuse.

The structure of the book

In Chapter 1 the focus is on how, throughout history, there have been different constructions and understandings of what constitutes childhood and child abuse and neglect. It is argued that careful analysis of historical research can help in the understanding of the present.

Chapters 2 and 3 concentrate on the recent history of child protection policy and practice from 1870 up to the present time. Detailed consideration is given to how social and political forces have shaped the way in which we respond to child abuse allegations today. The aim is to help those currently involved in this field of activity to understand the reasons for the complex and often contradictory nature of that response.

Chapter 4 considers the issue of child abuse and neglect definitions, and the impact of different definitions on policy, practice and research.

Chapter 5 looks critically at the question of the likely perpetrators of child abuse and in what circumstances child abuse is more likely to occur. This is an area of considerable development since the previous edition.

Chapter 6 considers a range of social and psychological theories and ideologies that have been applied to child abuse and neglect to explain why it happens.

Chapter 7 reviews research into the consequences and aftermath of the abuse and neglect of children, with implications for both practice and policy in ongoing child protection work.

Chapter 8 describes empirical research into child protection practice, examining key studies which demonstrate the effectiveness of different forms of intervention and the perspective of service users. The impact of research on policy and practice is particularly emphasised.

Chapter 9 considers global and cultural perspectives on child abuse and how these areas relate to practice in the UK, for example, the issues of trafficked children and forced marriages.

Finally, Chapter 10 aims to bring together the main themes from preceding chapters and identify key topics and themes for the future.

Childhood, child abuse and history

Key points in this chapter

- Contemporary accounts of child abuse often overlook the deep historical roots of similar problems and challenges.
- Children have suffered abuse in many forms throughout history and across all major societies.
- By looking back in history, with careful reflection and critical thought, we can develop a more informed view of contemporary debates and definitions of child abuse.

Introduction

The activities and concerns of the helping professions are, by and large, very *present-oriented*. Such professionals, including social workers, nurses, teachers and health visitors, are committed to tackling *current* social, health, educational and personal problems and need to have useful and pragmatic tools to support them in this endeavour. Such is their determination to find solutions to these problems, they may at times find it hard to consider what has gone before and become overly concerned with what is *new* (or what is presented as such). Yet there is much we can learn from an examination of the way in which the same sort of problems have been considered and addressed in the past, provided this is done with care and an awareness of the importance of different contexts.

If we consider the field of child protection work, ignorance of the past is often all too evident. Many accounts of the history of child abuse and neglect begin with Henry Kempe and the '(re)discovery' of 'battered child syndrome' in the early 1960s (Kempe et al. 1962). This approach to an historical overview implies the problem either did not exist beforehand or had somehow lain dormant. However, accounts of the child protection movement in the late nineteenth and early twentieth centuries (Behlmer 1982; Rose 1986, 1991; Ferguson 1990, 2004) demonstrate that very similar things were taking place then as are taking place in Britain now, in the early part of the twenty-first century. The National Society for the Prevention of Cruelty to Children (NSPCC) and other philanthropic agencies were emphasising the widespread nature of child abuse and seeking to convince the public of the need to protect children in the late nineteenth century, much as they do today. They were then decrying that the law and practice were deficient in dealing with the problem – and, again, continue to do so today. The experiences of our late Victorian predecessors, considered in more detail in Chapter 2, provide us with a rich source of insightful material regarding child abuse and protection, as well as a helpful lens for thinking about our more recent responses to many of the same problems. In order to benefit properly from this approach, however, we must cautiously interpret historical information in a critical and reflective manner.

Interpreting history

Historians themselves are fully aware of the difficulties of learning from the past:

> The study of past attitudes, of modes of thought and feeling is one of the most difficult branches of historiography. Not only is evidence patchy and often indirect, particularly where intimate family matters or the mentality of the inarticulate or the illiterate are concerned, but the interpretation of such evidence requires an empathy, a feeling for nuances, and above all an objectivity, a deliberate attempt to set aside one's own cultural assumptions that is not easy to attain . . . Huge generalisations have been hoisted on the slenderest foundations, evidence that is not congenial has been ignored or brushed aside, while other testimony has been crudely or carelessly misinterpreted. All of which suggests the need

for a reminder that bad history can still mislead the 'general public' as well as other scholars and students.

(Wilson 1984: 198)

All historical writing is selective as the range of sources available is often vast. Historians, like all of us, have their favoured viewpoints and theories, which influence the way they interpret data. This results in different emphases being given to certain types of evidence and a lack of careful consideration being afforded to others. Historical writing varies considerably in how much attention is paid to different forms of structural oppression, different forms of identity (including race, class, gender and age), and their impact on attitudes and behaviours. It is often all too easy to reassess the past based on contemporary filters.

When history is used as a means of casting light on present issues, there are two broad perspectives one might take. The first views the present as hard-won, far from inevitable, improvement on the past (Pinker 2012). Adherents of this viewpoint draw comfort from the ignorance and mistakes (as they see them) of previous generations. The second presents a more favourable picture of yesteryear and sees the present not as progress but as regression (Hinsliff 2016). The first perspective views the past as sometimes barbaric and often highly challenged, the second views it as a golden age; the first views the present as an improvement, the second views it as a deterioration. It is important to understand different viewpoints of this kind in order to maximise the usefulness of historical material and how it has been interpreted for a modern audience.

Childhood and history

The issues of childhood and child abuse are closely linked. Although only children can suffer *child* abuse, not every person under the age of 18 has always and everywhere been considered a child in this legal or social sense. Views about the status and rights of children have considerable influence over the ways in which they are treated by adults and determine, to some extent, what is considered abuse.

Our shared understanding of what a child is and what their status ought to be is in many ways socially constructed and, while an informed awareness of the socially constructed nature of childhood may not solve immediate issues – what should be done to protect a young child left home alone, or how a teenager running away from his or her foster placement can be most effectively helped – it should nevertheless enable child care professionals to reflect more fully on the social and political underpinnings of these situations. As one historian puts it:

One possible spin-off of a historical approach is that it can prevent us from taking any particular set of attitudes or behaviours as 'natural' or 'normal'. By examining the historical variety of the position of children and of ideas about childhood and by tracing back some of the steps by which we arrived at our present situation, we can achieve a more dispassionate analysis.

(Jordanova 1989: 4–5)

On the other hand, to some, our current notion of childhood is self-evident – we 'know' a child when we see one. It might become a little more difficult in the case of adolescents, but most people would consider childhood to be an age-related phenomenon. This is reflected in British law, which prescribes a series of legal rights and responsibilities taking effect at different ages. These statutes provide protection for children, place duties on their parents, impose prohibitions on certain activities and later lift them.

There are all sorts of anomalies though. For instance, in England, a 16-year-old is legally permitted to get married (with parental permission); join the armed forces (ditto); buy a lottery ticket; have sexual intercourse (and, by implication, have children of their own); consent to various medical procedures; leave home without parental permission; and drink beer, cider or wine as part of a meal in a restaurant or pub (provided an adult is present and paying). Yet, they cannot buy their own alcoholic drinks, watch certain films or, at the time of writing, vote in elections until the age of 18. Some age-related prohibitions last longer. It is not until the age of 21 that a person in England can stand for election as a councillor or Member of Parliament, apply for a licence to sell alcohol, have a heavy goods vehicle licence or apply to adopt a child. Such is the power of chronological age and the implications for people's status in society.

Despite these age-related demarcations, we know that children develop and mature, physically and psychologically, at different rates. We also know that in countries and societies other than the UK, childhood is construed differently. The age of sexual consent in Germany is 14, as it is in Italy, Portugal and Austria. In France, Greece and Sweden, it is 15 and in Turkey and Malta, 18.

In many of the world's poorer countries, childhood may be seen as much briefer, particularly if the child is poor, black and female (Ennew 1986). Children generally assume what we might term 'adult responsibilities' at an earlier age in poorer societies than in developed ones – they are more likely to fend for themselves on the streets (Panter-Brick 2002) and work for a living (UNICEF 2011). In richer societies, childhood, in the sense of being free from such demands, has been progressively extended. The trend in these countries is to keep young people in education for longer and longer, perhaps because of the reduced demand for manual labour and the increased demand for a better-trained workforce. It may also stem from a desire to protect children for as long as possible before exposing them fully to the adult world.

Since the 1960s, historians seem to have paid more attention than ever before to children and the concept of childhood. This may reflect the apparent growth in concerns about children and childhood in contemporary society during this period. We need to be careful in our interpretations, however, because there is evidence even from the earliest societies of child-centred concerns on the part of parents, which perhaps should not be so surprising. Sommerville (1982) notes that in Mesopotamia, in 1800 BCE, parents expressed the same sort of worries about their children as many parents do now: that they were not obedient or hard working enough at school. Our concerns about children often do seem to be perennial.

Philippe Ariès and childhood

Some of the most influential work of this period has been that of the French social historian, Philippe Ariès, probably the most oft-quoted historian in child care and child protection textbooks. The popular view put forward about Ariès' ideas (with one notable exception: Frost and Stein 1989) is that the notion of childhood is a relatively recent one, perhaps a product of the sixteenth and seventeenth centuries. This is usually said in order to demonstrate how we have become more sensitive to children and their needs than in the past. This is almost a total misreading of what Ariès was arguing, however. For example, in *Centuries of Childhood*, he wrote:

> In medieval society, the idea of childhood did not exist [but] this is not to suggest that children were neglected, forsaken or despised. The idea of childhood is not to be confused with affection for children: it corresponds to an awareness of the particular nature of childhood, that particular nature which distinguishes the child from the adult, even the young adult. In medieval society, this awareness was lacking.
>
> (Ariès 1962: 125)

Indeed, even the normally meticulous (and often very funny) social commentator, Bill Bryson, gets him wrong in his popular book *At Home* when he wryly quotes Ariès as stating, 'The idea of childhood did not exist' (2011: 566). Bryson goes on to say that, following Ariès, historians began to claim that children were viewed with something akin to indifference or even dislike. However, Ariès did not see the absence of *the concept* of childhood as detrimental to children. Indeed, he thought quite the opposite. According to Ariès, in the Middle Ages, children mingled with adults as soon as they were physically able; the concept of childhood as distinct from adulthood was not so prominent. As such, children, as we might understand them, and adults spent much time together in both work and play. It was only gradually, in the sixteenth and seventeenth centuries with the advent of formal education dominated by religious morality, that children became conceptually and societally separated from adults in ways we would recognise today. The increasing separation of children from adults in the public sphere was seen by Ariès as a backward step, placing greater restrictions on children in their formative years. The concept of childhood can be seen, therefore, as a potentially limiting force, placing children *more* at the mercy of adults who have greater power and influence over the concept of childhood and its concomitant status. Ariès is in some respects a child liberationist. He would have liked to undo the 'chains' imposed by our modern concept of childhood and return to a more varied, open and liberated past.

Many historians have found this account to be implausible (Pollock 1983; Hanawalt 1995). Archard accused Ariès of judging the past by the standards of the present:

> Ariès judges that the past lacked a concept of childhood. In fact what the past lacked was our concept of childhood. Previous society did not fail to think of children as different from adults; it merely thought about the difference in different ways from ours.
>
> (Archard 2004: 27)

Pollock (1983) summarises these criticisms in her excellent study, *Forgotten Children*. Her main argument is that Ariès' sources of evidence are not sufficient to substantiate his wide-ranging claims. First, he placed heavy reliance on paintings that could have been analysed in a variety of different ways, yet he interpreted them only in support of his views. Second, he used Héroard's diary of the early years of the future Louis XIII of France to show how children were viewed as 'little adults' from a very early age, particularly in relation to sexuality. He argues that this supports a more general thesis of the non-existence of childhood at that time. Pollock (1983) argues that this case is by definition *atypical* and tells us little about how children in general were viewed and treated. Consider what impression the diary of Queen Elizabeth II's nanny would give of child-rearing practices in the early twentieth century and how unrelated this would be to the more general experience of children at this time (Crawford 2003). Pollock (1983) is also critical of Ariès' rather rosy view of family life in the Middle Ages and points out that Ariès has nothing to say about the care of children who are physically dependent on their parents. He gives the impression that until the age of 7, children do not count and, once they reach this age, they are fully mature and ready to be assimilated into adult life without problem. Hanawalt, another historian, supports this critique:

> For children to survive, they need not only to be nursed, fed, and kept warm (biology), but also to be played with and talked to (culture), or they cannot be socialized. It matters not whether a mother or her surrogate perform these basic tasks or whether or not a sentimental attitude toward a childish state is present; it is simply that these activities must take place for the child to survive. Likewise, it is very difficult to set children of seven to skilled labor such as smelting, plowing, or carpentry.
>
> (Hanawalt 1995: 9)

These debates highlight the potential dangers of a historical perspective on children's issues and the meaning of and status afforded 'child'. While Ariès clearly sensitises us to the fact that childhood is a social construction, and that 'problems' of childhood can be socially created, he does not explain why this happens and makes rather sweeping statements on the basis of limited sources.

The barbaric past perspective

Many historians have used Ariès' argument that childhood did not exist until the sixteenth and seventeenth centuries to show that children in history have been subject to, at least, detached emotional upbringings and, at most, severe abuse, including infanticide (de Mause 1976; Shorter 1976; Stone 1977). De Mause notably argues that the more remote the period being examined, the crueller the treatment of children becomes:

> The history of childhood is a nightmare from which we have only recently begun to awaken. The further back in history one goes, the lower the level of child care, and the more likely children are to be killed, abandoned, beaten, terrorised and sexually abused.
>
> (de Mause 1976: 1)

De Mause shares with Ariès a belief that childhood is a product of relatively recent times, but there the similarity ends. Whereas Ariès sees the development of a more modern concept of childhood as repressive, de Mause sees it as highly progressive. For him, childhood has evolved from the dark ages to a golden present and he outlines seven evolutionary stages – from what he terms the 'infanticidal' mode, which existed until the fourth century, to the 'helping' mode, which commenced in the middle of the twentieth century. Gradually, over many generations, we have progressed from a state where parents were unable to see their children as separate beings with any particular needs, to one where they regard them as distinct and different and deserving of special rights. Stone (1977), focusing on the sixteenth- to nineteenth-century period, provides some support for this thesis. He argues that affection and love between parents and their children were impossible before the eighteenth century because of the material conditions of pre-industrial life. Parents and other adults did not invest emotionally in children because it was not considered worthwhile – child mortality rates were so high that 'to preserve their mental stability, parents were obliged to limit the degree of their psychological involvement with their infant children' (Stone 1977: 70). It was only in the nineteenth century, in Stone's view, that children were first seen as vulnerable individuals with distinctive needs. This change stemmed initially from the upper and middle classes, who had acquired more leisure time to devote to child care concerns, and was gradually filtered down to the poorer classes.

These and similar views have again been heavily criticised by other historians. Demos (1986) is critical of de Mause for the selectivity of his material and for ignoring the significance of context. Macfarlane's (1979) review of Stone's work is particularly telling. He quotes many examples of parents expressing love and affection for their children before the eighteenth century. In particular, Macfarlane (1970) refers to the diary of a seventeenth-century Puritan vicar, Ralph Josselin, and the grief that he evidently felt at the death of his 8-year-old daughter, Mary.[1] Macfarlane (1979) argues that Stone ignores evidence from poorer modern societies and from social anthropological studies that demonstrate considerable evidence of close child–adult emotional ties despite gross material poverty and high rates of child mortality. In short, Macfarlane does not accept Stone's view that affective relationships are determined totally by economics.

Indeed, there is a growing body of evidence to suggest that a concept of childhood necessitating a form of response and different treatment from adults has always existed. Boswell, in his study of the abandonment of children in antiquity, argues: 'It is clear . . . there was no general absence of tender feeling for children as special beings among any pre-modern European peoples' (Boswell 1990: 37). Hanawalt's description of fifteenth-century family life based on city records and literary sources also helps dispel the notion of parental detachment and lack of child-centredness (Hanawalt 1995). Pollock (1983), drawing on a study of 496 published diaries and autobiographies written between 1500 and 1900, argues that, while the concept of childhood changed and developed during this period, it existed throughout. The sources she considered all demonstrate a certain amount of parental ambivalence towards children, considering them to be a mixture of good and bad, innocence and depravity. But they all demonstrated human concern and a sense of responsibility, as well as finding their children wearisome and exasperating at times (some things never change, apparently!). In particular, the diaries she examined showed how the death of a child created similar and relatable heartfelt reactions throughout the centuries. We must conclude, therefore, that although children in former times were expected to take on what we would today consider adult responsibilities at an early age, it is not the case that notions of childhood were non-existent until relatively recently. It seems likely, instead, that children have always had a special status, particularly when they are physically dependent on adults for survival. As societies develop economically, there is a tendency for childhood, as we know it today, to be extended and obtain (even) greater recognition as a separate category, a process testified to by the growth of child welfare legislation. For example, there have been 15 major pieces of legislation in England alone on child protection and welfare established between 1989 and 2017 (NSPCC).

A major flaw in many historical analyses of childhood is that they tend to generalise the way in which children were perceived, as if all children's experiences were similar at a given time. This is as unlikely to be true of historical periods as it is for contemporary societies. Children of different classes, genders, races and abilities are likely to have widely different experiences in every period of history. A good example of this variation is provided by looking at the period of industrialisation in Britain in the nineteenth century, during which the development of greater sensitivity and sentiment towards middle-class children coincided with appalling working conditions for children of the labouring classes in mills, factories and on the street (Davin 1990).

Child abuse and history

What do historians tell us about child abuse? The existence of child maltreatment in history – infanticide, abandonment, severe physical chastisement, child sexual exploitation (sometimes called child prostitution) and harsh labour – is indisputable. Yet, the extent of such maltreatment and how societies have interpreted it at the time are issues of great contention. Some historians consider that the vast majority of children in the past were callously treated and that this was seen as relatively normal or acceptable because there was little sense of childhood as a protected status. Others take the view that callous maltreatment of children was not as common or as typically acceptable in recorded history as might be assumed. They argue that, although living conditions and general standards of care for children were generally far lower in the past, and although far greater expectations were placed on most children in terms of hard labour, this was predominantly a consequence of harsh economic conditions; gross child maltreatment has never been accepted as normal by any society. A distinction should be drawn, in this view, between harsh living conditions and cruel treatment, much as we might draw a similar distinction today. Within the prevailing standards of each age, there have been a relatively small number of cruel and unloving adults, and children in close contact with these adults were more likely to be abused, but society did not necessarily condone or accept such treatment.

Cruel treatment of children in antiquity

De Mause (1976), whose ideas we explored earlier in this chapter, placed the Roman Empire in his infanticide mode, one of the most severe forms of child abuse. Infanticide was not legally a crime until 318 CE (made punishable by death in 374 CE). De Mause concludes from this that it was not only common practice but evidence of the cruelty of the times more generally. Boswell, whose study, *The Kindness of Strangers* (1990), is concerned with abandonment rather than infanticide, a distinction he is keen to maintain, is far less critical. Whereas de Mause judges the Romans by the standards of the late twentieth century (using psychoanalytic theory as his baseline), Boswell takes into account the contemporary meaning of different forms of behaviour that, on the face of it, seem wholly barbaric. Undoubtedly, the Romans practised infanticide. However, seen in a context of no adequate contraceptive techniques and the absence of medical knowledge regarding abortion, it becomes clear that much (though not all) infanticide was a crude, though arguably in certain cases callous, means of controlling family size. Abandoning a child was another method of achieving the same end.

Boswell demonstrates that abandonment was much more 'popular' than infanticide for two reasons. First, the average Roman probably took no more pleasure in actively killing new-born babies than any other morally sound person would. Second, abandonment, which was usually carried out in a public place, frequently led to the child being rescued and looked after by someone else who, presumably, was better placed to provide at least some level of care. This was in most cases a desirable and even the intended outcome.[2] Contrasting sharply with de Mause's more lurid views, Boswell offers a sympathetic account of abandonment:

> Parents abandoned their offspring in desperation when they were unable to support them, due to poverty or disaster; in shame, when they were unwilling to keep them because of their physical condition or ancestry (for example, illegitimate or incestuous); in self-interest or the interest of another child, when inheritance or domestic resources would be compromised by another mouth; in hope, when they believed that someone of greater means or higher standing might find them and bring them up in better circumstances; in resignation, when a child was of unwelcome gender or ominous auspices; or in callousness, if they simply could not be bothered with parenthood.
> (1990: 428)

Child cruelty in the Middle Ages

Boswell's (1990) study also covers the Renaissance period. He argues that abandonment continued to be a common practice throughout Europe, never openly approved of but not officially outlawed either. Gradually, the Church became more involved and began to organise and regulate the activity. Monasteries provided havens for unwanted children through the practice of oblation (a presentation or offering to a deity). In the early thirteenth century, foundling homes were established, and the process of abandonment became centralised around these institutions. However, what were intended to be progressive developments did not always achieve their goals. Boswell argued that the death rate through disease in such places was probably higher than that resulting from the previous practice of abandonment.

How common infanticide was during the Renaissance period is uncertain. Although it was prohibited by ecclesiastical law in most European societies, there is evidence to show it was still not an uncommon occurrence. Shahar comments:

> The scope of the phenomenon cannot be gauged, but the number of cases was certainly too great for all of them to be attributed to murderous impulses resulting from post-partum depression or other grave mental disturbances (although these factors were certainly involved in some cases).
> (1990: 127)

There can be little doubt that infanticide and abandonment of children continued to be a crude means of 'disposing' of unwanted babies and that Church authorities generally sought to counter it with different levels of rigour at different points in history. Sharpe notes that, by the sixteenth century, infanticide was singled out for severe punishment by most European states and comments that: 'The "infanticide wave", in England at least, may have resulted in more executions than the more familiar witch craze' (1984: 61).

The issues of infanticide and child abandonment persisted right through to the early twentieth century in England and there was ambivalence about whether offenders should be punished or pitied. Both are now, of course, relatively rare events, sufficiently so that they are often reported in the national press (Hartley-Parkinson 2017). Sherr and colleagues (2009) estimated that between 1998 and 2005 in the UK, there were 16 babies abandoned per year, with the majority (77.4 per cent) aged less than one week old.

Another concern in the Middle Ages was that of child deaths in the home, ostensibly as a result of accidents. Hanawalt (1977) refers to ecclesiastical legislation of the thirteenth century warning parents not to sleep with their children and not to leave them alone or unattended near fires. Parents were viewed with considerable suspicion in cases where children did die as a consequence of such events. Langer (1974), drawing on court records across Europe, shows that a common response to such deaths was to require the mothers of the dead infants to do penance (an outward expression of repentance for wrongdoing). Shahar (1990) notes, however, that once children had achieved greater independence, their security was more assured, and that the deliberate killing of children other than newborns was very rare during the Middle Ages.

Sexual abuse of children in antiquity and the Middle Ages

There is little clear evidence about sexual abuse of children in antiquity and medieval times, although de Mause is unequivocal about the former: children in antiquity lived their early years in an atmosphere of sexual abuse, with older men in Greece or Rome often sexually abusing children (1976: 43). Wiedemann holds an equally unequivocal *contrary* position:

> ... *the occasional references to the sexual exploitation of children by perverts [do not] prove that Roman society as a whole was imbued either with a psychotic hatred of childhood, or with a degree of sexual freedom to put modern California to shame.*
>
> (1989: 30)

He points out that sexual activity between a man and a boy was not socially acceptable in Roman society and, if it involved a boy with citizen status, it was apparently a criminal offence.[3]

It is also clear that the Greeks and Romans operated a strict incest taboo. Sophocles' *Oedipus Rex* displays the horror that accompanied unwitting incest between a mother and her son. Boswell's (1990) study of abandonment was inspired by an inscription that warned men that by going to brothels they might be committing incest with children they had abandoned many years before. Such anxieties demonstrate how deep-seated the taboo really was. However, we simply do not know to what extent the sexual abuse of children within or outside of families was a feature in ancient societies. As we shall see in Chapter 2, it is only since the 1980s that there has been concerted attempts to focus on preventing intra-familial sexual abuse in Britain and the USA and to measure its true extent.

Similarly, and no doubt for the same reasons, there is also very little information on the subject of sexual abuse during the Middle Ages. Incest did not become a legal offence in England until 1908 (except for a brief period during the regency of Cromwell). However, it should not be assumed that an absence of legislation indicates a lack of concern or an acceptance of such behaviour. Prior to our more secular times, for nearly two millennia the Church played a leading role in the policing of sexual activity in England through the pulpit, the confessional and the ecclesiastical courts (Gagnon and Parker 1995). In Scotland, incest was made a crime punishable by death much earlier, in 1757, and was originally outlawed in 1567. Yet, however it was policed in practice, the incest taboo persisted throughout Europe in this period.

Child abuse from the Middle Ages to Victorian times

Evidence for this period is as scanty as that for earlier ages. Demos (1986) carried out a study of court records in New England in the seventeenth century and found a conspicuous absence of child abuse cases. Such a finding is usually attributed to the belief that cruelty to children in this period of history was so much the norm that court action was a rarity. Demos argues this could not have been the case, because he also found several instances of master–servant violence, which resulted in action being taken to prevent its continuation. He comes to the conclusion that child abuse was probably less prevalent in New England village communities at this time than is generally the case in the USA today. He attributes this to the fact that families were larger and less introverted and intense, children's labour value was high, filial duty was greater and there was more communal oversight.[4] Similarly, Kroll and Bachrach (1986) reported that considerable attention, effort and expense were devoted to seeking help for sick and disabled children in this period, showing, they argue, how valued children were in these societies.

Pollock (1983) demonstrated that public concern about cruelty to children in Britain existed well before the time it is generally thought to have been discovered, that is, in the last three decades of the nineteenth century. She carried out a study of child cruelty reports in *The Times* between 1785 and 1860 and found 385 cases of child neglect, physical abuse and sexual abuse, of which only 27 (7 per cent) were found not guilty. She commented:

> *The manner in which the cases were reported by the newspaper provides an indication of the attitudes of the time to cruelty to children. The fact that the majority of cases were also found guilty meant that law and society condemned child abuse long before the specific Prevention of Cruelty to Children Act appeared in 1889. Parents who abused their offspring were generally considered 'unnatural' and the cruelty as 'horrific' or 'barbaric'.*
>
> (Pollock 1983: 93)

However, there can be little doubt that for large numbers of poor children in the seventeenth, eighteenth and early nineteenth centuries, life was harsh by contemporary standards, even though the cruelty was not necessarily or intentionally inflicted by their parents. Accounts of the opening of the London Foundling Hospital in 1741 (McClure 1981) and of conditions for children in workhouses at the end of the eighteenth century (Cunningham 1991) are just two reminders of this harsh reality.

Changing definitions of child abuse

Here, before concluding the chapter, we offer a brief word on changing definitions of child abuse. As our understandings of childhood change and develop, so our definition of what constitutes child abuse also changes and develops. When we think about the phrase 'child abuse', we might 'naturally' think of some of the examples outlined in this chapter, of children being physically hurt, taken advantage of sexually or simply abandoned. But many contemporary understandings of child abuse include a much wider perspective. For example, childhood obesity is a growing problem in the UK, as it is in many other developed countries, and there has been some debate about whether and at what point childhood obesity might be characterised as a form of child abuse (Viner et al. 2010). On the other hand, children may experience harm because of parental mental health problems or because of social policies, without this necessarily constituting child abuse. There are also debates around the role of mind control, trauma and neglect.

Conclusion

This brief excursion into the early history of child abuse proves nothing definitely. Yet, it should dispel at least two commonly held beliefs: first, the notion that the further one goes back in history, the worse the treatment of children; second, that it is only in recent times that societies have taken concerted steps to deal with the problem.

With regard to the first point, there was undoubtedly a great deal of harsh treatment of children in previous eras that would not be tolerated now. Nor is there any doubt that present-day children on the whole are much more likely to survive infancy and enjoy far better health than their predecessors. On the other hand, there is evidence that children in every era have been valued, cared for and nurtured, often extensively and to the economic detriment of their families. Many historians and other writers have underestimated the degree of concern that parents of previous generations have shown for their children. There is also ample evidence of official concern and state action to protect children from abuse by their parents (Hanawalt 1977; Demos 1986; Boswell 1990). However, this evidence often seems to go unnoticed, which can perhaps be explained by the desire of each new generation to believe it has improved on the past.

Careful analysis of the history of child abuse helps serve to dispel myths and put current problems into a better perspective. What emerges is that every society has taken some steps to deal with the issue of care for children and has devised some means of intervention into family life to ensure this. These efforts have been influenced by the cultures, material circumstances, technologies and politics impinging on those societies. Examining these efforts with regard to contextual factors can enhance our understanding of current approaches to the same and similar problems.

Recommended reading

Ariès, P. (1962) *Centuries of Childhood*. Harmondsworth: Penguin.

Boswell, J. (1990) *The Kindness of Strangers: The Abandonment of Children in Western Europe from Late Antiquity to the Renaissance*. New York: Vintage.

Cunningham, H. (2005) *Children and Childhood in Western Society Since 1500*, 2nd edn. Harlow: Pearson.

de Mause, L. (ed.) (1976) *The History of Childhood*. London: Souvenir Press.

Heywood, C. (2001) *A History of Childhood: Children and Childhood in the West from Medieval to Modern Times*. Cambridge: Polity Press.

Pinker, S. (2012) *The Better Angels of Our Nature: A History of Violence and Humanity*. London: Penguin Books.

Pollock, L. (1983) *Forgotten Children: Parent–Child Relations from 1500 to 1900*. Cambridge: Cambridge University Press.

Shahar, S. (1990) *Childhood in the Middle Ages*. London: Routledge.

Woodhead, M. and Montgomery, H. (2003) *Understanding Childhood: An Interdisciplinary Approach*. Chichester: Wiley.

2 A history of child abuse and neglect: 1870 to the present day

Key points in this chapter

- In the 1970s, a national system of child protection was established for the first time.
- System-level reforms since the 1970s have primarily been reactive, particularly in response to child deaths.
- Over time, a pattern of repeated criticisms has developed that the system is either too intrusive or not intrusive enough into private family life.

Introduction

As we saw in Chapter 1, child abuse is not a new phenomenon, and neither is public nor state concern about it. The focus of this chapter is on how society has responded to child abuse and neglect between 1870 and the present day, from Victorian and Edwardian era responses to the formation of the sophisticated, modern systems for monitoring child welfare that we now see. We shall consider how these responses are often shaped by wider social, economic and political factors but also how they are often overtly reactive to individual events. The year 1870 has been selected as the starting date because of the clear thread between the social organisation around the problem of child abuse that started at this time.

Late Victorian and Edwardian responses to child abuse

The late Victorian age saw a flurry of activity around the issue of child protection. Throughout the nineteenth century, there were dramatic changes in terms of population growth, industrialisation and urbanisation in Britain. Between 1801 and 1861, the population almost doubled from 10.5 million to 20 million, of whom 7 million were under the age of 15. By 1901, the population was 38.3 million (including Northern Ireland), of whom more than 10 million were under the age of 15. Children formed one-third of the population throughout most of this period compared with one-fifth at the present time. On the topic of mortality, infant mortality rates were around 15 per cent throughout most of the nineteenth century and Rose tells us: 'Even as late as 1895 half the children up to 5 would die in the worst slums, compared with 19 per cent in a healthy district like Dulwich' (1991: 2).

Until the passing of the Education Act 1880, when schooling became compulsory for children up to the age of 10, children from poorer families were likely to spend more time labouring than being educated. The 1861 census showed that one-third of all children aged 5–9 and nearly half of 10- to 14-year-olds were working. Figures for working-class children alone, had they been collated, would have been much higher.

By any measure, the nineteenth century was a time of great upheaval and traumatic change for poorer families. These changes led to new problems and concerns about the upbringing of children and new forms of state intervention into family life. We will explore some of these in the following section.

Child care concerns up to 1870

There were four broad categories of children causing concern to the state up to the end of the 1860s: (1) children of the street ('vagabonds', 'beggars' or 'street traders'); (2) young offenders; (3) children at work;

and (4) children 'looked after' in Poor Law authority institutions. The main pattern of response was for such issues to be taken up initially by philanthropic societies of different religious persuasions acting as pressure groups, followed by government intervention and state legislation (Dingwall et al. 1984).

Note that none of these issues involved direct intervention into family life. Although there was a considerable concern to control the unruliness of children on the street (prompted by public order anxieties) and to influence the nature and amount of work that children could undertake (prompted by concerns about exposure to immorality as well as by concerns about exploitation), there was little thought given to more direct state intervention into family life to protect children from ill-treatment by their parents. Behlmer argued that to 'patrol industry on behalf of the young was [seen as] England's Christian duty. To patrol the home was a sacrilege' (1982: 9).

While this analysis of societal perceptions of paternalism is generally correct, it is important to note that the sacrosanctity of domestic privacy had always been more applicable to wealthier families than poorer ones. In the pre-industrialised period, the latter were subject to Church and community controls. The breakdown in these mechanisms that accompanied industrialisation created the need for new ways of maintaining moral and social order among poorer families, which is where the philanthropists came in. The question was how best to establish this new form of intervention, one that did not intrude on family affairs but did control the unruliness of children on the street and influenced the nature of child labour, without undermining parental responsibility.

Baby farming

In the late 1860s and early 1870s, this new form of intervention into family life began tentatively, with its focus on the issue of 'baby farming'. This term was used to describe the then common practice of paying for babies to be nursed and reared by substitute parents. The practice was widespread because of the absence of adequate contraception, the illegality and risks associated with abortion, the stigma attached to 'illegitimacy' and the need for poorer unmarried women to be at work. It was a free-market enterprise uncontrolled by state regulation. However, there were several infamous cases of babies being murdered by their 'carers', which created widespread public concern (Rose 1986).

In 1870, the Infant Life Protection Society was established with a view to controlling the practice of baby farming via a system of registration and inspection. By 1872, they had succeeded in pushing through the Infant Life Protection Act, which required any adult who 'fostered' more than one child under the age of 1 to register with the local authority and meet certain standards of care. In practice, the Act proved ineffective as the resources needed to enforce it were not made available. London County Council took the issue more seriously than most, though even they appointed only one inspector, in 1878, to cover the whole of the metropolitan area. Further Acts followed: the Infant Life Protection Act 1897, the Children Act 1908 and the Children and Young Persons Act 1933. These required official registration as soon as the first child was placed with a carer, the 'protected age' of the child was raised to 9, and inspection was made more thorough and comprehensive (Hendrick 1994).

The Infant Life Protection Society's concern with baby farming did not meet massive resistance from the establishment, although it was still seen by some as an unnecessary interference into what should be governed by private arrangements.

The formation of the NSPCC

In 1881, Thomas Agnew, a banker from Liverpool, travelled to New York where he visited the New York Society for the Prevention of Cruelty to Children. Agnew was impressed with what he saw and, when he returned to the UK, he set up the Liverpool Society for the Prevention of Cruelty to Children (SPCC). In 1884, the London SPCC was established and, by 1889, had opened 32 branches or aid committees across England, Wales and Scotland. In the same year, the organisation was renamed the National Society for the Prevention of Cruelty to Children (NSPCC). While other philanthropic societies, including Dr Barnardo's (founded in 1866), had been 'rescuing' children living outside their families for many years, the NSPCC's concern was to 'rescue' children living *within* their own homes.

The early NSPCC protagonists considered the existing arrangements for the reporting of child ill-treatment and neglect and the subsequent impeachment of parents to be something of a lottery. They argued that there were no statutory means of protecting children before cases of parental cruelty were tried and no means of ensuring continued protection once convicted parents had served their sentences.[1]

In an attempt to remedy this, an initially small number of NSPCC inspectors were appointed to seek out and report to the police instances of abuse and neglect, even though, until the passing of legislation in 1889, they had no legal authority or mandate to carry out this task. Shelters were established to provide places of safety for children pending prosecutions. They would not be established in law, however, for several more years. Shocking cases of child mistreatment were publicised in order to influence public opinion, alongside a relentless campaign of parliamentary lobbying to change the law, the outcome of which was the Prevention of Cruelty to Children Act 1889. The NSPCC, with the best of intentions, still uses comparable tactics today.

The Prevention of Cruelty to Children Act 1889 defined specific parental misdemeanours against children and created penalties for wilful ill-treatment or neglect leading to unnecessary suffering or injury to health. It empowered the police to arrest anyone found to be ill-treating a child and obtain warrants to enter the homes of children who might be in danger. The Act also legalised the removal of children to places of safety and enabled 'fit person' orders (a forerunner of modern-day care orders) to be imposed on children whose parents had been convicted of offences against them.

Further Acts followed in 1894, 1904 and 1908. By 1908, some of the main components of child protection law that still exist today were already in place. As Dingwall and colleagues put it:

> [T]here have been virtually no fundamental changes in the categories of children covered by the interventionist legislation since 1894. Subsequent legislation has consolidated the Victorian statutes and occasionally modernised their wording. It has introduced a few new types of disposition and redistributed enforcement duties. Nevertheless, the issues of principle were mostly settled in Victorian times.
>
> (Dingwall et al. 1984: 220)

The foundations were set even then for much of the form and style of current intervention practices in child protection work. In Ferguson's (1990) lucid account of an NSPCC case in the north-east of England in 1898, he depicts an inspector grappling with many of the same contradictions and complexities as present-day professionals must do. There was an emphasis on providing advice, support and material help, with court action viewed as a last resort. This approach developed as a result of two main factors: first, NSPCC inspectors had to gain acceptance in communities if they were to be effective; second, their ultimate concern and that of the state was to inculcate a sense of parental responsibility without undermining family life. Advice, persuasion and the threat of prosecution were methods thought to be in tune with these twin goals. Echoes of such approaches can be found in at least some aspects of contemporary child protection practice (Forrester et al. 2008a).

By 1914, the NSPCC had established itself as a fully-fledged national institution. Its officers covered the whole of the British Isles. Despite being feared in many communities, the NSPCC was also widely respected, and this was reflected in the high percentage of referrals that came from neighbours and relatives, with 58 per cent of cases reported to the NSPCC in 1986–87 originating from such sources (Behlmer, 1982).

Responding to sexual abuse

During this era, child sexual abuse within the family, previously widely ignored as an issue, was also being tackled by the NSPCC. Behlmer (1982: 70) notes that the London SPCC in its first year dealt with 95 cases involving 'domestic victims', of which 12 concerned 'an evil which is altogether too unmentionable' (meaning sexual assault or incest). Despite this slowly growing awareness, the NSPCC did not overtly bring child sexual abuse to public attention in the same way as physical abuse and neglect. The response was akin to a conspiracy of silence.

In contrast, 'child prostitution' received far more public attention. Following a series of articles in the *Pall Mall Gazette* in 1885, exposing a child prostitution ring that lured young English girls to brothels in Belgium, legislation was introduced to raise the age of lawful consent for girls from 13 to 16.

The issue of intra-familial sexual abuse continued to receive little public attention. Where it was acknowledged, it was seen as linked to low intelligence and resulting from the overcrowded sleeping conditions of the poorer classes (Wohl 1978). Arguably, it was Sigmund Freud, rather than the NSPCC, who should be credited with much of the effort in presenting childhood sexual abuse as one potent source of adult psychological difficulties. Freud did much to publicise not only the prevalence of child maltreatment in general and child sexual abuse in particular, but also the harm these behaviours were causing to individuals and society.

Following Freud's work, it became more common for specialist organisations, if not the wider society as a whole, to discuss and publicise the problem of sexual abuse. This led to the NSPCC, along with the National Vigilance Association, formed in 1885, to press for new laws to criminalise incest, which was not at this time a specific crime. This pressure resulted in the passing of the Incest Act 1908 and, although the impact of this Act was limited, incest was now, at least, officially recognised as a crime.

Protecting children within the family

There were other considerable shifts in thinking about state intervention into family life between 1870 and 1914. We have focused on the child protection aspects, but one could look at a range of areas, including education, working conditions and health, and notice similar developments. According to Parton:

> *In the last quarter of the nineteenth century the political debate increasingly focused on the need to address a growing number of social problems, such as crime, vagrancy and disease without imposing a strong (sovereign) state on the wishes and activities of individuals.*
>
> (2005: 11)

While these problems could be addressed, to an extent, without state intrusion into private family life, it was increasingly apparent that the family was a crucially important area for intervention in its own right. This development in political thinking created the conditions in which the NSPCC operated at this time. NSPCC inspectors tried to protect children by educating parents and encouraging them to modify their behaviour (much like many contemporary services do now). There is no doubt, however, that questioning parental behaviour inside the home posed a dilemma for NSPCC workers, namely, how best to influence the family and improve conditions for children without undermining parental independence and responsibility (see Behlmer 1982; Gordon 1989). Similarities between the late Victorian approach of the NSPCC and that of present-day responses by practising social workers are readily apparent.

Between the two World Wars

A shift in focus

In contrast to the significant changes that occurred between 1870 and 1914, there was a definite shift in focus away from these issues between the two World Wars. A 1923 Home Office report on the work of the Children's Branch noted that, despite a broader set of grounds for proceedings, the number of parental prosecutions had dropped from 4,106 in 1900 to 2,052 by 1921. Similarly, in 1913–14, the NSPCC dealt with 54,772 cases, but the number of prosecutions as a result was just over 4 per cent, compared to a rate of 10 per cent in 1895–96.

Several possible reasons for these changes have been advanced. For example, the 1923 Home Office report cited improved standards of parenting:

> *The children of the poorer classes are better cared for than they used to be, and it is now unusual to see dirty and ragged children in the streets of our great cities. Cases of extreme brutality which were all too common not so many years ago are now becoming less frequent.*
> (Home Office 1923: 69–70)

These improved standards were said to result from better welfare provision (including school meals, health and child maternity services), changes in working-class habits (such as reduced alcohol consumption) and the work of agencies like the NSPCC.

However, one cannot ignore the fact that average living standards also improved during this period, despite the recession that struck in the 1930s. By 1939, the average family in the UK was better fed, better housed and healthier than they had been two decades before. A sharp increase in car ownership and the popularity of leisure activities such as travel and sporting events also indicate a growing sense of prosperity (Stevenson and Cook 1977).[2] These factors point to the likelihood of less abuse taking place but also to the possibility that the kind of abject poverty noted in the Home Office report in 1923 ('dirty and ragged children') had reduced not as a consequence of improved parenting standards but as a natural by-product of a reduction in gross material deprivation.

Rose (1991) attributed the perceived reduction in child abuse to a decline in the birth rate. The average number of children born to families in 1915 was 2.5 compared with 6 in the 1860s: 'children being born from the Edwardian period were more "expected" and therefore on the whole more wanted than before' (Rose 1991: 243).

Ferguson (2004) used the term 'sequestration' to describe what was happening during this period. The NSPCC and others in the field were carrying out their work relatively free from scrutiny and criticism. Child deaths from neglect and abuse had reduced considerably since before the First World War. Ill-treatment of children was, therefore, seen to be a containable problem best left to specialists. In his view, this process persisted until the 'rediscovery' of child abuse in the 1960s and 1970s.

Dingwall and colleagues (1984) argued that child protection had never been a major concern of the state, except in the 1880–1900 period. Its real worry was the threat arising from the inadequate moral socialisation of children and the maintenance of social order. Neglect was seen as a cause of delinquency and was an important target of intervention primarily for that reason.[3]

Gordon (1989) argued that, while the extent and nature of child abuse did not change significantly during the period 1880–1960, social and state responses to it did change. Gordon linked societal concerns about child abuse and other forms of family violence to the strength of feminist thinking, arguing that when women have a stronger voice, as in the late Victorian and early Edwardian eras, this leads to more awareness of and tougher responses to the issue (although she did not suggest this means the agencies and workers themselves employed a feminist analysis). Her explanation for the lack of an overt focus on child abuse in the Depression-era in the USA is as follows:

> One of the major characteristics of depression-era social work was a policy of defending the 'conventional' nuclear family . . . A sympathy arose for the unemployed husband, the stress and role-conflict that frequently engendered his violence; remarkably less sympathy was mustered for the situation of mothers doing double shifts – at home and at work – in attempts to hold the family together . . . Indeed violence altogether was de-emphasized, and the SPCCs devoted themselves almost exclusively to child neglect, now conceived primarily in terms of economic neglect, such as malnutrition or inadequate medical care.
>
> (Gordon 1989: 22–3)

This argument also has good explanatory value for the British situation. Certainly, between the two World Wars, the government's focus was understandably and predictably on national security. As Gordon argues, its focus on 'women's issues', such as childrearing and the family or the violence of men at home, was reduced.

There is no way of knowing for certain whether the incidence of child abuse during this era was lower than before. However, it is clear that there was a much less evangelical approach to the problem than in previous decades and a good probability that a large amount of abuse therefore went unnoticed (see Ferguson 2004).

Sexual abuse

Gordon (1989) provides one of the few accounts of official responses to child sexual abuse during this period. The case records she studied show that such abuse persisted throughout the period 1880–1960. The 1880–1910 records showed that the SPCC workers of the time more readily accepted allegations of sexual abuse and judged child sexual abusers as socially and morally inferior beings. From 1910 onwards, there was a much more tentative approach to the issue, with far greater emphasis on abuse by strangers, on supposed sexual delinquency and a good deal of victim-blaming. The problem of child sexual abuse, though never high on the agenda, went even further underground for much of this time (Gordon 1989). Nevertheless, the number of prosecutions under the Incest Act 1908 gradually increased, reaching 100 a year by the beginning of the Second World War, and there is clear evidence of the vigorous pursuit of sexual abuse cases in some NSPCC accounts (Housden 1955).[4]

1945–74: The rise of the children's departments and rediscovery of child abuse

The Curtis Committee

There was an upsurge of interest in the welfare of deprived children after the Second World War. The report of the Curtis Committee, set up to inquire into the conditions of children 'deprived of a normal home life with their own parents and relatives' (Curtis 1946: 5), provided a comprehensive account of the child care concerns of the day. It is again notable that child neglect is referred to primarily because of its link with subsequent delinquent behaviour rather than because of alarm about harm to the child per se. This despite the fact that one of the catalysts for concern at the time was the death of a 12-year-old child, Dennis O'Neill, killed by his foster father (Home Office 1945).

Child care work under the Children Act 1948

The Children Act 1948 was greatly influenced by the findings of the Curtis Committee. In 1950, a joint circular was issued to local authorities, proposing the setting up of coordinating committees for overseeing 'problem family' cases that were being visited by a wide range of departments (Home Office 1950), an idea at least superficially similar to the contemporary 'troubled families' agenda. Under the Children and Young Persons (Amendment) Act 1952, the powers of children's departments to intervene were also broadened. This Act empowered authorities to seek fit person orders without the requirement that parents first be prose-cuted for cruelty or neglect. This change enabled authorities to protect children more easily and further reduced the need to prosecute parents, in tune with the less punitive approach towards families that character-ised this period.

The other major development was the push for a preventative approach. This notion was attractive to a wide variety of constituencies. Child care officers believed that admissions to care were preventable, given suffi-cient levels of support before the point of crisis. Central government departments, concerned by a dramatic rise in the number of children in care following the implementation of the 1948 Act, saw it as a cost-effective option. In addition, they were concerned about the link between neglect and delinquency and what they perceived as the pressing need to do something about the latter. Bowlby's study of institutional care for children and his theories about maternal deprivation were also influential (Bowlby 1951; Bowlby et al. 1965).

Packman (1975) has shown how, throughout the 1950s, child care officers spent more and more of their time working with families to pre-vent receptions into care. Such work received legal backing with the passing of the Children and Young Persons Act 1963, Section 1 of which empowered local authorities to provide material and financial assistance to keep children at home when this was thought to be in their best interests.

The main concern for the remainder of the 1960s continued to be delin-quency, the cause of which was seen to be neglect, and the solution, increased support for the family. (This mode of thought was reflected in the Children and Young Persons Act 1969.) Neglected children were treated by the law in the same way as children beyond control, children in moral danger, children refusing to go to school and children committing offences. In the mid-1970s, when attention switched more directly to the ill-treatment of children by their parents, this legislation proved to be inadequate in many respects.

With regard to professional responses, there were moves towards a broader family perspective. Deprived children were seen to be the product of deprived families, and a family-based service was felt to be essential. It was within this context that the Seebohm Report of 1968 recommended the formation of new unified social services departments comprising the former health and welfare and children's departments. These new depart-ments were set up to 'meet the social needs of individuals, families, and communities' (Seebohm 1968: 43).

The 'rediscovery' of child abuse in the USA

In the USA, child abuse was formally rediscovered in 1962 when the paediatrician Henry Kempe and his associates coined the term 'the bat-tered child syndrome' in their eponymous paper. This described and sought to explain the process by which parents (primarily mothers) physically assaulted their babies and young children (Kempe et al. 1962). Although paediatric radiologists had already recognised this problem (Pfohl 1977), Kempe and his colleagues were the first to confidently attribute children's injuries to deliberate mistreatment rather than to the outcome of accident or disease. Kempe argued that such physical abuse of children was far more widespread than anyone had previously considered and that professionals (doctors, in particular) had been ignoring it.

Kempe's original thinking also stressed the psychological aspects of child abuse. His view was that child abuse resulted from the parent's emotional or psychological problems, which in turn stemmed from their own emotionally deprived childhood experiences. This view was far more in keeping with prevailing social mores, with child abuse said to result from psychological problems rather than because of cruelty, poverty or ignorance. Kempe argued that parents needed psychological treatment or therapy, that their children needed temporary protection and that in most cases rehabilitation should be possible. His main exceptions to this rule were parents diagnosed as having psychotic illnesses.

This model of child abuse was remarkably influential throughout the USA in the 1970s and 1980s. What's more, thanks to the tireless campaigning of Kempe and others, the physical abuse of children became a major social issue, attracting national publicity and funding (Nelson 1984). As early as 1967, every state in the USA had mandatory reporting laws and the Children's Bureau was spending considerable amounts of money on research into the problem.

It is hard to pinpoint the reasons for the re-emergence of this age-old problem. Technological developments, such as the use of X-rays, played a part. However, Pfohl (1977) attributed much to the professional aspirations of paediatricians, who in an era of better physical health among children were in search of a new role. Nevertheless, broader social factors need to be taken into account as well. The climate was right for greater focus on the care and well-being of children. The relative affluence of the 1960s created the conditions for people to pay greater attention to the needs of children and the quality of parent–child relationships. By giving child abuse a medical label and seeing it as treatable, new forms of intervention into family life were not seen as threatening in general because they would be aimed only at families that had 'the illness'.

The re-emergence of child abuse as a problem in Britain

Parton (1979, 1981, 1985) provided a detailed account of the development of child abuse as a social problem in Britain in the late 1960s and the 1970s. The pattern of development was similar to (and influenced by) that in the USA. He saw the growth of the problem as very closely linked to professional aspirations and the politics of the family and the state.

There were two main professional groupings involved in the 1960s: medical doctors (notably paediatricians) and the NSPCC. In 1963, Griffiths and Moynihan, two orthopaedic surgeons, used the term 'battered baby syndrome' in an influential article in the *British Medical Journal*. The amount of medical literature devoted to this topic developed steadily throughout the 1960s, but the problem was not responded to at a wider level at this stage.

Despite this growing interest (albeit in narrowly-defined terms), at the same time, the NSPCC faced an identity crisis. Throughout the 1950s and 1960s, the new statutory children's departments grew in size and stature and there was considerable overlap between their responsibilities and those of the NSPCC. Both were tackling similar problems and in similar ways, but the children's departments were better resourced and had a broader mandate. The emergence of a direct focus on physical child mistreatment offered the NSPCC an opportunity to develop a more specialist and separate role. Contact was made with Henry Kempe and his associates and a project was established in London to provide specialist help for families referred for child abuse (see Baher et al. 1976). During this period, the NSPCC was highly influential in placing the issue firmly on the social agenda (see Parton 1985).

Summary

On the face of it, the period between 1945 and 1974 was one in which family policy and practice, in general, were relatively benign. The style of the time was unequivocally family-oriented. Families identified as being at risk expected to be the recipients of help (Ingleby 1960). Whether such a policy served the interests of children is an open question. Gordon's account of the US situation is instructive, given the dearth of British studies of child protection during this period:

> The defend-the-conventional-family policy in social work continued through the 1940s and 1950s. These decades represented the low point in public awareness of family-violence problems and in the status of child-protection work within the social-work profession.
>
> (Gordon 1989: 23)

Gordon also described the increasing influence of psychoanalysis. In Britain, the influence of psychoanalytical theory has always been much less than in the USA (Yelloly 1980) but there can be little doubt that the work of Bowlby (1951) focused attention on the emotional qualities of parenting and emphasised an apparent need to bolster families with advice and support.

Sexual abuse, as we now perceive it, continued to receive limited focus. The main forms of perceived sexual abuse at this time were incest, seen as a rare and pathological phenomenon, or girls in 'moral danger' (Greenland 1958; Allen and Morton 1961). From a feminist perspective, policy responses to child abuse during this time were deficient in terms of protecting women and children from male violence.

The period and the events that followed substantially challenged this 'family support' model and created a momentum towards 'child protection' with which professionals are still grappling today. What occurred in policy and practice terms can be attributed substantially, if not entirely, to the death of (and subsequent public inquiry into) one child: Maria Colwell.

1974–90: The establishment of a child protection system

Maria Colwell

Maria Colwell, aged 7, was killed by her step-father in 1973 (Department of Health and Social Security 1974). She had been in the care of East Sussex County Council for five years following a period of general neglect and low standards of care, and for nearly all of this time had been looked after by her aunt. Her mother had, meanwhile, remarried and given birth to three more children. In 1971, she was determined to have Maria back home. The County Council agreed a plan of rehabilitation and supported Maria's mother to discharge the care order. Maria, who had been very resistant to returning home, died 13 months later, grossly under-nourished and severely beaten by her step-father. This was despite the fact that throughout this period there had been many professionals involved in her care, all of whom failed to detect the neglect and ill-treatment that were taking place over some considerable time.

We can have a fuller understanding of how the Maria Colwell case came to have such an impact on the practice of social work through the work of Parton (1979). He argued that her death did not immediately cause a great deal of national concern; however, the decision of the then minister of the Department of Health and Social Security (DHSS), Sir Keith Joseph, to hold a public inquiry brought the case into the national spotlight. Parton pinpointed the influence of a group called the Tunbridge Wells Study Group, consisting of paediatricians, lawyers and social workers, as a key factor in instigating this inquiry. Sir Joseph himself was very much in tune with the ideas of this group, as he promulgated a more general thesis about cycles of deprivation among poor families and the need for specialist intervention (Joseph 1972).

The resulting public inquiry – the first of its kind – aided by media reporting, caught the attention of the general public and established a precedent for many subsequent inquiries, focusing on individual failure and not wider issues of child abuse. Diane Lees, Maria's social worker, was particularly vilified. The social work profession was considered to be too soft and permissive. The more benign family approach, prevalent since 1948, was called into question and the professional autonomy afforded to those working with children for over half a century was forfeited.

The establishment of a system for dealing with child abuse

As a consequence of the Maria Colwell inquiry report, the DHSS laid the foundations of the system that largely still exists for protecting children. The aim of these changes were to raise awareness of child abuse, to ensure that allegations of abuse were promptly responded to, to improve inter-agency cooperation and to put in place more thorough systems for monitoring children judged to be at risk, while the mechanisms for achieving these aims included:

- area review committees, consisting of higher and middle managers from all agencies with a role to play in the protection of children, whose function was to coordinate and oversee all work in this area;
- case conferences involving all front-door professionals, whose function was to assess new cases and to review ongoing casework; and
- registers of all children considered to be abused or at risk of abuse.

Intervention became more focused and more intrusive. The concerns of the previous era – to avoid the separation of parents and children and to support the family as a whole – were now officially called into question. The Children Act 1975, largely concerned with more general child care issues, reflected the mood of the times. Drawing on a study of children in long-term care (Rowe and Lambert 1973), it emphasised the needs of children as distinct from parents. The Act also made two major changes to child protection practice. First, it allowed for care proceedings to be issued when a child was or might be living in the same household as a person who had committed violent or indecent (Schedule 1) offences under the Children and Young Persons Act 1933. This particular response was a direct result of the death of another child, Susan Auckland, at the hands of her father, previously convicted for the manslaughter of another of his children (Department of Health and Social Security 1975). Second, it required the appointment of guardians *ad litem* to act exclusively on behalf of the child in legal proceedings. This change was made out of concern for cases such as Maria Colwell's, where parents sought to discharge legal orders and the local authority did not oppose them. In other words, the changes were intended to ensure that the views and interests of the child were separately represented in court from those of their parents or the local authority. These changes reflected a new emphasis on the abuse of children and the deficiencies of the Children and Young Persons Act 1969 for the purposes of protecting them.

Child abuse work, 1975–85

For the remainder of the 1970s, the pressure to create more effective detection, investigation and monitoring systems for child abuse continued. From 1973 to 1981, there were 26 further inquiries into the deaths and serious abuse of children in Britain at the hands of their carers (Corby et al. 2001). In almost all of these cases, various health and welfare agencies were involved, often in a statutory capacity (Department of Health and Social Security 1982). By means of further advice and circulars from the DHSS, considerable effort was made to incorporate lessons from these inquiries into practice. From relatively small beginnings, child abuse work developed into a major preoccupation of social services departments. By this time, social services departments were firmly in the lead role in this field, despite official concern to emphasise inter-professional practice.

The definition of what counted as child abuse also broadened over time. By 1980, the term 'child abuse' had replaced 'baby battering' and the subsequent term 'non-accidental injury'. The 1980 DHSS circular, entitled *Child Abuse: Central Register Systems*, outlined four categories of abuse or risk of abuse:

• physical injury;
• physical neglect;
• failure to thrive incorporated with emotional abuse; and
• living in the same household as someone convicted of Schedule 1 offences of the Children and Young Persons Act 1933.

It is notable that the sexual abuse of children was not considered as a category for registration at this time.

In the first half of the 1980s, there was some relaxation in the drive to establish better systems for responding to child abuse. There were fewer public inquiries (Corby et al. 2001) and a general consolidation of the rash of changes that had taken place in the 1970s.

Intrusive social work practice?

By 1985, state intervention into family life to protect children had become more systematic, but had it become more intrusive?

The most comprehensive research into practice during this period was that of Dingwall and colleagues (1983), who argued that the 'new' response to child abuse, characterised by public inquiries and more formal categorisation of instances of abuse, was tougher in theory than in practice. They tried to demonstrate that, despite greater concerns for children at risk, social workers were still operating in a relatively benign way with families. They identified a 'rule of optimism', whereby social workers were expected to make the best interpretation of an allegation of abuse. This 'rule', they argued, was not an individual one of social workers' own making; it reflected prevailing liberal views about the respective roles of the state and the family, namely, that while the state needs to ensure the protection of children, this should be done only with due regard to the rights of parents balanced against the needs of children. Thus, the liberal approach they identified was in line with the general requirements of the state as seen by the general population. However, Parton (1985) argued that an increase in the use of place of safety orders in the 1970s and the gross numbers of children in care were evidence of a more intrusive approach towards families. Corby (1987) found that from the parents' point of view, interventions were punitive and severe. Parents suspected of abusing their children were often treated with suspicion and poorly informed of what was happening and had no right to attend case conferences. Yet, relatively few cases resulted in court action. Thus, it can be argued that increased state intervention into family life between 1975 and 1985, while officially encouraged, was in practice tentatively implemented as far as judicial escalation was concerned.

The Short inquiry, 1984

At the same time, there were counter-concerns being put forward about the dangers of over-intrusive and heavy-handed practice. Parton (1991) dated these concerns from 1978. First, a series of studies was commissioned by the DHSS, resulting in a number of publications summarised in a report entitled *Social Work Decisions in Child Care* (Department of Health and Social Security 1985a). These studies, while not directly focused on child abuse, came to the general conclusion that not enough attention was paid to the needs of families (Packman 1986). Second, in 1984, the House of Commons Social Services Committee, chaired by Renée Short, undertook an inquiry into children in care, during which its major concern was the perennial problem of the relationship between the state, children and the family, and how best the state can protect children without undermining family independence. In particular, it was vexed by the relative weight to be given to professional discretionary powers (especially those of social workers) and to a legally-enforced rights-based approach and came to the conclusion that there should be a shift towards the latter (see Parton 1991). The Short inquiry also recommended the establishment of a working party on child care law, whose report in 1985 (Department of Health and Social Security 1985b) laid the foundations for the Children Act 1989.

The Beckford inquiry, 1985

Against this backdrop of reports and parliamentary focus, it was the death of Jasmine Beckford and the subsequent public inquiry (Brent (London Borough of) 1985) that had the most significant impact on social work practice of this period. Jasmine, aged 4, died in July 1984, emaciated and horrifically beaten over an extended period of time by her step-father, Morris Beckford. Jasmine and her younger sister, Louise, had both suffered severe injuries in 1981, for which Morris was given a suspended sentence. The children were taken into care by Brent Borough Council and lived with foster carers for six months. They were returned on a trial basis to the care of their parents and the family was supported by social services somewhat sporadically for the next two years, although Jasmine was seen only once by her social worker in the last 10 months of her life. The judge at the trial of Morris Beckford and Jasmine's mother described the social worker as being 'naïve beyond belief'.

The inquiry into Jasmine's death found that the social worker had regarded Jasmine's parents as the primary clients and that Jasmine's parents' explanations of why she could not be seen had been uncritically accepted. The final report of the inquiry made 68 recommendations, aimed primarily at combating the over-optimism of social workers. Dingwall and colleagues' (1983) 'rule of optimism' was mistakenly interpreted to support this view. The report stressed that too much emphasis was placed on the rehabilitation of Jasmine and her sister, and that evidence to suggest the likelihood of further abuse was ignored. The report was unequivocal that the primary task of social work was the protection of children and that, where necessary, the full force of the law should be employed to this end.

The findings of the Beckford inquiry had an immediate impact on policy and practice. The DHSS (1986) published draft guidelines setting out recommendations for improving inter-professional coordination in child abuse work. The main proposed changes consisted of reframing child *abuse* work as child *protection* work, emphasising the statutory obligation placed on local authorities to act primarily on behalf of children at risk. It was also proposed that area review committees should be renamed 'joint child abuse committees', although in the end they were renamed 'area child protection committees'. Social services departments were given primary responsibility for coordinating a protection plan for children whose names appeared on the child protection register. Despite these changes, it is notable that parental attendance at formal case conferences was still considered to be inappropriate, despite a range of professionals feeling the opposite (Brown and Waters 1985). The aim was to focus attention on the protection of children first and the consideration of the needs and rights of parents firmly second.

There was also a significant rise in the numbers of children assessed as being at risk. The number of place of safety orders increased dramatically in 1986 and 1987 after nine years at roughly the same level, and there was a significant rise in the number of children coming into care.

Between 1985 and 1989, there were a further 12 inquiries following child deaths (Department of Health 1991a; Corby et al. 2001), all of which further emphasised the need for a child-focused and risk-conscious approach.

The increasing importance of child sexual abuse

Support for those in favour of a return to a more family-focused approach was augmented from an unlikely source. In the summer of 1987, newspapers reported a child sexual abuse scandal in Cleveland. Over a period of six months, 121 children had been brought into care on the recommendation of two paediatricians who, using a physical test pioneered in Leeds (see Hobbs and Wynne 1986), diagnosed the majority as having been sexually abused by anal penetration. The parents of these children were in uproar and attracted the attention of the local MP, Stuart Bell, to their cause. He raised the matter in Parliament and another public inquiry, this time with a very different focus, was established.

Up to this time, the issue of child sexual abuse had been a relatively minor concern for child protection agencies in Britain. As with physical abuse, concerns about the sexual abuse of children originally stemmed from experience in the USA where the main protagonists were survivors of sexual abuse (Armstrong 1978; Brady 1979; Angelou 1983), feminist writers such as Rush (1980) and the medical profession (Kempe and Kempe 1978).

Another approach was developed by Giaretto and colleagues (1978), who had a major influence in Britain, in particular on the work of child psychiatrists, psychologists and social workers at Great Ormond Street Hospital (see Bentovim et al. 1988; Furniss 1991). Their approach was to develop a method of intervention based on family therapy principles. In addition, they developed techniques (again, pioneered in the USA) for helping children disclose sexual abuse, using drawings, play, anatomically correct dolls and video-recordings. These techniques were adapted by social workers in several statutory agencies and employed in Cleveland.

By 1987, child sexual abuse was beginning to feature as part of the official child protection agenda, although responses to the problem nationally were patchy and variable. An Ipsos MORI survey commissioned by Channel 4 claimed that 1 in 10 children had experienced some form of sexual abuse by the age of 15 and in half of these cases the abuse had been committed by a family member or somebody known and previously trusted by the child (Baker and Duncan 1985). Paediatricians developed the reflex anal dilatation (RAD) test (Hobbs and Wynne 1986), which was seen as a breakthrough in providing definite physical evidence of sexual abuse.

The Cleveland inquiry, 1987

These developments set the scene for the Cleveland scandal of 1987. The plethora of child sexual abuse diagnoses and the subsequent removal of children into statutory care can be attributed to a combination of factors. First, there was heightened awareness of the possible extent of child sexual abuse among key social services personnel and community paediatricians. Second, paediatricians were aware of the newly-developed RAD test, convinced of its validity and determined to use it. Third, other agencies, particularly the police and police surgeons, were more traditional in their approach and did not accept the new thinking, thus creating a major split in the inter-professional approach. Fourth, the social services department had recently reorganised its child protection system in response to the findings of the Beckford inquiry (Brent (London Borough of) 1985). The result of these factors was that paediatricians diagnosed far more cases of sexual abuse than had previously been the case, the social services department acted swiftly to remove the children, and the police, who would usually have been closely involved in gathering evidence, dissociated themselves from what was happening.

As a result, large numbers of children were taken into care. Although all the children had been 'diagnosed' as being abused, it was not clear who had abused them. Social workers, using the techniques developed at Great Ormond Street Hospital (Bentovim et al. 1988), held a series of interviews with the children to find out, and parents were denied access to them to ensure they did not influence their evidence.

The main findings of the Cleveland inquiry report (Butler-Sloss 1988) confirmed that child sexual abuse was a more widespread phenomenon than previously thought and the chair of the inquiry, Lord Justice Elizabeth Butler-Sloss, was at pains to stress that child sexual abuse must remain on the policy agenda. However, the report criticised every agency and profession for not working together more cooperatively as well as the specific use of the reflex anal dilatation test without supporting evidence.

Social workers were singled out for particular criticism. The more direct approach that had been encouraged in the case of physical abuse was seen as inappropriate with regard to sexual abuse. Those concerned with more general child care matters lobbied for more legal rights for parents and more legal control over social workers (Campbell 1988). The Cleveland Report broadly agreed with the need for parental rights to be placed upon a firmer footing and that parents should be fully informed of decision-making, particularly with regard to medical examinations.[5]

Although the Cleveland inquiry added momentum to the view that a more family-supportive approach was needed, other sources, such as the Short Report (House of Commons 1984), had already been advocating just such a shift. Other social developments taking place in the 1980s were also viewed with concern by politicians. The traditional family was said to be under threat as a result of recession and unemployment, high divorce rates and the growth of lone-parent families. It was estimated that by the early 1990s there were 3 million children living in poverty (Kumar 1993). Concerns about teenage pregnancy and violent teenagers also came to the fore. Factors such as these were cited as evidence of the need for a change in direction.

Draft *Working Together* guidelines issued in 1986 were hastily amended to incorporate the recommendations of the Cleveland Report (Department of Health and Social Security 1988), some of which created a complete U-turn in policy, most notably parental participation in formal case conferences. Whereas the 1986 draft stated that it was inappropriate for parents to attend, the 1988 guidelines said they should be invited unless their presence would impact negatively on the child's best interests. These guidelines placed greater emphasis on interdisciplinary consultation and recommended joint police and social services department investigations as the norm.

The Children Act 1989

The Cleveland Report also impacted on the passage of the Children Act 1989 through Parliament. This Act, for the most part implemented on 14 October 1991, remains fundamental to the practice of child protection, particularly in England. The key concepts of the Act include parental responsibility; the paramountcy principle; and partnership working between parents and professionals and between local authorities, the National Health Service (NHS) and other agencies. The key tension of the Act is the attempt to draw a balance between ensuring that children are given sufficient support to remain within their own families and that children at risk are identified and protected. The Act also aimed to consolidate all child care law, public and private, within one piece of legislation as well as address various other concerns, such as the need to increase the use of voluntary care arrangements (see Lowe 1989).

Amendments were made in light of the events in Cleveland, such as empowering children to refuse to undergo medical assessments if they so wished (Sec. 44(7)) and enabling local authorities to provide or pay for accommodation for alleged abusers so that children could remain at home during investigations (Schedule 2, para. 5). The legal rights of parents were strengthened, and the discretionary powers of professionals reduced. These rights included making provision for parents to have contact with children in care. All of these changes – increased parental participation, more voluntary approaches and greater legal control over professional discretion – were reinforced by the events in Cleveland.

The implementation of the Children Act was also affected by case law, in some instances preceding 1989. For example, the case of *Gillick* v. *West Norfolk and Wisbech Area Health Authority and another* (1986) established the notion of 'Gillick' competence, which set the parameters for deciding when a child is able to consent to medical treatment without the need for parental consent or knowledge. This judgment also established the broader principle that parental power over a child exists for the benefit of the child and not for the benefit of the parent. The Act was therefore more concerned with parental *responsibility* than parental *power*, but clearly the two are interrelated. This can be seen in the case of *Re M (Minors) (Residence Order: Jurisdiction)* (1993), which separated the right of a parent to determine where the child should live from their responsibility to provide a decent home for the child. In particular, it ruled that parental power does not extend to being able to accommodate the child in clearly unsuitable accommodation, because the responsibility of the parent to provide suitable accommodation intersects and overrides their power to choose not to.

1991–2010: Embedding the Children Act 1989 and the development of safeguarding

Following the implementation of the Children Act 1989, the practice of child protection entered a new era, underpinned by new powers and duties given to local authorities and the new legal concept of 'parental responsibility'. The early 1990s saw social workers and other professionals operating with a much greater degree of uncertainty in relation to issues of neglect within the family and physical and sexual abuse. In the first two years following the implementation of the Act, the numbers of care proceedings and applications for emergency care orders reduced considerably. There was a fair degree of tentativeness in pursuing allegations of sexual abuse within the family following the fallout from Cleveland (Corby 1998). Greater attempts were being made to work with families. Parental participation at formal case conferences gradually became more common, as did parental involvement in the period following initial interventions. While there were those who queried the nature of this partnership-focused approach (Corby et al. 1996), it cannot be denied that the introduction of the Act and the new *Working Together* guidelines were impacting on practice. Very quickly, this new approach was subjected to an unexpected 'stress test' in the form of concerns about 'satanic' and 'institutional' abuse of children.[6]

Concerns over satanic abuse

Interest in satanic abuse originated in the USA where a series of allegations and publications about the phenomenon arose in the 1980s (Smith and Prader 1980; Spencer 1989). Social workers in the UK, when faced with very disturbing and strange accounts of child abuse, took note of these publications, and several major investigations took place in the 1990s into cases of suspected satanic abuse in Congleton, Rochdale, Manchester, Liverpool and Nottingham, among many others. The shared features of these cases were accounts by young children of being involved in rituals with adults dressed in cloaks and various black magic paraphernalia and being subjected to (or witnessing) acts of sexual indecency and physical cruelty. Often, social workers and the police responded by removing the children and interviewing them. At first, the considerable public interest in these cases was supportive of this approach and professionals praised them for their bravery. However, this support quickly turned to criticism.

Matters came to a head following a case in the Orkneys in 1991. A number of children suspected of involvement in ritualistic sexual abuse were removed by police and social services from their families in dramatic dawn raids. The children were moved to mainland Scotland and placed into foster care where they were subjected to intensive interviewing and denied any contact with their parents.[7] Six weeks later, a decision was reached that the legal proceedings were incompetent, and the children were returned home.

The subsequent public inquiry (Clyde 1992) did not make a judgment as to whether abuse had taken place but instead examined whether the professional response was reasonable in light of the information available at the time. The overall findings were consistent with those of Cleveland: Lord Clyde was particularly critical of the style and quantity of the interviewing of children (considered to be insufficiently objective and far too frequent and intense); the manner of the removal of the children from their homes; and the ban on contact between parents and children (considered to be traumatic for both and unnecessary). The outcome of the inquiry was confirmation of the need for a less intrusive style of intervention into child abuse cases.

Following the Orkney case, concerns about satanic abuse dissipated almost as quickly as they had arisen. The Department of Health (DoH) commissioned research into all 84 cases of alleged ritual abuse from 1987 to 1992 and found no hard evidence to support the notion that satanic cults were torturing or killing children. However, there was evidence of sexual abuse in a large number of these cases, often by multiple perpetrators either from extended family networks or, in a few examples, by organised paedophile rings (La Fontaine 1994). La Fontaine explained the rise and fall of these concerns as stemming from a unique combination of circumstances involving Christian fundamentalism, the influence of North American writing about such abuse and the readiness of professionals to take literally what La Fontaine (1998) clearly thought were the fantasies of disturbed and deprived children, many of whom were being subjected to appalling sexual (but not *satanist*) abuse.

Concerns over institutional abuse

The 1990s also saw a significant growth in concern about the abuse of children in settings other than their own homes, including those in the care of local authorities and in day nurseries. In this decade, there were at least 12 public inquiries into abuse in institutional settings, outstripping the number of inquiries regarding the abuse of children in their own homes (Corby et al. 2001). This was in stark contrast to the 1970s and 1980s when there were just three inquiries into institutional abuse (Lewisham in 1985, Belfast in 1985 and Greenwich in 1987), compared with nearly 50 regarding family-based abuse.

One notable example related to a system known as 'Pindown', in use at the time in children's homes in Staffordshire (Staffordshire County

Council 1991). Pindown was a crude method of controlling children in care who were considered to be 'challenging'. Pindown was essentially a form of solitary confinement based very loosely on sensory deprivation principles. Children were kept in poorly furnished rooms, not spoken to by staff, and forced to complete tedious and repetitive tasks. This system operated in some places for over six years with the tacit approval of Staffordshire Social Services Department. A total of 132 children were subjected to the Pindown regime, including one 9-year-old. Another child was kept under this regime for 84 continuous days. Not surprisingly, the subsequent inquiry report found the Pindown regime to be abusive in the extreme (Staffordshire County Council 1991).

In the immediate aftermath, a series of other concerns were raised about regimes in Southwark, Brentwood, Bradford, Lincolnshire, Kirklees, North Wales, Islington, Sheffield, Lambeth and Chepstow, indicating that the events in Staffordshire were not isolated examples. Inquiries were also started in Leicestershire and Gwent regarding the sexual abuse of children in residential care.

The DoH responded to this flurry of concern by commissioning a general inquiry into the state of residential children's services in England (Utting 1991; Warner 1992), with similar inquiries taking place in Wales and Scotland (Social Services Inspectorate, Wales, and Social Information Systems 1991; Skinner 1992). The Utting Report provided an overview of the strengths and weaknesses of residential care at the time, reaffirming its low status and the low levels of qualified staff (Utting 1991). With regard to abuse, the report seemed satisfied that changes in the Children Act 1989, particularly those related to inspections and independent visitors for children in care were sufficient to prevent the sort of ill-treatment evidenced.

These initiatives, however, did not stem the flow of new concerns about the abuse of children in residential settings. Allegations of sexual abuse and physical mistreatment of children resulted in inquiries into the Shieldfield day nursery in Newcastle (Hunt 1994) and at a residential boarding school for children with learning difficulties in Northumbria (Kilgallon 1995), as well as wide-scale police investigations into almost all children's homes in Merseyside, Cheshire, Clwyd and Gwynedd. In response, the DoH commissioned a further inquiry into the situation of all children living away from home, including children in long-term hospitals, residential schools and foster care (Utting 1997). The main message of this report was to reaffirm the need for considerable vigilance, but also that measures were being put into place to ensure greater safety for children not living in their family homes.

A particular set of concerns about institutional abuse in North Wales eventually led to the establishment of a tribunal of inquiry. This type of inquiry was the most formidable means of carrying out quasi-judicial investigations into matters of national concern and had never previously been used in connection with child abuse. The tribunal was set up following a series of allegations regarding the widespread sexual abuse of children in residential homes in North Wales, possibly involving a large-scale cover-up. Its establishment undoubtedly reflected not only the need to examine events in North Wales but also the extent of the concern that abuse of children in care had raised more generally.

The inquiry commenced in 1996 and reported in 2000 (Waterhouse 2000). It examined all allegations of abuse taking place in 84 statutory, voluntary and private residential settings between 1974 and 1996, as well as those arising from foster care placements. It eventually focused on 29 children's homes and 15 foster homes. The tribunal found evidence of widespread sexual and physical abuse of boys and girls in Clwyd during this period and evidence of some physical abuse in Gwynedd. However, contrary to the views of many, the tribunal found no evidence of a paedophile ring operating in Clwyd or in Bryn Estyn.

Despite these findings, the tribunal did not have a great effect on policy and practice developments, largely because by the time it came to report, new initiatives had been or were already being introduced.

Working Together (1991) and the Memorandum of Good Practice (1992)

In response to Cleveland and some of the other concerns about child abuse discussed previously, new child protection guidelines were produced in 1991 outlining the need for more measured, planned and coordinated interventions. This guidance revised and updated the previous Working Together guidelines, issued in 1988, and aimed to strike a balance between the kind of overzealous intervention seen in Cleveland and the limited intervention seen in the cases of Maria Colwell, Jasmine Beckford and others. It promoted inter-agency working, setting out how to manage child protection services at a strategic level, and provided guidance for individual cases. It was made a requirement that social workers and the police conduct joint investigations into all serious allegations of physical abuse and into all allegations *without exception* of sexual abuse. In 1992, guidelines were issued setting out in detail the requirements for videoed joint interviews, which, following the recommendations of the Pigot Committee, were to be allowed as evidence-in-chief at the criminal trials of alleged abusers in order to ease the trauma for child witnesses in court (Home Office/Department of Health 1992). For the first time, serious case reviews were introduced to help local authorities and others learn from instances of death or serious injury to a child where abuse or neglect was suspected to be a factor. These guidelines were updated again in 1999 following the publication of Child Protection: Messages from Research in 1995 (Department of Health 1995).

Child Protection: Messages from Research (1995)

In 1995, the research projects set up by the DoH following the Cleveland inquiry report were published individually (20 in all) and summarised in

Child Protection: Messages from Research (Department of Health 1995). This summary report argued that the child protection system acted like a giant sieve, responding to a broad spectrum of referrals about the care of children, from relatively minor concerns about the demeanour of toddlers in nurseries through to extremely serious allegations of sexual abuse and incest. Some 24 per cent of referrals resulted in child protection conferences, with slightly more than half resulting in the child's name being placed on the at-risk register (Gibbons et al. 1995a). The remaining 76 per cent of families, those for whom no conference was arranged or for whom the child's name was not placed on the at-risk register, received minimal levels of support. Thus, services were said to be overly focused on children and their families who had been placed on the register (Gibbons et al. 1995b). Nearly all families subject to initial child protection investigations were poor; had experienced problems, such as the death of loved ones, divorces, accidents and illnesses (physical and mental); and had previously been referred to social services departments or were current service users. The children in most of these families were 'in need', as defined by the Children Act 1989 (Farmer and Owen 1995). Parents on the receiving end of child protection investigations found them to be difficult and stigmatising. Many parents felt that they were being unfairly labelled as child abusers, rather than recognised as parents struggling to cope in difficult and impoverished circumstances (Farmer and Owen 1995). There were too few attempts to engage parents in the process either by giving adequate information or by enabling meaningful participation at child protection conferences. There was thus little evidence of partnership working between professionals and parents (Thoburn et al. 1995).

These findings largely echoed those reported a year earlier by the Audit Commission (1994), who found that spending on child protection work was concentrated on a relatively small number of families, often resulting in the wider obligation to provide resources for children in need, under Section 17 of the Children Act, going unfulfilled.

The general picture created by these two influential sources was that child protection work had become too bureaucratised, proceduralised and focused on overt incidents of child abuse, such as bruising or sexual abuse allegations. As a consequence, wider family problems and in particular the issue of neglect tended to be overlooked. If more obvious forms of abuse were not present or went unnoticed, families could expect minimal help and support. The *Child Protection: Messages from Research* (Department of Health 1995) report also noted that children living in neglectful situations often suffered worse long-term consequences than the majority of those who were physically and sexually abused (see Egeland et al. 1983). The point was that standards of care in neglectful families tended to persist throughout childhood, whereas other forms of abuse might be isolated or sporadic, albeit still serious. Overall, it was deemed that children living in persistently adverse conditions, possibly experiencing the most psychologically damaging effects, were among those least likely to receive supportive services.

1997–2010: From child protection to safeguarding

This situation might almost have been 'tailor-made' for the incoming New Labour government, with its self-proclaimed progressive and reforming intent. The new administration quickly set about introducing a significant number of changes, the main aim of which was to improve the circumstances of large numbers of children, rather than focusing on particular and relatively small groups. Indeed, the government sought to shift the debate entirely away from a narrow concentration on child protection and towards the broader concept of 'safeguarding'. One of the cornerstones of this approach was a determination to tackle the legacy of child poverty left by the outgoing Conservative government in 1997 by introducing a range of community-based projects and services, initially targeted on poorer districts, but with a view to universal coverage in the future. These projects, including Sure Start, the Children's Fund and the Connexions Service, covered the age range from 0 to 18. Later initiatives included improved nursery and after-school provision, particularly for disabled children, and the introduction of tax credits to promote greater opportunities for mothers to work. Other key goals included tackling youth crime and reducing teenage pregnancy.

Over a relatively short period of time, a range of new policy initiatives were introduced, including the Quality Protects programme (Department of Health 1998) to tackle issues relating to the health, educational and social development of children in care; the Leaving Care Act 2000, to provide better follow-up services and support for young people previously in care; and the Care Standards Act 2000, to achieve a greater element of independence in residential care inspection. A new framework for assessing children in need and their families was implemented in 2001 (Department of Health 2000) and the qualifying education of social workers was lengthened, alongside the introduction of specialised post-qualifying child care programmes and new practice guidelines (Department of Health 1999). The response of many social workers to this raft of new initiatives was to 'play safe' and retain a focus on what they saw as the most serious and concerning cases (Platt 2001; Spratt 2001).

At the same time, there continued to be many pressing concerns about children in care coming out of the North Wales tribunal of inquiry, and concerns about child protection work in the community, with highly-publicised serious case reviews into the death of Rikki Neave in Cambridgeshire (Bridge 1997) and the gross neglect of young children in a family in Caerphilly in Wales (Bridge 1998).

New government, familiar challenges

Despite this reforming intent, many of the challenges that were high on the agenda in the mid-1990s persisted. The sexual exploitation of children was one such issue. Much of the campaigning work in relation to child sexual exploitation has been carried out by voluntary agencies such as Barnardo's and The Children's Society (Lee and O'Brien 1995; Swann 1998). They presented a model of children being groomed for exploitation by older males frequently posing as boyfriends. The image created was one of victimisation and exploitation, and it has had a powerful effect on policy development in Britain. In 2000, the DoH and other government departments produced new guidance requiring children exploited via 'prostitution' to be treated as victims of child abuse rather than offenders and pointed to the need for law enforcement measures to be targeted on those exploiting them (Department of Health/Home Office/Department of Education and Employment/National Assembly for Wales 2000). The issue of the commercial sexual exploitation of children also gained a global perspective with public concern raised about sex tourism in Southeast Asia (Munir and Yasin 1997) and the trafficking of children, particularly from Eastern European countries (Manion 2002) (see Chapter 9).

The late 1990s also saw a rise in concerns about the production and distribution of images (including videos) of child sexual abuse. While this form of abuse is often considered under an extra-familial abuse heading, Itzin (1997) has demonstrated that the production of child sexual abuse images frequently commences within the family. She also demonstrated the links between child sexual abuse images and organised abuse, sexual exploitation and sexual offending more generally. It had long been suspected that there was a link between viewing images of child sexual abuse and direct acts of sexual abuse. In 2009, Bourke and Hernandez published the results of a study of 155 offenders sentenced for the possession of child abuse images, the majority of whom claimed to have committed no previous acts of direct sexual abuse. After an 18-month programme, the researchers established that in fact 131 of the 155 offenders had committed direct sexual abuse (a 2,369 per cent increase in the number of admitted offences).

Megan's Law in the UK

The death of Sarah Payne in July 2000 in Sussex also contributed to an outbreak of public anxiety about the risks to children from sex offenders. Fuelled by a campaign organised by the now-defunct *News of the World* tabloid newspaper, there followed a demand for the presence and location of all sex offenders living in the community to be made public, drawing on the model of 'Megan's Law', introduced across the USA in 1996 following the rape and murder of 7-year-old Megan Kanka in New Jersey by a neighbour with a history of sexual assault. In response, the government introduced the Criminal Justice and Court Services Act 2000, making it a requirement for agencies to work together to assess and monitor released prisoners thought to pose a risk to the public. These tasks were to be carried out by multi-agency public protection panels, consisting largely of police and probation officers (Lovell 2001). The pressure for maintaining and increasing the reach and scope of these measures increased following the murders of two 11-year-old girls, Jessica Chapman and Holly Wells, by their school caretaker, Ian Huntley, in Soham in 2002. At Huntley's trial, it was revealed that he had been investigated by the police on several occasions between 1995 and 1999 following allegations of rape, indecent assault and having sexual intercourse with girls under the legal age of consent. None of this information was shared when Huntley was appointed as a school care-taker in 2001. The Bichard inquiry, set up to investigate these matters, argued for better record-keeping and clear protocols for the sharing of information between relevant agencies (Bichard 2004), and in 2011 a national police database was set up to allow regional police forces to share data on convicted criminals, suspects and victims of crime, as well as the details of people questioned by the police but not charged. Civil liberties and the right to privacy were seen as irrelevant where the protection of children was concerned.

While many of these shifts towards improved information-sharing and assessment of risk are understandable in the light of the tragic deaths involved, there are potential unintended consequences. The first is much less emphasis being placed on understanding and differentiating between the reasons and motives for abusive activities and on treating the problem (Colton and Vanstone 1996; Featherstone and Lancaster 1997). Second, there is a danger that abuse becomes associated with individual pathology, while other factors and explanations become rela-tively invisible. Third, there is a danger that concern with extra-familial abuse could lead to less attention being given to the abuse of children within their families. The death of Victoria Climbié and the subsequent public inquiry served as the most shocking reminder, if one were needed, of the devastating harm that could result from overlooked intra-familial abuse.

The Climbié inquiry, 2003

The Climbié inquiry revealed a situation, unlike that found in many previ-ous inquiries, of relatively limited involvement with Victoria and her 'family' or guardians on the part of health, social care or police agencies. To some degree, this resulted from Victoria's unusual living arrangements. She was born in the Ivory Coast and in 1998, aged 7, was sent by her parents to live with her great-aunt, Marie Therese Kouao, in the suburbs of Paris (for her educational betterment). Marie was experiencing considerable domes-tic and financial difficulties, and in 1999 she departed for London, accom-panied by Victoria, to seek employment and a new life. Much of her and Victoria's early contact with professionals was concerned with securing accommodation. Marie eventually solved this herself by moving to live with Carl Manning, whom she met when he was driving a bus on which she and

Victoria were travelling. With the knowledge that was subsequently available to the inquiry, it was clear that physical abuse, including beatings, burns and hot water scalding, were inflicted on Victoria not long after moving into Carl's flat. However, there were only three contacts between health and social care professionals and Victoria from then until the time of her death (approximately eight months later). The first two (in July 1999) involved her being taken to two different hospitals with, first, scabs and cuts on her face and head and, second, scald marks (also on her face and head). At the first of these two contacts, Victoria was diagnosed as having scabies. At the second, Marie alleged that Victoria had poured hot water over herself to reduce the itching pain caused by the scabies. While there was more suspicion about what had happened to Victoria after this second contact, there was no definite assessment carried out and no proper follow-up. The third point of contact was in November when Marie alleged that Carl had sexually abused Victoria, perhaps motivated by a belief that this would result in her getting help with her housing difficulties. However, the allegation was subsequently withdrawn, and it was not followed up. There was no further contact with professionals until Victoria died in February 2000 as a result of physical beatings, hypothermia and gross neglect.

The Climbié inquiry, chaired by Lord Laming, who had a distinguished career in social services management and inspection, came to similar conclusions to those of many previous inquiries, namely that poor communication between agencies, lack of attention paid to children in their own right and a failure to follow-up concerns had led to disastrous consequences. What was different was Laming's complete and utter condemnation of the way in which child protection work was organised and conducted at all levels. Laming was at pains not only to point the finger at front-door workers but also at their senior managers, councillors and strategic bodies such as area child protection committees. He also pointed to the shortcomings of central government for failing to establish clear lines of accountability and was critical about standards of professional training. The inquiry report made 108 recommendations, with the aim of almost completely overhauling the policy and practice of child protection work. These included the creation of a national Children's Commissioner, the replacement of area child protection committees with Local Safeguarding Children Boards (LSCBs), the introduction of electronic multi-agency recording systems, increased managerial scrutiny and oversight of front-line practice, and greater emphasis on joint child protection training.

Legislative and policy changes following the Climbié inquiry

Following the publication of the Climbié report, the government published *Every Child Matters* (Department of Health 2003), which identified five outcomes for every child in the country: being healthy, staying safe, enjoying and achieving, making a positive contribution and achieving economic well-being. This Green Paper response was in keeping with the government's stated agenda of continuing to balance the need for protecting children with that of supporting families. In other words, the paper aligned with the agenda to continue with the policy direction of safeguarding rather than child protection, at least insofar as the latter was considered to prioritise the needs of children over those of their families or to view the two as necessarily being in competition.

The government also proposed the establishment of a national database of children in England; to introduce children's trusts in each local area to bring together the work of health, education and social services; and for local authorities to appoint directors of children's services to oversee services and establish clear lines of accountability. In 2003, responsibility for children's social services was transferred from the Department of Health to the Deparment for Education and Skills (DfES). In 2004, the Children Act placed these reforms on a statutory footing and Children's Commissioner posts were created in England, Northern Ireland, Scotland and Wales. In 2007, a further policy document was published, entitled *Every Parent Matters* (Department for Education and Skills 2007a), which set out how all parents and carers were to be supported from 'early years' intervention, through school and into their child's early adulthood. Three significant pieces of legislation were passed during this period:

- the Carers and Disabled Children Act 2000 applied to all carers aged 16 and over and placed a duty on local authorities to provide direct services for them, following an assessment of need;
- the Carers (Equal Opportunities) Act 2004 placed a duty on local authorities to inform carers of their rights and required carers' assessments to take account of whether carers wished to work, undertake training or education, or engage in leisure activities; and
- the Work and Families Act 2004 gave carers the right to request flexible working arrangements, if certain criteria were met.

These developments need to be understood as part of a wider agenda aimed at taking 'all children out of poverty by 2020' as well as to 'develop the potential of all children'. The focus on all children and all families, and on prevention, remains evident, even in the wake of the Climbié tragedy.

The *Working Together to Safeguard Children* guidelines were also updated and re-issued in light of these developments, in 2006 and again in 2010. The government sought to emphasise the responsibility of all agencies to promote the welfare of children, including to safeguard them from abuse and neglect. The guidance also set out in detail how individual cases were to be managed. Such levels of prescription would later be criticised by *The Munro Review of Child Protection* (Munro 2011a), which noted that *Working Together* was 55 times longer than the comparative guidance issued in 1974.

Although these developments were intended to develop and reinforce a system of family support (for most) and early intervention (for some), Parton (2005) argues that children were increasingly becoming the central concern of the state, with the parents moving increasingly into the background. Policy with regard to parents focused primarily on increasing their uptake of paid employment. A more balanced approach also had considerable implications for resources. Many of the families referred to social services were living in poverty and faced considerable material problems and difficulties. Until the publication of the Field Report in 2010 (Field 2010), there appeared to be little consideration of the cost implications of meeting the needs of these families in order that they in turn could meet the needs of their children (Tunstill and Aldgate 2000). The New Labour government did have ambitious targets for reducing child poverty, centred on supporting wider parental employment and the provision of tax credits and child care initiatives. Yet, whatever way such support was to be provided, there were always going to be clear cost implications in providing sufficient resources to meet the range of health, environmental, social and financial needs of poorer families. Despite significant increases in public spending over this period, calls for more were inevitable, just as there continued to be those who questioned whether the problems experienced by families and child welfare professionals were solvable simply by increased funding. As in many areas, the New Labour government tried to achieve a balance, making the case for increased spending alongside the need for public sector reform.

Peter Connelly

The death and subsequent public inquiry into the death of Maria Colwell led directly to the establishment of a national system of child protection, many elements of which are still apparent today. It is unlikely that there will ever be a repeat of such momentous changes as a result of one child's death, however tragic. And yet, in a different way, the death of Peter Connelly ('Baby P') in 2007, and the subsequent public and political outcry, were just as significant, albeit in a different way.

Peter was born in 2006 and lived with his mother, Tracey Connelly, her partner, Steven Barker, and his brother, Jason Owen. Peter's father left the family home when Peter was 4 months old. In December 2006, Peter was seen by a local doctor because of a head injury. He was subsequently examined at the Whittington Hospital in Islington, where bruising and scratch marks were observed on his body. This prompted the arrest of Peter's mother and maternal grandmother, and Peter's name was added to Haringey's child protection register. Peter was discharged from hospital and accommodated with a family friend. His mother was released on bail in January 2007, soon after which Peter returned to her care. In April, Peter attended North Middlesex Hospital in Enfield, where staff observed further bruising and scratches. The home environment was noted by social workers to be disorganised, smelly and dirty, and contained weapons, animal faeces, fleas, lice and Nazi paraphernalia. In total, Peter had contact with child welfare professionals on 60 separate occasions, not including hospital attendances, before he died in August 2007, aged 17 months. In November 2008, Steven and Jason were found guilty of causing or allowing the death of a child and Tracey pleaded guilty to the same offence.

Several local inquiries, a national task force and a national inquiry were held. A serious case review in Haringey was later criticised by the government, while an independent review reported on 1 December 2008 that Haringey's child protection services were 'wholly inadequate'. A second serious case review, published in 2010, found that Peter's death was 'preventable'. As a result of the national outcry that followed the publicity surrounding Peter's death, the government set up the Social Work Task Force (SWTF), tasked with undertaking a comprehensive review of national social work practice, as well as commissioning a second report by Lord Laming. Yet, the effects of Peter's death on the child welfare system went far beyond the changes in legislation and policy that followed.

The Social Work Task Force (SWTF) and Lord Laming's second report

The SWTF was a joint venture between the DoH and the Department for Children, Schools and Families (DfCSF) – later renamed the Department for Education (DfE) – and focused on four areas: recruitment and retention, training, quality and leadership. It was envisaged that the report of the SWTF would identify key ways to make improvements across these areas. Early proposals were for a recognised post-qualifying year to be introduced for social workers; to include a more manageable caseload and enhanced supervision; greater inspection of education and training courses; a programme to identify 'future leaders' in social work; a high-profile marketing campaign to raise the status of the social work profession; and extra pay for the best social workers to ensure they continued to work directly with parents and children, rather than moving into management. The final report of the SWTF – *Building a Safe, Confident Future* (Social Work Task Force 2009) – made a number of recommendations including higher criteria for entry to social work qualifying programmes; an assessed and supported first year in employment for newly-qualified social workers; a national framework for continuing professional development; the establishment of an independent national college of social work; and the introduction of a social work 'licence to practice'. In March 2010, an implementation plan – *Building a Safe and Confident Future* – was published by the DoH, the DfCSF and the Department for Business, Innovation and Skills (DfBIS) (Social Work Task Force 2010). £200 million of additional funding was provided to support recruitment, student bursaries and workforce development, and to improve information technology systems, to pilot new career structures and to support employers through the first year of reform.

In addition to the broad remit of the SWTF, Lord Laming was also asked to produce a second report, evaluating the changes that had taken place since his first report following the death of Victoria Climbié. *The Protection of Children in England: A Progress Report* was published in 2009 and sought to identify what had been achieved since the first Laming report, what barriers remained to effective safeguarding work and what actions could be taken by the government to overcome these barriers. In total, Laming made a further

58 recommendations. One of the most radical was that every referral from a professional should result in an initial assessment, to include direct contact with the child and their family. Although the government initially accepted this recommendation and indicated it would be included as part of an updated version of *Working Together*, research by Loughborough University estimated that this would lead to an increase in the number of initial assessments by between 4 and 479 per cent, depending on the authority (this is not a typographical error – the range really was this great), with an average increase of 91 per cent. This would require the services of an additional 2,000 social workers (Holmes et al. 2010). Once this became clear, the government concluded it could no longer accept this recommendation and it was not included in subsequent statutory guidance. The government did, however, accept many of the other recommendations. In practice, with the formation of a new Coalition government in 2010, many policy changes were scrapped before they had even been implemented, most notably the planned-for register of every child in England known as Contact Point.

2011–present day: The resurgence of child protection in an age of austerity

With the general election of May 2010 and the formation of the Coalition government, another shift in policy took place. Prompted by an economic desire to cut government spending and a political ambition to empower local decision-making, the new administration sought to discover ways in which child protection could be reformed to enable more local flexibility but without incurring significantly increased costs – the desire was to 'do more with less'. As a result of spending cuts for local authorities, early help and preventative services for families were significantly reduced in almost every area, although most especially in areas of high deprivation and need.

The Munro Review of Child Protection

Although the report of the SWTF and Lord Laming's second report were both significant in their own ways, *The Munro Review of Child Protection* is without question the most important consideration of the child protection system undertaken in the past 20 years. Munro's report, published in three parts, was based on an explicit attempt to take a different approach from previous inquiries and reviews and to avoid what Munro saw as their most common errors. Although in keeping with previous reports, Munro did make several recommendations to improve practice. These were meant to be predicated not only on a thorough understanding of 'the system' but also upon a similar understanding of human behaviour.

The first part of the report, published in 2010, was the result of an extensive 'listening exercise', which considered the views of children, families, carers, social workers and other professionals. This part of the report also set out the methodology employed to gain a fuller understanding of the entirety of the child protection system, rather than focusing on discrete elements in isolation. The report described the problem of unintended consequences resulting from such narrow approaches. For example, timescales for assessments were introduced to prevent 'drift' but helped contribute to what Munro saw as an unhelpful preoccupation with meeting performance indicators rather than evaluating the inherent quality of the assessments produced. Munro argued that child welfare professionals, especially social workers and their managers, were too focused on compliance with rules and regulations and that the exercise of professional judgement was stymied by this culture of targets.

The final part of the report, published in May 2011, set out 15 recommendations. The common thread between these recommendations was to remove unnecessary bureaucracy and targets, increase the potential for professionals to exercise their judgement and to focus more attention on the experiences of children and the outcomes achieved for them and their families. For example, the first recommendation was that *Working Together* guidelines should be revised and significantly simplified, while the third recommendation said that the government should introduce a new public inspection framework to examine how the wishes and experiences of children shape the provision of services.

The wider impact of Peter Connelly's death

Although Peter Connelly's death resulted in a number of important inquiries and reports, not least *The Munro Review of Child Protection*, it was the 'informal' impact of the tragedy that has proved more significant and longer-lasting. Warner (2012) and Jones (2014) have written extensively about this period and articulated many of the key points. The media and political response to Peter's tragic death was intense, beyond anything that had been seen before. *The Sun*, a national tabloid newspaper, ran a front-page story about the case entitled 'Blood on their hands' in reference to Haringey's social workers and, in particular, the then Director of Children's Services, Sharon Shoesmith (who, in 2016, published her own account of what happened after knowledge of Peter's death became public and what we might learn from it). Shoesmith was soon dismissed from her post by the then Education Secretary, Ed Balls, live on television. The leader of the Conservative Party at the time, David Cameron, who would later become Prime Minister, argued that the death of Peter was evidence of a 'broken society' in Britain. He described this situation as one in which there were families who could not nurture children, mothers who did not know how to love, fathers who were absent and children caught in cycles of abuse. This type of coverage and response intensified the sense of a blame culture within child protection social work, whereby many child welfare professionals became overwhelmed at the thought that they too might miss apparently obvious signs of abuse or neglect. The number of referrals to local authorities increased dramatically, as did the numbers of care proceedings. As an inevitable consequence, the number of children in care started to rise and has continued to do so between 2008 and 2018.

Child sexual exploitation, modern slavery, child trafficking and radicalisation

In addition to ongoing concerns about intra-familial abuse, awareness has also increased of 'new' forms of abuse outside of the family, including child sexual exploitation, modern slavery and child trafficking. These concerns may have emerged at least in part because of wider public concern about immigration more generally, although it is far from accurate to say that immigrants pose any more danger to children and young people than non-migrants. Yet in the media and public eye, such dangers may be easier to comprehend if they can be said to arise from outside the mainstream of society rather than from within it.

The two most notable concerns about child sexual exploitation to occur in recent years relate to Jimmy Savile and Rotherham, the latter having been described as the 'biggest child protection scandal in UK history' (Gladman and Heal 2017: 28). Jimmy Savile was a UK celebrity, becoming famous in the 1960s as a presenter of the BBC's *Top of the Pops*. Over the next three decades and beyond, Savile engaged in charity work, including with the Stoke Mandeville Hospital. Savile's fame and apparent good works gave him an unprecedented level of access to children and young people and, in 2013, two years after his death, Scotland Yard labelled Savile a 'prolific, predatory' sex offender, who was guilty of at least 214 criminal offences across 28 police forces and 14 medical establishments. For example, within the Leeds General Infirmary alone, Savile is thought to have abused at least 33 patients, ranging from 5 to 75 years of age. The Rotherham scandal was, if anything, on an even larger scale. From the 1980s to the second decade of the twenty-first century, an estimated 1,400 children were sexually abused by groups of predominantly British-Pakistani men. Children were 'picked up' from schools and residential homes and repeatedly sexually assaulted and raped. To make matters worse, it appeared that many in authority in the area were aware of what was happening and did little or nothing to intervene.

Conclusion

There are a variety of reasons for the somewhat bewildering developments between the publication of the Jasmine Beckford inquiry report, the passing of the Children Act 1989, the Victoria Climbié inquiry and *The Munro Review of Child Protection*. They can best be understood by reference to the way in which the issue of child abuse was responded to in earlier years.

Throughout the extensive period reviewed in this chapter, and continuing into the present day, there was and is ambivalence and uncertainty about the best way for the state to intervene in families to ensure that children are properly socialised and not ill-treated. Preserving the independence of the family and the rights of parents has always needed to be balanced against the welfare of children and their rights to be protected from abuse and neglect. For many years this task was left to the judgement of the NSPCC and later to child care officers in children's departments, with backing from the courts as and when required. This approach was deemed to be working well as long as support for the family remained the major goal.

The 'rediscovery' of child abuse challenged this consensus, just as it did in the late Victorian era. Social workers and others were increasingly pressed to intervene more authoritatively into families in light of a recognition that parental abuse of children was more widespread than had previously been imagined.

Looking back, there have been times when a specific focus on child protection has been the main concern (for example, the late Victorian era and 1970 to the present) and times when a broader family-support approach has predominated (for example, 1914 through to the end of the 1960s). Events at Cleveland and changes to family structure and cohesion created the basis of a shift back to more family-supportive approaches in the 1990s. This shift was reinforced between 1997 and 2010 before a return to child protection, with some more recent signs that we are again moving back to family support, at least in theory, if not in practice. However, the events of the preceding 30 years have done nothing if not create an awareness of the fact that, for at least some children, family homes are dangerous and distressing places and there can be no simple return to the primacy of family-support without a concurrent commitment to the safety of children. The search for the proper balance between the two will likely continue for as long as there is liberal democracy.

Child abuse: A historical timeline

Table 2.1 Timeline of child abuse, 1800 to 2017

Date	Event
1802	The Factory Acts regulated the number of hours children could spend at work
1861	Offences Against the Person Act consolidated provisions related to, in particular, offences of violence
1870	Compulsory school attendance introduced for 5- to 12-year-old children
1872	Baby farming and the Infant Life Protection Act
1884	Formation of the London Society for the Prevention of Cruelty to Children (SPCC)
1885	Criminal Law Amendment Act raised the age of sexual consent from 13 to 16 years old
1887	Formation of the National Society for the Prevention of Cruelty to Children (NSPCC)
1889	Prevention of Cruelty to, and Protection of, Children Act allowed police to arrest people for mistreating children and to enter homes to prevent harm to children
1908	Children Act introduced juvenile courts and Incest Act criminalised sexual abuse
1933	Children and Young Persons Act combined all existing child protection laws and added further restrictions such as a minimum working age for children (14)
1945	Dennis O'Neill inquiry
1946	Curtis Committee

Table 2.1 continued

Date	Event
1948	Children Act and the formation of children's departments
1950	Coordinating committees (cruelty and neglect)
1962	Henry Kempe and the battered child syndrome
1974	Maria Colwell inquiry. Formation of the child abuse prevention system. Area Child Protection Committees established
1975	Susan Auckland inquiry
1974–80	17 public inquiries into child abuse deaths
1981–85	15 public inquiries into child abuse deaths
1985	Jasmine Beckford inquiry
1986–91	12 public inquiries into child abuse deaths
1986	Draft *Working Together* guidelines (child protection)
1987	Kimberley Carlile and Tyra Henry inquiries
1988	Cleveland inquiry and new *Working Together* guidelines
1989	Children Act introduced the paramountcy principle of the child's welfare
1991	New *Working Together* guidelines
1992	UK ratified the UN Convention on the Rights of the Child
1995	Children (Scotland) Act
2000	Publication of the *Framework for the Assessment of Children in Need and Their Families* and the Waterhouse inquiry. Children (Leaving Care) Act and Care Standards Act
2002	Education Act required education services to safeguard and promote the welfare of children
2003	Victoria Climbié inquiry. Publication of *Every Child Matters*
2004	Children Act required local authorities to appoint a Children's Director and replaced Area Child Protection Committees with Local Safeguarding Children Boards
2008	Reporting restrictions on the death of Peter Connelly lifted
2009	Publication of *The Protection of Children in England: A Progress Report*
2010	New *Working Together* guidelines
2011	*The Munro Review of Child Protection.* Launch of the Troubled Families policy agenda
2014	Children and Families Act made changes in relation to adoption; introduced Education, Health and Care (EHC) plans for disabled children; formalised 'staying put' arrangements for foster care; and set a 26-week deadline for care proceedings. DoH published the results of investigations into widespread abuse perpetrated by Jimmy Savile. Publication of the Jay Report into the sexual exploitation of children in Rotherham
2017	Children and Social Work Act required local authorities to publish their support offer for young people with care experience and made further changes to adoption processes

Recommended reading

Davies, C. (2012) *The Ghost of Lily Painter*. London: Windmill Books.

Ferguson, H. (2004) *Protecting Children in Time: Child Abuse, Child Protection and the Consequences of Modernity*. Basingstoke: Palgrave Macmillan.

Gordon, L. (1989) *Heroes of Their Own Lives: The Politics and History of Family Violence, Boston, 1880–1960*. London: Virago.

Hendrick, H. (1994) *Child Welfare: England 1872–1989*. London: Routledge.

Jones, R. (2014) *The Story of Baby P*. Bristol: Policy Press.

Parton, N. (1991) *Governing the Family: Child Care, Child Protection and the State*. London: Macmillan.

Parton, N. (2014) *The Politics of Child Protection*. London: Palgrave Macmillan.

Reder, P., Duncan, S. and Gray, M. (1993) *Beyond Blame: Child Abuse Tragedies Revisited*. London: Routledge.

Warner, J. (2012) *The Emotional Politics of Social Work and Child Protection*. Bristol: Policy Press.

Protecting children and young people from harm: contemporary perspectives

3

Key points in this chapter

- Despite the focus on families and individuals, child abuse and neglect cannot be understood separately from social context.
- Sociological perspectives challenge the basis of many individualised and family-based responses to child maltreatment.
- Recent developments have helped reveal and confirm the troubling relationship between social deprivation and officially-recognised incidence rates of child abuse and neglect.

Children's rights, child abuse and neglect

Much of the discussion about child abuse focuses on individuals and families. However, social contexts have a major influence on the way in which child abuse and neglect are framed, understood and responded to in policy and practice. Changes in these social contexts can have a more profound impact than mere changes in systems and procedures.

Take, for example, the question of children's rights. The belief that children have inherent rights, in the same way as adults, and that these rights can be meaningfully separated from those of the child's parents, has important consequences. (As noted by Moran-Ellis (2010), this has not prevented the 'demonisation' of adolescents in particular in wider political and media discourse.) In world terms, the 1989 *UN Convention on the Rights of the Child* (UNCRC) was a landmark in this respect, setting out basic rights for nation states to adhere to. It stresses that children should be free from abuse, that they have the right to an education, that they should not be exploited as part of the labour market, and that they have a right to live with their families – rights that can only be curtailed by judicial means. Currently, 196 countries are party to the UNCRC, including every member of the United Nations, bar one: the USA.

In Britain, the rights of children were considerably enhanced in legal terms by the Children Act 1989 although the law is now different in the devolved regions of the UK. For example, in Wales, Part three of the Act, including Sections 17 and 20, has been repealed and replaced by the Social Services and Well-being (Wales) Act 2014. Further, Northern Ireland and Scotland did not pass their variations on the Children Act 1989 until 1995 (Tisdall and Plumtree 1997). The main effects of these changes have been in relation to seeking children's views about key decisions made about them. Thus, their wishes and feelings must be taken into account in court hearings, reviews and conferences, and in relation to decisions about placements and medicals. However, there are limits, most notably that the child's age and understanding must be taken into consideration, and while to some extent the need to place limits on a child's self-determination seems reasonable, there are dangers. A clear example of this is the scepticism that often surrounds accounts by children and teenagers in relation to sexual abuse and exploitation.

The rights of disabled children are even more likely to be infringed upon than those of other children. Disabled children are more vulnerable to physical and sexual abuse, particularly in out-of-home settings, which they frequent more than other children. Euser et al. (2015) reported that children with a 'mild intellectual disability' were significantly more likely to be victims of child sexual abuse in out-of-home care settings compared with other children in similar settings and the general child population. Compounding the problem, the abuse of disabled children is less likely to be reported (Stalker et al. 2015).

Nevertheless, efforts continue in this field. In 2008, UNICEF released a publication entitled *Handbook on Legislative Reform: Realising Children's Rights*, which set out how the Committee on the Rights of the Child, the body responsible for monitoring the implementation of the UNCRC, has achieved notable successes by way of nation states enacting laws on previously unlegislated areas of child abuse, such as female genital mutilation and child trafficking.

In general terms, however, while there have been some important developments in relation to children's rights at the level of conventions and research, there is still much to be done. Many professionals remain uneasy about relating to children and tend to work largely through parents (Ferguson 2017). This is despite reported exhortations in government guidance for child protection professionals to 'focus on the child'. Giving children's voices the same degree of credence as those of adults in judicial and quasi-judicial proceedings is still a long way off, particularly in regard to younger children. In addition, there are those who argue that children's rights cannot simply be separated from those of their parents or from embeddedness within particular communities. Although it is important to recognise and respect the fact that children have the right to be safe, to be heard and to partici-pate, none of us (children especially) should be considered merely as individual 'rights-bearers' without a concurrent recognition that such rights can only be meaningfully realised within specific family and social circum-stances. Archard (2004) thus distinguishes between 'liberationist' and 'caretaker' conceptions of children's rights, with the former emphasising that children should have equality in rights with adults, and the latter that children are relatively more dependent, vulnerable and incompetent.

Sociological perspectives on different forms of abuse

Sociological perspectives on child abuse did not have a major influence on child protection thinking and work in the UK before the 1990s, except in the case of sexual abuse and the question of gender. The reason for this is probably twofold. First, such perspectives do not provide clear indicators for practice because by definition they look broadly at the social and cultural conditions that create the climate for child abuse rather than at individual cases. Second, many sociological perspectives provide a (helpful) challenge to professionals who are intervening in families to protect children, because they question the ethics and politics of mainstream assumptions (Howe 1991). Thus, they can have an unsettling quality, locating the 'cause(s)' of the problem outside the individual sphere and posing uncom-fortable questions about the validity of much professional intervention.

For example, Straus and Gelles (1986) conducted several national inci-dence surveys in the USA of physical child abuse. In these studies, they and their colleagues reported high levels of intra-familial violence of all kinds. They came to the conclusion that such violence was the norm and that individuals were more likely to be subjected to violent acts within fami-lies than outside them. In an attempt to explain these high rates, they argued that violence is a socially-sanctioned form of maintaining order and is approved of as a form of child behavioural control or discipline by many in US society. It can be argued from this perspective that a society that approves of corporal punishment, including in schools, and endorses the adage 'spare the rod and spoil the child' sets the scene for a variety of other forms of violence. Child abuse is thus seen as being on the same spectrum as other socially-approved forms of violence rather than being a separate pathological phenomenon. This perspective may be troubling for many. It suggests that parents found to be physically abusive towards their children are not necessarily inherently damaged or pathological; rather, their behaviour may be part of a continuum with other forms of socially-accepted violence.

Such a perspective also suggests the need for high-level changes in the way we treat and think about children if we want to lower the incidence of physical child abuse, including the need to encourage non-violent means of enabling and encouraging pro-social behaviour – and indeed, there have been moves in this direction in the UK. Yet an outright national ban on the use of physical punishment has not been forthcoming in the UK, partly because many parents still use such punishment (or the threat of such punishment) as a form of discipline. While it is illegal to hit any other person for any reason other than defence of oneself or one's property, the Children Act 2004 provides parents with a potential legal defence, under Section 58, in the form of discipline: parents must show their actions amounted to 'reasonable punishment' of their child. The Scottish and Welsh governments announced in 2017 their intention to remove this legal defence for their citizens, potentially resulting in children in Wales and Scotland being less at risk of physical chastisement than their peers in England.

Support for physical punishment is more deeply entrenched in the USA, although some states do prohibit it in schools. In contrast, most countries in South America have outlawed corporal punishment in any setting, while many countries in southern Africa are committed to full prohibition, as are India and a number of other Asian countries. Other European countries have also been much more proactive than the UK in this respect. Sweden, where the ban on the use of physical punishment of children by parents has been in operation the longest, has seen reductions over time in youth involvement in crime and decreases in substance misuse, rape and suicide (Durrant 1999). Although, as noted by Beckett (2005), it does not follow that banning corporal punishment is *causally* related to lower rates of child maltreatment or deaths from child maltreatment.

Nevertheless, there are others who take the view that what they call 'non-abusive' corporal punishment does not inevitably or necessarily lead to aggression, and indeed this viewpoint informs the 'chastisement practices' within some cultural groups. One of the central tenets of this view is that Sweden's anti-spanking laws have never really been evaluated fully – indeed Lyons et al. (1993) argued that physical abuse increased after the ban in Sweden, because parents may have become even more violent when they felt 'mild spanking' was not available as a legal option (operating almost like a safety valve, of sorts). There are also fears that emotional abuse – in the form of excessive criticism, persistent mocking and derogation – could increase when 'non-abusive' corporal punishment is forbidden.

Returning to the question of how society sanctions or condones certain behaviours, whether implicitly or explicitly, the same sort of analysis can be applied to sexual abuse: because the sexual exploitation of women and, to a lesser extent, of children, is tolerated in, for instance, art, cinema, advertising, pornography and prostitution, a climate is set whereby sexual abuse results. Again, from this perspective, sexual abuse is seen as part of a continuum rather than a qualitatively distinctive act, with myriad attitudes towards what is acceptable and what ought to be condemned.

The clear strengths of these social and cultural perspectives are that they broaden our focus in comparison with psychological and social psychological theories and help us to understand how societal influences – such as the views of our friends and neighbours, the images we see on TV and online – can contribute to the incidence and form of child mistreatment, despite the fact that society officially aims to reduce and prevent such problems. The implication for social policy is the need to tackle these matters on a broad front and that repeated interventions with individuals and families alone are insufficient (and even potentially harmful). The major weakness of these perspectives, at least for professionals, lies in the fact that it cannot fully explain why some people within the same culture and society abuse children while others do not.

The social–structural perspective and child abuse

Gil's research and writing, already referred to, formed the cornerstone of this perspective. Gil's (1970) early work convinced him that child abuse was class-related and that 'psychological' explanations of abuse by themselves were too narrow and grossly underestimated the contribution of stress, particularly that caused by poverty and material deprivation, to the causation of child abuse. He developed his ideas further to lay some of the blame for child abuse on the policies of the state itself (Gil 1975, 1978).

Gil also put forward a broad definition of abuse that included failing to meet the developmental needs of children, whatever the reason. This definition clearly places responsibility for child abuse on the state over and above the person who actually abuses the child, on the grounds that it sanctions inequality and low standards of housing, health, education and leisure for the children of the poor. From this point of view, the state, far from being the benign rescuer of children when parents ill-treat them, is actually the villain of the piece because it abuses children by its failure to provide adequate facilities for them, and also creates stresses for parents that increase the likelihood of their committing physical acts of abuse or neglect. Nigel Parton (1985, 2007) has lent considerable support to this perspective in Britain:

> *Child abuse is strongly related to class, inequality and poverty both in terms of prevalence and severity ... Locating the problem in terms of social structural factors has important implications for the way we define the problem, the way we explain it and the best way of doing something about it. For solving the problem requires a realignment in social policy which recognises the necessity of attacking the social, economic and cultural conditions associated with the abuse.*
>
> (Parton 1985: 175–6)

The strength of the social–structural approach is that it does justice to the accepted fact that physical child abuse in particular has a close association with deprivation and especially so with regards to neglect (Wolock and Horowitz 1984). Its weakness lies in the fact that a minority of poor people abuse their children (and so do some rich people) and, therefore, it is not a sufficient explanation, essentially overlooking the importance of human agency and autonomy. Taken to the extreme, it offers child abusers a way of avoiding responsibility for their own actions. Finally, it does not address the aetiology of child sexual abuse, which is generally considered not to be linked to class and poverty and nor is emotional abuse.

Child protection policy in the UK during the 1990s began formally to take into account structural inequality and social exclusion through the third side of the (latterly non-statutory) 'assessment triangle', family and environmental factors, which incorporated family history and functioning, wider family, housing, employment, income, family's social integration and community resources into the family assessment. Thus, in addition to the child's developmental needs and parenting capacity, professionals involved in child protection and welfare services were required to take account of the 'world outside the family' (Parton 2005).

Feminist perspectives and child abuse

Feminist ideas have had a major impact on how we think about, and understand, all forms of child abuse and there are clear lessons to take from these contributions. First, men can be seen as a risk to children (and to women) and it is important that professionals working directly with families are aware of this. They must be careful not to assume shared values, concerns and interests between parents of different sex; in particular, they need to be attuned to the possibility of male violence to their partners.

Second, there is much that could be done to reduce the risk of child abuse by tackling issues of gender socialisation. It seems important to engage fathers in child protection work because, if the roots of violence to both children and women lie in part in male socialisation, then without men's involvement a target for change is being systematically missed (Scourfield 2003). There are some practical considerations, too. For example, research suggests that a large number of children live with a 'social father'. This term can be used to describe any father figure who is not biologically related to the child he is caring for, including men who are married to or cohabiting with the child's mother and who may previously have been referred to as 'step-fathers'. In some contexts, social fathers can exhibit significantly higher levels of cooperative caregiving, take on more shared responsibilities and be more engaged with the child than biological fathers (Berger et al. 2008).

However, engaging males in health and welfare interventions is a difficult task for a variety of reasons. There are barriers, such as the view that childrearing is 'female business', and the fact that males are more likely to be the abusive carer or bear responsibility for family violence. Also, many families referred to children's services are or are assumed to be headed by female lone parents, and any males involved with such families are seen as peripheral figures. Other barriers stem from the fact that we have a largely female workforce - approximately, 85 per cent of child and family social workers in the UK are female - and the difficulties this may pose in seeing family life from a male perspective, as well as the danger of trying to engage with violent men.

In recent years, there have been a number of developments in relation to the question of how best to engage fathers and men more generally in this kind of work. It has become clearer that of course for many men, becoming a father engenders moments of deep reflection and represents a clear and important point of transition in their lives (Ferguson and Gates 2015). The feminist perspective helps us understand that having predetermined roles for men and women in relation to the family can be just as problematic for fathers as it is undoubtedly for mothers (Silverstein 1996). It is also clear from a number of studies, summarised by Allen and Daly (2007), that, all other things being equal, children benefit in many and various ways from the positive involvement of fathers in their lives. This being the case, it is perhaps not surprising that many fathers whose children are suspected of being maltreated are committed to their well-being and are extremely distressed if their children are removed from the family home (Zanoni et al. 2014). As noted by Scourfield (2014), the difficulties that many child welfare professionals have in engaging with fathers is not, axiomatically, because of sexist or anti-feminist attitudes. Rather, the reasons for lack of engagement are complex and largely organisational. Expectations of fathers may be lower than for mothers, involving fathers may go 'against the grain' of the prevailing culture and the assumed responsibility of mothers for the welfare of their children has a deeply-rooted social legacy.

Thus, it is evident that *structural* feminism has been, and remains, an important means of raising awareness about child protection issues. Angelides (2004) has argued that concerns about sexual abuse of children come onto the policy agenda when feminism is strong and vice versa. Uncomfortable though the ideas of feminists may be for parts of mainstream society, nevertheless there can be little doubt that they have been highly influential in reshaping thinking about abuse in Britain over the past 30 years.

On the other hand, at the micro level, feminist-informed thinking is being used to understand the processes taking place within families leading to abuse and violence – for example, by studying the overlap between violence against women and child abuse in the same family (Edleson 1999) as well as examining why violence against children and violence against women are often treated decidedly differently (Messing 2011; see also Featherstone 1997; Featherstone and Trinder 1997).

One of the key developments during the past 20 years is that there is no longer consensus over the meaning of 'feminism' or indeed 'family' (Featherstone 2007). Most commentators agree that there are different emphases within an overall feminist discourse and some of the earlier forms of feminism have been criticised for being geared towards white, middle-class perspectives. But most of the perspectives so far outlined are considered by radical feminists, for example, to be gender-blind. From their point of view, all of the psychological perspectives commonly referred to by professionals, particularly attachment theory, assume that women are (or should be) the primary carers of children and that, if things go wrong, the spotlight falls on their behaviour.

A radical feminist perspective on child abuse began to emerge in the 1980s. The stimulus for this came from the 'discovery' of child sexual abuse, an act committed predominantly by males, and feminist explanations have been highly relevant. From this starting point, the feminist perspective has now been applied to all forms of abuse. This perspective has been articulated by many writers in the USA and the UK (for example, Dominelli 1986; Nelson 1987; Macleod and Saraga 1988; Driver and Droisen 1989; Cox et al. 2001; Smart et al. 2001; Ferguson 2004; Featherstone 2007).

There is little equivocation about the reason for the existence of child sexual abuse and the form that it takes from these researchers:

> *Generally boys and men learn to experience their sexuality as an overwhelming and uncontrollable force; they learn to focus their sexual feelings on submissive objects, and they learn the assertion of their sexual desires, the expectation of having them serviced.*
>
> (MacLeod and Saraga 1988: 41)

> *Abuse in the form of violence against women is a normal feature of patriarchal relations. It is a major vehicle that men use in controlling women. As such, it is the norm not an aberration. The widespread incidence of child sexual abuse reveals the extent to which men are prepared to wield sexual violence as a major weapon in asserting their authority over women.*
>
> (Dominelli 1986: 12)

The attention of these writers is not on individual males. Individual pathology is discounted as a cause of child abuse (as is family pathology). Rather, abuse is seen as an extreme example of institutionalised male power over females. The implications for policy of this perspective are similar in kind, if not focus, to those of the other sociological perspectives. Sexual abuse needs to be addressed and tackled at the societal level, as well as at the individual level. Men abuse children (and women) primarily because of the general power imbalance between the sexes and the different forms of socialisation that they experience, not because of psychiatric illness or emotional deficits.

With regard to physical abuse and neglect, feminist perspectives are less clear-cut (Featherstone 1997). The argument that such abuse is created by the conditions of patriarchy does not rest as easily in this case as with that of sexual abuse. However, women (still) spend far more time with children than do men and have to cope more directly with the stresses of child care. This argument has been taken further by some feminists in that they see the notion of motherhood, a product of patriarchy that reinforces the idea that children's welfare and needs are best met by mothers, as exacerbating the already existing stresses placed on women looking after children (Ong 1985). Under such conditions, it is surprising that the numbers of women who abuse and neglect children do not vastly exceed those of men and, from this point of view, men are disproportionately violent to children. The implication is that women's violence to children is much more likely to be stress-related than that of men. Another area opened up by the feminist perspective is that of domestic violence (Dobash and Dobash 1992) or domestic abuse and its linkage with child abuse (Mullender and Morley 1994). Exposure to domestic abuse is now widely recognised as a form of child abuse in and of itself and feminist perspectives have helped broaden our understanding of domestic abuse to include not 'only' physical and sexual violence but also more subtle forms of coercive control and domination (Stark 2009).

The strength of feminist perspectives on child abuse as a whole is that it opened up a dimension that had been missing from previous explanations about why child abuse occurs. We saw earlier that (in the case of physical abuse and neglect) men have been, until fairly recently, overlooked in terms of intervention. Feminist perspectives point to the error in this, in that understanding and challenging the nature of male–female power relations at an institutional and individual level are of major importance in the theory and practice of child protection work (Scourfield 2003). The challenge should be both to the impositions placed on women within the family and to the way in which males are socialised (Hearn 1990).

The weakness of 'the' feminist perspective is in assuming that there is one perspective. 'Post-feminist' perspectives have questioned the determinism of radical feminism and argued the need for more flexibility in understanding female identity and of the roles that this might play in child abuse, for instance (Featherstone and Trinder 1997).

Poverty and child protection

Whatever the actual incidence of child abuse across society and across different socio-economic classes, state intervention takes place almost exclusively with poor families. What accounts for this and what are the implications of it for future policy and practice?

One account is that abuse occurs across all social classes but is more likely to be identified in poorer families because they are less able to deal with and contain their problems. A related account is that abuse occurs across all social classes but is more likely to be identified in poorer families because poorer families are more likely to be the subject of state surveillance in various forms. A third account is that physical abuse and neglect are in fact positively correlated with poverty and poor families, i.e. child abuse and neglect are strongly related to harsh living standards and the stresses of living in them. Finally, drug and alcohol misuse are also much more common in poorer neighbourhoods and living in such conditions impacts on parenting and the treatment and care of children.

Of course, it is vital to note that not all poor families ill-treat their children, and it is clearly possible to live in even the most materially deprived of circumstances and not to ill-treat children – indeed, to love and nurture them. However, there are studies that show, unsurprisingly, that families most at risk within such poor environments are those exposed to multiple forms of disadvantage, including physical and mental illness, bereavements and disability (Brandon et al. 2010).

A fourth account linking child abuse and neglect to poverty is that which proposes a cyclical transmission of abuse and neglect, i.e. abuse and neglect go across generations in poor families. However, we also know that only a minority of ill-treated children go on to become neglectful or abusive parents themselves, suggesting again that the relationship is far from deterministic or causal.

All these accounts have some explanatory value. However, it is important not to get into either/or debates within the poverty explanations or between them and other explanations. It is likely that child abuse is more closely associated with living in poverty, with the possible exception of child sexual abuse. It is also likely that abuse and neglect of children outside poorer families remain much more hidden from official notice. Finally, it is likely that poor standards of care and ill-treatment of children go across generations in a small number of highly deprived and disadvantaged families.

However, important though poverty is, there are many other factors that, in different combinations, contribute to the causation of child abuse and neglect alongside poverty. Multi-dimensional explanations of child abuse and neglect have long been adopted by professionals in practice, emphasising the emotional and physical needs of children, in combination with assessments of parenting capacity and environmental factors.

Finally, another way of understanding the impact of poverty on child well-being is via the levels of inequality in a society, as well as relative deprivation. Wilkinson and Pickett (2010) have argued that a smaller gap between rich and poor leads to happier, healthier and more successful populations, including children. A range of health and social problems, including life expectancy, infant mortality, teenage births, mental illness and drug and alcohol addiction, are apparently worse in more unequal countries. (More recently, Wilkinson and Pickett's analysis has been criticised for cherry-picking the data and ignoring important outliers.) Even so, in the UK, the work of Bywaters et al. (2016, 2018) has revealed what they describe as an 'inverse intervention law', whereby families living in deprived areas in relatively affluent local authorities are more likely to experience state intervention than those living in similar circumstances in more deprived local authorities, resulting in more formal instances of child abuse and higher numbers of children in care.

Responding to child abuse

In 2019, our knowledge base about the abuse and neglect of children has developed into a vast array of scenarios. We are now aware of physical, sexual, emotional abuse and neglect of children in their own homes, in residential and hospital services and in sports clubs; of children being bullied at school; being abused by the clergy; living on the streets; being involved in sexual exploitation and the production of images and videos of child sexual abuse; being trafficked and economically exploited; being damaged by war experiences; and being assaulted and killed by strangers.

We know that some children and young people are exposed to many forms of abuse and that abuse can create a vulnerability to further abuse. We also know that the experience of abuse can lead to the abuse of others, including other children and siblings. We are beginning to realise that quite large proportions of adults experiencing everyday problems, including mental ill-heath and serious drug and alcohol dependency or use, have some history of being abused as children and into adulthood.

Given this, one of the most pressing problems is surely the need to develop responsive and readily available support services for abused children, for their parents and other carers, and for adults who have been abused or neglected in the past. It is important to bear in mind in this instance that what is supportive can also be preventive. Nevertheless, there is still little in the way of comprehensive support services available for those who have been abused or for members of their families. Which is not to suggest we are without any good examples of supportive responses to child abuse, particularly with regard to sexual abuse. The problem is that such support is only patchily available (Finkelhor and Tucker 2015).

In 2009, *The Lancet* published a review of interventions used in the prevention of child maltreatment and treatment of associated impairments (MacMillan et al. 2009). The results showed that cognitive-behavioural therapy (CBT) brought benefits for sexually abused children with post-traumatic stress symptoms and that child-focused therapy had some benefit for neglected children (although no interventions with neglected children were found to be significantly effective), whereas therapy involving mother and child was beneficial following situations of intimate partner violence. For physically abused children, the study found that parent–child interaction therapy was perhaps the most promising intervention. This finding has also been confirmed by other studies (Carr 2009), especially when the therapy also involved a non-abusive carer. For emotionally or psychologically abused children, no interventions were shown by this study to be particularly effective. In all areas, the study called for more research into 'what works', with a focus on clear outcome measures and studies that rely on methods other than self-reporting of benefits. Other interventions, such as eye movement desensitisation and reprocessing, have also begun to show some promise (Shapiro 2014).

More recently, the traumatic nature of child maltreatment has been highlighted, potentially widening the scope for supportive services to be provided, particularly for children in care, by learning from what works for people experiencing trauma resulting from other experiences (for example, soldiers returning from theatres of war). Services have also been developed specifically to help parents separated from their children, most notably mothers, although these are not entirely without controversy. For example, the Pause Project seeks to support mothers who have or could have multiple children removed because of concerns about child abuse, addressing the 'cliff edge' in support that so often accompanies the child's placement into public care. An initial evaluation of the Pause programme indicated a successful reduction in future child removals (McCracken et al. 2017), although some have criticised the requirement for mothers to take long-term, reversible contraceptive medication in order to be considered eligible for the programme. Other notable support options include Trevi House, which offers a unique rehabilitation unit for mothers experiencing drug and alcohol dependency, enabling them to engage in recovery and support services with their child, rather than having to be separated from them first. However, such services remain a long way from being universally available.

Conclusion

This overview of contemporary perspectives reveals, we hope, the utility and value of considering sociological perspectives on child abuse. Not because they easily and linearly translate into informing better individual practice, but because they help dispel the idea that psychological perspectives, no matter how dominant they may appear, are the only perspectives worth considering. While psychology can be very useful for understanding the behaviour of individuals, sociology is equally useful for understanding the 'behaviour' of large groups and patterns within broader society. Which is not to say that sociological perspectives cannot have an impact on policy or practice. Without the work of feminist thinkers, writers, academics, advocates, politicians and others, how under-developed might our conceptions of domestic abuse now currently be?

Careful analysis of contemporary perspectives can, though, help directly in practice too. Understanding more clearly the relationship between poverty, relative deprivation and child abuse should help professionals remain more aware of the role that poverty has in the lives of many families, particularly those formally recognised by the state to be mistreating their children. Although such awareness can make for personal discomfort, the goal of providing better support should help us remain open and reflective to these challenging alternative views.

Recommended reading

Featherstone, B., Gupta, A., Morris, K. and Warner, J. (2018) Let's stop feeding the risk monster: towards a social model of 'child protection', *Families, Relationships and Societies,* 7(1): 7–22.

Featherstone, B., Gupta, A., Morris, K. and White, S. (2018) *Protecting Children: A Social Model.* Bristol: Policy Press.

Firmin, C. (2017) *Contextual Safeguarding. An Overview of the Operational, Strategic and Conceptual Framework.* Luton: University of Bedfordshire.

Munro, E. (2011) *The Munro Review of Child Protection: Final Report.* London: The Stationery Office.

Parton, N. (2005) *Safeguarding Childhood: Early Intervention and Surveillance in Late Modern Society.* London: Palgrave Macmillan.

Sidebotham, P., Brandon, M., Bailey, S., Belderson, P., Dodsworth, J., Garstang, J., Harrison, E., Retzer, A. and Sorensen, P. (2016) *Pathways to Harm, Pathways to Protection: A Triennial Analysis of Serious Case Reviews 2011 to 2014.* London: The Stationery Office.

Stark, E. (2009) *Coercive Control: How Men Entrap Women in Personal Life.* Oxford: Oxford University Press.

4

Defining child abuse

Key points in this chapter

- Child protection practice in the UK is still primarily based on the four major categories of maltreatment long identified as such: physical abuse, emotional abuse, sexual abuse (including child sexual exploitation) and neglect.
- Obtaining an agreed definition of these four types of maltreatment between professionals, across different professional groups and between professionals and lay persons represents an ongoing challenge.
- New forms of abuse and neglect continue to emerge and further complicate our efforts to agree formal definitions and to work effectively in practice to safeguard children and young people.

Introduction

Any logical approach to a problem entails describing its nature and size, so that the response to it can be appropriate and sufficiently well-resourced to ensure an effective solution. However, it should be clear from reading the preceding chapters that notions of child abuse and neglect are nothing if not complex, as well as being subject to constant change, debate and realignment. They are highly contested concepts, underpinned by and subject to a range of political and cultural factors particular to the society in which they occur. In much of the literature on this subject, the words 'abuse', 'neglect' and 'maltreatment' are used apparently interchangeably, indicating that we are far from establishing a consensus on what they might mean (Mennen et al. 2010). For these reasons, child abuse and neglect are not phenomena that lend themselves to easy definition or measurement. Although the two phenomena are closely interrelated, for the purposes of analysis, they will, as far as possible, be considered separately. Before we look at different categories of child maltreatment, some general considerations should be taken into account.

The cultural context of a child abuse definition

Child abuse and neglect are socially defined constructs. They are products of a particular culture and context and are not absolute unchanging phenomena. As we have seen in the historical chapters, what is considered to be abusive or neglectful in a particular society at a particular moment may not be considered abusive or neglectful in a different society or in the same society some time later. Korbin (1981) cites examples of culturally approved practices in societies in the southern hemisphere that we would almost certainly define as abusive:

> These include extremely hot baths, designed to inculcate culturally valued traits; punishments, such as severe beatings, to impress the child with the necessity of adherence to cultural rules; and harsh initiation rites that include genital operations, deprivation of food and sleep, and induced bleeding and vomiting.
>
> (Korbin 1981: 4)

She points out that the reverse is also true:

> Practices such as isolating infants and small children in rooms or beds of their own at night, making them wait for readily available food until a schedule dictates that they can satisfy their hunger, or allowing them to cry without immediately attending to their needs or desires would be at odds with the child-rearing philosophies of most of the cultures discussed.
>
> (Korbin 1981: 4)

The lesson to be learned from anthropological studies is that the cultural context within which behaviour takes place and the meaning attributed to it by those sharing that culture are important factors to be taken into account when labelling certain acts as abusive or neglectful. In an attempt to solve this conundrum, Kempe argued that children everywhere have the right to be protected from parents who are unable to cope at a level deemed reasonable by the society in which they reside (Kempe and Kempe 1978). However, the question of what is 'reasonable' has no fixed answer, and neither is it entirely clear why children might need to be protected *only* from 'unreasonable' parents, as opposed to from anyone who might be able to seriously harm them.

Although such examples and comparisons rightly sensitise us to the cultural nature of child abuse and neglect, this does not mean there can be no common standards whatsoever. Korbin (1981) stresses that the sort of abuse described by Kempe et al. (1962) as the 'battered child syndrome' would not be sanctioned by any society. Other research seems to confirm this point – Korbin et al. (2000) studied the views of African-American parents and compared them with European-American parents. They found that although there were differences in emphasis, there was a remarkable degree of agreement regarding behaviours that most respondents viewed as abusive or neglectful. Finkelhor and Korbin (1988) argue strongly that other 'culturally approved' practices, such as ritual circumcision and female genital mutilation, should also be seen universally as abusive and addressed as such.[1]

Differing definitions are not, however, only a challenge when comparing between different societies. Within the same society too, different definitions are often readily apparent. Calheiros and colleagues (2016) argue that although different perspectives evidently do exist, finding shared operating definitions is important, not least for the question of mutually comprehensible assessments and interventions. They found that far more consensus was evident in relation to definitions and the severity of physical abuse and sexual abuse, and much less in relation to emotional or psychological abuse and neglect. Hence, just the same sort of care needs to be taken with a culturally relativist approach in these circumstances.

Webb et al. (2002) show how a whole range of factors, such as cultural stereotyping, misplaced cultural sensitivity, fear of being seen to be racist and inadequate training can result in professional workers failing to protect children in black and ethnic minority families from abuse. The cases of Tyra Henry (Lambeth 1987)[2] and Victoria Climbié (Laming 2003)[3] provide examples of this and, more recently, the widespread sexual exploitation and abuse of young girls in Rotherham provides another.

The concerns of the definers

Legislators, by and large, favour non-specific definitions of abuse because they allow flexibility and room for manoeuvre. Therefore, most legal definitions of child abuse are phrased in very general terms, such as 'improper treatment' or 'significant harm'. However, researchers into child abuse are very much concerned with achieving precision and consistency. Clear identification of the object of research and common standards of measurement are important ingredients of such work. Definitional inconsistencies between studies may well account for major differences in estimates of prevalence (Finkelhor and Baron 1986).

Defining child abuse and neglect in practice

A further general issue relates to the process by which child abuse and neglect are actually defined in practice. Here we are considering what Gelles (1982) termed *operational* as opposed to *nominal* definitions (that is, those used in law and research). How do social workers and other professional groups decide in practice what does and does not constitute abuse or neglect from the large (and seemingly ever-increasing) number of referrals they receive?

While it is now a somewhat dated study, the issues raised and examined by Giovannoni and Becerra (1979) remain pertinent today. They were of the opinion that there were no adequate definitions of abuse or neglect that could be operationalised by professionals: 'A major thesis of this book is that child abuse and neglect are matters of social definition and that the problems that inhere in the establishment of those definitions ultimately rest on value decisions' (Giovannoni and Becerra 1979: 5). To test this hypothesis, they devised 78 pairs of vignettes briefly describing potentially abusive situations.[4] The researchers assigned 60 vignettes at random to four groups of professionals (police, social workers, paediatricians and lawyers) and also to a number of lay inhabitants of Los Angeles, who were asked to rate them on a 1–9 scale of seriousness. The main finding was that there was little agreement between the professional groupings about the seriousness of the various types of maltreatment. Overall, there was most agreement between the police and social workers, who together took a more serious view of nearly all the incidents than did paediatricians or lawyers (in that order). This lack of agreement was attributed to the different requirements of the various occupational roles. The reason for higher ratings on the part of police and social workers was seen to be their greater involvement in the early investigative stages of maltreatment. The police rated vignettes where a crime had been alleged as more serious than the other professionals. Social workers were ahead of the others with regard to emotional abuse and lawyers tended to rate everything lower than the rest because their concern was whether there was enough evidence to prove a case in a court of law.

With regard to the lay participants, Giovannoni and Becerra found that, as a whole, they were more likely to judge the scenarios as more serious than all the professionals and that those from poorer social groups 'generally saw mistreatment as more serious than did those of higher socioeconomic status' (Giovannoni and Becerra 1979: 189). This is in contrast to the widely held perception that professionals have higher standards in this respect than the general public. The main conclusion drawn from Giovannoni and Becerra's study was that there was much confusion among professionals when deciding whether cases were sufficiently abusive or neglectful to justify mandatory intervention.

Later studies have highlighted a related difficulty, namely, that the heterogeneous nature of child maltreatment does not lend itself to very strict operational definitions, even when the study involves only one type of professional group. Mennen et al. (2010) studied the case records of 303 children identified as being maltreated by a child protection social work agency. The study also identified five areas of parental behaviour deemed by the agency to be neglectful: neglect of basic care, environmental neglect, medical neglect, educational neglect and supervisory neglect. Based on these measures, they found that 71 per cent of the case records contained evidence of neglect, compared with only 41 per cent of the children who were formally classified as being neglected. The conclusion of the study was that even based on the agency's own definition of neglect, they had not formally identified a large number of children who fitted their own definition, despite a high level of involvement and recognition that other forms of maltreatment were present.

In recent years, there has also been a growing recognition of different types of harm that may lie outside normally accepted definitions of maltreatment, and yet which can still have potentially very serious and lasting effects on children's health and well-being. For instance, in the UK and the USA, among other countries, child obesity is being recognised as a major public health issue. Some have advocated for a recognition of child obesity as a child protection concern (Jones et al. 2013). Others have argued that obesity is not the result of individual parenting failures but arises instead from gross social inequalities (Mulderrig 2016). Nevertheless, this debate over the proper limits of definitions of child maltreatment highlights the ever-changing nature not only of recognised childhood problems (in this case, obesity) but also differing conceptions of the role and extent of parental rather than social responsibility. Abuse, in the minds of many, suggests some deliberate act on the part of, usually, a parent. Neglect, similarly, may suggest to many a deliberate form of omission. Considering whether childhood obesity is a form of maltreatment involves the possibility that some forms of abuse may involve no intentionality on the part of the parent, indeed may even result from good intentions.

Considerable effort has been made to tighten official definitions over the last 30 years in the UK. There have also been constant attempts to get various professionals to work closely together to achieve greater consistency. However, on the basis of these sources of evidence, the only safe definition is that it is a judgement reached by a group of professionals on the examination of the circumstances of a child, normally (in the UK) at a child protection conference.

Formal definitions of child abuse

The Children Act 1989

In the UK, child abuse and neglect are not clearly defined anywhere in primary legislation. The nearest it comes to a definition is in Section 31(2) of the Children Act 1989 when setting out the grounds for care proceedings, which states:

> A court may only make a care order or supervision order if it is satisfied –
>
> (a) that the child concerned is suffering, or is likely to suffer, significant harm; and
> (b) that the harm, or likelihood of harm, is attributable to –
>
>   (i) the care given to the child, or likely to be given to him if the order were not made, not being what it would be reasonable to expect a parent to give to him; or
>   (ii) the child's being beyond parental control.

The key legal concept in relation to abuse and neglect is the notion of *significant harm*. Harm is defined in Section 31(9) (as amended by the Adoption and Children Act 2002) as follows:

> 'harm' means ill-treatment or the impairment of health or develop-ment [including, for example, impairment suffered from seeing or hearing the ill-treatment of another];
> 'development' means physical, intellectual, emotional, social or behavioural development;
> 'health' means physical or mental health; and
> 'ill-treatment' includes sexual abuse and forms of ill-treatment which are not physical.

Section 31(10) then addresses the issue of how to measure 'significant harm', as follows:

> Where the question of whether harm suffered by a child is significant turns on the child's health or development, his health or development shall be compared with that which could reasonably be expected of a similar child.

As Lyon points out, the sort of comparisons being required are 'invidious, if not well-nigh impossible, but do raise incredible spectres of class, cul-tural, racial, religious and ethnic considerations' (1989: 205).

As operational definitions, therefore, the law offers little help, and much is left to the judgement of professionals and ultimately of the courts to decide on whether child mistreatment is sufficiently serious to warrant making care or supervision orders.

Working Together guidelines

However, formal definitions of child abuse and neglect are to be found in secondary legislation guidelines and these will be used as a framework for the rest of this discussion. Five categories of maltreatment are identified in the 2018 *Working Together* guidelines: (1) physical abuse; (2) emotional abuse; (3) sexual abuse; (4) child sexual exploitation; and (5) neglect. (Extremism is also identified and is considered below under the heading 'radicalisation').

Physical abuse

Physical abuse was the original concern of those who brought child abuse to public attention in the 1960s. In the 2018 guidelines, physical abuse is defined as involving:

> A form of abuse which may involve hitting, shaking, throwing, poison-ing, burning or scalding, drowning, suffocating or otherwise causing

physical harm to a child. Physical harm may also be caused when a parent or carer fabricates the symptoms of, or deliberately induces, illness in a child.

(HM Government 2018: 102)

As a nominal definition, this categorisation is relatively specific but is still not particularly useful as an operational definition for professionals because there is little guidance as to when behaviour such as hitting becomes serious enough to warrant protective intervention, especially when considering that smacking children is not a criminal offence everywhere in the UK. Clearly, for physically abusive behaviour such as poisoning or drowning, single incidents will always be enough to warrant statutory intervention. Although the defence of 'reasonable chastisement' has been removed, Section 58 of the Children Act 2004 only states that the battery of a child resulting in actual or grievous bodily harm cannot be justified on these grounds. It is still permissible to hit a child as long as the consequences are so minor that they would not provide sufficient evidence to warrant an assault charge. This is open to different interpretations but satisfies the demands of those who wish to retain the right to smack children. Fabricating the symptoms of illness or deliberately inducing illness in a child (fabricated or induced illness, FII) is thought to be a rare form of abuse and may also be known as Munchausen's syndrome by proxy (see below).

Therefore, the only guidance in this respect comes from the concept of significant harm in the Children Act 1989, which, as noted above, is still relatively vague, particularly for practice.

Seriousness

The seriousness of the injury must clearly play a part. Minor bruising, for instance, is generally not seen as sufficiently serious to require a child protection plan, whereas a series of unexplained bruises is more likely, under the same circumstances, to be considered sufficient cause for such action.

Intention

Intention has generally been considered to be a key variable in deciding whether an action is abusive or not (although it is not one that is specified in the 2018 guidelines). Again, there is variation with regard to this. Dingwall et al. identified among some hospital doctors what they termed a strict liability approach (1983: 36). From this point of view, if a child suffers a serious injury, even accidentally, the child's carer at the time should accept responsibility for the outcome and can be judged to be abusive. For the majority of child protection workers, however, intentionality is seen as an influential factor. For example, if the child suffers minor bruising but the adult intended much more serious harm, the fact that the actual harm was relatively minimal would not detract from the seriousness of the intent.

As noted above, however, more recent developments in our understanding of the impact of trauma on behaviour pose a challenge to these ideas about intentionality, as do recent developments in our understanding of empathy (Baron-Cohen 2011). If a parent has experienced an unresolved loss or trauma that leads them to display disconnected and/or extremely insensitive caregiving, which their child experiences as maltreatment, one can question how useful the concept of intentionality is. Similarly, a parent might misuse drugs or alcohol in order to manage their own experiences of trauma and by so doing, place their child at significant risk, without the parent ever contemplating, let alone desiring, to do harm to their child. Which is not to say that harmful behaviour towards children should be excused or overlooked or that there is no difference between genuine accidents and intentional abuse; however, it does suggest that the question of intentionality is less clear-cut than one might otherwise wish it to be.

Age of child

A factor often taken into consideration in defining physical abuse is the age of the child. Generally, the younger the child, the greater the likelihood of official recognition of physical abuse. This response is frequently justified by the fact that young children (particularly those under school age) are physically more vulnerable and less frequently monitored by child welfare professionals.

Context and risk

An analysis of the circumstances surrounding the reporting of a physical injury is also important in deciding whether or not to define it as abusive. Much reliance here is placed on professional judgement. Factors to be taken into account about physical injuries include their actual nature and the likelihood that they are inflicted intentionally, the coherence of the account given by a parent or carer about how the injury occurred, whether there has been any delay in reporting the injury and whether or not there has been a previous history of abuse (Meadow 1997).

Fabricated or induced illness (FII)

The official definition of physical abuse in the *Working Together* guidelines includes fabricated or induced illness (FII). The deliberate administration of harmful substances was included in Kempe's early descriptions of child abuse (Kempe and Kempe 1978). There has been some controversy in the UK about whether FII actually exists, primarily because of a series of court cases in which a number of women, including Sally Clark and Angela Cannings, were originally convicted of murdering their children; convictions which were later overturned by the Court of Appeal. Despite the cases of Clark and Canning being unrelated to FII, some media commentators drew the mistaken conclusion that their exonerations undermined the evidence of FII as a real phenomenon.

Taking the case of Sally Clark as an example, she was accused of murdering two of her children, the first in 1996 and the second in 1998. Both died in a similar manner and Meadow, a British paediatrician and author, testified that the chance of two children from the same family dying of sudden infant death syndrome (SIDS) was 1 in 73 million. Clark was convicted in 1999 but this was overturned in 2003. In 2001, the Royal Statistical Society had released a public statement saying that Meadow had no statistical basis for his claims and, in the appeal trial in 2003, it became apparent that the prosecution had failed to disclose evidence that the second child may have died of natural causes.

The controversy surrounding these and other cases led to a review of how cases of suspected FII should be managed, both in the court arena and by local authorities. The 2010 judgment of HHJ Clifford Bellamy (made in regard to three children, known as X, Y and Z) set out a number of case management points, including reminding local authorities of the seriousness of accusing a parent or carer of FII, that the views of health professionals involved with the child should be sought, in addition to any reports from independent experts, that independent experts should have regard to *Fabricated or Induced Illness by Carers (FII): A Practical Guide for Paediatricians* (Royal College of Paediatrics and Child Health 2009) and that any reports from independent experts should be examined thoroughly. A review of these guidelines in 2013 confirmed that they remained relevant, valid and up-to-date.

Emotional abuse

Emotional abuse for the purposes of registration is defined in the 2018 guidelines as:

> The persistent emotional maltreatment of a child such as to cause severe and persistent adverse effects on the child's emotional development. It may involve conveying to a child that they are worthless or unloved, inadequate, or valued only insofar as they meet the needs of another person. It may include not giving the child opportunities to express their views, deliberately silencing them or 'making fun' of what they say or how they communicate. It may feature age or developmentally inappropriate expectations being imposed on children. These may include interactions that are beyond a child's developmental capability, as well as overprotection and limitation of exploration and learning, or preventing the child participating in normal social interaction. It may

involve seeing or hearing the ill-treatment of another. It may involve serious bullying (including cyber bullying), causing children frequently to feel frightened or in danger, or the exploitation or corruption of children. Some level of emotional abuse is involved in all types of maltreatment of a child, though it may occur alone.

(HM Government 2018: 103)

Defining emotional abuse for practical intervention purposes is extremely difficult. Social workers seem to be particularly aware of, and concerned about, the emotional ill-treatment of children, but may find it very hard to pinpoint their concerns. This is because they are tackling areas of major uncertainty and sensitivity, which are both controversial and difficult to prove. Styles of parenting are brought into question by the issue of emotional abuse. For instance, are authoritarian or extremely permissive parenting styles abusive? Is constant criticism of a child a form of abuse? Can it be shown that such parenting styles have ill-effects? Where is the line between acceptable and unacceptable psychological parenting to be drawn? Is it abusive actively to prejudice a child against people of different races and sexes? Some would argue that it is but would be hard pressed to prove that such upbringings are actively harmful to the individual, even though it is likely that society as a whole will be the poorer for such forms of socialisation. It is difficult to prove links between causes and effects in this area; Garbarino and Vondra (1987) describe 'stress-resistant' children who, despite apparently rejecting parents, survive to be reasonably well-adjusted adults and there is a growing body of literature on the nature and effect of childhood resilience more generally.

In the USA, Wald (1982) has argued that there should be intervention only where a child is suffering serious emotional damage, evidenced by severe anxiety, depression or withdrawal, or aggressive behaviour or hostility towards others, and the parents are unwilling to provide treatment for the child. Burnett (1993) has tried to develop a specific set of definitions of emotional abuse. Using vignettes with the public and professionals in a moderate-sized city in northeast USA, he found general agreement on nine forms of what he termed psychological abuse:

- confining a child in a small place
- severe public humiliation
- the 'Cinderella' syndrome
- severe verbal abuse
- encouraging or coercing a child into delinquency
- threatening a child
- refusal of psychiatric treatment
- not allowing social and emotional growth
- not providing a loving, nurturing atmosphere.

(Burnett 1993: 446)

In Britain, greater emphasis has been placed on emotional abuse following the refocusing shift in child protection work that took place in the second half of the 1990s, and this is reflected in the official reporting statistics, which show that in March 2017, 1 in 5 children in need were identified as being at risk of emotional abuse (Department of Education 2017a: 8). Glaser (2002), however, notes that there are continuing uncertainties over definition. She points to the need for careful psychological assessment of children whose parents are thought to be emotionally abusive using the following areas of focus on their behaviour:

- emotional unavailability, unresponsiveness and neglect
- negative attributions and misattributions to the child
- developmentally inappropriate or inconsistent interactions with the child
- failure to recognise or acknowledge the child's individuality and psychological boundary
- failing to promote the child's social adaptation.

(Glaser 2002: 703–4)

Such a framework seems to be a useful aid in raising practitioner awareness and structuring assessment and intervention, but it would still be hard to prove emotional abuse in care proceedings on this basis. Indeed, in 2006, Justice McFarlane found that cases of emotional abuse will rarely, if ever, warrant an application for an emergency protection order, and even rarer still would be an application for such without giving notice to the child's carers. In 2008, the Ministry of Justice published research into the profiles of children and families involved in care proceedings under Section 31 of the Children Act 1989 (Masson et al. 2008). In considering the concerns of children's services, it found that maternal emotional abuse was present in 59 per cent of cases and paternal emotional abuse in 50.8 per cent of cases. These data tell us that, contrary to the *Working Together* guidance, many applications for care orders were made without considering the emotionally abusive aspects of the child's care (as *Working Together* states that some level of emotional abuse is involved in all types of child maltreatment), but what they cannot tell us is on how many occasions care proceedings were issued solely on the basis of emotional abuse.

The risk of future emotional harm

Another issue that can arise particularly in relation to emotional abuse is the question of future significant harm. Recall that the Children Act 1989 says a court may make a care order or supervision order so long as it is satisfied the child is currently suffering significant harm or is *likely to suffer* significant harm in future. Thus, a child may be removed from home via a care order without having suffered serious harm of any kind but because, for example, an older sibling has been sexually or physically abused and there is reason to suspect that any other child in the same household will experience the same. Yet in relation to emotional abuse, the question of how one can meaningfully predict future significant harm is far less obvious, not least because the results of emotional harm may take many years to become apparent, lacking the immediate impact of physical or sexual abuse.

In 2013, the Supreme Court of the UK gave what was anticipated to be a significant judgment in relation to this question, having been asked to consider the case of a child removed at birth from her mother on the grounds that she would otherwise suffer emotional and social harm in the future. The Supreme Court did not overturn the care order, yet they also did not, as some had hoped they might, engage seriously with the question of what constitutes emotional harm as opposed to *significant* emotional harm, nor with the question of likelihood. Lady Hale, one of the Supreme Court judges to hear the case, now President of the Supreme Court, gave a dissenting judgment and concluded that the original judge was mistaken to have made the care order:

> *This case raises some profound questions about the scope of courts' powers to take away children from their birth families when what is feared is, not physical abuse or neglect, but emotional or psychological harm. We are all frail human beings, with our fair share of unattractive character traits, which sometimes manifest themselves in bad behaviours which may be copied by our children. But the State does not and cannot take away the children of all the people who commit crimes, who abuse alcohol or drugs, who suffer from physical or mental illnesses or disabilities, or who espouse anti-social political or religious beliefs . . . How is the law to distinguish between emotional or psychological harm, which warrants the compulsory intervention of the State, and the normal and natural tendency of children to grow up to be and behave like their parents? Added to this is the problem that the harm which is feared may take many years to materialise, if indeed it ever does. Every child is an individual, with her own character and personality. Many children are remarkably resilient. They do not all inherit their parents' less attractive characters or copy their less attractive behaviours. Indeed, some will consciously reject them. They have many other positive influences in their lives which can help them to resist the negative, whether it is their schools, their friends, or other people around them. How confident do we have to be that a child will indeed suffer harm because of her parents' character and behaviour before we separate them for good?*

The position of the child protection social worker trying to address and respond to these most pertinent of questions in practice with many different families in many different social contexts is surely an unenviable one.

Sexual abuse and child sexual exploitation

Sexual abuse is defined in the 2018 guidelines as follows:

> *[Sexual abuse] involves forcing or enticing a child or young person to take part in sexual activities, not necessarily involving a high level of violence, whether or not the child is aware of what is happening. The activities may involve physical contact, including assault by penetration (for example, rape or oral sex) or non-penetrative acts such as masturbation, kissing, rubbing and touching outside of clothing. They may also include non-contact activities, such as involving children in looking at, or in the production of, sexual images, watching sexual activities, encouraging children to behave in sexually inappropriate ways, or grooming a child in preparation for abuse (including via the internet). Sexual abuse is not solely perpetrated by adult males. Women can also commit acts of sexual abuse, as can other children.*
>
> (HM Government 2018: 103)

In addition, child sexual exploitation is defined as follows:

> *Child sexual exploitation is a form of child sexual abuse. It occurs where an individual or group takes advantage of an imbalance of power to coerce, manipulate or deceive a child or young person under the age of 18 into sexual activity (a) in exchange for something the victim needs or wants, and/or (b) for the financial advantage or increased status of the perpetrator or facilitator. The victim may have been sexually exploited even if the sexual activity appears consensual. Child sexual exploitation does not always involve physical contact; it can also occur through the use of technology.*
>
> (HM Government 2018: 103)

These definitions specify the fact that sexual abuse need not involve physical contact and it provides some specific examples of such non-contact abuse. Both refer to the issue of grooming a child in preparation for abuse, something that was not present in the 1999 version of these guidelines (although it was in 2006). The inclusion was made in response to the growing awareness then of children being contacted by potential abusers via the internet, a possibility that most child welfare professionals will by now be all too familiar with. However, there are still many gaps to be filled. For instance, the definition makes no distinction between intra-familial and extra-familial abuse, and says nothing about the age of the perpetrator, other than to point out that sexual abuse may be perpetrated by children as well as adults, both male and female. Glaser and Frosh's (1988) definition still seems more comprehensive than those offered in official guidance:

> *Any child below the age of consent may be deemed to have been sexually abused when a sexually mature person has, by design or by neglect of their usual societal or specific responsibilities in relation to the child,*

engaged or permitted the engagement of that child in any activity of a sexual nature which is intended to lead to the sexual gratification of the sexually mature person. This definition pertains whether or not it involves genital contact or physical contact, and whether or not there is discernible harmful outcome in the short-term.

(Glaser and Frosh 1988: 5)

In 2017, the government issued supplementary guidance regarding sexual exploitation, *Child Sexual Exploitation: Definition and a Guide for Practitioners, Local Leaders and Decision Makers Working to Protect Children from Child Sexual Exploitation* (Department for Education 2017c), updating previous guidance issued in 2009 (Department for Children, Schools and Families 2009). This guidance notes that child sexual exploitation is a complex form of abuse and can be difficult to identify. It further stresses that the issue of consent is far from straightforward, noting that just because the child is legally able to consent to sexual activity does not mean that all sexual activity engaged in by the child is necessarily consensual. Perhaps most importantly, the guidance emphasises that child sexual exploitation is never the fault of the victim (while also cautioning that some children may be perpetrators as well as victims). This emphasis was included to challenge the idea that some victims of child sexual exploitation have actually been willing participants. Such ideas may have influenced responses to many well-known child sexual exploitation scandals including Rotherham, Rochdale and Oxford (see Jay 2014). The guidance gives the following (non-exhaustive list of) scenarios or examples of child sexual exploitation:

- A 44-year-old female posing as a 17-year-old female online and persuading a 12-year-old male to send her a sexual image, and then threatening to tell his parents if he doesn't continue to send more explicit images.
- A 14-year-old male giving a 17-year-old male oral sex because the older male has threatened to tell his parents he is gay if he refuses.
- A 14-year-old female having sex with a 16-year-old gang member and his two friends in return for the protection of the gang.
- A 13-year-old female offering and giving an adult male taxi driver sexual intercourse in return for a taxi fare home.
- A 21-year-old male persuading his 17-year-old 'girlfriend' to have sex with his friends to pay off a drug debt.
- A mother letting other adults abuse her 8-year-old child in return for money.
- A group of men bringing two 17-year-old females to a hotel in another town and charging others to have sex with them.
- Three 15-year-old females being taken to a house party and given 'free' alcohol and drugs, then made to have sex with six adult males to pay for this.

The issue of defining sexual abuse, sexual exploitation and sexual commercialisation in practice is both complex and problematical. There is now a general awareness not only that child sexual abuse is far more common than was previously thought, but also that it affects very young children as well as older ones (Macfarlane and Waterman 1986). As well as responding to intra-familial abuse, the importance of responding to the needs of children and families where the former have experienced abuse outside the family should not be underestimated (Bolen 2001).

Medical, social and behavioural factors in defining sexual abuse

There are few clear-cut medical signs of sexual abuse. Thus, most medical examinations of children suspected of having been abused yield little by way of concrete evidence. It is now generally accepted that medical evidence without some form of corroboration from a social and behavioural assessment is not sufficient to prove child sexual abuse in court.

With regard to behavioural indicators, a variety of factors have been identified as associated with sexual abuse of children, for example, withdrawn presentation, para-suicide and suicide, running away from home and eating disorders (see Porter 1984). However, these correlations do not prove connections and can, therefore, only sensitise professionals to the possibility of sexual abuse. They have limited value in terms of the standard of evidence required in courts. The best indicator, particularly in younger children, is that of precocious sexual behaviour (see Brilleslijper-Kater et al. 2004). However, even sexual behaviour in children is not a clear indicator of sexual abuse. The development and exhibition of sexual behaviour are, after all, a normal part of healthy development. Children aged between 0 and 4 will normally kiss or hug other children, as well as show an interest in and talk about body parts, including genitalia, and they may engage in masturbatory behaviour. As in many cases, the best way for professionals to ensure they do not mistake normal childhood behaviour for a sign of something more worrying is to educate themselves as fully as possible about child development and to develop trusting and reliable relationships with young people (Bovarnick et al. 2017).

The child's testimony

As a consequence of the fact that there are few reliable external indicators of child sexual abuse, considerable emphasis has been placed on the child's account of events. While there is now much more openness among professionals to listening and responding to these accounts, there are still many problems in substantiating that abuse has occurred, particularly if it is alleged to have taken place within the family. As was seen in Chapter 2, following the Cleveland and the Orkney inquiries, there was concern that social workers and clinical psychologists were too willing to believe children and were possibly guilty of leading them too much. In America, the case of Frederico Macias raised similar concerns. Macias was convicted of murder in 1984 and was given the death penalty. The prosecution relied heavily on the testimony of a 13-year-old witness. Four years later, the same witness reported:

> Because different people asked me so many questions about what I saw I became confused. I thought I might have seen something that would be helpful to the police. I didn't realize that it would become so important. I thought they wanted me to be certain, so I said I was certain even though I wasn't . . . the more questions I was asked, the more confused I became.
>
> (Ceci and Bruck 1995: 304)

Fortunately, this statement was made two weeks before Macias' scheduled execution and he was later exonerated in 1993.

The concerns highlighted by the Cleveland and Orkney inquiries led to the introduction, in 1992, of the *Memorandum of Good Practice* for interviewing children which was to be used in all child abuse cases where a serious crime had been alleged (Home Office/Department of Health 1992). This document was revised in 2001 and then replaced by *Achieving Best Evidence in Criminal Proceedings* (Ministry of Justice 2011), for use when interviewing all children under the age of 17, regardless of the offence involved. The Achieving Best Evidence (ABE) protocol is a semi-structured interview and aims at eliciting as much free recall as possible by the interviewee. For example, the interviewer asks, 'What shall we talk about?' rather than employing more direct questions. Many studies have indicated the benefits of this approach in providing the required information (for example, Korkman et al. 2006). In spite of the supposed widespread usage of the ABE protocol, research has found that, in practice, closed questions, suggestive summaries, inappropriate prompts and the repetition of questions remain prevalent (see Westcott and Kynan 2006; Westcott et al. 2006). As we saw in the example of the Macias case from the USA, the use of repetitive questions has been shown to result in changes to the interviewee's responses and a decline in accuracy and consistency (Krähenbühl and Blades 2006). Children giving evidence in court also continue to be placed under tremendous pressure (Westcott and Page 2002).

Neglect

Neglect is defined in the 2018 *Working Together* guidelines as:

> the persistent failure to meet a child's basic physical and/or psychological needs, likely to result in the serious impairment of the child's health or development. Neglect may occur during pregnancy as a result of maternal substance abuse. Once a child is born, neglect may involve a parent or carer failing to:

> - provide adequate food, clothing and shelter (including exclusion from home or abandonment);
> - protect a child from physical and emotional harm or danger;

- ensure adequate supervision (including the use of inadequate care-givers); or
- ensure access to appropriate medical care or treatment.

It may also include neglect of, or unresponsiveness to, a child's basic emotional needs.

(HM Government 2018: 104)

As an operational definition, this is no less problematic than the definitions of abuse given in the same guidance and outlined above. Practitioners must determine on a case-by-case basis what counts as 'persistent failure' and 'serious impairment'. They must also be able to define basic psychological and emotional needs.

In the USA, following on from the pioneering work of Polansky and his colleagues (1985), there have been some recent attempts to develop more specific models on which to base child neglect work. For instance, Burke and her colleagues define child abuse and neglect as:

Deficits or omissions in the parental role performance related to inadequate use of the parental environment that results in a serious threat to or observable decline in the well-being of the child.

(Burke et al. 1998: 394)

Such a definition clearly places a great deal of responsibility on the parents and this has always been an area of some dispute in dealing with neglect, perhaps more so in Britain than in the USA.

To what extent, for instance, should consideration be given to notions of cultural difference, material resources and intellectual capacity in assessing whether a parent is neglectful or not? Stevenson (1998) considers whether we can distinguish between low standards of care brought about by poverty and ignorance, and those that result from lack of parental care or concern. She concludes that we often cannot.

A more recent study considered the relationship between child experiences characterised as neglectful prior to age 4 and child outcomes at age 4, and found that certain problems (such as a poor level of home safety, cleanliness and a failure to provide adequate shelter) resulted in impaired language and other developmental difficulties. Other problems (a high turnover of caregivers and medical neglect) resulted in less developmental concerns (English et al. 2005). The conclusion to take from this is that children's experiences of serious neglect and its consequences should override, at least initially, concerns about parental culpability and the rights and wrongs of intervention.

Other researchers take a different view – Straus and Kantor give the following definition:

Neglectful behavior is behavior by a caregiver that constitutes a failure to act in ways that are presumed by the culture of a society to be necessary to meet the developmental needs of a child and which are the responsibility of a caregiver to provide.

(2005: 20)

They recognise themselves the 'controversial' part of this definition as being 'behavior by a caregiver', which they explain is included to rule out other possible causes of neglect such as poverty, mental illness or malevolent motives. Straus and Kantor go on to argue that they have attempted to define neglectful behaviour without considering harm – actual or potential – to the child. They do so not only because, in their view, this makes the phenomenon easier to study but also because it is important in practice. They give the example of a carer who repeatedly leaves a child unsupervised but, via good fortune, the child remains unharmed. On the other hand, a child could be left alone on just one occasion and could die as a result. Clearly, the more often a developmentally young child is left unsupervised, the greater the *chance* of harm and this is why they highlight the importance of *chronicity*; it is also why professionals are often concerned in practice with establishing the pattern of behaviours as the basis for a judgement regarding the significance or otherwise of the risk of harm.

All the same, the issue of standards of care and the concerns about parental culpability make tackling neglect a very problematic issue for health and social care workers. A further problem lies with the difficulty of proving neglect in care proceedings. As a consequence of these uncertainties, neglect cases have been less likely to be vigorously pursued than other forms of abuse.[5]

Clearly there is much work to be done in clarifying what is meant by neglect but, as has been noted, chronic neglect has been overlooked to a large degree because of the focus on more specific forms of abuse – yet neglected children are likely to suffer worse outcomes in the long term.

Failure to thrive

The problem of 'failure to thrive' has not been included in official definitions of maltreatment in the UK since 1999. Yet the term continues to receive much attention, particularly in medical journals more so than in social work or child abuse journals. Whether recognised formally or not, and whether described in such terms or not, a failure to thrive in babies is a serious and potentially life-threatening form of neglect. Because it can be subjected to measurement, it is technically easier to define and can be thought of as easier to prove than general neglect (Iwaniec et al. 1985). Babies have an expected normal level of growth (weight and length), which is based upon their birth weight and size. Those that fall well below this expectation, with no apparent physical explanation, can be considered to be at risk; neglect (both physical and emotional) is thought to be a likely cause of this.[6]

Various medical causes for failure to thrive have, of course, been identified (with cystic fibrosis and Russell-Silver syndrome being two of the most common); nevertheless, there are other, rarer medical causes, such as Classic Bartter syndrome (see Samayam et al. 2011), which are harder to detect, and which could potentially cause difficulties for professionals wishing to be clear about the reasons for a child failing to thrive. Close monitoring of a child's physical growth when placed away from the parents may show that, with reasonable care and feeding, normal development will take place, thus proving that some form of neglect lies at the heart of the problem. However, this form of intervention is clearly not without cost, both financially and also – more importantly – to the child and his or her parents, especially if there was no improvement in their development in substitute care.

More recently, the usefulness of the dichotomy between 'organic' failure to thrive (cases where an underlying medical condition is found) and 'non-organic' failure to thrive (cases in which no underlying medical diagnosis can be made) has been called into question. This is because the dichotomy often leads to children undergoing a battery of extensive medical tests, some involving prolonged hospitalisations. Jaffe (2011) argues that any investigation into a suspected case of failure to thrive must take a multi-factorial approach, considering the child's caregiving environment as much as their physical condition – the argument being that whether or not a child has an underlying medical condition, it is important that this does not preclude an investigation as to whether they are receiving good enough care at home.

Other forms of abuse

Outside of these long-standing categories, it is now increasingly recognised that child maltreatment may come in many different forms - including child trafficking, gang activity, female genital mutilation, forced marriage and radicalisation.

Child trafficking

Children may be trafficked for a variety of reasons – child sexual exploitation, forced marriage (see below), domestic work or other forced labour or to involve them in criminal activity such as drug dealing. Prosecutions are rare, despite the often large-scale criminal networks involved (McRedmond 2010). Child trafficking, contrary to popular imagination, may not always involve violence or even the threat of violence. Sometimes, families in poorer parts of the world may simply be tricked into 'agreeing' for their child to be taken away, perhaps with the promise of a formal education or a better life (Europol 2011). Although the Modern Slavery Act 2015 consolidated a number of offences related to trafficking and slavery, the most recent practice guidance from the Department for Education and the Home Office was published in 2011. This guidance defines trafficking based upon the Palermo protocol to Prevent, Suppress and Punish Trafficking in Persons:

> 'Trafficking of persons' shall mean the recruitment, transportation, transfer, harbouring or receipt of persons, by means of the threat or use of force or other forms of coercion, of abduction, of fraud, of deception,

of the abuse of power or of a position of vulnerability or of the giving or receiving of payments or benefits to achieve the consent of a person having control over another person, for the purpose of exploitation. Exploitation shall include, at a minimum, the exploitation or the prostitution of others or other forms of sexual exploitation, forced labour or services, slavery or practices similar to slavery, servitude or the removal of organs.

(Department for Education and the Home Office 2011: 4)

As with child sexual exploitation, this guidance makes clear that the child cannot consent to their own trafficking, any more than they can consent to their own exploitation, even if they have not been overtly deceived. Given the nature of the problem, it is unsurprising that we do not have a clear idea of how many children are trafficked into or out of the UK in any given year, although in 2017, around 1,200 children were identified by the National Crime Agency as being potential victims of trafficking.

Gang activity

How can a gang be defined and how does one differentiate between a gang and other forms of youth groupings? The Centre for Social Justice has defined a gang as follows:

A relatively durable, predominantly street-based group of young people who: 1. see themselves (and are seen by others) as a discernible group; 2. engage in criminal activity and violence; and may also 3. lay claim over territory (not necessarily geographical, but can include an illegal economy territory); 4. have some form of identifying structural feature; and/or 5. be in conflict with other, similar, gangs.

(Centre for Social Justice 2009: 21)

In addition, the Policing and Crime Act 2009 (updated by the Serious Crime Act 2015) defines gang-related violence as follows:

Violence or a threat of violence which occurs in the course of, or is otherwise related to, the activities of a group that:

a) consists of at least 3 people; and,
b) has one or more characteristics that enable its members to be identified by others as a group.

(Early Intervention Foundation and the Home Office 2015: 5)

In 2010, the government published non-statutory guidance, *Safeguarding Children and Young People Who May Have Been Affected by Gang Activity* (Department for Children, Schools and Families/Home Office 2010) and, despite growing concerns and evidence of more gang-related activity, it has not been updated since. This guidance recognises that young people in or around gangs can be both perpetrators and victims of harm. Indeed, the guidance explicitly states that 'children who harm others are both victims and perpetrators' (p. 6). This point is supported by research undertaken on behalf of Victim Support (Owen and Sweeting 2007), which highlighted three pathways from victimisation to offending behaviour, namely, retaliatory violence, displaced retaliation, or the victim befriending offenders (partly in order to seek protection from future victimisation). The same research highlighted two pathways from offending behaviour to victimisation, namely, being subject to retaliatory violence and a lack of protection from adults in authority.

In 2017, the Children's Commissioner for England released a report estimating that up to 46,000 children may be involved with gangs and in the following year, media reports began to emerge of 'county lines' (drug networks operating in provincial towns and involving local young people from those areas). Clearly, gang involvement is a serious and growing problem for many children and young people, and not just those residing in inner city areas.

Female genital mutilation (FGM)

Female genital mutilation (FGM) has been a criminal act in the UK since 1985 but the more recent Female Genital Mutilation Act 2003 added a new offence, prohibiting any UK nationals or permanent UK residents from carrying out FGM abroad or aiding, abetting or otherwise allowing the carrying out of FGM abroad, including in countries where the practice is legal.

The World Health Organization (WHO) defines FGM as procedures that intentionally modify or injure female genital organs (for non-medical reasons).The impact of FGM can include serious bleeding, difficulties urinating and potential childbirth complications in the future. In 2008, the WHO expressed concern about the increasing trend for trained medical professionals performing FGM. In 2010, it was widely reported in the media that the practice of FGM was growing in the UK, with girls being especially at risk during the longer summer school holiday, when their absence from the UK or their recovery from the procedure would be less noticeable. One story in the *Observer* newspaper (2010) stated that 63,000 girls and women in the UK have already undergone FGM.

The NHS describes four types of FGM, all of which are illegal and constitute child abuse. Type 1 (clitoridectomy) involves removing part of all of the clitoris. Type 2 (excision) involves the removal of part of all of the clitoris and the inner labia. Type 3 (infibulation) involves narrowing the vaginal opening and Type 4 is 'other procedures' including pricking, piercing, cutting, scraping or burning the area. There are no health benefits to FGM and the effects can include pain, difficulty having sex, infections, bleeding, incontinence, depression, self-harm and trauma. In some cases, FGM can cause death by blood loss or infection. FGM practices are largely concentrated in Africa, Middle Eastern or Asian countries and communities and more than 200 million women and girls worldwide are thought to have undergone FGM.

Forced marriage

The Forced Marriage Unit was set up in the UK in 2005 to lead on the government's forced marriage policy. The Anti-social Behaviour, Crime and Policing Act 2014 made it a criminal offence to force someone to get married, adult or child. In 2017, the Forced Marriages Unit identified 1,196 cases in which someone needed advice or support in relation to forced marriage. This included 355 cases involving a child (aged below 18 years of age). In 2014, the Home Office issued practice guidance which included the following definition:

> There is a clear distinction between a forced marriage and an arranged marriage. In arranged marriages, the families of both spouses take a leading role in arranging the marriage, but the choice of whether or not to accept the arrangement still remains with the prospective spouses. However, in forced marriage, one or both spouses do not consent to the marriage but are coerced into it. Duress can include physical, psychological, financial, sexual and emotional pressure. In the cases of some vulnerable adults who lack the capacity to consent, coercion is not required for a marriage to be forced.
>
> (Home Office 2014: 1)

Radicalisation

Concerns about the radicalisation of children have emerged as a result of the growing threat to the UK (and other countries) from Islamic terrorism (for example, Al-Qaeda and ISIS). The Counter-Terrorism and Security Act 2015 placed a duty on many public authorities in England and Wales, including many local authorities, to prevent people from being drawn into terrorism. In practice, this has meant the involvement of many social workers, working to prevent children and young people from being radicalised into supporting the kind of extremist ideologies associated with terrorist groups. According to the relevant guidance, extremism can be defined as:

> Vocal or active opposition to fundamental British values, including democracy, the rule of law, individual liberty and mutual respect and tolerance of different faiths and beliefs. We also include in our definition of extremism calls for the death of members of our armed forces, whether in this country or overseas.
>
> (HM Government 2015: 21)

While radicalisation can be defined as:

> *The process by which a person comes to support terrorism and extremist ideologies associated with terrorist groups.*
>
> (HM Government 2015: 21)

To counter extremism and radicalisation, the government widened the *Prevent* strategy in 2011 (it having been initially introduced in 2003), to deal with all forms of terrorism and non-violent extremism. In 2015–16, about 7,500 referrals were made to the scheme, with action being taken in about one in every 10 cases. The government has said the scheme has prevented about 50 children from entering conflict zones in Iraq or Syria, while the Muslim Council of Britain has said it is too intrusive and over-zealous.

However, radicalisation and extremism are not wholly related to terrorism. As defined in the 2018 Working Together guidelines:

> *Extremism goes beyond terrorism and includes people who target the vulnerable - including the young - by seeking to sow divison between communities on the basis of faith or denomination.*
>
> (2018, p. 104).

Conclusion

As can be seen, what is defined as child maltreatment has grown from the battered child of 1962 to a vast range of practices and behaviours, ranging from the 'obvious' (physical and sexual abuse), to the contested (emotional abuse and neglect) to the contextual and overtly political (radicalisation). The field is increasingly complex with child welfare professionals expected to take on new issues and concerns, even though for most their primary focus may well continue to be on physical, sexual, emotional abuse and neglect within the family. The emphasis now is on truly protecting children from a wide range of threats and increasingly the anticipation is that professionals will work together proactively to prevent harm to children both within and outside the family. Not only is the breadth of concerns now facing child protection professionals breath-taking, but so is the speed with which new issues arise – currently there are concerns being raised in relation to gang activity, radicalisation, forced marriages and coercive control. Undoubtedly other concerns will also arise in future, and just as unexpectedly.

Despite this breadth of focus, Harris (1995) has argued that what we choose to focus on in terms of concerns about children are culturally specific. While this undoubtedly remains true, consideration of the international scene should provide some perspective on domestic concerns without reducing any commitment to tackling them. Awareness of these matters and of the complexities involved in defining child abuse in our own society which have been thus far reviewed should sensitise professionals to the ever-changing nature of this challenging area of work.

Recommended reading

Daniels, H. and Livingstone, M. (2014) *Hackney Child*. London: Simon & Schuster.

Ferguson, H. (2004) *Protecting Children in Time: Child Abuse, Child Protection and the Consequences of Modernity*. London: Palgrave Macmillan.

HM Government (2018) *Working Together to Safeguard Children: A Guide to Inter-agency Working to Safeguard and Promote the Welfare of Children*. London: The Stationery Office.

Lyon, C. (2003) *Child Abuse*, 3rd edn. Bristol: Jordan Publishing.

May-Chahal, C. and Cawson, P. (2005) Measuring child maltreatment in the United Kingdom: a study of the prevalence of child abuse and neglect, *Child Abuse and Neglect*, 29(9): 969–84.

Stevenson, O. (2007) *Neglected Children and Their Families*. Oxford: Blackwell.

Perpetrators of child abuse

5

Key points in this chapter

- Contemporary research has sought to answer questions about perpetrators of child abuse, and the children who are abused; much of this focus has been upon correlation, rather than causation.
- Evaluation of associated factors needs to be nuanced, if the 'hows and whys' of child abuse are to be correctly understood, and children effectively safeguarded.
- With the exception of child sexual abuse, almost all studies of abuse and neglect point to the importance of diminished socio-economic backgrounds.

Introduction

A myriad of research has been conducted into the characteristics of perpetrators of child abuse and neglect, as well as into the characteristics of the children most likely to become victims of such maltreatment. The driving force behind much of this research has largely been to predict and prevent future abuse and neglect.

First, if it is possible to identify those adults who are most likely to abuse or neglect children, then early and decisive intervention is likely to afford those children greater protection.

Second, it is clear that there is a close association between who is most likely to be the victim of abuse or neglect and the question of perpetration. Children in close proximity to likely perpetrators are obviously those who are most at risk. However, not all children in these situations appear to be equally at risk. Some children seem to have more resilience, while others seem to be singled out for mistreatment.

Third, the causation of child abuse and neglect is very closely linked to the question of perpetration and the interrelationship between these three aspects of child abuse cannot be sufficiently emphasised. However, for the purposes of analysis, these issues will be looked at separately. In this chapter, the first and second questions will be considered. Theories of causation will be the subject of Chapter 6.

Researchers have considered a wide range of variables that seem likely to be associated with abusive and neglectful behaviour towards children. Inevitably, given the amount of research carried out, this summary will be a selective one. The factors selected for closer analysis in respect of those who abuse are as follows:

• gender
• age
• poverty and race
• adults who have themselves been abused
• family structure
• psychological capacities
• the impact of alcohol and drugs
• mental health difficulties
• domestic violence.

While much of the research focuses upon abusers within family settings, extra-familial abuse is also significant, and will therefore be addressed. That said, it should be noted that, with the exception of child sexual abuse, children are most likely to be abused or neglected by their parents and/or carers (Lamont 2011; US Department of Health and Human Services 2017). Indeed, most children who are seriously or fatally maltreated, experience this harm while living with relatives or at home – the very location in which we might hope children would be safe (Sidebotham et al. 2016).

Causal connections

Before considering the characteristics of perpetrators and victims of child abuse and neglect, special comment needs to be made regarding the absence of causal connections. Often, research finds an association or a correlation between a certain characteristic or variable – such as 'parents with mental health difficulties' or 'a child aged under 12 months' – and child abuse or neglect. While helpful, this is very different from being able to claim that the presence of these types of characteristics or variables is causally *predictive* of child abuse or neglect.

For those unfamiliar with statistical language, there are precise differences between the terms 'association' or 'correlation', and 'causation'. An association or correlation between two or more things indicates any statistically dependent relationship between them. Two (or more) things are associated (or correlated) if some of the variability in one can be accounted for by the other(s). For example, there is an association between personal wealth and voting for right-wing political parties and a similar association between personal poverty and voting for left-wing political parties (Huber and Stanig 2009). However, while this association is demonstrably accurate, it does not allow one to draw conclusions about the voting records or future voting intentions of individuals. All it allows you to say is that if you picked one wealthy person at random (ignoring all other variables), he or she would be more *likely* to vote for a right-wing party than a left-wing party, but in many cases you would be wrong. The same holds true for less wealthy individuals.

The relationship between the types of variable in this example is not causal. The saying 'correlation does not imply causation' is well known and absolutely accurate. Indeed, to say that correlation does imply causation is a logical fallacy. Further examples of this mistaken belief are the numerous studies which found that women taking a certain type of hormone replacement therapy (HRT) had a lower risk of heart disease. This led to the proposition that HRT might in some way protect women against heart disease. However, a randomised trial showed that HRT actually raised the risk of heart disease. A deeper analysis of the original data showed that women who took HRT were more likely to be from higher socio-economic groups and as a result they tended to have better diets and engage in more exercise. Both the use of HRT and a reduced incidence of heart disease were caused by being a member of a higher socio-economic group.

Munro (2008) has explored these issues in relation to the field of child protection. Many people intuitively think that the more risk factors are identified for a particular family or child, the stronger the prediction of future harm – Munro points out that this is incorrect. In addition to knowing about the factors identified in relation to perpetrators or victims of abuse, we also need to be able to compare this to the incidence of the relevant factors in the general population (the 'base rate'). Take poverty as an example (as Munro does). In 2001, in the UK, around 21 per cent of children lived in poverty. To understand how strong a predictive factor poverty is for child abuse, we need to compare this general level of poverty with the incidence of poverty in abusive families. If found at the same level in abusive families as in the general population, poverty would have no predictive value in terms of abuse. If found to be more common in abusive families, poverty would be a predictive factor and the more common it was in abusive families, compared with the general population, the stronger the predictive value would become. If found to be less prevalent in abusive families than in the general population, poverty would be contra-indicative of abuse. Munro identifies a variety of factors that do seem to be relatively strong predictors for perpetration of abuse or neglect, many of which are discussed below, such as a record of previous violence, personality disorder, a history of mental health problems and being male. Munro also identifies a variety of risk factors for victims, including being young and being born prematurely – again, these are discussed in more detail below. As Munro argues, the best predictor of abuse would be a factor that occurs in all abusive families and very rarely in the general population. Munro concludes that given the ambiguous nature of child abuse and neglect (as discussed in Chapter 4), one commonly identifiable factor of causation is unlikely.

In summary, research into the characteristics and variables related to perpetrators and victims of abuse has so far identified associations or correlations rather than causal connections. Munro's argument about the importance of appreciating the base rate of any given factor is also of significance. The greater the differential between the incidence of a particular factor in abusive families and in the general population, the more predictive it is of abuse (either as an indicator or a contra-indicator). Unless we understand the base rate of that factor, we cannot say whether or not it is a stronger or weaker predictor of abuse or neglect. We must consider the association and correlation between the variety of factors discussed below, rather than causal links.

The gender of those who abuse and neglect

Overall, children are more likely to be maltreated by females than males. Given that it remains the case that mothers and other female carers spend more time with children than fathers and other male carers, this may not be surprising. Statistics from the US Department of Health and Human Services show that most perpetrators of child maltreatment are female. In 2009, 53.8 per cent of recorded cases of child abuse or neglect were believed to have been perpetrated by a female (and 44.4 per cent by males; in the remaining 1.8 per cent of cases, the gender of the perpetrator was unknown). In 2008, the figures were 56.2 per cent female, 42.6 per cent male; in 2007, 56.5 per cent female, 42.4 per cent male; in 2006, 57.9 per cent female, 42.1 per cent male; and in 2005, 57.8 per cent female and 42.2 per cent male. In 2016, 53.7 per cent of perpetrators were women and 45.3 per cent were men; 1.0 per cent were of unknown sex (US Department of Health & Human Services, Administration for Children & Families 2017).

Physical abuse

Nevertheless, in situations of physical abuse, fathers or social fathers are generally seen as the more likely perpetrators when compared with mothers. Men are almost universally conceptualised as being more violent than women, which probably accounts for this perception. In a study of an accident and emergency hospital department over a two-year period, Steen and Hunskaar (2004) found that out of 1,680 assault victims, the vast majority (1,588 or 94.5 per cent) reported that they had been the victims of male-perpetrated violence. In the UK, a nationally representative study, on behalf of the NSPCC, by Radford et al. (2011) found that 86.4 per cent of the children and young people aged up to 24 years of age who self-reported severe physical violence, attributed this violence to a male parent or guardian. Notwithstanding these findings, in practice, social workers and other professionals tend to carry out much of their work in such cases almost exclusively with women (Scourfield 2001; Brewsaugh and Strozier 2016).

The physical abuse of children is not solely perpetrated by men, however. In 2005, a survey of over 15 million Australians aged 15 and over found that while 55.6 per cent of respondents reported having been physically abused by their father/step-father before the age of 15, 25.9 per cent reported having been physically abused by their mother/stepmother. A British study found that mothers were more likely to physically abuse their children than fathers (49 per cent of recorded incidents by mothers compared with 40 per cent by fathers – May-Chahal and Cawson 2005). More recently still, a study by Sidebotham et al. (2016) found that in nearly a quarter of Serious Case Reviews, the primary perpetrator of abuse was the child's mother, the largest single category. Fathers caused harm in 29 (17 per cent) of the cases, while male partners or other social fathers were cited in 18 cases (9.7 per cent). Where the physical assault proved fatal or where the child was seriously injured, the perpetrator was most likely to be male – the second most consistently high proportion of perpetrator category was mother and father together, 21.8 per cent (2014), 22.3 per cent (2015) and 20.1 per cent (2016). On balance, the evidence does suggest that fathers or social fathers are more likely to be responsible for serious injuries or fatalities (US Department of Health and Human Services, Administration on Children, Youth and Families 2007a, 2008, 2009). For example, Kajese et al. (2011) studied 170 child homicides in Kansas, USA, between 1994 and 1997. The most commonly identified perpetrator was the child's biological father (in 26.6 per cent of cases), with slightly fewer killed by their biological mother (24.9 per cent) and fewer again by the child's mother's male partner (19.8 per cent). These figures are more 'balanced' than those of an earlier study by Brewster et al. (1998), who studied 32 cases of infanticide on United States Air Force bases between 1989 and 1995 and found that 84 per cent of the perpetrators were men looking after children on their own at the time of the fatal abuse episodes.

Sexual abuse

Fathers or social fathers are also seen as more likely to be responsible for nearly all acts of intra-familial sexual abuse of children (Bornstein et al. 2007). Assumptions about the nature of female sexuality are the likely reason for this, with women generally thought far less likely to abuse children sexually (Clements et al. 2014). This assumption may go some way to explain why the research literature on women's sexual crime perpetration remains underdeveloped relative to that of men, with the knowledge gap being particularly pronounced for perpetrators of child sexual abuse (Burgess-Proctor et al. 2017). It is notable that, despite the perception that women are less likely to be perpetrators, they are still held to be partly responsible for what happens – hence the term 'collusive mothers'[1] (McLaren 2013; Zagrodney and Cummings 2017).

The evidence to support this widely held view is quite clear-cut; overwhelmingly, sexual abuse is perpetrated by males (Australian Bureau of Statistics 2005; McCloskey and Raphael 2005; Hassan et al. 2015). Of 411 sexually abused children referred to the Great Ormond Street Hospital for Sick Children between 1980 and 1986, only 8 children (2 per cent) had been abused by females (Bentovim et al. 1988).

Intra-familial sexual abuse implicates not only fathers; there have been studies of abuse by grandfathers (Margolin 1992), uncles (Margolin 1994) and male siblings (Adler and Schutz 1995). Some writers have considered there to be important distinctions between male intra- and extra-familial abusers. Becker and Quinsey (1993), for instance, point out that perpetrators who abuse extra-familial children have a higher recidivism rate than those who solely abuse children within their families. They also found that men who abused boys were more likely to reoffend than those who abused girls. More recently, Hanson and Morton-Bourgon (2005) found that when studying persistent sexual offenders, deviant sexual preferences (for children) combined with anti-social attitudes were the major predictors of sexual recidivism. Furthermore, in Sweden, Nilsson et al. (2014) undertook a 10- to 15-year follow-up study of a population-based cohort (196 individuals, all men) and a clinic-referred study group (185 individuals, of whom 182 were men and 3 were women) of convicted intra- and extra-familial child sexual abuse perpetrators. The study found extra-familial offenders at index to be significantly more likely to reoffend sexually and violently than intra-familial offenders.

Others, particularly from a feminist perspective, see little distinction between intra- and extra-familial abuse. Bolen (2001) notes that although intra-familial abuse accounts for between 11 and 40 per cent of all sexual abuse of children, and between 7 and 8 per cent of all sexual abuse is committed by parental figures, nevertheless this model of abuse dominates our thinking. From her perspective there is little in the way of a qualitative difference between intra- and extra-familial abuse.

There are a small number of studies of intra-familial female sex abusers. Krug (1989) studied eight cases in detail and came to the conclusion that female sexual abuse of children mirrored that of male sexual abuse: motivation was assessed to be the mothers seeking to satisfy their emotional and physical need for intimacy and possibly power, by actively seeking out their sons during times of conflict in their relationships with their partners.

In 2011, Testa et al. noted that as most victims of child sexual abuse are girls and most perpetrators are male, the likelihood of the abuse being transmitted inter-generationally is low when compared with other types of abuse. However, the same paper, echoed more recently in the findings of Baril et al. (2016), also notes that when a female child is sexually abused, it is more likely her mother was also sexually abused in childhood.

There is a need for some degree of perspective when considering the likely gender of child sex abuse perpetrators. While it is wrong to assume that women do not sexually abuse children, one should not fall into the trap of seeing such abuse as perpetrated equally by men and women.

We know much less about women who sexually abuse outside the family, but turning finally to male extra-familial abusers, we move into the terrain of 'paedophiles'. Pritchard (2004: 57) identifies three types of extra-familial child abuser, including those deemed career paedophiles, who dedicate their lives to covert sexual pursuit of children, casual offenders with disorganised personalities, and violent offenders. Sullivan et al. (2011) found that, when compared with intra-familial abusers, extra-familial abusers were likely to be significantly more preoccupied with sex and to emotionally over-identify with children.

The research distinguishes between internet sex offenders (ISOs), who view child abuse images, and general sex offenders (GSOs). Tomak et al. (2009) argue that the former are a different group of offenders from the latter – that is, ISOs are not 'just' GSOs making use of a new technology. ISOs are less deviant, less physically aggressive and less impulsive compared to GSOs. However, they are still overwhelmingly male. In the USA, there were 3,672 arrests for possession of child abuse images in 2006 compared with 1,713 in 2000. Almost all those arrested were male (Wolak et al. 2011).

Emotional abuse

Although the World Health Organization (WHO) (Mikton et al. 2014) claims that 36 per cent of adults worldwide have experienced emotional abuse as a child, and the UK's NSPCC 2017 annual report confirmed emotional abuse to be the second most common reason for children being made subject to a child protection plan in England and Wales (Bentley et al. 2017), there is surprisingly little research into the gender of this category of perpetrator, their demographic features and wider characteristics relating to neglect (see below); there is even less where emotional abuse is concerned. Initially conceptualised as 'mental injury', emotional abuse did not become more widely recognised until the late 1970s and early 1980s, which may partially explain the relative paucity of research into this abuse category generally, and perpetrator characteristics in particular (Simmel and Shpiegel 2013). One exception to the relative dearth of empirical research on caregiver characteristics associated with emotional abuse, is the correspondence of this type of abuse with domestic violence in some studies. In 2005, national child welfare data revealed an association between reports of domestic violence, failure to supervise, physical abuse and emotional abuse, recently echoed by Simmel and Shpiegel (2013). More males were found to perpetrate emotional abuse, possibly reflecting the higher rates of domestic violence perpetrated by males in which context emotional abuse is often a feature.

Neglect

Neglect continues to be the most frequent category of child maltreatment recorded by child protection agencies, accounting for three-quarters of child victims (74.8 per cent), reflected in the annual US *Child Maltreatment Report 2016* (US Department of Health and Human Services 2017). In England, a Department for Education (2017a) cites neglect as the most common category of maltreatment for children who were the subject of a child protection plan, constituting 48.1 per cent such plans. Despite the incidence of this category of concern, neglect is itself, assessed as being neglected as a subject of specific empirical research (Stoltenborgh et al. 2013b). It is generally held that mothers are mainly responsible for mistreating children in cases of neglect (Daniel and Taylor 2006). This is likely to be because of common assumptions about parenting roles, with child care still largely seen as the responsibility of women and may reflect the fact that mothers may, in many instances be the child's sole or main carer (Sidebotham et al. 2016). When things go wrong, responsibility is often attributed to mothers. When faced with suspected or proven child neglect, professional practice is almost solely focused on mothers (Daniel and Taylor 2006). However, there is little direct separate research into the issues of gender and neglect. In 2008, Dufour et al. undertook an in-depth analysis of parents involved in neglect and found that children of single mothers do seem particularly vulnerable (Dufour et al. 2008). The WHO's (2014) report estimates that 16 per cent of adults have experienced physical neglect in childhood, with little difference reported between the genders. Self-reported emotional neglect was estimated to be 18 per cent (Mikton et al. 2014). Possibly in part because not all countries undertake population-based surveys, and those that do use inconsistent definitions, measurement techniques and study designs, the report does not include commentary about the gender or relationships of those responsible. The limited nature of our knowledge as to the gender of the perpetrators of neglect should lead us to be cautious about making assumptions as to the responsibility for it, especially in situations where more than one carer is involved. Nevertheless, it can be concluded that for a variety of reasons, associated largely with male gender-biased assumptions, women are thought to be more implicated in the neglect of children than is in fact the case.

The age of those who abuse and neglect

Traditionally, the physical abuse and neglect of children have been associated with young and immature parents (Greenland 1987). By contrast, Gil's sample of 1,380 cases of reported abuse in the USA in the late 1960s led him to conclude that the age distribution of parents did not, as observed in a number of earlier studies of physically abused children and their families, support the finding that the parents tended to be particularly young (Gil 1970).

A more recent study carried out in Northern Ireland investigated children subject to a child protection plan for a long period of time (over 23 months), with more than one child protection plan (i.e. sequentially registered, then de-registered, then registered again), or who suffered further significant harm while already subject to a child protection plan. This study (Devaney 2009) found that 21 per cent of the children's mothers had been aged 20 or under at the time of the child's birth and 9 per cent of fathers had also been aged 20 or under. This would indicate that a significant proportion of children subject to child protection plans in these circumstances were born to relatively young parents. However, the same study also considered the age of parents at the time of registration and found that the mean age of mothers was 31 and the mean age of fathers was 36. The study does not provide a breakdown of these figures and a mean age can provide a distorted result, depending on the distribution of ages in the sample (for example, a small number of much older parents would increase the mean disproportionately). Sidebotham and Heron (2006) found that neglected children tended to have younger parents than other children. However, the Devaney (2009) study did not support this. Instead, Devaney found that children made subject to child protection plans for sexual abuse and emotional abuse had the youngest mothers and fathers respectively at the time of the child's birth. At point of registration, children made subject to child protection plans for physical abuse and sexual abuse had the youngest mothers and fathers respectively. Devaney also found that teenage parents who had made use of family support were far less likely to experience these types of difficulties than other young parents. Recently, Sidebotham et al. (2016) found some evidence of the additional pressures of young parenthood, particularly young motherhood, for parents caring for their baby or young child. In a sub-set of 24 serious case reviews where the family had only one child and where the age of the mother was recorded, the mother was found to be aged 19 or younger at the time of her child's birth in 54 per cent of cases. In comparison, the average age of first-time mothers in England and Wales was 28.5 years in 2014. Age was itself not the only factor; issues raised in relation to the mother's age included estrangement from the new mother's parents; denial of pregnancy and/or concealed birth of the baby; temporary housing or supported accommodation; and lack of support from the baby's father and/or an unstable relationship with the baby's father. Therefore, the evidence about low parental age per se and abuse and neglect is not consistent enough to provide clear connections. It may be convenient to associate child abuse with young parenthood. However, the evidence is not nearly strong enough to have much predictive value, even in association with other factors considered indicative of risk.

Abuse by adolescents and children

The sexual abuse of children by other children and adolescents has been the most common focus of attention by researchers – less so physical or emotional abuse. This focus on maltreatment by adolescents and children includes the abuse of children by siblings – 'sibling abuse'. By some measures, sibling abuse is more prevalent than the abuse of children by adults (and, indeed, more prevalent than the abuse of children and spousal abuse combined – Wiehe 1991). In considering children subjected to multiple forms of maltreatment and victimisation (known as polyvictimisation), research would indicate that exposure to multiple forms of maltreatment has a greater impact upon the emotional well-being of children than repeated instances of a single type of victimisation or maltreatment. In their nationally representative study of the prevalence and impact of the maltreatment of children in the United Kingdom, Radford et al. (2011) found that physical violence and victimisation by a sibling or peer was the most prevalent forms of victimisation experienced by infants, children, young people and young adults who were classed as victims. Given the prevalence of maltreatment experienced from siblings and peers, it is perhaps surprising to find, as illustrated in the research carried out by Meyers (2015) 24 years after the publication of Wiehe's study, that survivors of physical and emotional abuse by their siblings still questioned the validity of qualifying their own experiences as being abusive. Just as worryingly, Hotaling et al. (1990) found that in abusive families of more than one child, 100 per cent of children in their study had committed at least one act of serious abuse against their sibling. More recently, Irfan and Cowburn (2004) found that among the British Pakistani community, 35 per cent of physically abusive acts were committed by siblings, as compared with 33 per cent by mothers and 19 per cent by fathers. Several studies demonstrate that brothers are more likely to abuse their sisters, although sisters do also abuse their brothers (Graham-Bermann et al. 1994), and indeed, their sisters (Meyers 2015). It is postulated that parents may view aggression by their sons as more significant than similar acts of aggression by their daughters (Schwartz et al. 1997).

Research into the sexual abuse of children by other children paints a similar picture, in that over a third of child sexual abuse is thought to be committed by someone aged under 18 (i.e. another child; Stop It Now 2007).

In the USA, Fehrenbach et al. (1986) found in their study of adolescent sexual offenders that 95 per cent were male. In the UK, Masson et al. (2015) reviewed a sample of 700 young people who had exhibited sexually harmful behaviours who were referred to nine residential or specialist community-based services across the UK in the 1990s. Of these, 676 (97 per cent) were male and 24 (3 per cent) female. In Fehrenbach's study, 19 per cent had been sexually abused themselves, the bulk of their victims were known to them and one-third were relatives. Johnson (1989) carried out a study of 13 female child perpetrators aged between 4 and 12. Her main findings were that, first, these girls had all been severely sexually abused over long periods of time and, second, most of their victims were members of their own families. Considering the differences between young people and children who sexually abuse younger children and those who abuse their peers, Gunby and Woodhams (2010) found that peer abusers were more likely to have witnessed family violence and had family members more likely to be associated with criminal activity. Young people and children who sexually abused younger children had greater deficits in self-esteem and social isolation and were also more likely to know the victim, to lack age-appropriate friends and to be the victims of peer abuse. The study by Masson et al. (2015) found the female sample were likely to be referred for support at a younger age than the male sample: aged 10–13, as opposed to a modal age of 15 years for males. Girls were significantly less likely to have previous criminal convictions at the point of referral and had experienced higher rates of sexual victimisation in their histories. The female sample were found to have fewer victims who were younger and known to them, whether or not related. In comparison with the male sample, the females had high levels of reported learning difficulties. Radford et al. (2011) concluded that, of those children who experienced contact sexual abuse from a peer, in four out of five cases (82.7 per cent), nobody else was aware, suggesting the prevalence of peer-on-peer sexual abuse may be significantly higher than that which is officially recorded.

Peer abuse, or bullying, of children by other children outside the family would appear to be a widespread phenomenon. Yet Information about its extent is mixed, and much depends on definition, reporting practices and recording. A previous survey of 4,000 children in the UK, aged between 5 and 16, indicated that 60 per cent of children reported having been bullied, with 38 per cent reporting that they had been bullied severely at least twice (Elliot 2002). In an earlier NSPCC study, 43 per cent of respondents said they had been physically bullied, discriminated against or made to feel like an outsider by other young people (Cawson et al. 2000). The most recent NSPCC study (Bentley et al. 2017) breaks down the types of bullying experienced by children, and which are found at times to overlap. In 2015–16, the NSPCC saw a 13 per cent increase in counselling sessions relating to online bullying on the previous year. Online bullying ranged from abusive comments about the child's appearance to encouraging the child to kill themselves. While online bullying attracts much public and media attention, the NSPCC reported having delivered more counselling sessions about physical bullying (4,723 sessions) than online bullying (4,541 sessions). A third bullying type is cited as peer pressure and blackmail, when children fear that declining involvement in certain behaviours. such as joining a gang, participating in criminal and antisocial behaviours, sharing sexual images and carrying out sexual acts online and offline, will result in their being bullied. Together, these bullying behaviours are the second most common reason for boys, and the third most common reason for girls, making contact with Childline in the UK, comprising 9 per cent of overall counselling sessions offered in 2015–16.

In summary, we know more about young sexual abusers than we do about young people who are physically aggressive, even though research indicates the latter probably far outnumber the former.

Poverty, ethnicity and child abuse

Neglect

Partly because of a traditional focus on individual and psychological factors in the understanding of child abuse, there has been less direct attention paid to the association between broader social factors, such as poverty and class, and child abuse. However, as we saw in Chapter 3, connections between social exclusion and child abuse are evident; research consistently identifies an association between economic disadvantage and the increased likelihood of a child being subject to a child protection plan or looked after in out-of-home public care (Featherstone et al. 2017; Bywaters et al. 2018). In an extensive longitudinal study of 3,835 children in the USA, Slack et al. (2011) found that indicators of poverty were linked to an increase in the likelihood of neglect, even when the indicator of poverty might be interpreted as a family asking for support (such as receiving financial support from family members). Slack et al. also found that the association between poverty and neglect was not significantly affected by parental stress, parental involvement with the child's activities (for example, playing sports or games with the child), or the use of physical chastisement. This could indicate that interventions based on modifying these types of parenting concerns will not prove as successful as a more targeted, anti-poverty intervention. Slack notes that poor economic indicators should be used as a warning sign that the family is likely to be struggling in other areas as well. In a population-based birth cohort study of 2,443 Australian children and their parents, Doidge et al. (2017) undertook to examine the possible correlation between socioeconomic disadvantage and child maltreatment, using as their focus the Australian Temperament Project. While economic factors were found to be significant predictors of physical and sexual abuse, witnessing domestic violence and economic factors were, conversely, not found to be associated with emotional abuse or neglect.

Abuse

As we have seen, it is not just neglect which can be associated with poverty. In the USA in 2010, the fourth National Incidence Study of Child Abuse and Neglect (NIS-4) (Sedlak et al. 2010) found that children living in low socio-economic households (those with household income below $15,000 per year, parents with low educational attainment or members of the household reliant on food stamps, subsidised school meals, and so on) were more than three times as likely to be psychologically, physically or sexually abused than other children and more than seven times as likely to be neglected. In Britain, Cawson et al. (2000), in a large-scale survey, found that children from lower socio-economic backgrounds were more likely to report being physically or emotionally abused (and neglected) than other children. In considering those children subject to serious case reviews in England, Sidebotham et al.'s (2016) data show a statistically significant trend towards higher SCR rates in local authorities with higher recorded levels of deprivation, including for those in which the child's death was directly related to child maltreatment. Further, they found family socio-economic circumstances, measured by neighbourhood deprivation, to be strongly correlated with the proportion of children either subject to child protection plans, or who were in public care as of 31 March 2015. Indeed, children living in the most deprived decile were found to be around 13 times more likely to be on a child protection plan, and 11 times more likely to be in public care, than a child residing in the least deprived decile.

Nevertheless, it has been argued that physical abuse and neglect of children is a cross-class phenomenon and that the high proportions of lower-class families being suspected of such abuse result from the fact that they are more open to state surveillance. This is because of their need for state resources, application for which is at the cost of reduced privacy and independence. Through this lens, as identified by Bywaters et al. (2018), the official figures merely demonstrate that the children of the poor who are being abused are more likely to be *spotted* than those in the higher social classes.

NIS-4 also found that, for the first time in the history of National Incidence Studies (previous studies having been produced in 1981, 1988 and 1996), there were race differences in the incidence of maltreatment, with higher rates reported for black children. These differences were found across a variety of measures, including overall maltreatment, overall abuse and overall neglect and physical abuse. The report notes the need for further analyses of whether these race differences remain once the effect of family circumstances is taken into account.

By contrast, in the UK and Europe, there has been found to be a notable dearth of research into the identified differences in intervention rates of child protection services in the lives of children and their families between broad ethnic categories. This contrasts with the substantial research record in North America focusing on the disparity and over-representation of black and ethnic minority children in the child welfare system in the context of child protection and out-of-home care (Bywaters et al. 2017). Maguire-Jack et al. (2015) examined the complex interactions underpinning the root causes of this disparity. Their findings suggest that the disparity in maltreatment of black, white and Hispanic children may be the result of differences in risk, rather than solely the bias of reporters and individual child protection service workers. The paper contributes to a developing body of research implicating income inequality in higher rates of child maltreatment, with groups at the lower end of the income distribution being found to be at greater risk of maltreatment. Less recently, data from serious case reviews (SCRs) indicate that while black or black British children made up 3 per cent of the under-16 population (Office for National Statistics 2001), they accounted for 13 per cent of SCRs in 2003–5 and 8 per cent in 2005–7. Comparable figures for children of mixed ethnicity were 3 per cent (general population), 6 per cent (percentage of SCRs, 2003–5) and 13 per cent (percentage of SCRs, 2005–7); for Asian or Asian British children, the figures were 6 per cent, 6 per cent and 5 per cent and for children from other ethnic groups, the figures were 1 per cent, 1 per cent and 2 per cent respectively.

In the UK, data from the triennial analysis of SCRs between 2011 to 2014 (Sidebotham et al. 2016) indicate that of the 293 SCR notifications subject to the review, 79 per cent of those children were white, of which 76 per cent were white British; 6 per cent were black or black British and 5 per cent Asian or Asian British. Children with a mixed ethnicity background accounted for 8 per cent of the total. In 11 cases (4 per cent of the notifications), ethnicity was not stated.

Several factors could account for this over-representation. Black and ethnic minority families are likely to be more open to state surveillance as a result of figuring highly among indices of deprivation.[2] Lack of cultural knowledge and awareness and the operation of both institutional and direct racism may increase the chances of suspicions of abuse in black families being confirmed. On the other hand, issues of cultural sensitivity and stereotyping have resulted in less vigorous pursuit of child protection concerns particularly in respect of Asian families (Webb et al. 2002).

Whatever the genuine situation with regard to physical abuse, most incidence studies of child sexual abuse point to its existence among all strata of society. Finkelhor et al. (1986, 1993) argue that class, ethnic and regional factors do not seem to affect the incidence of sexual abuse of children in the USA. In a national survey held in 1985, the only exceptions to this were boys of English or Scandinavian heritage, who were at higher risk than those from other ethnic groupings (Finkelhor et al. 1990). The NSPCC incidence study in the UK also found that sexual abuse was spread across social classes (Cawson et al. 2000).

Most reported child sexual abuse is located disproportionately among poorer families. In the USA, the 2010 NIS-4 found that child sexual abuse rates were 0.7 children per 1,000 for children not in low socio-economic status families but 2.4 children per 1,000 for children in low socio-economic status families, a rate nearly 3.5 times as high (Sedlak et al. 2010). However, in comparison with earlier National Incidence Studies, this was a relatively minor difference, with the 1996 study finding a rate 18 times as high for children from low socio-economic status families (Sedlak and Broadhurst 1996).The 2010 survey authors comment that in part this decline in the rate of difference is consistent with declines overall in sexual and physical abuse and they conclude that these declines are real, as they are supported by other sources of data (such as US Department of Health and Human Services Administration on Children, Youth and Families 2007b, 2008, 2009).The bulk of families coming to the notice of the NSPCC in the UK as a result of child sexual abuse were also from the poorer classes (Creighton and Noyes 1989: 18–19).

The argument that high rates of physical abuse and neglect are found among poorer families simply because they are more exposed to state surveillance could, it seems, be more justifiably applied in the case of child sexual abuse. Finkelhor is unequivocal about the implications of the disparity of findings between research studies and officially reported statistics, arguing that professionals need to be cautious about using inaccurate, class-biased stereotypes in their work, and that detecting and reporting abuse in higher social classes needs to be improved (Finkelhor 2008).

Parents who have been abused

The issue of the inter-generational transmission of abuse is a thorny one indeed (Kaufman and Zigler 1989). Because of what we know about the impact of abuse on self-esteem, it seems reasonable to believe that parents who have been abused are likely, all other things being equal, to find it harder to provide good enough parenting for their children. However, attention needs to be paid to the discontinuities as well as the continuities, and knowledge of the circumstances in which abused parents do *not* abuse their own children is of as much importance to child protection professionals as that of the circumstances in which they do. Yet there has been scant research, particularly recently, addressing this issue.

Physical abuse and neglect

Oliver (1985), using official records, uncovered 147 families out of a population of 200,000 in north Wiltshire where abuse of children had happened in successive generations. However, the potential usefulness of this study, as with many others, is diminished by the fact that we are not told how many of the parents who were abused themselves in the first generation did *not* go on to abuse their own children. In other words, studying parents who have already abused their children tells us nothing about the proportion of parents who have been abused but do not go on to be abusive themselves.

A study by Hunter and Kilstrom (1979) neatly illustrates this. They interviewed 282 parents of new-born children admitted to a regional intensive care nursery for premature and ill infants. Of these parents, 49 (17 per cent) had themselves been abused. At follow-up a year later, 9 of these had abused their children. Only one child from the rest of the sample had been abused. Thus, the inter-generational rate in this prospective study was 18 per cent. However, if the 10 children who were abused had become the subject of a *retrospective* study, it would have been found that 90 per cent of their parents had been abused and this could give an exaggerated impression of the extent of inter-generational abuse.

It is worth noting an issue raised earlier: that all these studies focus almost entirely on transmission of violence and abuse through mothers whereas, to the best of our knowledge, men are responsible for at least half of all physical abuse. There is very little research into the antecedents of adult males who physically abuse.

Sexual abuse

The picture is only slightly better in this respect with regard to sexual abuse. Despite the fact that males are responsible for nearly all such abuse and that girls are by far the most likely victims, there is still considerable focus on women as the key link between sexual abuse over two generations. Faller (1989) found that nearly half the mothers of a sample of 154 sexually abused children either had experienced or knew of sexual abuse in their own families of origin. This study is particularly useful in that it also checked the experiences of the male offenders in these cases; nearly 40 per cent of them had also experienced or knew of sexual abuse in their families as children.

Studies of male perpetrators of sexual abuse who have been imprisoned show relatively high proportions of these men having been sexually abused themselves as children. Simons et al. (2008) found that 73 per cent of their sample of convicted child sex abusers had themselves experienced sexual abuse in childhood. Yet in an earlier study, only 5 out of 274 perpetrators reported having been sexually abused themselves (Bentovim and Boston 1988). The differences may be explained by the fact that these studies were looking at two different types of sexual abuser: persistent offenders who are a danger to many children outside their families, and offenders who have targeted children within their own family. However, one should not assume that intra- and extra-familial sexual abuse are totally unconnected phenomena.[3]

It is also worth noting that although sexual and physical abuse have been considered separately, several of the studies point to sexual abusers having themselves experienced both forms of abuse in childhood, although Simons et al. (2008), echoed latterly by di Giacomo and Clerici

(2013), found that adult sex abusers (rapists) were more likely to have experienced physical abuse in childhood than child sex abusers, and they were also more likely to have experienced emotional abuse and parental violence.

Emotional abuse

As with the other areas, there is a paucity of research on the inter-generational transmission of emotional abuse. Various documents make an assumption that emotional abuse is transmitted in this way (such as Prevent Child Abuse America 2005) but there is limited empirical research either way. Given that emotional abuse is generally held to play a part in both physical and sexual abuse (a child abused in these ways is also being emotionally abused), then the discussion above would also apply, in some form, to the inter-generational transmission of emotional abuse.

The topic of inter-generational transmission of abuse of all types is clearly a problematic one. It has been argued that focusing on this issue is pessimistic so far as those who have been abused are concerned. That continuities exist is not in dispute; however, as Straus pointed out in the late 1970s, the more pertinent question to be asked is not whether abused children become abusive parents; rather, what conditions need to exist for the transmission of abuse to occur (Straus 1979).

Family structure, child abuse and neglect

There is considerable debate about how child abuse is related to different family structures. Official statistics show that lone parenthood has increased dramatically since the 1960s, as has divorce. For instance, in 2016, divorces among opposite sex couples in England and Wales increased by 5.8 per cent, compared with 2015. In context, this follows a significant fall in the number of divorces between 2014 and 2015 (9.1 per cent). By 2016, the divorce rate was 30 per cent lower than the 2003 peak in divorce numbers in the UK (Office for National Statistics 2016). This is a relevant consideration given the two features of family structure that have been most often studied: lone parenthood and step-parenting (particularly with regard to sexual abuse).

Lone-parent families

In the USA, the NIS-4 (Sedlak et al. 2010) stated that children residing with their married, biological parents, experienced the lowest maltreatment rates overall – 6.8 per 1,000 children. Conversely, the report continues, children living with one of their parents who had an unmarried partner experienced the highest incidence of overall maltreatment at 57.2 per

1,000 – a rate more than eight times greater than experienced by children living with two married, biological parents. The incidence of overall maltreatment for children living with just one parent (and no partner) was found to be 28.4 per 1,000.

The rate of abuse for children living with two married biological parents was found to be 2.9 children per 1,000, compared to 33.6 per 1,000 for children living with one parent and that parent's unmarried partner. The rate for children living with just one parent was 10.2 per 1,000. For neglect, the figures are reported in a slightly different way but do show that the rate for children living with two married biological parents was 4.2 per 1,000 and 19.6 per 1,000 for children living with just one parent. Simon et al. (2018) analysed pooled data from three cross-sectional national telephone surveys comprising 13,052 children in 2016. Findings indicated that of the 8.4 per cent of children overall reporting they had experienced physical abuse by a caregiver, of these, 27.1 per cent of victims reported they were living with two parents, while 53.8 per cent of those reporting physical abuse said they were living in 'other family structures'. In both studies, the overall figures mask some differences between the incidence of abuse and neglect.

In England and Wales, an analysis of SCRs (Brandon et al. 2008) found that of the 161 published between April 2003 and March 2005, 73 per cent of the children were living with two biological parents at the time of the significant infliction of harm, compared with 13 per cent who were living with one biological parent and their partner and 20 per cent who were living with just their mother.

These results do not generally fit with earlier findings from research. For example, Sack et al. (1985) carried out a study of 802 adults in Oregon, USA, and found the prevalence of abuse to be twice as high in single-parent households as in those with two parents. Creighton and Noyes (1989) found that one-fifth of children registered for sexual abuse came from lone-female-headed homes.

Therefore, on the one hand, children in lone-parent families can appear as significantly more at risk of abuse and neglect than their counterparts in two-parent families, but there is some evidence, especially from recent official reports, that this is not necessarily so. Such statistics also cannot tell us anything about the dynamics or processes that might help to account for variations in abuse rates between these two family types. Clearly, as indicated above, economic stress is likely to be an important factor. The higher incidence of neglect cases among lone-parent families shown up in the NIS-4 (Sedlak et al. 2010) could support this, although rates of neglect for children living with two married biological parents were also found to be higher than rates of abuse for the same children.

With regard to sexual abuse, Finkelhor et al. (1986) argue that children in lone-female-headed households could be exposed to a greater number of male adult figures than those in two-parent households and that this could place them at statistically greater risk of being sexually abused. This rather contributes to a somewhat negative picture of lone parenting. The advantages of such families should also be taken into account, such as the potential for less interpersonal conflict between parents, a factor that has been associated with emotional abuse. There is a need for much more research into the impact of lone parenting (benefits and costs) on childrearing in general.

Step-parents and social fathers

The term 'social father' is a relatively new one and is used to describe a person (male) who has responsibility for caring for a child to whom they are not biologically related. Therefore, the category of social father is in some senses wider than just step-fathers (that is, fathers who have married the child's mother), and refers to any male figure with caring responsibility for a child to whom they are not genetically related.

The research evidence on the effect of a social father or a step-parent on a family is mixed. Starting with step-parents, the term 'Cinderella effect' has been used to describe the significantly increased incidence of children being abused by step-parents than by genetic parents (Daly and Wilson 2005). A wealth of data has found links between step-parents and child abuse. It has also been found that in families in which the parent has both step-children and genetically related children, it is the step-children who are more likely to be abused (Crawford and Krebs 2008). Other studies have also shown that not only are step-children more likely to be abused, they are also more likely to experience neglect, especially in the form of lack of parental supervision. For example, based on information from Australia, step-children aged under 5 are more likely to experience unintentional injuries than genetic children. Comparing data from lone-parent families to that of two-parent families suggests that the absence of a biological parent does not increase the risk but adding a step-parent to a family does (Tooley et al. 2006).

Reconstituted families are thus highly over-represented in these abuse statistics, but there has been little follow-up research as to why this is the case or into the process of abuse in such families. In any event, one hugely significant caveat needs to be borne in mind – there is a danger of assuming that all step-parents present a risk to children, and clearly this is not true. The majority of step-parents do not abuse or neglect their step-children.

However, there is other research, focused specifically on social fathers, which indicates that this group of male carers is likely to exhibit at least as good care as biological fathers and, in many cases, higher quality care. Social fathers who married the child's mother (in other words, step-fathers) appeared to engage more with the children in the family, take on more responsibility for their care and were more trusted by mothers than non-married social fathers (Berger et al. 2008). However, on closer analysis, much of this difference could be attributed to background individual or family characteristics – although, significantly, not all of it.

There is clearly a need for more broad-based research into the impact of family structure on children in reconstituted families and, as with lone-parent families, attention needs to be paid to positive features and adaptations as well as to negative consequences.

Other significant factors associated with those who abuse or neglect children

This section looks at four other significant factors associated with child abuse and neglect: learning difficulties and the so-called (and deeply unhelpfully named) 'toxic trio' of mental health difficulties, substance misuse and domestic violence. Finally, research into the psychological make-up of child sexual abusers will be considered.

Abuse and neglect: parents with learning difficulties

In their studies of SCRs between 2005 and 2007 (Brandon et al. 2009) and latterly between 2011 and 2014, Sidebotham et al. (2016), in considering parental mental health difficulties, did not highlight any significant incidence of parental learning difficulties. However, parents with learning disabilities have, nevertheless, typically been viewed as posing an increased risk to children (Social Services Inspectorate 1999). In some studies, this view has been justified by the data. For example, research suggests that parents with learning difficulties are disproportionately represented in care proceedings, experience increased likelihood of being involved in child protection investigations, are more frequently subject to care applications and are more likely than any other group to lose their children in this context (Booth et al. 2005; Jones 2013; LaLiberte et al. 2017). However, Booth and Booth (1998) studied 30 adults who had been cared for by a parent with a learning difficulty and found that over half reported childhood physical or sexual abuse, although primarily the abuse was perpetrated not by their parent but by a partner of their parent. In other words, it appeared that parents with learning difficulties were more vulnerable to being targeted by perpetrators, rather than being perpetrators themselves. In general terms, while it is safe to assume – as with all groups of parents – that some parents with learning difficulties will abuse or neglect their children, few studies have actually assessed whether the risk for children is significantly greater than for any other group of parents. What is clear is that parents with learning difficulties are over-represented in terms of having children subject to child protection plans. Creighton and Noyes (1989) found that 10 per cent of mothers and 5 per cent of fathers of children listed on child protection registers (now replaced by child protection plans) had attended special schools, which points to a significant correlation between learning disability and officially reported child abuse.

There are, however, several factors that could account for this association, the most obvious being that the heightened concern that exists with regard to people with learning difficulties bringing up their own children results in their child care practices being exposed to greater scrutiny than those of parents without learning difficulties. Care should be taken not to see people with learning difficulties as a homogeneous group with similar characteristics. They do share some common problems, but these stem mainly from their potential for being undervalued and exploited by others. Indeed, previously issued government advice on this topic, entitled *Good Practice Guidance on Working with Parents with a Learning Disability* (Department of Health/Department for Education and Skills 2007), still seems pertinent, noting that parents with learning difficulties often face other difficulties as well, including mental or physical health difficulties, domestic violence and substance abuse.

Research that demonstrates the circumstances in which parents with learning difficulties abuse their children is more useful than research that simply demonstrates correlation rates between low intelligence and child abuse. Booth and Booth (1993) argue that disentangling fears about parents with learning difficulties from the reality of their parenting behaviours is highly problematic – they note that a parent with learning difficulties should be seen as a more vulnerable parent, rather than as a different kind of parent. Certainly, this is borne out by the experiences of such parents in court care proceedings in the USA and elsewhere where the rates of child removal are around 50 per cent (McConnell and Llewellyn 2000).

The 'toxic trio': mental health difficulties, substance misuse and domestic violence

In their two previous studies of over 350 SCRs, held between 2005 and 2009, Brandon et al. (2009, 2010) identified what has been referred to as a 'toxic trio' of risk factors for child abuse, namely, domestic violence, mental health difficulties and substance misuse. They also included a fourth factor: poverty or poor living conditions. The authors found that in nearly 75 per cent of cases from the 2009 study, one or more of these factors was present. In their most recent analysis, Sidebotham et al. (2016) found that of 175 SCRs completed between 2011 and 2014, 138 (79 per cent) had one or more of the three problems recorded as being present. Therefore, it appeared to them that these factors, especially in combination, increase the risk to children. Before we consider the wider evidence base for this 'toxic trio', it is worth noting, as discussed above in the section on the lack of causal connections for child abuse and neglect, that Brandon et al. and more recently, Sidebotham et al. (2016), are not claiming that to detect and prevent child abuse we only need identify families where these factors are present; by way of illustration, they note that in 2016, 36 families (21 per cent of the 175 SCRs) were identified as not having any of the three problems present. Brandon et al., in their (2009) review of SCRs reiterated again as previously in the 2003–5 study, that even where parental challenges of mental ill-health, domestic violence, substance misuse and poverty do co-exist, they do not *predict* serious maltreatment or death of a child. It seems also important to note that people are not toxic, and that there are many important differences between the three issues linked together by this increasingly troubling phrase.

Mental health difficulties

In considering all of the SCRs held in England and Wales between 2005 and 2007, Brandon et al. (2009), confirmed again between 2011 and 2014 by Sidebotham et al. (2016), found that of all the characteristics of parents involved, mental health difficulties were the second most frequently cited, only just behind domestic violence. In a detailed study of 40 of the 2005 and 2007 cases, the same authors found that nearly 75 per cent of the children lived with domestic violence and/or parental mental health difficulties, and/or parental substance misuse. In the 2016 review, 39 families (22 per cent) were identified as having all three factors recorded as being present. Two of the three factors were noted for 53 families (30 per cent). Finally, there were 47 families (27 per cent) where only one of the factors was noted.

These findings are very similar to those for SCRs held between 2003 and 2005, in which mental health difficulties (including personality disorders) were identified in over 50 per cent of the cases selected for more in-depth study (Brandon et al. 2008). So (relatively) common is the occurrence of parental mental health difficulties in cases of serious child abuse and/or child deaths that it is perhaps hard to remember that the 'obviousness' of this link was not always recognised. Early child abuse pioneers, such as Steele and Pollock (1974), were of the view that parents who abused their children had psychological incapacities to nurture and care for their babies and children because of their own emotionally poor upbringing (and not because of specific mental health difficulties).

However, this was primarily the case because of a fairly strict definition of what constituted mental health difficulties. Studies that have taken a broader definition of mental illness have demonstrated a closer association with physical child abuse. For example, Oliver (1985) found that 50 out of 147 mothers (34 per cent) had been treated psychiatrically for depression, as had seven of the fathers (5 per cent). In a more recent study, Stith et al. (2009) conducted a meta-analysis of 155 studies into parental characteristics identified with child abuse and found that addressing the mental health needs of parents who abuse or neglect their children was likely to be important. However, as with other areas (such as step-parents), certain caveats must be borne in mind. As reflected in the Social Care Institute for Excellence (SCIE) report *Think Child, Think Parent, Think Family: A Guide to Parental Mental Health and Child Welfare* (Diggins 2009, updated 2011), children are not simply at risk because carers have mental health difficulties - that would be far too linear a conclusion. Instead, research indicates that other factors, including parental drug and alcohol misuse and domestic violence, are often apparent in situations of serious abuse or neglect.

It may be the case that there are some forms of psychological state, such as depression, the effects of which are underestimated as contributory factors to the abuse and neglect of children. Sheppard (2003) has demonstrated in a series of studies that between 36 and 46 per cent of mothers receiving child welfare services are clinically depressed (using the Beck Depression Inventory). Indeed, parental depression, as a specific mental health difficulty, has been studied quite widely and it has been shown that it is associated with emotional and behavioural difficulties for children (National Research Council and Institute of Medicine 2009: Diggins 2009). The literature on the negative effects of parental depression for children is relatively consistent (see Jaser et al. 2005; Burns et al. 2009; Galbally and Lewis 2017). The female carers of children, such as Christine Mason (Lambeth, Lewisham and Southwark 1989), Beatrice Henry (Lambeth 1987) and Rosemary Koseda (Hillingdon 1986), have all been described as showing symptoms of depression.[4]

However, one of the key questions – and certainly the key question here – is how much does child abuse and neglect account for (or mediate) the negative effect of parental depression? Two main parenting styles have been found to be associated with parental depression: harsh parenting and disengaged parenting. Harsh parenting occurs when a parent is more negative towards their child, more likely to be irritated by them and/or to be verbally or physically aggressive towards the child (Lyons-Ruth et al. 2002). Disengaged parenting occurs when a parent is more likely to withdraw from their child, less likely to respond to emotional needs and less likely to engage in positive interactions with the child (Goodman and Brumley 1990). Although the research base for clear links with abusive or neglectful behaviour is less clear, harsh parenting behaviours associated with parental depression may, in certain circumstances, escalate to the threshold of physically abusive behaviour (Silverstein et al. 2009). Perhaps surprisingly, the link between parental depression and neglect is less clear than the link between parental depression and abuse (Knutson and Schartz 1997). A more recent study, which sought to examine in more detail the mediation between parental depression and poor outcomes for children, actually found little evidence to support the view that physically abusive parental behaviour was a mediating variable, finding instead that neglectful parenting partially mediated the link (Mustillo et al. 2011).

In Britain, with the broadening of focus onto children in need in the last two decades, there has been a significant shift in thinking about the importance of adult mental health in the safeguarding of children. In 2003, SCIE released a protocol for partnership working for local agencies working with adults with mental health difficulties (and other issues), and agencies with specific child protection functions, noting that effective coordination between these two different types of agency was a key way of promoting the well-being of children by ensuring appropriate support was available for parents (Kearney et al. 2003). There is of course a danger that focusing on the role of depression in child abuse could serve to place even more emphasis on women as key carers. Nevertheless, both in relation to serious and fatal abuse of children and more general concerns about good-enough parenting, there is clearly a need to make much more use of the growing awareness and knowledge base about the links between mental health and child abuse and neglect (Stanley et al. 2003).

Substance misuse: alcohol

Alcohol has been closely linked with child abuse from the early days of the NSPCC at the time when the temperance movement had a high profile and it has long been cited as a contributory factor to physical child abuse (Browne and Saqi 1988). In a study of all SCRs between 2005 and 2007, Brandon et al. (2009) found that alcohol misuse was a feature in 19 cases, less than domestic violence (49), mental health problems (32) and drug misuse (28) but more than the parent being a teenager (18), the parent being formally in care (5) or the parent currently being in care (4). Similarly, in the more recent study of SCRs, Sidebotham et al. (2016), between 2011 and 2014, found alcohol misuse to be present in 65 of the SCRs (37 per cent), fewer than domestic violence, 94 cases (54 per cent), and parental mental health problems, 92 cases (53 per cent). The NSPCC reported a 16 per cent increase in calls relating to concerns about substance misuse near children in 2015–16, compared to 2013–14, although the summary did not specify how the proportion related to alcohol or drug misuse respectively (*NSPCC News*, 13 February 2017).

However, contrary to common perceptions, research findings linking alcohol misuse with child abuse or neglect are inconsistent. There is a much stronger relationship between adult alcohol abuse and a childhood history of abuse, i.e. adults abused as children have a higher likelihood of misusing alcohol (Choi et al. 2016; Fuller-Thompson et al. 2016). A history of abuse in childhood has also been found to be a significant risk factor for adolescent binge drinking (defined as five or more drinks in a row, at least two to three times a month; Shin et al. 2009, 2015).

Alcohol misuse does have a higher association with child neglect. Studies in the USA point to as many as half of all families known to the public welfare system being affected by alcohol or drug misuse (see Curtis and McCullough 1993). However, as we have seen, there are major difficulties involved in defining neglect, and the term 'alcohol problems' is also open to widely varied interpretation.

As we develop broader concerns about the care and development of children beyond abuse, the issue of alcohol misuse and its effect on children also grows in importance. Research shows that a million children could be living with parents with problematic drinking habits in Britain and that such children have higher levels of behavioural problems, school problems, emotional disturbances, lower self-esteem, anxiety and depression, and disrupted routines. They are likely to experience more disrupted routines, less supervision, more financial problems and witness more domestic violence (Kroll and Taylor 2003). Pregnant women who misuse alcohol can cause problems for the foetus; foetal alcohol syndrome (FAS) is the leading known environmental cause of learning disability in the Western world (National Institute of Alcohol Abuse and Alcoholism 1993; Wilhoit et al. 2017).

While there are no causal links between alcohol abuse and all these problems, the fact that they are so prominently correlated means that awareness of alcohol misuse in families is increasingly becoming a warning signal about children being at risk of neglect.

Substance misuse: drugs

As noted above, in SCRs, parental drug misuse is a common feature; in a review of SCRs from 2011–14, parental drug misuse was recorded as present in 66 (38 per cent) of the 175 reviews (Sidebotham et al. 2016). That this is so is not a new phenomenon; in 1995, Dore et al. pointed to very high rates of drug misuse among substantiated child mistreatment cases in the USA. As with alcohol, it is not clear from these figures whether drug misuse is associated more with physical abuse or with neglect. It is probably the latter. However, research also suggests that drug misuse (and alcohol misuse) feature in the majority of cases of emotional abuse as well (Bijur et al. 1992).

As with alcohol, there are concerns about the impact of drug misuse on the foetus. However, research into this topic is inconclusive in that it is not easy to separate the impact of drugs from other frequently associated factors such as poor nutrition and lack of proper antenatal care (Keen and Alison 2001). Again, most of the concerns centre around the issue of neglect. There is little research directly linking problem drug use with physical or sexual abuse. The key concerns are supervision, the impact of drug-seeking lifestyles and the longer-term psychological impact on the child (Kroll 2004). In broad terms, the research suggests that children of substance-misusing parents are likely to suffer deficits in their development which has clear implications for preventive and supportive programmes.

Domestic violence

Domestic violence typically involves patterns of physical, sexual or emotional abuse, and can be understood as the misuse and exercise of power and control by one partner over another. As noted previously, the definition of harm derived from the Children Act 1989 now includes 'impairment suffered from seeing or hearing the ill-treatment of another' (as amended by the 2002

Adoption and Children Act). Addressing a recognised gap in safeguarding and public protection within the context of non-violent intimate partner relationships, the Serious Crime Act 2015 created a new offence in England and Wales of 'controlling or coercive behaviour in an ongoing relationship between intimate partners or family members' (Home Office 2015). Given the relatively recent recognition of this offence, specific data and research into the impact of this particular non-physical aspect of abusive behaviour towards children are limited. Nonetheless, what is known is that while legislation is gender-neutral, statistics to date repeatedly highlight women and girls being disproportionately affected by crimes committed within the domestic violence context. The Crown Prosecution Service's *Violence Against Women and Girls Crime Report* (2016/17) confirmed, that of the 93,590 defendants prosecuted, 85,280 (91.8 per cent) were male and 7,656 (8.2 per cent) were female. The Crown Prosecution Services' report for 2015/16 (deemed to have more fully recorded data) identified the proportion of female victims remaining steady at 84 per cent (Crown Prosecution Service 2016). However, in the report entitled *Domestic Abuse in England and Wales* (Office for National Statistics 2017), men accounted for 33.6 per cent of victims of domestic abuse, while women accounted for 66.4 per cent. Of these households, 43.7 per cent identified children as being present. In her qualitative study of 15 mothers and 15 of their children aged between 10 and 14 years of age, Katz (2016) posits that research into children's experience of domestic abuse disproportionately focuses upon their experiences of physical domestic violence, at the expense of the insidious, agency-corroding nature of coercieve and controlling abuse, characterised by perpetrators intimidating, isolating and controlling their victims (Stark 2007). By extension, perpetrators were found to isolate and monitor children as well as their mothers, emotionally abusing them and controlling the family finances, impacting directly and vicariously upon children. In such circumstances, Katz found children being prevented from spending time with their mother, grandparents and peers, not being allowed time with friends or to participate in extra-curricular activities.

Children living with domestic violence are over-represented among those referred to children's services and domestic violence is a factor in up to two-thirds of cases discussed at child protection conferences (Humphreys 2006). In the Department for Education's (2017a) report, 49.9 per cent of children assessed to be in need, at 31 March 2017, had domestic violence as the most commonly identified factor. In the report by Sidebotham et al. (2016), of the panoply of risk factors discussed, the most prominent factor – as in previous SCR biennial reports – is the ongoing risk to children inherent in domestic abuse contexts: it was a factor present in 2011–14 cases from all categories of serious and fatal maltreatment, including nearly all cases of overt filicide. Domestic violence can also affect unborn children: Gazmararian et al. (2000) estimated that 324,000 pregnant women are physically victimised by their male partners each year, leading, in some instances, to subsequent birth problems and depression in mothers.

In Britain, research has indicated that between 30 and 66 per cent of children living with domestic violence experience direct abuse (Humphreys 2006). Children and adolescents exposed to domestic violence can present with a range of difficulties; childhood trauma symptoms have been linked to such exposure, as has the presence of externalising behaviour problems, especially in boys (Evans et al. 2008).

An additional, compelling and many-faceted lens through which to identify possible indicators of child maltreatment and domestic violence, in the absence of explicit disclosure, is the developing body of research and clinical evidence indicating the at-times, inter-relationship between the abuse of children, vulnerable adults and animals within the domestic violence context (NSPCC 2005; Bright et al. 2018). The categories of animal abuse include their sexual and physical abuse, and neglect (NSPCC 2005). The study of animal abuse in intimate partner violence (IPV) contexts and its relationships to other forms of violence, including child maltreatment, is important to consider and hold in professional view for a number of reasons: animal victims suffer pain, violence and terrifying deaths within the domestic violence context. In 2011, the Humane Society of the United States estimated that nearly one million animals a year were abused or killed in the context of IPV. Despite the scale of this recorded abuse, animal victims of IPV are often overlooked, both in criminology and victimology literatures, and are often inconsistently understood and considered in professional child protection practice, indicating that the prevalence of animal maltreatment is likely to be significantly higher than that which is officially recorded (Knight et al. 2014). These 'links' or associations are various, with equally important inter-related implications for collaborative professional practice for those working to safeguard children and animals alike. Research indicates that children perpetrating cruelty to animals may be suggestive of their having experienced serious physical abuse (McEwen et al. 2014; Bright et al. 2018). In addition, some research indicates the younger a child begins committing animal cruelty, including having sex with animals, to be predictive of adult interpersonal violence (Henderson et al. 2011). DeViney et al. (1983) identified that where serious animal abuse had been perpetrated within a household by an adult, there may be an increased likelihood of another form of violence within the family taking place, leaving the child also at risk of harm. In their 2016 study of 150 adult men charged with physically and sexually abusing and/or neglecting animals between 2004 and 2009, Levitt et al. (2016) found in the majority of cases, the animals were victimised by their 'owners' or by their owner's former or current partner – strongly suggestive of a domestic violence context. Much research has focused on women who have experienced domestic violence also experiencing cruelty to their animals – and at times, death of their pets at the hands of domestic violence perpetrators as a means of exerting intimidatory coercive control (Newberry 2017). Less research has focused directly upon the impact on children whose companion animals are abused in this environment. However, McDonald et al. (2015), in their study of 291 ethnically diverse children (55 per cent Latino or Hispanic) between the ages of 7 and 12 recruited from a community-based domestic violence service., indicated that exposure to companion animal maltreatment was associated with callousness in the child witnesses. This was in turn associated with greater internalising and externalising problems. The impact of their exposure to animal maltreatment on externalising problems was mediated through callousness, being uncaring and unemotional. They found this exposure to have enduring negative impacts for the child witnesses, being associated with psychopathology in childhood, extending into adulthood. McDonald et al. (2015) identified that more than half of children living in families with intimate partner violence are exposed to abuse of their pets – not only traumatic and at times fatal for the animal, but experienced as traumatic in childhood, and beyond.

Separating victims from their domestic abuser offers no guarantee of their own, or their children's protection; control and direct violence are at times perpetrated following separation. Futher, the prospect or reality of restrictions placed on contact between the father and his children has been assessed, in some instances, as a trigger for serious and fatal violence to the child (Stanley et al. 2010; Sidebotham et al. 2016).

However, as with much of the other research referred to in this chapter, there is a pressing need for studies that go beyond correlations and explore in greater depth the dynamics of the family processes where child abuse, animal abuse and partner abuse coexist, so that child and wider protection intervention in these circumstances across and between agencies can be better informed (Coohey and Braun 1997).

Sexual abuse

There has been little connection made between particular psychological characteristics and child sexual abuse, and much more emphasis on interactive rather than individualistic factors than in the case of physical abuse and neglect. There has been no research linking mental illness with sexual abuse. Traditionally, incest has been linked to families of low intelligence, but there is little research evidence to show this to be the case.

In 2008, Whitaker et al. undertook a meta-analysis of 89 studies, published between 1990 and 2003, examining risk factors for the perpetration of child sex abuse. They compared the characteristics of sex offenders against children, sex offenders against adults, non-sex offenders and non-offenders. They found that while sex offenders against children were different from non-sex offenders and non-offenders, with regard to categories such as family factors, externalising behaviours, sexual problems and attitudes and beliefs, they were not significantly different from sex offenders against adults. As noted by the study's authors, this strongly suggests that the presence of general risk factors can lead to a variety of extremely negative behavioural outcomes, including sex offences against children, but does not support the view that there are qualitative differences between offenders against children and offenders against adults, despite perhaps fairly strongly held and common views to the contrary.

Who is abused?

All children are potentially vulnerable to abuse by those adults who look after them throughout childhood because they are dependent on them for all aspects of physical and emotional protection and care. Most children are not mistreated by their parents because protective behaviour is considered natural and instinctive (Bowlby 1971). Finkelhor and Korbin (1988), writing from an international perspective but with an eye to poorer countries, point out that children are most vulnerable to abuse and neglect if they are:

- less healthy than others;
- disabled (although in a few societies, disabled children are protected by being accorded a special status);
- female;
- born in unusual, stigmatised or difficult conditions;
- unwanted;
- born with 'dis-valued' traits and behaviours;
- considered to be 'illegitimate' in some way;
- born in situations of rapid economic change.

While such children are less obviously at risk in richer societies, they are still more vulnerable to abuse and neglect than those who do not share these characteristics. Many of the factors listed above have been considered in the first section of this chapter. The factors that remain to briefly be discussed are: age, gender, factors inherent to the child and disability.

Age

Children and young people are vulnerable to maltreatment in different ways, at different ages. The age groups especially vulnerable to serious harm, however, are infants and pre-school children (4,980 children aged under 1; 13,540 aged 1–4 years), and adolescents (14,300 children aged 10–15 years and 2,010 aged 16 and over) (Department for Education 2017a). Using Department for Education statistics (Department for Education 2017a), the age breakdown of children subject to child protection plans are presented in Table 5.1. This includes the unborn category of children (1,130), including those about to be born to parents who have already seriously abused siblings and, increasingly, those due to be born to parents involved in substance misuse or domestic violence. Concerns about children under 1 are largely in relation to emotional abuse and neglect. Children in this age group are more likely to be made subject to child protection under these categories due to their inherent vulnerability and dependence upon others. Around 70 per cent of children who die from abuse in the USA, and the UK, are under the age of 4, with the highest death rate among children aged less than 1 year (Department for Education 2017a; US Department of Health and Human Services 2017).

The age group most likely to be made subject to child protection plans in the UK for sexual abuse are those between 10 and 15. However, one must be careful when using these figures not to assume that certain forms of abuse are confined to certain age ranges. For example, Boyer and Fine (1992) found that 24 per cent of female child sexual abuse survivors were first abused at age 5 or younger. Finkelhor (1993) also notes that children under 6 constitute at least 10 per cent of child sexual abuse victims in the USA.

Gender

The gender breakdown for children subject to child protection plans in the UK on 31 March 2017 shows boys being slightly more likely than girls to be made subject to a child protection plan generally, and under the categories of physical abuse, neglect and emotional abuse specifically so. There seem to be no obvious reasons why this is so. It could be speculated that, in the case of physical abuse, physical punishment of boys is more generally sanctioned as a means of control in our society than of girls and that this cultural norm leads to more excessive violence in their case. It has generally been thought to be the case that the sexual abuse of boys is less likely to be officially reported than that of girls.

In many of the poorer societies throughout the world (southern India, for example), girls are more likely to be subjected to abuse because they are less valued for their economic utility.

Factors inherent to the child

Difficult though it may be to contemplate, there are certain factors that make some children more likely to be the victim of child abuse than others. In other words, aside from the factors related to parents and to the environment, many of which we have discussed above, there are certain inherent characteristics that make some children more at risk of maltreatment. Infants and children who cry persistently are more at risk of physical abuse (being shaken). Disabled children are more likely to be abused or neglected but we will consider this group separately below. Children with more difficult temperaments, children with aggressive behaviour, attention deficits and other behavioural problems are also more likely to be abused. On the other hand, children with robust and high self-esteem, higher intelligence, creativity, humour and independence have a level of resilience against any abuse and this also makes abuse less likely to occur (Masten et al. 1990; Benard 1995).

Table 5.1 Number of children who were the subject of a child protection plan at 31 March 2017, gender, initial category of abuse and ethnicity

	Total children who were the subject of a child protection plan at 31 March 2017	Initial category of abuse[1]				
		Neglect	Physical abuse	Sexual abuse	Emotional abuse	Multiple[2]
All children[3]	51,080	24,590	3,950	2,260	17,280	3,010
Breakdown by gender:						
Male	25,610	12,432	2,087	838	8,731	1,524
Female	24,300	11,391	1,764	1,381	8,327	1,441
Missing/Indeterminate[4]	1,170	766	101	37	217	45
Breakdown by age at 31 March:[5]						
Unborn	1,130	752	100	36	201	43
Under 1	4,980	2,796	496	160	1,312	213
1–4	13,540	6,666	1,137	389	4,636	714
5–9	15,120	6,878	1,092	566	5,652	929
10–15	14,300	6,593	972	900	4,894	945
16 and over	2,010	903	155	205	579	166
Breakdown by ethnicity:[6]						
Total known ethnicity[7]	49,470	23,691	3,832	2,200	16,827	2,916
White[8]	38,280	19,439	2,559	1,817	12,146	2,323

Table 5.1 Continued

	Total children who were the subject of a child protection plan at 31 March 2017	Initial category of abuse[1]				
		Neglect	Physical abuse	Sexual abuse	Emotional abuse	Multiple[2]
Mixed[9]	4,590	2,077	323	138	1,821	231
Asian or Asian British[10]	3,210	911	460	112	1,564	158
Black or black British[11]	2,600	998	391	97	950	162
Other ethnic group[12]	790	266	99	36	346	42

Source: Children in Need census.

Notes:

1. Category of abuse as assessed when the child protection plan commenced.
2. 'Multiple' refers to instances where there is more than one main category of abuse. These children are not counted under the other abuse headings so a child can appear only once in this table.
3. Sub-totals/totals are rounded to the nearest 10. Sub-totals may not add up to totals due to rounding.
4. Includes unborn children.
5. Excludes a small number of children of unknown age who are included in the 'all children' total.
6. Due to low numbers involved and to protect confidentiality ethnicity is aggregated into groups.
7. Excludes children of refused/not known ethnicity.
8. White comprises of white British, white Irish traveller of Irish heritage any other white background and Gypsy/Roma.
9. Mixed comprises of white and black Caribbean, white and black African, white and Asian any other mixed background.
10. Asian or Asian British comprises of Indian, Pakistani, Bangladeshi and any other Asian background.
11. Black or black British comprises of Caribbean African or any other black background.
12. Other ethnic groups comprises of Chinese and any other ethnic group.

Behaviourists and family therapists are interested in the dynamics of child abuse and why certain children are 'selected' for such abuse and not others. Children who are not wanted or who are considered to be the wrong sex by their parents are seen to be at greater risk (Roberts et al. 1980). The dynamics of the situation are effectively summarised by Belsky and Vondra (1989): they assess the undermining impact of a 'difficult' child on parental functioning will be reduced when the parent has a plethora of personal psychological resources. Conversely, an 'easy-to-rear' child can compensate for limited parental personal resources in maintaining parental effectiveness (Belsky and Vondra 1989).

Turning to extra-familial sexual abuse, including that which takes place in institutions, Finkelhor's observations seem pertinent; a child is increasingly vulnerable to abuse when their activities and contacts are insufficiently supervised and monitored. Increasing a child's susceptibility further is the impact of emotional neglect or physical or psychological abuse, coalescing to make them more vulnerable to perpetrators who offer the promise of attention, affection, 'love', safety and acceptance – but equally, to intimidation and threats – in exchange for sex (Finkelhor 1993). The behaviour which Finkelhor describes can be conceptualised as grooming and is an important theme in the context of child exploitation, which will be explored in Chapter 9.

Disabled children

One of the key problems with research into disability and child abuse lies with the problem of a consistent definition of the two concepts. It is further complicated by the challenge of accurate identification of abuse or neglect in this population; focusing support and intervention through the lens of the child's health or disability needs, their unhygienic living conditions, developmental delay, poor growth, challenging behaviour and physical injuries risks, inadvertently, being attributed to the child's disability, rather than understood as indicators symptomatic of possible chronic neglect or abuse (Sidebotham et al. 2016). Notwithstanding these challenges, sufficient evidence has been generated over the last decade or so to conclude that disabled children are disproportionately at risk of child abuse and neglect of all kinds (Slayter 2016). In the USA, where it is estimated that 8 per cent of children have disabilities, official reports of abuse show considerable differences between the extent of abuse of disabled and non-disabled children. Kendall-Tackett et al. (2005) show that across the USA, in the late 1980s, the rate per 1,000 for all kinds of abuse of disabled children was 35.5 compared with 21.3 for the non-disabled population. Sullivan and Knutson (2000a) studied 40,000 children in an American city and found that disabled children were 3.4 times more likely to be abused or neglected than non-disabled children; 31 per cent of disabled children in their sample had been abused or neglected.

In Britain, there are few large-scale studies of this kind to give a clear picture of abuse and neglect of disabled children (Miller 2002). It is estimated that 3 per cent of all Looked After children in England were Looked After as of 31 March 2017 because of their disability (Department for Education 2017b). Among the reasons for this are a combination of complexity of need and a lack of local support services, along with abuse or neglect. In the UK, Radford et al. (2011) identified that children with disabilities were assessed to be over three times more likely to be abused than children without disabilities.

Children who are disabled and living away from home are seen to be particularly at risk. Gordon et al. (2000) found that disabled children are more likely to be in residential care than are non-disabled children and Utting (1997) found some time ago that children in residential care are extremely vulnerable to abuse of all kinds.

There is clearly much that needs to be done in terms of researching the extent of such abuse and the reporting of it. Equally important is the need for a whole range of better supportive facilities for families with children with disabilities, particularly in relation to those at the lower end of the socio-economic scale.

Conclusion

The research studies considered in this chapter have all sought to answer questions about the perpetrators of abuse and who is abused. As we have seen, there are weaknesses and biases in most of the research studies that pose questions about their usefulness for practice. The main weaknesses of these studies have been repeatedly stressed. They are, first, that they have focused too much on general correlations and not enough on particular details. We know, for example, that children living in reconstituted families are overall more at risk than those living with both natural parents. Yet we know little about the degree of risk, which factors exacerbate the risk or in what conditions reconstituted families do a good job of rearing children. These sorts of criticism apply to almost all of the factors that have been associated in the research studies with child abuse and neglect. The reasons for this weakness lie in the misplaced emphasis on predicting and targeting the problem, the constant need to note the difference between correlation and causation and the need to consider the hows and whys of child abuse. Second, many of the studies demonstrate gender bias and slip into the easy assumption that the mother is the key figure in the child abuse process. Again, such a view does not do justice to the hows and whys of child abuse.

This does not invalidate the work that has been done, but stresses that it needs to be used in a careful and critical manner. If used in this way, such research can sensitise professionals to risk potential, but so far it provides a basic starting-point only.

One overriding factor that pervades much of the research and many of the findings is the impact of poverty, stress and deprivation. Except in the case of sexual abuse, which is commonly agreed to be more broadly spread across classes, almost all studies of abuse and neglect point to one or more of these factors being significant. It has been argued that known cases are likely to be found disproportionately in poorer families because of the nature of state surveillance. While this may be so to some extent, the evidence from incidence and prevalence studies on abuse and neglect (apart from sexual abuse) suggests that maltreatment of children is closely linked to socio-economic background and the strains and deprivations that are associated with this for many people.

Recommended reading

Howe, D. (2005) *Child Abuse and Neglect: Attachment, Development and Intervention*. Basingstoke: Palgrave Macmillan.

Humphreys, C. and Stanley, N. (2006) *Domestic Violence and Child Protection: Directions for Good Practice*. London: Jessica Kingsley Publications.

Pritchard, C. (2004) *The Child Abusers: Research and Controversy*. Maidenhead: Open University Press.

The causation of child abuse

6

Key points in this chapter

* A variety of theoretical paradigms are reviewed and analysed and it appears that no single explanation is sufficient.
* Combined and integrated, however, a number of connections between the different perspectives percolate to the surface.
* By looking at the unique contributions of different theories we begin to see explanatory patterns which can help practitioners.

Introduction

Health and welfare professionals involved in the field of child abuse have arguably paid less attention to why such abuse happens than they have to the type of person who abuses and the type of child who is most vulnerable to abuse. This is probably because these two questions seem to have a more direct impact on prediction and prevention: if we can identify those most likely to be at risk, then we can do something about it. Also, the question of why child abuse happens is not always considered as directly relevant to the day-to-day practicalities of child protection work. Such an inquiry has traditionally been seen to be more the province of theorists than of practitioners. This state of affairs is understandable, given the increased volume of child protection work and the pressures on practitioners not to make mistakes. However, endeavouring to understand why the abuse of children takes place serves three main functions: (1) it gives a greater sense of control to the worker over events that may otherwise seem inexplicable; (2) it gives a sense of direction for intervention and treatment; and (3) it informs those responsible for policy-making in this field. For these reasons, understanding why abuse has happened has a very important contribution to make to child protection work.

There are complex problems, however, when attempting to identify 'causes' of something. It is often claimed, for instance, that 'ice' causes 'road accidents'. However, if we stop to think about this for a moment, we can see the problem. Most of us have lots of ice in our freezers . . . and it's perfectly harmless! Of course, what we meant was 'ice on the road', but the ice is not, in and of itself, the sole 'cause' of an accident. If we all stayed in until it thawed, then there would be no problem. The problem, i.e. the 'cause' of accidents, is usually a series of other intervening, moderating or mediating variables (as they are called). What leads to accidents is a range of such variables, including the condition of the tyres and their depth of tread; the condition of the brakes and the braking system; the condition and state of repair of the road surface; the visibility at the time of the accident; the level of concentration of the driver; or whether the driver was drunk or on drugs. And there may be many other variables; and if that state of affairs was not complicated enough in itself, these variables may be interconnected (or there are 'interaction effects', to use statistical language). This is the case with road accidents, where many of the variables identified above can be measured or verified in some way. Now consider how much more complex child maltreatment – in all its different forms and, as we have seen, with all its definitional complexity, ambiguity and imprecision – is likely to be explained causally.

The ever-present problem of causation – or aetiology – is, to some extent, tackled in contemporary research by newer methodologies, such as meta-analysis, structural equation modelling and path analysis, allowing the more precise isolation of moderating and mediating variables which was only possible in the past by rigorous experimental design (but which is often impracticable or unethical in the field of child maltreatment).

A broad range of theoretical perspectives has been brought to bear on the aetiology of child abuse. They derive from diverse sources, survey the problem at different levels and, as a consequence, do not necessarily complement each other. Indeed, there is a good deal of conflict and disagreement between adherents of different approaches. On the other hand, there are those whose theoretical focus has been on the development of integrative approaches to understanding why child abuse happens (Garbarino 1977; Jack 2000; Belsky and Jaffee 2006), and there is some evidence of the adoption of this type of thinking in the *Framework for the Assessment of Children in Need and Their Families* which was introduced in April 2001 in England (Department of Health 2000) and which is still used in the assessment of need in many organisations around the world. Although we have seen that *The Munro Review of Child Protection* in the UK (Munro 2011a) promoted a rethink about the timing of an assessment of need during the early stages of an inquiry, arguing that, initially, the assessment of risk in the context of family strengths and gaps is paramount, it nevertheless recognises the importance of a more comprehensive understanding of the family's circumstances and the child's developmental needs later on.

One potential drawback of the integrative approach is that, although it provides a richer explanatory account of the problem of child abuse, it is inevitably more complex, and practitioners can find this harder to apply than single-cause accounts. Overall, however, and especially given the contested nature of a good deal of child protection work (see Chapters 3 and 4), the fact that multidimensional theories of child abuse causation may lead to questioning about certainty and the need for greater caution in practice may be no bad thing.

There are three main groups of broad theoretical perspective used to explain child abuse, neglect and maltreatment:

1. *Psychological theories*: those that focus on the instinctive and psychological qualities of individuals who abuse.
2. *Social psychological theories*: those that focus on the dynamics of the interaction between abuser, child and the immediate environment.
3. *Sociological perspectives*: those that emphasise social and political conditions as the most important reason for the existence of child abuse.

This categorisation will be used as the structure for this chapter. In addition, consideration will be given to attempts to combine these perspectives to provide a more holistic picture. As we are primarily discussing *theoretical* approaches in this chapter, as their authors proposed them some years ago (for example, Freud), references to their work may appear somewhat dated, but that is not to downplay or minimise their influence. Furthermore, in this chapter we have given more prominence and weight to the writings of the originators of each of the theories discussed.

Psychological theories

In this section consideration will be given to the contributions of the disciplines of biology, attachment theory, psychodynamic theory, learning theory and cognitive approaches.

Biology and child abuse

Biological explanations were not applied directly to the understanding of child abuse until the late 1980s, although they did underpin some key theories such as that of attachment and psychodynamics. They now find their latest application in approaches which link evolutionary psychology, neuroscience, biochemistry and genetics to our understanding of child abuse and neglect.

Sociobiologists have, in a very general way, applied these principles to the question of step-parenting, substitute parenting and child abuse. Some non-genetic parents in the animal world have been noted to be very cruel to infants. Hrdy (1977, 2009) found that in one species of monkey, males seeking to mate with females already with litters, but with no male protectors, killed the young. The explanation for this behaviour, according to sociobiological theory, is simply that, as these monkeys have no investment in the genes of these infants, the sooner they are out of the way, the more quickly the male adults can produce offspring of their own. On the other hand, sociobiologists point to examples of altruism where infant birds and animals are nurtured and protected by non-relatives. In a subsequent study, Maestripieri et al. (1997) found evidence of inter-generational transmission of physical abuse of infant macaque monkeys in a longitudinal study covering 30 years.

Talk of a 'child abuse gene' seems somewhat far-fetched, but research into the impact of sensory deprivation on the growth and development of the brains of young children does provide food for thought. 'Feral' children, i.e. children who have been abandoned or severely neglected, and either partially or wholly reared by animals, have been shown to have suffered irreparable brain damage, affecting their capacities to communicate and relate emotionally to humans later on. While these are very rare and extreme cases, they have led to greater concern about the impact of serious neglect and institutionalisation on the capacity of children psychologically and emotionally to overcome early deprivation (Glaser 2000; Schore 2000, 2001; Perry 2002). With the use of technology, including functional magnetic resonance imaging (fMRI), electroencephalography (EEG) and positron emission tomography (PET) scans, we can now see these processes in operation. For example, EEG maps comparing maltreated and non-maltreated children shown photos of angry, happy and neutral faces demonstrate that maltreated children process the images in a different part of the brain – behind the eyes – compared with non-maltreated children (McCrory et al. 2010). This means that they tend to think, 'What have *I* done to make him so cross?' when looking at the 'angry face'. The non-maltreated child thinks, 'What's made *him* angry?' because they make sense of the image using brain circuits in the centre of the brain, allowing the image to be processed in a more balanced and measured way.

Similarly, genetic research is beginning to indicate that certain genes, especially (1) the DRD4 7-repeat polymorphism – a dopamine neurotransmitter responsible for how we deal with reward and pleasure; (2) the MAO-A, the so-called 'aggression' gene; and (3) the 5HTT 'depression' gene, all play a part in explaining some of the variation in the causes and consequences of abuse and neglect. There will never be a single genetic rationale to explain child maltreatment; and current indications are that 'gene x environment' interactions and the notion of 'differential susceptibility' (Belsky et al. 2007) – that the interaction of genes and environment operates differently within different people under different circumstances – are likely to offer the most convincing explanations.

Initially, much of the theorising of sociobiologists appeared to be reductionist, even overstated, but today neurological, biochemical and genetic research is beginning to be accepted by researchers across all disciplines. Although this brand of child abuse research has its critics, it does remind us of the part that genetic capacity and instinct can play in certain behaviours and it is a variable not to be overlooked. Unthinking and indiscriminate use of such theory could, however, fuel prejudice and lead to over-reliance on instinct as a tool for understanding the way in which people behave. We will return to neurobiological, biochemical and genetic research in Chapter 7 when we look at the consequences of abuse.

Attachment theory and child abuse

The main theoretical tenets of attachment theory are derived from the work of one person, John Bowlby. In the period immediately after the Second World War, he carried out studies into the nature and effects of 'maternal' deprivation on young children (Bowlby 1951). Although attachment researchers would now use terms such as 'parental' or 'caregiver' instead of 'maternal', Bowlby initially hypothesised that any significant separation of a child from the mother in the first five years of life could have deleterious effects on its emotional development and could lead to a variety of psychological and social difficulties in later life, such as the development of an affectionless personality. Originally, the reasoning for this process was derived from psychodynamic theory; that is, that the child developed a psychologically healthy sense of self through consistently rewarding emotional contact with the mother. As his work developed, Bowlby drew more and more on the biological sciences and ethology, thus placing more emphasis on the physical aspects of carer-to-child bonding and child-to-carer attachment. In the final analysis he argued that a child securely attached to the mother gains the dual benefit of physical protection and psychological security.

While retaining many of Bowlby's initial insights, contemporary attachment theory has its critics (as we shall see) but it remains an important lens through which to better understand the parent/carer–child relationship. It is described by Shemmings and Shemmings (2011) as:

> [a] behavioural system ... responsible for regulating the infant's propensity to monitor physically and psychologically the accessibility of the attachment figure. Bowlby concluded that from a very early stage the attachment system acts initially to protect the child from harm, threat and, in particular, fear and danger, but later provides a 'secure base' from which the child can explore the environment ... Attachment behaviours intended to increase proximity – such as crying, gazing and calling – are unconsciously selected if the child cannot reach their attachment figure, depending not just on the physical distance from the attachment figure but also their perceived emotional availability: the fact that a parent is nearby physically does not assuage attachment needs unless s/he is emotionally present. Perceived emotional closeness also determines how much hugging, clinging and smiling is required to ensure the caregiver stays near. When attachment is de-activated, it is replaced by exploration, feeding, etc.
>
> (Shemmings and Shemmings 2011: 18)

Bowlby's early theorising was criticised by Rutter (1978) for not taking into account that the child could become attached to other significant figures as well as the mother: Hrdy's concept of the 'alloparent' (Hrdy 2009). According to Rutter's argument, the consistency and positive nature of the relationship were more important. Thus, the roles of the father and other relatives in the emotional development of the child needed to be given more consideration. This is now seen as a 'given' in modern attachment theory.

Feminists initially criticised attachment theory on the grounds that it had limiting and restrictive implications for women, because of its prescription that mothers should be in close proximity to their children for the whole of their infancy. Most attachment theorists now agree that children at around the age of 3 can cope with separation because they can, by use of language and reasoning, understand and accept explanations of what is happening.

Until the late 1980s, attachment theory was not directly applied to the problem of child abuse, although it has had a major influence on general child care policy and practice. Crittenden and Ainsworth (1989) argued that repeated consistent and rewarding interactions between a caregiver and child lead to high self-esteem and the capacity to trust. Conversely, non-responsive, rejecting and inconsistent responses lead to anxiety, insecurity, a lack of self-worth and a restricted ability to relate to others. This problematic interaction is considered to lessen the child's chances of making satisfying peer relationships later on in life because a sense of self and trust of others, which are essential to this process, do not exist. The pattern may then be repeated with the child's own children, thus providing some explanation of how abuse is transmitted from one generation to the next (Bakermans-Kranenburg and Van IJzendoorn 1997; Morton and Browne 1998). This process is not considered inevitable because the effects of poor early attachment experiences are thought to be remediable by attachment to a surrogate figure or by successful counselling.

However, because over 40 per cent of the world's population is likely to show an insecure-avoidant or insecure-ambivalent attachment in close relationships, contemporary attachment research instead now stresses the role of *unresolved loss and trauma* (see Madigan et al. 2006), extremely *insensitive and disconnected caregiving* (see Lyons-Ruth and Jacobvitz 2008; Out et al. 2009) and *low mentalisation capacity* (the inability to appreciate that others have different thoughts, feelings, hopes and intentions from one's own) (see Fonagy and Target 2005; Allen et al. 2008).

The misuse and misunderstanding of attachment theory and research concern many commentators. Indeed, it was Mary Main – one of the early pioneers of attachment theory and research, along with John Bowlby and Mary Ainsworth – who co-edited a special issue of the *Family Court Review* which was devoted to the question of attachment theory and research in welfare and protection decisions about children. In their Introduction, Main, Hesse and Hesse (2011) examine a number of misconceptions about attachment.

What are the strengths and gaps in this theoretical approach? The strengths lie in its convincing and detailed explanation of the process whereby abuse and neglect potential can be derived from particular dynamics within adult–child relationships (Howe 2005; Cassidy and Shaver 2008; Crittenden 2008; Shemmings 2016b; Shemmings and Shemmings 2011, 2018a forthcoming, 2018b forthcoming). Initially the gaps were, first, its inability to account more fully for the fact that the majority of parents who have been abused do *not* go on to abuse their own children and, second, the fact that insufficient account is taken of the total dynamics of the family. Nowadays, these gaps have to some extent been filled and certainly the focus is no longer exclusively on the mother–child – or even caregiver–child – pairing. The challenge for attachment theory in the coming years will be to explain the interactions between genes and the immediate caregiving environment, as well as the connection between social factors, such as poverty and unemployment, and attachment and the combined effect upon child abuse and neglect.

Psychodynamic theory, physical child abuse and neglect

Freud's work forms the kernel of psychodynamic thought, but it has been subjected to considerable variation by his followers. There are several good overviews of Freudian theory (e.g. Kahn, 2002). The key arguments of this perspective are that human beings mentally adapt their instinctive drives to the demands and requirements of their social circumstances. In the process of so doing, they develop personality traits that persist throughout life and influence their relationships with others. Freud's belief was that the dominant human instinctual drive was libidinal, or sexual. He also theorised that very young children had such sexual drives and he devised an elaborate explanation of how these were moulded into pro-social behaviours and internalised to shape an individual's character.

Summarised very briefly, Freud postulated that in the first five years of life infants go through three psychosexual stages: the oral, the anal and the genital. These stages of development are linked to sources of physical plea-sure – the oral stage to feeding, the anal stage to elimination and the genital stage to sexual stimulation. For Freud, socialisation meant the suppression of these pleasures in order to function as a responsible person in society. Parents carry out this socialising task. As a result, childhood sexuality goes through a latency stage only to reassert itself in adolescence, by which time individuals are considered to be more able to manage their libido for them-selves. As a result of this process, the psyche of each individual is made up of the id (the libidinal drive), the superego (the conscience or voice of the parent, which represses the id) and the ego (the integrating element which balances the id and superego and forms the visible or social aspect of the personality). The personality is also made up of different levels of conscious-ness as a result of this socialising process – the conscious (that part of the mind used in everyday life), the preconscious (that part of the mind from which past material could be summoned with prompting) and the uncon-scious (that part of the mind to which libidinal drives and urges have been exiled; these are normally unavailable to consciousness).

How does this relate to child abuse? With regard to physical abuse, Freudian or psychodynamic theory has arguably been the most dominant explanatory model since its rediscovery in the early 1960s (see, for exam-ple, Letourneau 1981; Halston and Richards 1982). It saw a decline during the 1990s but has since seen a resurgence as a result of a series of texts which approach child welfare and protection practice from a psychody-namic perspective (see, for example, McCluskey 2005; Ruch et al. 2010; Cooper 2018).

In terms of Freudian psychodynamics, from the very early stages, the children of abusing parents are not responded to in a way that helps them to progress through all the necessary psychosexual stages. They are frustrated by a lack of adequate response almost from the first contact and, therefore, are unlikely to develop the sort of integrated personality that enables them to relate responsively to others.

Thus, put simply, child abuse is seen to be the result of excessive super-ego demands. The carer's psychological make-up is the key. Psychological treatment, focusing on improving his or her ability to relate to other people, is seen to be the solution to the problem. Such treatment is to be achieved by insight development (through a psychotherapist) and by the effects of a rewarding relationship with a practitioner over a period of time.

The strengths of this approach, as with attachment theory, are that it can help professionals to understand the intra-personal and inter-personal dynamics of child abuse and point to intervention aims and strategies (Searing 2003). It is still hard for many in the child protection field to comprehend and tolerate violence to children; the psychodynamic approach provides a tool for this purpose. The weaknesses lie in the very heavy focus placed on the individual without sufficient consideration of the circumstances in which they are operating and in the lack of attention to social and environmental factors.

Psychodynamic theory and child sexual abuse

With regard to the sexual abuse of children, psychodynamic thought has rather a mixed history. According to Jeffrey Masson (1984), before Freud developed the psychosexual personality theories outlined above, he hypothesised that 'hysteria' in women might have been caused by them having been sexually abused as children. This hypothesis, according to Masson, was based on disclosures to him by women whom he was treating. He relayed his ideas to his fellow doctors in Vienna but they rejected his hypothesis, mainly because, as 'hysteria' was such a commonly diagnosed illness, the implication was that incestuous abuse was of epidemic proportions. Freud's response was to go away and look at his material again. Soon after, he laid the foundations of the theory of psychosexual development. Reference has already been made to the oral, anal and genital stages. With regard to the last, Freud hypothesised that, as part of their normal development, boys and girls at the genital stage 'desired' their parents of the opposite sex. This desire was repressed and the repression led to modelling along the lines of the same-sex parent. When this process was disturbed, this led to developmental problems and the possibility of neurosis. Thus, Freud argued that when he dealt with adults with such neuroses and tried to help them unlock these childhood repressions, it was not surprising that a lot of sexual material should arise. However, contrary to his original view, he saw these accounts as fantasies or wish fulfilments rather than as recollections of fact.

Such theorising was initially very influential in psychoanalytic circles and was one factor in predisposing psychotherapists and psychiatrists for many years to disbelieve accounts of sexual abuse. However, throughout the mid-1980s, influenced by the writings of Rush (1980), Herman (1981) and Masson (1984), there was a major shift in psychodynamic thinking with the development of a 'believing' school among psychoanalysts, the most famous example being Alice Miller (1985). Indeed, psychoanalysts and others went to great lengths to elicit accounts of child sexual abuse based on beliefs that many of their patients and clients had repressed events. Particularly in the USA (Loftus and Ketcham 1994), this so-called 'repressed memory syndrome' was challenged in the 1990s by critics (and lawyers) who argued that therapists had 'persuaded' their clients that they had been abused when they had not ('false memory syndrome').

Psychoanalysts as a whole, however, have still not theorised in great depth about why child sexual abuse happens. Most would consider such abuse to have a very damaging effect on personality development, particularly if it took place in the first five years of a child's life, because of its distorting effect on the process of psychosexual development, but little has been written from this point of view about the causation of sexual abuse. Finkelhor et al. (1986), reviewing research on child sexual abusers, found two main views among psychoanalytic writing on this subject: first, that child sexual abusers have arrested psychosexual development and choose to relate at a child's emotional level; second, that they have general low self-esteem and, therefore, gain a sense of dominance and control by victimising children. However, neither explanation properly explains why such people resort to sexual abuse in response to these emotional difficulties.

Learning theory and child abuse

Learning theory, while embracing many different approaches, is based on the view that behaviour is shaped, or learned, by the interaction of an individual with the environment. The internal processes described by psychoanalysts are completely rejected. Classical learning theorists (Pavlov 1927; Skinner 1953) see behaviour as a response conditioned by external stimuli or reinforcers and dismiss the notion of any internal functioning at all. From this point of view, what is not observable does not exist. However, since this early theorising, learning theorists such as Bandura (1965) and Michenbaum (1977) have incorporated social modelling and the notion of internal cognitive reasoning processes into their analyses of how behaviour operates, and these more complex theories are generally accepted by most learning theorists now. An example of how social learning theory has been applied to modern-day child protection practice – specifically in the London Borough of Hackney's Reclaiming Social Work (RSW) innovation – can be found in McCafferty (2011). The RSW approach also incorporates elements of a 'strengths-based' orientation (see Gaughan and Kalyniak 2011), which is to say that as the past cannot be changed, it is often more productive to concentrate on how the future could be different. This orientation partly derives from the late Steve de Shazer's pioneering work on 'solution-focused therapy' (de Shazer 2005); there are also similarities with some of the tenets of 'motivational interviewing' (Miller and Rolnick 2002), as well as Andrew Turnell's 'signs of safety' (Turnell 2009). Some of these ideas were first articulated for use in practice in Parton and O'Byrne's (2000) notion of 'constructive social work' for social workers. Along with RSW, many of these ideas are referred to in the Munro report in the UK (Munro 2011a), and we return to them in Chapter 8 when we consider the evidence base for interventions.

From this general perspective, child abuse is a problem resulting neither from personality traits nor from lack of attachment. Rather, it is largely the result of having learned dysfunctional child care practices or, alternatively, of not having learned functional child care practices. The question of punishment looms large here. Adults who have themselves experienced punitive treatment may well rely on such methods to discipline their own children. Most learning theorists see punishment as effective in the short term, but less so in the long term. It also has unwanted side-effects for both the punisher and the punished. The dysfunctional effects of punishment have been put forward as important reasons for banning all forms of corporal punishment (Leach 1999). Positive reinforcement of pro-social behaviours and negative reinforcement (such as ignoring) of anti-social behaviours are seen as more effective and enduring influences on behaviour.

Dubanoski et al. (1978) described a set of behavioural explanations of why children are physically abused:

- parents may lack effective child management techniques;
- parents may deliberately use punitive childrearing practices;
- the abuse may result from explosive acts triggered by the child;
- there may be a high level of stress;
- parents may have seriously negative attitudes towards the child.

Each of these problems might lead to the need for a variety of responses, including teaching new techniques, teaching self-control and focusing on attitude change.

Learning theorists have been applying their ideas to child abuse cases in the USA and the UK since the mid-1970s. Early British studies (Reavley and Gilbert 1979; Smith and Rachman 1984), for example, proved mostly unsuccessful. They found that simply teaching new child management techniques was in many cases inadequate, and stressed the need for attitudinal change on the part of parents as well, particularly where problems had been well established over a long period of time and motivation for change was low. Pure behaviourist interventions are rare now, having largely been replaced by cognitive and cognitive-behavioural therapies (see below). Today social learning theory underpins many aspects of the 'Incredible Years', one of the most popular parenting programmes available (Webster-Stratton and Reid 2005).

The strengths of the learning theory perspective lie to some extent in its clarity and specificity. The learning theorist intervening in a case of child abuse would, for instance, focus on the actuality of the abuse, the situational factors, the antecedents and the consequences of the event, the attributions placed on the child by the parents, and their attitudes towards punishment and control. The personality of the parents and their developmental history would not be a major concern. There is also more potential for change than with the psychodynamic perspective, in that early experiences are not considered to be as deterministic.

Learning theory suffers from the same weaknesses as those of other psychological theories so far reviewed, namely, that it often focuses on the individual abuser to the exclusion of the impact of wider networks. It may be that the strength of learning theory with regard to child abuse is also its weakness: it runs the risk of oversimplifying the problem in its search for clarity. In addition, it has so far paid little direct attention to child sexual abuse.

Cognitive approaches to child abuse

There has been an increase in interest, particularly in the USA (Newberger and White 1989), in the application of cognitive theory principles to the understanding and treatment of child abuse. The essential feature of this approach is that the way people perceive, order, construct and think about the world is an important key to their behaviour. It was noted earlier that parental attitudes were perceived to be important, as well as their actual behaviour. Cognitive theorists point to the value of finding out how parents who have abused children perceive their children's behaviour. Larrance and Twentyman (1983) argue that attribution theory could help to explain why parents who have not been abused as children do abuse as adults. Their argument is that they may have developed a 'frame' or view on a child and/ or on themselves that leads on to child abuse.

Newberger and White (1989) put forward a useful model of levels of parental awareness. At the first level, the child is seen by the parents purely as an extension of themselves. At the second level, the parents ascribe conventional roles to the child. At the third level, the child is seen by the parents as an individual with its own changing needs. They argue that abuse is more likely to take place when parents are at the first level. Although most parents progress to the highest level with time and experience and without outside help or intervention, this is not true in all cases. According to this view, intervention must be focused on helping parents to perceive their children differently, and such activity can help to prevent recurrence of abuse.

Deblinger and her colleagues (1999) successfully used cognitive-behavioural interventions in the treatment of 100 sexually abused children diagnosed as experiencing post-traumatic stress disorder (PTSD) in New Jersey, and this success was maintained over a two-year follow-up period. The therapy involved gradually encouraging children mentally to confront their abuse and to develop everyday coping strategies. Non-abusing parents were also helped by similar means with a view to increasing supportive behaviour to their children. It was found that where both parents and children were involved in the therapy, there were most improvements in terms of the child's psychological health.

Until relatively recently there was little evidence of the use of cognitive approaches with abused children in the UK (Verduyn and Calam 1999) but cognitive-behavioural therapy (CBT) is now increasingly being used with traumatised children (see Trickey and Black 2009). Scott (1989) developed such work in relation to families with more general child care problems with some success, though mainly with parents who had less complex and less well-established problems. Cognitive-behavioural approaches have been used with adult sex offenders (for example, Chesin et al. 2010).

American studies suggest that, particularly in relation to treatment, there are encouraging possibilities for cognitive-behavioural interventions. While cognitive theory shares with other psychological theories the danger of not paying sufficient attention to the social context, nevertheless its approach to child abuse problems is clear and understandable and supports individuals in taking responsibility for their own futures.

Social psychological theories

In this section, attention will be paid to theories that consider behaviour as follows:

- as a product of interaction between individuals;
- as determined by family dynamics;
- as influenced by social networks and supports.

These approaches may be termed 'middle range' in that they fall between a focus on the individual and a focus on broader social factors. Essentially the relationships between individuals and their immediate environments are seen as key determinants from these perspectives. The three areas of interaction have been separated from each other for analytic purposes, but many theorists of these persuasions see close links between them.

Individual interactionist perspectives and child abuse

The key defining factor of the individual interactionist approach is that behaviour is seen to be determined less by intra-personal factors such as prior experiences, or by learning, and more by interactions between people (Deacon and Gocke 1999). From this perspective, greater attention is placed on the dynamics of current relationships than on parental background or characteristics. Thus, interactionists take the child's contribution to situations of abuse much more into account, and also that of the spouse or partner (Kadushin and Martin 1981).

A climate of abuse can result from parents lacking skills to cope with difficult behaviour and from certain children continually exposing that

inadequacy. From this perspective, the combination of factors is as important as the weight of them, if not more so. Thus, a difficult crying baby with
two parents with low tolerance of stress and high aggression levels is
particularly at risk, whereas a more easily comforted and responsive child
with parents who have the same characteristics may not be. The child can,
from this perspective, reward the parents and enhance their skills or further de-skill them and lower their self-esteem. Similarly, the parents'
responses will affect the responses of the child, in a circular process.

Wolfe (1985) argues that parents do not have to have been abused
themselves as children for them to abuse their own children, because he
sees violence as a product of interactional events rather than a result of
factors such as parental upbringing. He argues that it is possible for a
frame of violence to develop within families. Similarly, Dibble and Straus
(1980) point out that violence to children can and does take place in families where parental attitudes are disapproving of such violence. This, they
argue, is because such violence is often situational, not a product of attitudes. Their study involved only families with two parents and they found
that violent behaviour on the part of one parent was likely to influence the
other parent to be violent even if he or she was personally opposed to
using violence against children. These studies lend support to the view
that violence breeds violence.

This perspective on violence in the family offers another dimension with
regard to the dynamics of why and how physical abuse of children occurs
and persists. However, as is true of all the perspectives so far considered,
a major weakness is that individuals are seen in isolation from wider social
influences and stresses.

Family dysfunction theory, physical child abuse and neglect

Family dysfunction theory broadens the focus a little more in that its concern is with the impact of family dynamics on the behaviour of its members. This theory and family therapy, the treatment method derived from
it, originated within the field of psychiatry and the aetiology of mental
illness.

Family therapy is a theoretically eclectic discipline. Initially, it drew
mainly from psychodynamic theory and concentrated on the impact of
family life on the psychological development of the individual (Dallos and
Draper 2005). Many practitioners adopt a systems perspective based on
the work of Minuchin (1974), which theorises that there are two main sub-
systems within the family, that of the parents and that of children, and
emphasises the need for boundaries (with some degree of permeability) to
be maintained between the two in order to ensure a healthy climate for all
family members. Therapy is focused on examining the nature of current
boundaries and on improving communication between family members.

Another family therapy approach is termed 'strategic'. Family therapists
of this school see the family as a powerful system that resists attempts

to change it from the outside (Dale et al. 1983). Carefully worked-out tactics and strategies are needed to break down this resistance to create the best conditions for change.

Dysfunctional family theory has been used in the UK to help explain the dynamics of physical abuse of children within the family and the interplay between professionals and parents where serious abuse has taken place. Asen et al. (1989) refer to the notion of 'stand-in abuse' where the child is subjected to violence by one parent as a means of 'getting at' the other parent. The notion of a child as scapegoat, the bad one in the family and the reason for all the family's ills, is another example of a family dysfunction explanation of child mistreatment. Reder et al. (1993) used material from public inquiry reports to examine both intra-familial dynamics and the way in which parents relate to professionals involved in working with them. They focused particularly on the way in which parents tend to oscillate between revealing what is going on (what are termed 'covert warnings') and concealing it.

Family therapy techniques have also been used in the assessment of families. Dale et al. (1986) reported on successfully using strategic family therapy to determine whether it was safe for children who had been abused to return to the care of their families.

There is a general lack of focus on causes of behaviour among family therapists. Their concern is with the here-and-now dynamics of family life and how to break or change patterns of behaviour. From this point of view, the notion of 'cause' in the linear cause-and-effect sense is seen to be less relevant than the process.

Family therapy and child sexual abuse

Family therapy thinking has played a major role in the explanation of the causes of child sexual abuse. This is largely due to the pioneering work of Arnon Bentovim (see Bentovim et al. 1988) at the Great Ormond Street Hospital, referred to in Chapter 2. This approach, which incorporates both psychodynamic and systems theories, is broadly based on the hypothesis that child sexual abuse serves the function of keeping together families that would otherwise collapse. The classic scenario is that of the abuse of a teenage daughter by her father, who is considered to be seeking emotional and sexual gratification because communication and sexual relations with his wife have broken down. It is believed in many cases that the wife/mother knows (whether consciously or subconsciously is not made clear) what is happening and passively colludes in the continuance of this situation. This collusion is thought to serve the function of freeing her from responsibility without sacrificing the unity of the family. The solution to the problem is seen to be one of opening up the secret to all family members, disentangling the knotted relationships and freeing individuals to decide on their futures. The means of achieving this is by family meetings and the use of family therapy techniques.

The strengths of the family dysfunction approach are that it heightens awareness of the powerful nexus of relationships that the family can be sheltering and demonstrates how it can sustain unacceptable forms of abuse. However, it suffers from the problem of many systems-based theories, in that, although it well describes how dysfunctional families operate, it is much more limited in explaining the reason why they function in the way that they do. The Great Ormond Street team explained sexual abuse by reference to the emotional need of the perpetrator and the structural dependence on adults of the child victim. Feminist critiques of family dysfunction theory stress the lack of attention paid to gender power relations. Family therapy thinking has also been criticised for focusing too much on the family as a closed system cut off from wider systems and social influences. There is evidence of the development of more flexible family dysfunction approaches that take into account both of these concerns (Barratt et al. 1990; Masson and O'Byrne 1990; Jenkins and Asen 1992).

A final criticism is that the explanatory value of the family dysfunction approach is limited to the types of abuse situation outlined above. It does not help to explain the wide range of forms of sexual abuse that can take place in families, such as abuse of infants and abuse by siblings, uncles and grandparents (Corby 1998) and, of course, it contributes little to our understanding of abuse outside the family (but it does not set out to).

Social ecological approaches

General systems theory was adapted by social work theorists in the USA and the UK in the early 1970s to broaden this profession's traditional emphasis on personal problems and to move away from concentration on personal pathology (Pincus and Minahan 1973; Hingley-Jones and Mandin 2007). The influence of systems theory and ecological approaches (see Jack 2000) in understanding and interpreting social problems has been particularly influential in the USA with the development of general concerns about the environment.

From this perspective, human behaviour is influenced, or determined, more by the context in which a person lives than by intra-personal or inter-personal factors. In the particular case of child abuse, it is hypothesised that where environmental conditions are unfavourable to families, the incidence of abuse is likely to be higher. In the USA, Garbarino (1977, 1982) has been particularly active in exploring these connections. He found in both rural and urban areas that officially reported abuse was higher in those neighbourhoods where indicators of social stress, population mobility and poverty were highest. A major factor was seen to be isolation from possible support systems, be they the extended family or community-based systems such as neighbourhood centres and day-care facilities.

Garbarino (1977) linked this theoretical approach to others in that he did not preclude individual history as an additional causative factor and he acknowledged the impact of culture. Nevertheless, given these factors, stress, created from living in environments that are not conducive to psychological health and development, is seen to be a major contributory factor to child mistreatment and points to solutions other than a focus on the individual, most notably community-based initiatives to break down isolation and create a sense of belonging and shared problems.

There are difficulties with 'proving' the validity of social ecological theories in relation to child abuse causation, not least because of the fact that poorer communities are more likely to come under the close surveillance of public authorities and, therefore, produce higher official rates of abuse. There is also a need for closer attention to be paid to which particular deficits in what circumstances contribute to child maltreatment and the process by which this happens (Seagull 1987; Coohey 1996). In Britain, Department of Health initiatives in the second half of the 1990s (see Chapter 2) led to greater attention being paid to social stress as a causative factor in certain types of child abuse and to the use of broader-based assessments of families referred for child protection concerns (Department of Health 1995). In the early 1990s there were developments to support families at risk by use of community-based projects such as the Sure Start and Children's Fund programmes, but critics of these schemes alleged that they did not reach the families for whom they were intended. Social ecological thinking underpins these developments (Jack 2000). In the USA, where they have a longer-established community-based programme (Healthy Start/Healthy Families), concerns have been raised that too much reliance is being placed on broad-based initiatives of this kind (Chaffin 2004).

Despite this type of reminder about not putting all your eggs in one basket, the main strength of the social ecological approach lies in the way in which it broadens the scope of thinking about why the abuse of children occurs. It shifts the focus from individual pathology to the influence of the immediate environment and the need to tackle the problem at that level. At the other end of the spectrum, however, it is argued that exponents of this approach pay little attention to political factors that contribute to the deterioration of neighbourhoods and the disorganisation and break-up of social networks. Attention to these points might well lead to quite different solutions to the problem.

Sociological perspectives

Arguably, sociological perspectives on child abuse did not have a major influence on child protection thinking and work in the UK before the 1990s, except in the case of sexual abuse and the question of gender. The reason for this is probably twofold. First, such perspectives do not provide clear indicators for practice in that they look broadly at the conditions that create the climate for child abuse rather than at how this works out in individual cases. Second, many sociological perspectives provide a challenge to those who are intervening in families to protect children, in that they question the ethics and politics of mainstream assumptions (Howe 1991). Thus, they have an unsettling quality in that they locate the 'cause' of the problem outside the sphere of influence of the professional worker and they consequently pose uncomfortable questions about the validity of that professional intervention. The main sociological perspectives to be considered in this section are those that have been articulated by researchers and others involved in the child abuse field:

- the social–cultural perspective, which points to links between child abuse and general social approval of the use of violence to maintain control and order;
- the social–structural perspective, which relates child abuse to the maintenance of general inequality in northern industrialised societies;
- perspectives that link child abuse to gender and generational inequality – that is, feminist and children's rights perspectives.

The social–cultural perspective and child abuse and social approval of violence

The work of Straus and Gelles (1986) in the USA has already been referred to several times in relation to their national surveys into the incidence of physical child abuse. In these studies, they and their colleagues reported high levels of intra-familial violence of all kinds. They came to the conclusion that such violence was the norm and that individuals were more likely to be subjected to violent acts within families than outside them. In an attempt to explain these high rates, they argued that violence is a socially sanctioned general form of maintaining order and that it is approved of as a form of child control by most people in US society (and, of course, elsewhere). It can be argued from this perspective that a society that approves of the corporal punishment of children in schools and endorses the old adage 'spare the rod and spoil the child' sets the scene for a variety of unwanted forms of violence, of which physical child abuse is one. Child abuse, therefore, is seen as being on the same spectrum as socially-approved forms of violence rather than as a separate pathological phenomenon.

Adherents of these views point to the dysfunctions of physical punishment for individuals in later life (which can include lowered self-esteem and poor social relationship skills), their families (as a result of the inter-generational transmission of punitive parenting) and for society as a whole, which is increasingly looking in the job market for individuals with flexible problem-solving skills, a style of behaviour not generally created by the use of physical punishment as a key form of discipline (Straus 1994).

From this perspective, it is clear that there is a need for change at a broad societal level to the way in which we treat and control children. There is a need to encourage non-violent means of ensuring pro-social behaviour. There have been moves in this direction in the UK and Scotland, for example, passed legislation in October 2017 banning smacking. As has been seen, other European countries have been much more proactive in this respect. In Sweden, where the ban on the use of physical punishment of children by parents has been in operation the longest, there have been reductions over time in youth involvement in crime and decreases in substance misuse, rape and suicide (Durrant 1999).

The clear strengths of the social–cultural perspective are that it broadens the focus in comparison with psychological and social psychological theories and helps in the understanding of how societal influences can contribute to the incidence and form of child mistreatment despite the fact that society officially sets out to reduce and prevent such occurrences. The implications for social policy are that there is a need to tackle matters on a broader front and that intervention into individual cases alone is not sufficient for dealing with the problem. The major weakness of this perspective lies in the fact that it does not always help to explain why some people within our inevitably flawed cultures abuse and yet others do not.

The social–structural perspective and child abuse and maintenance of general inequality

Gil's research and writing, already referred to, form the cornerstone of this perspective. Gil's (1970) early work convinced him that child abuse was class-related and that 'psychological' explanations of abuse by themselves were too narrow and grossly underestimated the contribution of stress, caused by poverty and material deprivation, to the causation of child abuse.

He developed his ideas further to lay some of the blame for child abuse on the policies of the state (Gil 1975, 1978). He put forward a broad definition of abuse which included all children whose developmental needs could not be met, whatever the reason.

This definition clearly places responsibility for child abuse on the state over and above the person who actually abuses, on the grounds that it sanctions inequality and low standards of housing, health, education and leisure for the children of the poor. From this point of view, the state, far from being the benign rescuer of children when parents ill-treat them, is actually the villain of the piece because it abuses children directly by its failure to provide adequate facilities for them to lead a fulfilling life, and also creates stresses for parents that increase the likelihood of their committing acts of abuse or neglect.

More recently, the work of Sue White, Brid Featherstone, Anna Gupta, Kate Wilson, Paul Bywaters and Andy Bilson in the UK has added greatly to our understanding of the role of poverty and adversity on responses to allegations of child maltreatment (Featherstone et al. 2014, 2015) and their differential effects on how governments, organisations and practitioners alike have on families caught up in the system (Mason and Bywaters 2016; Bilson and Martin 2017).

The strength of the social–structural approach is that it does justice to the accepted fact that physical child abuse has a close association with deprivation. As we have seen, this is particularly so with regard to neglect (Wolock and Horowitz 1984). Its weakness lies in the fact that not all poor people abuse their children and, therefore, it is not a sufficient explanation. Also, until relatively recently, this perspective had not taken into account structural factors other than class and poverty. There are signs that post-structuralist and post-modernist understandings may complement the social–structural approach (see, for example, White 1997; Fook 2002); they certainly include gender and cultural dimensions.

The social–structural approach has not had a great deal of support in child abuse circles. Pelton (1978) pointed to the fact that structural inequality explanations pose a threat to those who espouse clinical and medical approaches to child abuse. Other writers have seen Gil's views as 'idealistic' (Greenland 1987) or beyond the scope of the helping professions and, therefore, not applicable to day-to-day practice.

Child protection policy in the UK during the 1990s began formally to take into account structural inequality and social exclusion through the third side of the 'assessment triangle' – family and environment factors – which incorporates family history and functioning, wider family, housing, employment, income, family's social integration and community resources into the family assessment. Thus, in addition to the components of the other two sides of the triangle – the child's developmental needs and parenting capacity – professionals involved in child protection and welfare are required to take account of the 'world outside the family'.

Feminist perspectives and child abuse

One of the key developments during the past 10 years has been that there is no longer consensus over the existence of one 'feminism' or indeed 'family' (Featherstone 2007). Many commentators argue that there are different distinct emphases within an overall feminist discourse and some of the earlier forms of feminism have been criticised for being geared towards white, middle-class perspectives. But most of the perspectives so far outlined are considered by radical feminists, for example, to be gender-blind. From their point of view, all of the psychological perspectives assume that women are the key carers of children and that, if things go wrong, then the spotlight falls, very unevenly, on their behaviour. The interactionist perspectives broaden the focus but assume an equal power base between men and women.

The radical feminist perspective on child abuse began to emerge in the 1980s. The stimulus for this came from the 'discovery' of child sexual abuse, an act committed predominantly by males, and feminist explanations have been highly relevant to it. From this starting point, the feminist perspective has now been applied to all forms of abuse. This perspective on child sexual abuse has been articulated by many writers in the USA and the UK (for example, Dominelli 1986; Nelson 1987; Macleod and Saraga 1988; Driver and Droisen 1989; Cox et al. 2001; Smart et al. 2001; Ferguson 2004; Featherstone 2007).

The attention of these writers is not on individual males. Individual pathology is discounted as a cause of child abuse (as is family pathology). Rather, abuse is seen as an extreme example of institutionalised male power over females. The implications for policy of this perspective are similar in kind, if not focus, to those of the other sociological perspectives. Sexual abuse needs to be tackled at a societal level as well as at the individual level. Men abuse children because of the general power imbalance between the sexes and the different forms of socialisation that they experience as a result, not because of psychiatric illness or emotional deficits.

With regard to physical abuse and neglect, feminist perspectives are less clear-cut (Featherstone 1997). The argument that such abuse is created by the conditions of patriarchy does not rest as easily in this case as with that of sexual abuse. However, women spend far more time with children than do men and cope with the stresses of child care, often with little support. The argument has been taken further by some feminists in that they see the notion of motherhood, a product of patriarchy which reinforces the idea that children's welfare and needs are best met by mothers, as exacerbating the already existing stresses placed on women looking after children (Ong 1985). Under such conditions, it is surprising that the numbers of women who abuse and neglect children do not vastly exceed those of men, and, from this point of view, men are disproportionately violent to children. The implication is that women's violence to children is much more likely to be stress-related than that of men. Another area opened up by the feminist perspective is that of domestic violence (Dobash and Dobash 1992) – or as it tends now to be referred to 'domestic abuse' (to take account of the more outwardly 'non-violent' forms of abuse, such as emotional and coercive abuse) and its linkage with child abuse (Mullender and Morley 1994).

The strength of feminist perspectives on child abuse as a whole is that it opened up a dimension that had been missing from previous explanations about why child abuse occurs. We saw earlier that (in the case of physical abuse and neglect) men have been, until fairly recently, overlooked in terms of intervention. Feminist perspectives point to the error in this, in that understanding, and see challenging the nature of male–female power relations at an institutional and individual level as of major importance in the theory and practice of child protection work (Scourfield 2003). The challenge should be both to the impositions placed on women within the family and to the way in which males are socialised (Hearn 1990).

The weakness of any critique of *the* feminist perspective is in assuming that there is one perspective. 'Post-feminist' perspectives have questioned the determinism of radical feminism and argued the need for more flexibility in understanding female identity and of the roles that this might play in child abuse (Featherstone and Trinder 1997). This goes a long way to counter the argument that feminist perspectives can be used in a reductionist and exclusive way, attributing everything to patriarchy, thus overriding other explanatory accounts.

The children's rights perspective and child abuse

Freeman (1983) identified two main schools of thought on children's rights: the protectionist and the liberationist. Protectionist thinking about children has been applied to the question of child care through legislation since the late nineteenth century and still underlies much of current policy and practice in the field of child abuse. Essentially the argument from this viewpoint is that children have the right to protection from their parents by outside bodies in circumstances where their health and welfare are at risk. In the absence of these conditions, parents have the responsibility of determining their children's rights up to prescribed ages.

The liberationist perspective is a product of the late 1960s and derives mainly from the field of education. Holt (1974) provided a good example of the extreme end of this type of thinking. His argument is that childhood is an oppressed status and that the current state of affairs in which parents grant concessions to children who have little redress against their actions and decisions is unjust and reinforces their oppression. He proposed a series of rights that children should have, such as the right to choose where to live, the right to vote and the right to have the same financial status as adults. In short, his view is that children should have exactly the same rights as adults. Age is seen as irrelevant and self-determination as paramount.

In the late 1980s and 1990s, there was a shift in official thinking about children's rights away from a traditional protectionist perspective towards viewing children in a more independent light. The Children Act 1989 took children's rights of this kind into consideration. However, it could not possibly be seen as liberationist in the way in which Holt (1974) proposed. In fact, it reflects a half-way house position between the protectionist and liberationist viewpoints. Children's views are to be taken into account, but there is no suggestion that they should prevail.

In respect of physical abuse, the development of anti-corporal punishment legislation and policy reflects the influence of liberationist views. The thinking is clear: if children had the same rights in society as adults and, therefore, similar individual status (one that was not prescribed by family relations), they would be less likely to be the object of physical abuse and neglect. For instance, we do not consider it proper to smack adults for misbehaving. Were children to have individual rights without reference to their parents, we would not consider such treatment to be acceptable in their case either.

The main strength of the children's rights perspective is that it compels us to consider matters from the child's point of view as an individual rather than purely as a family member, and points to changes in the status of children at a societal level as a solution to the widespread problem of child abuse. While the relevance of this perspective has no bounds, it should be stressed that the notion of children's rights has a particular role to play in the protection of children living away from home. Various reports (Utting 1991, 1997; Warner 1992) on the care of children being looked after in local authority care and elsewhere demonstrate the consequences of children not being able to assert rights of complaint against those in power over them.

There were considerable general developments in the 1990s to establish and assert children's rights, for instance, the UN Convention on the Rights of the Child, adopted by the United Nations in 1989 and ratified by the UK government in 1991, and the setting up of a formal representations procedure in the Children Act 1989. However, a UK Children's Commissioner position has existed for nearly 20 years and the post of Minister of State for Children in the UK was established in 2003.

The weakness of the children's rights perspective lies in the fact that most children living at home cannot easily be seen in isolation from their parents because of their dependence on them. Children's rights protagonists tend to ignore this fact and also the fact that many parents do not have the means to achieve the high standards that the children's rights perspective properly demands.

Attempts at integration and ecological perspectives

Social workers and other professional workers in the field of child protection need to be open to a wide range of explanations of child abuse in order to intervene effectively into families where children are thought to be at risk, even though this approach may be more complex than that of following a single theory. Attempts to integrate the different approaches to child abuse have been made. Using an ecological framework, Belsky (1980) and Belsky and Jaffee (2006) pointed to a four-level approach, similar to that of Bronfenbrenner (1979):

1. Ontogenic development is concerned with what the individual parents bring to the situation, their developmental background and experiences.
2. The microsystem is concerned with the interaction of individuals within the family.
3. The exosystem is concerned with the immediate social environment within which the family functions.
4. The macrosystem takes into account broader structural factors, such as cultural attitudes to violence.

The way in which these different systems interact is the key to the likelihood of abuse occurring or not. Wiehe (1989) and Coohey and Braun (1997) have developed integrative models in relation to physical abuse. Finkelhor et al. (1986) provided a similar type of model for child sexual abuse. The way forward is clearly in the direction of further attempts at integrating ongoing research into the aetiology of child abuse. While practitioners may be more concerned with what is directly relevant to practice, it should be borne in mind that a broad range of integrated knowledge provides a strong base from which to operate.

Integrated thinking about the causation of child abuse does of course have implications for far more people than child protection workers. However much we develop understandings of abuse and neglect at the micro level, the implications of the broader sociological theories of child abuse causation cannot be avoided by society as a whole. A more concerted effort needs to be made to give consideration to child abuse prevention in all areas of planning and policing of society.

Most researchers in the field of child abuse point to the dangers of adopting single-cause explanations of the phenomenon. While some explanations may seem to be particularly useful for the understanding of certain forms of abuse (for example, attachment theory appears to have particular relevance in the case of physical abuse or emotional rejection of young babies), they are unlikely to be sufficient in themselves.

One recent example of an approach to research which attempted to combine 'opposing' perspectives is offered by Matias et al. (2014). The authors compared the capacity of attachment and social learning theory to predict certain developmental outcomes in a sample of 113 children aged 5–6. They found that 'parent–child mutuality predicted secure child narratives independently of social learning theory-based measures; in contrast, criticism predicted peer-nominated fighting independently of attachment theory-based measures' (2014, p. 77). Thus, the study offers practitioners some guidance from attachment theory about what to encourage parents to do more of, and from social learning theory what parents would be wise to minimise and do less of.

Conclusion

There has been (and still is) a polarisation between different perspectives on why child abuse occurs, with single explanations dominating within different 'camps'. In the field of physical abuse, for example, the cases of Victoria Climbié, Peter Connelly, Daniel Pelka and Kyra Ishaq highlight the clash between different perspectives, especially those of the needs of the child and the rights of carers. Social workers and other child protection professionals, in each of these tragedies, were heavily criticised for overlooking what, with hindsight, were key indicators of abuse. Similarly, the social workers in the Jasmine Beckford case (Brent 1985) focused on improving the social circumstances of the parents of the child by helping them find more suitable accommodation, by providing Jasmine's mother with supportive help at home and by obtaining nursery school provision for Jasmine. The focus was on external factors improving the quality of life which, it was assumed, would reduce stress and enhance parent–child relationships.

The report criticised the social workers on a variety of grounds, including not taking into account the psychological background of the parents. Again, with the value of hindsight, this criticism was justified and greater attention to inter-personal and intra-personal factors might have led to greater caution in decision-making.

It is often said tragedy should, generally speaking, not be used to create new legislation and governmental guidance. The Munro report in the UK (Munro 2011a) was not requested as a result of such tragedies and, hence, the hope is that it will produce more lasting changes in policy and practice.

Recommended reading

Cassidy, J. and Shaver, P. R. (2008) *Handbook of Attachment: Theory, Research and Clinical Applications*, 2nd edn. New York: Guilford.

McCrory, E., De Brito, S. A. and Viding, E. (2010) Research review: the neurobiology and genetics of maltreatment and adversity, *Journal of Child Psychology and Psychiatry*, 51(10): 1079–95.

Trickey, D. and Black, D. (2009) Child trauma, in M. Gelder et al. (eds) *New Oxford Textbook of Psychiatry*, 2nd edn. Oxford: Oxford University Press.

Turnell, A. (2009) *Of Houses, Wizards and Fairies: Involving Children in Child Protection Casework*. Perth: Resolutions Consultancy.

7 The consequences of child abuse

Key points in this chapter

- The consequences and sequelae of abuse and maltreatment are not always easy to predict and many children who were maltreated are able, despite the abuse, to lead fulfilling lives.
- Sometimes the effects of maltreatment can appear later, if the child experiences more optimal, nurturing relationships: within an abusive environment the child may develop short-term strategies to cope with what is happening but they may leave emotional scars that can re-emerge later.
- There is much room for optimism regarding how to help and support children and families where there is maltreatment.

Introduction

In the past, less attention has been paid to the consequences or effects on a child of being abused than to ways of preventing such abuse happening in the first place. This is no longer the case. Particularly since the recent greater emphasis paid to child sexual abuse – including online sexual abuse and child sexual exploitation – there has been an explosion of interest in, and studies about, the consequences of both these forms of abuse and all others as well. This concern with the effects of sexual abuse initially was largely attributable to the pressure of the feminist movement, but it may also reflect increasing societal concerns about risk to individuals identified by, among others, Ulrich Beck (1992, 2008). Beck argued that such concerns are characteristic of modern, more affluent societies which possess increasingly more effective technological means of controlling broad aspects of life and which thereby create a strong desire to reduce risk to a minimum. This argument has been applied to child abuse concerns generally (for example, Parton 2007). However, it seems particularly persuasive in explaining the increase in attention paid to the consequences of abuse, because in relation, for example, to the physical punishment of children, it is not only those who are abused who may pay a cost, but their relatives and society as well.

Moving on to the concerns of child protection policy-makers and practitioners, there are several good reasons for the careful study of the consequences of child abuse. First, the support and treatment needs of children, young people and adults who have been abused must be considered.

Awareness of the short- and long-term impacts of various forms of abuse and neglect is central to the development of appropriate resources and services for meeting such needs.

Second, there is a preventive aspect to focusing on the consequences of abuse, and the question of the inter-generational transmission of abuse was discussed earlier. Greater focus on the effects of abuse and the consequent development of better ways to help and support families stay together whenever possible can help reduce the likelihood of abuse being repeated in the next generation (even though many children who are abused do not go on to become abusers).

Third, informed knowledge about the consequences of different forms and intensities of abuse and neglect can shape support and intervention practices, although it is important to bear in mind that some forms of intervention may add to the harm already created by the abuse that the child has suffered rather than alleviate it (for example, being taken into care – certainly in the short term – and with more 'invasive' forms of therapy).

As we saw in Chapter 6, the nature of causality is complicated, and it is difficult to isolate precisely what is actually 'causing' which outcome. The same is true when we explore the effects or 'consequences' of child abuse and neglect. For example, some emotionally abusive experiences can result in mental illness for one person but leave another relatively unscarred. Similarly, many people are mentally ill who were not abused, as with the more heritable conditions such as schizophrenia and bipolar depression. But there are some forms of abuse that can lead more directly to certain outcomes: 'non-organic failure to thrive' often results in restricted growth, for example; shaking a baby can damage the spinal cord and neck or *in extremis* lead to brain damage, or even death. But with emotional abuse, and even sexual abuse, it is more difficult to say accurately whether a particular outcome in adulthood was the direct result of the events in childhood. A child's resilience, for example, can be a key factor in determining whether she or he will be able to 'bounce back' – or is it better understood as 'bounce forward'? – from adversity (for an excellent website devoted to resilience in children, visit www. boingboing.org.uk).

As with the 'causes' of maltreatment, in this chapter, we consider the mediating connections and pathways that we can more confidently expect to exist between abusive acts towards a child and the outcomes later on in adolescence and adulthood, in order to begin to understand more fully how abuse affects individuals in different ways.

Whatever the consequences of child maltreatment may be, they can be profound and may endure long after the abuse or neglect occurs; they may include minor physical injuries, low self-esteem and an inability to focus attention, or brain damage, extremely violent behaviour and, in extreme situations, suicide.

Up until the past 5–10 years most quantitative studies of the consequences of child abuse were correlational in design. That is to say, they looked for statistical connections between the types of abuse and outcomes. Few involved control groups of children who were *not* abused.

The use of control groups has not significantly increased in the recent past, which is partly due to the considerable ethical problems involved when contemplating such research, but two other developments have been noted. First, using meta-analytic statistical methods and systematic reviews allows researchers to combine many studies if certain design features and parameters are present across them. Second, there has been an increase in neurological, biochemical and genetic research into the causes and consequences of abuse, and such techniques permit the isolation of mediating processes more than any other. For example, a typical contemporary research study into consequences of early abuse can be found in Kim and Cicchetti (2010). Their very precise focus was the longitudinal pathways linking child maltreatment, emotion regulation, peer relations and psychopathology with 215 maltreated and 206 non-maltreated children (aged 6–12 years) from low-income families (again, a very precise sample). The study involved exploring boundaried research questions aimed not at a broad inquiry such as 'is mental illness an effect of child abuse?' but with the much tighter focus of the mediating effect of 'emotion regulation' and 'peer support'. The findings indicated how important the contribution of affect regulation was as a protective factor between child maltreatment and the development of subsequent psychological problems.

Confidence is a key theme in this edition; this is why it is prominent in the subtitle of this volume. For practitioners and policy-makers to feel more confident in their practice, they need to be able to rely upon sound, robustly designed research. To date, and as we shall see in some of what follows, research has often produced ambiguous and conflicting results, sometimes as the result of poor design, an imprecise sample focus or the research questions simply being too wide-ranging.

Although we have tended to concentrate on quantitative research, qualitative research that is similarly focused also produces findings which are capable of being used directly by practitioners and policy-makers alike. Bernard's (1999) study of child sexual abuse and black children with a disability is a good example. Similarly, in separate areas of child protection, Sue White's critical study of the micro-worlds of practitioners' responses to the UK's Integrated Children's System (see, for example, White et al. 2010; Wastell et al. 2011) and Brid Featherstone and Jonathan Scourfield's work on men as parents and carers (Featherstone et al. 2010), as well as Scourfield's on self-harm among young people (Scourfield et al. 2011) are excellent examples of how qualitative research can help practitioners feel more informed and, hence, more confident.

We first summarise correlationally-based studies, incorporating, where relevant, meta-analyses and systematic reviews, and we then move on to consider more recent 'biopsychosocial' studies. A number of caveats exist with most of the studies. First, samples have tended to be drawn from lower socio-economic backgrounds, prisoners, mental health patients or other clinical populations. Other than attachment-based research (for example, Out et al. 2009), it is rare to find examples of research conducted in so-called 'low-risk' populations. Second, data collection is often achieved through the use of official records or by the self-reporting of current or past child maltreatment and this may result in a misrepresentation of the true prevalence levels of child abuse and neglect. Third, as we have seen earlier, there are problems about agreed definitions of what constitutes abuse. Lack of definitional clarity makes comparability between different studies difficult; it is not always possible to be sure that you are comparing like with like. Some studies are careful to differentiate between types of abuse and degrees of severity, while others are not. Fourth, the difficulty of deciding on the length of time to be allowed for follow-up of cases is a problem. Research that is carried out soon after the abuse has occurred will obviously miss out on evaluating longer-term effects. On the other hand, the greater the gap between the abuse event and subsequent behaviour, the less chance there is of causally linking the two because of the existence of more intervening variables.

The consequences of physical abuse and neglect

Research into the consequences of physical abuse and neglect has been patchy, particularly in the UK. There has been a generally held view that the consequences of physical abuse are self-evident, with provision of protection and security in serious cases being the key requirements, and studies of the consequences of neglect have been few and far between. More recently, however, more interest began to be shown into the effects of physical child abuse, and particularly into the effects of neglect, as policy has shifted from a focus on abusive events to a broader consideration of ongoing neglectful (and abusive) climates within families.

Separating out the effects of physical abuse and neglect in order to pinpoint which causes what, however, is highly problematic in that the two are often closely linked. It would be rare for a child experiencing regular physical ill-treatment not to be experiencing neglect (especially emotional harm). On the other hand, parents can be seriously neglectful without actually physically abusing children. This needs to be borne in mind throughout the following commentaries.

Beginning with physical abuse, it tends to be associated with:

various types of injuries, particularly when exposure to such abuse occurs in the first three years of life (Vinchon et al. 2005). Shaking an infant may result in bruising, bleeding, and swelling in the brain. The physical consequences of 'shaken baby syndrome' can range from vomiting or irritability to more severe effects, such as concussions, respiratory distress, seizures, and death (Conway 1998). Two-thirds of subdural haemorrhages in children under two are caused by physical abuse (Vinchon et al. 2005). It is estimated that 10 per cent of admissions to paediatric burns and plastic surgery units are related to child maltreatment (Chester et al. 2006).

(Lazenbatt 2010: 5)

Other possible consequences of physical abuse include partial loss of vision or blindness, learning disabilities and paralysis (Conway et al. 1998). Neglected infants may experience 'non-organic failure to thrive', resulting in the child's weight, height and motor development being significantly below that expected for the child's age, as well as learning and psychological problems.

Short- and medium-term effects on emotional development

The emotional impact of physical abuse

Physically maltreated children will often become passive and withdrawn (internalising behaviours) or, alternatively, overactive and aggressive (externalising behaviours). Both physically and sexually abused children sometimes exhibit both extremes (Kaplan et al. 1999) but Fearon et al. (2010) found that attachment insecurity was strongly associated with externalising problems, with the effects greater for boys than girls. Children demonstrating disorganisation of attachment had the most elevated risk. Emotional and psychosocial problems identified among individuals who were maltreated as children include: low self-esteem; depression and anxiety; post-traumatic stress disorder (PTSD); attachment disorganisation or disorders; eating disorders; and self-harming behaviour, including suicide attempts (Silva et al. 2000; Widom 2000).

Calam and Franchi (1987) provide a useful – and timeless – overview of psychological characteristics displayed in the short term by children who are physically abused. Many of these characteristics can be seen as survival tactics adopted by the powerless in the face of harsh treatment. Such abused children can develop a form of 'pseudo-maturity' that manifests itself in behaviour aimed at keeping their parents happy. Generally, they have a lack of appetite for, or confidence in, play. Such children become self-critical and lack self-esteem. 'Frozen watchfulness' is another response, usually to more extreme forms of abuse and deprivation; that is, the child seems to be wary of human contact and to lack emotional reaction. Hyperactivity and inability to settle for any substantial length of time have also been seen as typical of the behaviour of physically abused children.

These initial responses may or may not persist. Early negative psychological development is thought to be caused not so much by the actual physical abuse as by the way in which parents relate emotionally to their children, and it is maintained by the way in which they continue to interact with them, regardless of whether they use physical violence again or not.

In the USA, Steele (1986), arguing along similar lines, stressed that the main feature of being an abused child is inconsistent care, which in general terms leads to a sense of insecurity. This manifests itself in low self-esteem, problems in developing a sense of self-identity, a diminution in the ability to cope with life and its stresses, a lack of ability to take pleasure in things and to make lasting attachments, depression, delinquency and masochism. For many researchers and practitioners, it is the *emotional quality* of parenting that is the key. The emotionally incapacitating effects of this type of early mistreatment can be alleviated only by positive interpersonal experiences. In both these accounts, therefore, physical abuse is seen more as a symptom of emotional abuse, and the important consequences, provided a child's physical safety is ensured, are linked to the child's emotional and relationship needs.

The emotional impact of neglect

The impact of neglect alone on children (i.e. unaccompanied by any specific incident of physical or sexual abuse) has been relatively under-researched (Hildyard and Wolfe 2002). However, the Minnesota Longitudinal Study of Parents and Children (Egeland et al. 1983; Erickson et al. 1989; Sroufe et al. 2009) – which included emotional abuse – began in 1975 and has been of considerable influence in the development of child protection policy in the UK. The Minnesota Study is still running and in 2009 the researchers summarised the findings in *The Developing Child* (Sroufe et al. 2009).

This longitudinal study followed the development of 267 children born to first-time mothers identified as being at risk for parenting problems over a period of six years. The study focused on 84 of these children, all of whom had been reported as being abused, and used 85 non-abused children, selected from the original sample of at-risk mothers, as a control group. The researchers categorised their experimental group children under four main abuse headings:

1. Children who were physically abused.
2. Children whose parents were hostile and verbally abusive.
3. Children who were neglected.
4. Children whose parents were psychologically unavailable (that is, they were emotionally abusive).

Children from all the 'abused' groups were generally rated as having less confidence and lower self-esteem than those in the control group. However, the main aim of the study was to see whether there were differences between the experiences of children who were abused and neglected. The study found that there were differences, though not as great as between the abused and non-abused groups as a whole. At age 4, the neglected and emotionally abused children were the cause of most concern.

However, at age 6, these children, whose parents were described as psychologically unavailable, fared as well as the other groups of abused children. The group giving most cause for concern at this stage was the neglected children, who were very low achievers in school. Such children were found to show disorganised attachment behaviour with their parents, negative self-representations, to be isolated and withdrawn in social situations and to have poor problem-solving skills. The study pointed to the persistent and ongoing nature of neglect as the cause of the severity of the outcome compared with that of other forms of abuse. Other studies have also pointed to the fact that neglected children seem to be lower in self-esteem than children who have been physically abused (for example, Toth et al. 1997).

Summary

What comes across clearly from research into the early effects of child abuse and neglect is that it is the emotional impact of children's experiences that debilitates and disadvantages them. This provides a focus for treatment for all abused children. It tells us that with regard to children who are being physically ill-treated, it is not sufficient just to ensure their physical safety (important though this is). With regard to neglected children, it tells us clearly that, even though there are no incidents of inflicted abuse, they may have major emotional deficits that need attending to, arguably of greater severity than for other abused children.

Before moving on to the next section, which considers social and intellectual functioning, it should be noted that the consequences of abuse and neglect considered above lay the foundation for what is to follow. Children who are psychologically disturbed or emotionally deprived at an early age lack the internal cognitive map and hence behavioural skills needed to develop socially and intellectually. As will be seen, the deficits in these areas result in frustrations and avoidance behaviours which elicit further negative responses from those with whom they interact, and so on.

Medium-term effects on social and intellectual functioning

Relationships with peers

As children get older, peer relationships take on an increasingly important role (Tajima et al. 2011). Children who have been mistreated seem to fare badly in peer relationships, according to research findings (Camras and Rappaport 1993; Bolger et al. 1998). These studies find that physically abused and neglected children are either more aggressive or more withdrawn than their non-maltreated peers and that they are likely to experience more conflict and hostility in their relationships with them. Higher levels of aggression are found among physically ill-treated children; neglected children tend to be more withdrawn (Erickson and Egeland 1996). Bolger et al. (1998), in a study of 107 maltreated children, found that the earlier the onset of maltreatment and the longer it persists, the less likely such children are to be popular with their peers. They also note that maltreated children find it harder to maintain friendships in adolescence as these become more intimate and complex.

The reason for poor social functioning on the part of abused children might not be the result of the psychologically incapacitating effects of being poorly cared for or ill-treated. An alternative explanation is that their parents are themselves socially isolated and do not provide, or value, peer contacts for their children. There could be factors other than these that mark out ill-treated children for fractured peer relationships. They may have been disruptive in school, poorly dressed by the standards of the rest of the neighbourhood and avoided by their peers for these reasons.

Clearly both psychological and social factors need to be taken into account. However, the research leaves us in little doubt that abused and deprived children do not generally enjoy good peer relationships and this, therefore, can add to the difficulties they may already be experiencing in their intra-familial relationships.

School performance

Differences exist among the findings on the consequences of maltreatment on cognitive development, verbal abilities and problem-solving skills. Some studies have found evidence of lowered intellectual and cognitive functioning in abused children compared with children who have not been abused (Veltman and Browne 2001; Porter et al. 2005), whereas others found no differences (Allen and Oliver 1982). This may be connected with confounding variables such as the timing, nature and severity of the abuse.

Far less equivocal is the finding that child abuse results in lower academic achievement as well as impaired school performance generally, for example, through lower grades. This finding has emerged consistently over the years, including from the Minnesota Study (Sroufe et al. 2009). Poor educational achievement has also been found among children in care in the UK, many of whom are likely to have experienced some form of abuse or neglect (see Jackson 1996).

Two important messages come across from research into the short- and medium-term effects of physical abuse and neglect so far reviewed. The first is that early depriving experiences can set up a cycle of events that can reinforce the ill-effects of those early events (Howe 2011). The second, linked to the first, is that incidents of abuse, while traumatic and occasionally causing lasting physical damage, even death, are not as such the major determinants of negative consequences. The ongoing climate within the family seems to be of prime importance in determining whether or not such consequences persist.

'Runaways'

Both in the USA and in Britain, an association between physical abuse and neglect has been found with children who run away from home and are then homeless. Kaufman and Widom (1999), in a study of 587 reported runaways, found that just under half had been physically abused. In the UK, there has been a series of studies carried out by the Children's Society into the backgrounds and experiences of children and young people who have run away from home (Rees 1993; Rees and Smeaton 2001). Rees (1993), in a study of 80 children staying in a safe house, found that physical violence was the most commonly cited reason for running away from home, occurring in just under a half of all those interviewed. In a sample of 416 adolescents drawn from a longitudinal study conducted in Pennsylvania, Kim et al. (2009: 19) found that 'physical and psychological abuse predicts a child's running away from home and that running away predicts later delinquency and victimisation as well as partially mediating the effect of earlier abuse'. In a study in the USA, Sullivan and Knutson (2000b) found very high levels of children with disabilities among their sample of runaways, with maltreatment being seen as the main cause in the majority of these cases. Today, 'Railway Children' (www.railwaychildren.org.uk) acts as an awareness-raising organisation in 24 countries.

Resilient children

Not every child who is maltreated experiences the negative consequences presented so far. 'Protective factors', such as optimism, high self-esteem, high intelligence or a sense of hopefulness can insulate or 'buffer' some children (Heller et al. 1999). The Minnesota data also found that relationships with supportive adults and friends also helped (Sroufe et al. 2009). Mrazek and Mrazek (1987) list 12 factors that can account for resilient survival behaviours. Most of these are associated with the child's personality and intelligence, but some are linked to situational circumstances, such as access to good educational and health facilities. However, a number of commentators are now questioning whether this 'trait-based' operational construction of 'resilience' is the most appropriate one (Liebenberg and Ungar 2009). They prefer instead to conceptualise resilience as the ability to recognise, seek, acquire and then negotiate successfully the right kind of help and support when it is needed; they see it as a dynamic process, not a static personal attribute, even though it contains a genetic component.

Kinard (1998), however, poses the following important questions about resilience in children, particularly in relation to defining the concept. Are there objective measures of resilience? Who decides whether a child is resilient? How long does a child have to be resilient to be termed as such? She also notes that resilience does not necessarily signify emotional health in that a child could simply be internalising problems, factors that need to be borne in mind when supporting families where children are acting as carers (Dearden and Becker 2001; Cree 2003).

Clearly, therefore, much care is needed on the part of professionals in using the notion of resilience. On the positive side, it may inform supportive help given to children coping with adverse circumstances, but there are dangers that children could be too easily identified as resilient and not be helped in an effective way.

Severe psychological difficulties and impairments to young children as a result of physical abuse

Studies have linked physical abuse with hyperactivity in children (Whitmore et al. 1993). Originating in the USA, the diagnosis of PTSD is increasingly being used elsewhere (Perrin et al. 1999). This diagnosis has been applied to adults and children experiencing disturbingly high levels of stress, following either being the victim of or witnessing extreme violence or threat of it, or some form of catastrophe (Seng et al. 2011). Symptoms of PTSD in children include sleep disturbance, loss of concentration, constant re-experiencing of the trauma-inducing events and separation anxiety. PTSD is usually seen as an extreme reaction to an event – or events – that an individual finds to be too much to cope with. Clearly there are many variations in relation to PTSD – often connected with the under-identification of mediating factors, making diagnosis problematic. However, there is sufficient evidence to link PTSD to children exposed to physical and sexual violence within and outside the family.

Longer-term pathological effects of physical abuse and neglect

As was stressed in the introduction to this chapter, the longer the gap between the abusive incident and the behaviour associated with it, the greater the uncertainty about the link. This is demonstrated in the case of child sexual abuse and prostitution, for example, and should be borne in mind throughout this discussion, in which two long-term effects linked to physical abuse and neglect are considered: mental illness, and general life experiences and outlook. Drug-taking, delinquency and violent crime are not explored in any detail because the trajectories and pathways are too loosely coupled to be reliably considered as direct effects of child abuse; although, clearly, many children who are abused follow criminal pathways and abuse drugs – the problem is that so do lots of children who have not been abused (and, also, many abused children do not go on to follow criminal pathways or abuse drugs). These particular outcomes are notoriously hard to pin down, and that is why they have been excluded from the discussion.

Mental illness

The link between parental mental illness and physical child abuse and neglect was considered in an earlier chapter. Here the concern is whether mental illness is a consequence of being abused or neglected as a child. Because of the impact of mediator variables, we often encounter wide variation in results – and this is why there are few studies today which consider such research questions as 'Does child abuse lead to . . . ?' Here are two examples which illustrate this problem.

An early study into the prevalence of the experience of child abuse among a sample of mentally ill participants was undertaken by Carmen et al. (1984). They analysed the case records of 188 in-patients in a US psychiatric hospital to see if there was evidence of abuse (as children or adults) in their backgrounds. They found that 80 (43 per cent) of these patients had histories of some form of abuse; 64 of these (80 per cent) had been physically abused and half sexually abused; 72 (90 per cent) had been victimised by family members; 52 (65 per cent) were female. The researchers argue that these figures are probably an underestimation of the real incidence of abuse in this population because they included only those cases where there was unequivocal evidence that abuse had occurred. But some years later Read (1998), reporting on an examination of the records of 100 consecutive admissions to an acute psychiatric in-patient unit in New Zealand, found a considerably lower rate of abuse than Carmen et al. – namely, 22 per cent. However, patients who had been physically or sexually abused, or both, were more likely to be suicidal, to have longer stays in hospital and to show the most severe disturbances in symptoms and behaviour.

Greater sensitisation to the fact that such relatively high numbers of people who are treated as psychiatric patients are likely to have been ill-treated as children can only be of benefit to them and their treatment. However, it should be noted that there are many other possible factors apart from childhood abuse that could account for the psychiatric illnesses found in these studies and, as we have demonstrated, by no means all physically and sexually abused children develop psychiatric illnesses. There are also problems relating to the definitions and diagnoses of psychiatric illness.

A more promising approach to the study of pathways between child abuse and subsequent mental ill-health looked at the 'impact of child abuse on neuro-endocrine functioning and the structure of the brain, in particular on the amygdala, hippocampus, left hemisphere, and corpus callosum' (Coates 2010: 391), and then considered the effects on mental disorders. All were implicated to a greater or lesser degree in moderating the effect on adult mental health. The author went on to look specifically at what the implications were for practitioners and in essence stressed the need for stability, consistency and predictability in close relationships.

More recently, Bailey et al. (2018) found using meta-analysis that childhood trauma was associated with severity of hallucinations and delusions in psychotic disorders in adulthood.

General life experiences and outlook

Most of the studies looking at how abuse impacts on victims when they reach adulthood are retrospective ones. As was discussed in Chapter 6, such studies tend to exaggerate the extent of the influence of abuse on later life. Also, there is a problem with retrospective studies that the memory of the research respondents becomes less accurate over time (Widom et al. 2004). Indeed, such lapses in memory and recall could be as a result of a defensive process, to unconsciously repress or deny the effects of an abusive childhood. In a study of 1,196 substantiated physical abuse and neglect cases (followed up after 20 years), Colman and Widom (2004) found that they were more likely to have experienced problems in close relationships with other adults than those in a control group. This was indicated by higher rates of cohabitation, separation and divorce.

A British study by Gibbons et al. (1995b) followed up 144 children 10 years after they had been placed on child abuse registers for physical abuse. They used a control group of a similar number of children from similar backgrounds and came to the conclusion that there was little sign that the severity of abuse had any direct effects on the child's development 9 or 10 years later.

A 20-year follow-up study of 44 children identified with 'non-organic failure to thrive' showed that some children had by adulthood developed more positive attachment styles where others had not (Iwaniec and Sneddon 2001). Key variables were seen to be the type of professional support that these individuals had received and their experience of rewarding close relationships.

As can be seen, therefore, important though these prospective studies are, the findings are not sufficiently consistent to provide the basis for safe judgements about the long-term effects of child physical abuse and neglect.

The consequences of extra-familial physical abuse: bullying

Bullying in the twenty-first century is more complex and covers more examples than previously. For example, it can be physical or emotional bullying; and it can also involve cyberbullying and sexting or sending nude photos or 'trolling' messages about a child (or an adult). The dangers and consequences of bullying have increased rapidly over the past few years. For example, in the USA, suicide is the third highest cause of death among young people. And in the UK at least half of suicides among young people are related to bullying.

Clearly, not all children by any means will develop this disorder following school bullying and the emphasis of central government policy in England is on prevention. Nevertheless, the consequences of school bullying are likely to be severe in the short term for a small number of children and it is important to ensure a prompt and appropriate response where it occurs.

Summary

Many of the studies reviewed here suffer from the problems of causally linking abuse and outcome, from weak and vague definitions of abuse and from a lack of attention to social factors as influences on behaviour, such as the differential impact of abuse on women. Having noted these problems, however, the following general picture of the consequences of physical abuse and neglect emerges from the research that exists. Many physically abused children suffer considerable emotional and psychological problems in their early childhood, leading them to have problems in trusting other people and to suffer from a sense of personal worthlessness. Socially and intellectually, they do not perform well because of this. Many physically abused children tend to be both aggressive and withdrawn; neglected children as a whole seem to be less aggressive but are more likely to exhibit withdrawn behaviour. A relatively small number of children suffer permanently from the physical effects of injury and severe neglect. Some children seem to survive well and cope despite all the odds.

Much depends on the quality of their relationships with members of their family and others during childhood and also on the individual personality and intelligence of the child in question. In the longer term, there is evidence of links between being physically abused and mental illness, drug abuse, delinquency and violent criminality and general adjustment to life. The connection between child abuse and these behaviours in adult lives is harder to prove, but nevertheless, particularly in the field of mental illness, the consistency of the findings is persuasive and has important implications for psychiatric practices.

The consequences of child sexual abuse

Research into the impact of sexual abuse on victims has been, and continues to be, more in evidence than that into physical abuse and neglect. This stems to a large extent from the way in which sexual abuse was emphasised in the 1980s, often as a result of women recounting their childhood experiences and the effects these continued to have in their adult lives. Such accounts have led to greater sensitivity to the consequences of such abuse, particularly with regard to its long-term effects. Generally, although there are the same methodological problems as in studies of the consequences of physical abuse, particularly in relation to definitions and the use of control groups, research into the effects of child sexual abuse seems to be more systematic and detailed. Nevertheless, there are still major difficulties in sifting out the direct impact of the abuse from that which may be attributed to other variables, such as pre-existing problems, responses to the abuse by significant adults (including professionals) and later depriving experiences.

From the mid-1980s, studies tended to differentiate between short-term and long-term effects (Browne and Finkelhor 1986; Beitchman et al. 1991, 1992). Also, clear distinctions are made between the impact of intra-familial and extra-familial sexual abuse of children in only a few of the research studies.

Short-term effects

These include a higher level of severe consequences for children of all ages who have been sexually abused, in particular: fearfulness, depression and withdrawal, hostility and aggression, low self-esteem, guilt and shame, physical symptoms, cognitive disability, developmental delay, impaired school performance and showing inappropriate sexual behaviour.

Two conclusions can be drawn. The first is that, while an appreciable number of sexually abused children do experience behavioural and emotional problems in the two years following abuse, compared with children who have not been abused, the link between these behaviours and sexual abuse is weak and other factors could account for them.

The only relatively clear direct outcome is that of inappropriately sexualised behaviour, which occurs in between 25 and 33 per cent of all sexually abused children (see also Brilleslijper-Kater et al. 2004).

The second conclusion is that sexual abuse per se has different effects on children. Browne and Finkelhor note that: 'In the immediate aftermath of sexual abuse one-fifth to two-fifths of abused children seen by clinicians manifest some noticeable disturbance' (1986: 164). It should be stressed that this apparently strange conclusion may result from the fact that a broad definition of sexual abuse is used in most of the studies, including, for instance, various degrees of seriousness and both intra-familial and extra-familial abuse. It should be noted that the timing of the research is also important. Calam et al. (1998) found that, overall, their sample of children experienced more problems two years after the abuse incident than they did at four weeks afterwards. It has to be stressed that research into this area is still relatively new and experimental; it is important, therefore, to interpret the findings carefully and not to draw hasty conclusions from them.

Long-term effects

Many of the behaviours and emotions discussed in relation to short-term effects of sexual abuse are also to be found in studies of long-term effects. As stressed at the start of this chapter, the links, seen to be problematic in the case of short-term effects, are even more problematic with regard to long-term effects because of the greater length of time between the abuse and the observed behaviour and because of the possible effect of a much wider range of intervening variables. Nevertheless, there are a number of consequences that have emerged. For example, Swanston et al. (2003), in a nine-year follow-up of 103 sexually abused children in Sydney, Australia, found that they suffered significantly more from *fear and anxiety* than individuals in their non-abused control group.

The same authors also found high rates of *depression and low self-esteem* in their study. Again, in Australia, Martin et al. (2004) carried out a study of 2,485 14-year-olds. They found that 5.4 per cent of girls and 2 per cent of boys in their sample had been sexually abused and that those who had been sexually abused were far more likely than their non-abused peers to entertain *suicidal thoughts*. Boys who had been sexually abused were more likely than girls to attempt suicide (55 per cent compared to 29 per cent).

Low self-esteem is another longer-term consequence of sexual abuse in childhood. Swanston et al. (2003) confirm a significant link between self-esteem and sexual abuse in their study. For the same reasons as outlined earlier, it is very difficult to untangle the links between childhood sexual abuse and longer-term psychiatric problems; the same applies to connections with sexual abuse and eating disorders, abusing other children as adults and running away from home. Less problematic, however, is the almost self-evident finding that there are physical consequences of sexual abuse. For example, Jaudes and Morris (1990) collected data from a sample of 138 sexually abused children referred to hospital between 1979 and 1987 and found that one-third of them had a sexually transmitted disease. Their average age was just over 6 years. Although, despite their name, it is possible for sexually transmitted diseases to be passed on in non-sexual ways, the chances of this are very small (Neursten et al. 1984). Interestingly, and perhaps somewhat controversially, for 'the most part, physical symptoms were of no value in differentiating between those who had been sexually abused and those who had not' (Kelly and Koh 2006: 112).

The findings of research into the general long-term effects confirm that women who have been sexually abused are more likely than women who have not to have problems in later life with regard to fear, anxiety, self-esteem, depression, satisfactory sexual relations, substance misuse and general mental health, and to be vulnerable to further abuse. However, such consequences are not inevitable. In the section that follows, the focus is on those factors that can be influential in leading to the worst outcomes.

A number of other variables have been associated in the literature with influence on the harmful effects of child sexual abuse: age at onset of abuse; gender of child; degree of seriousness of the abuse; duration of abuse; relationship of the abuser to the abused; abuse accompanied by violence; and the way in which the abused child was helped and responded to at and after the time of disclosure. However, today the only *relatively* consistent finding among these variables is that concerning the gender of the victim, but we need bear in mind that in recent years a significant number of young boys have been sexually abused within religious settings (see, for example, Jay 2014; Harper and Perkins 2017) and this may now affect these findings.

For example, according to the Fourth National Incidence Study of Child Abuse and Neglect (NIS-4) (Sedlak et al. 2010; $n = 16,875$), girls are now sexually abused five times more often than boys (but to illustrate the point about variation, in the third study – only a decade earlier – it was three times more prevalent). The NIS-4 survey still confirms David Finkelhor's earlier finding that both boys and girls are most vulnerable if sexual abuse occurs between the ages of 7 and 13 (Finkelhor 1994).

Beitchman et al. (1991, 1992) referred to several other studies that confirmed the influence of family response on both short- and long-term harm. Their view was that victims of child sexual abuse are more likely than non-victims to come from disturbed families and, therefore, that they are particularly likely to be responded to by their families in a negative way. Clearly this argument is more relevant to intra-familial abuse. Also of importance in this area is the response of professionals to allegations of sexual abuse. Elwell and Ephloss (1987) found that bad handling of intervention by the police and other professionals was associated with increased short-term trauma. Gomes-Schwartz et al. (1990) found that children removed from their families showed the most short-term problems but, as Browne and Finkelhor (1986) comment, these might have been the most problematic cases in the first place.

There seems, therefore, to be reasonable evidence to suggest that sexual abuse is likely to be most harmful in the following instances:

- where the abusive act involves penetration;
- where the abuse has persisted for some time;
- where the abuser is a father-figure;
- where the abuse is accompanied by violence, force and/or the threat of it;
- where the response of the family is negative.

While the age and sex of the abused child do have some impact on the outcome, the research does not provide clear indications of the direction of the effects of these variables. There is not sufficient information on the impact of professional intervention to evaluate conclusively its effect for good or ill.

For some health and welfare practitioners, the degree of detail of all this research may seem unnecessary, in that child sexual abuse of the type in which they frequently become involved – largely intra-familial and often of a very serious nature – clearly has harmful effects on the child. It can seem to be somewhat hair-splitting to separate which element of abuse in a generally abusive situation causes the most harm. Similarly, research that suggests that children who are removed from families do less well than those who remain can be frustrating when it is apparent that removal is the only feasible course of action. Nevertheless, there are some important and relevant findings, in particular, that sexual abuse of children is not necessarily incapacitating for them in later life. There is a tendency among professionals to make this assumption, which can in itself have negative effects. In particular, awareness of the impact of the variables just discussed is an important starting-point for assessing the consequences for the child and how to organise a response. Such knowledge provides a framework for intervention, not a blueprint. Children whom one would expect to suffer less harmful effects on the basis of known research findings may in fact experience considerable trauma. As has been repeatedly stressed, there are weaknesses in the research, and findings need to be carefully interpreted. Nevertheless, despite its limitations, this is the best formal available knowledge and it should, therefore, have relevance for policy and practice in this field.

The question of disorganised attachment behaviour

There is a general consensus in attachment research that mere 'insecurity' of attachment is unlikely *on its own* to lead to mental health disorders but until recently it was thought that 'the only clear connections between infant attachment and adult psychopathology are between disorganised attachment and dissociative symptoms in adolescence and early adulthood' (Dozier et al. 2008: 736). (For a more detailed account of what disorganised attachment is – and is not – see Duschinsky 2015.)

Over the last two years the position of researchers has changed due to some new evidence alongside a reconsideration of earlier findings (see Duschinsky 2015; Duschinsky and Solomon 2017; Granqvist et al. 2017; Reisz et al. 2017; Reijman et al. 2018). These papers conclude that disorganised attachment (referred to as 'D') may occur through different 'pathways'. These different 'Pathways to D' (Granqvist et al. 2017) do not necessarily stem from abuse, which was until recently assumed to be its most likely source. Children can show 'fear' when needing a primary attachment figure to be a safe haven and secure base for reasons other than 'direct' abuse. As a result of the work undertaken in the research papers listed above, Shemmings summarised the position as follows:

I propose the following conceptualisation of the different 'pathways to D':

- Abusive Parental Behaviour experiences, such as physical or sexual abuse and some extreme forms of intentional emotional abuse or neglect.
- Unintentional Parental Maltreatment, comprising caregiving which is inadvertently frightening to the child, extensive unplanned care (see Main et al. 2011), frequent over-night separations (see Main et al. 2011), the combined effect of socio-economic risk factors (Gedaly and Leerkes 2016; Cyr et al. 2010) as well as gene–environment interaction (but more research is needed here).
- Pathways Involving No Maltreatment, such as some children with autism (but as yet it isn't clear precisely what the mechanism might be that produces D behaviours) and the possibility of a more direct genetic influence (again, more research is needed).

(Shemmings 2016a: 34)

As we have seen at various points throughout this book, a number of research findings depend heavily on the definitions of 'abuse', 'neglect' and 'maltreatment' being used. This is true in this discussion about attachment disorganisation which Shemmings explained as follows:

the definition of 'maltreatment' I have used is the one outlined in the UK's Guidance entitled Working Together to Safeguard Children (revised 2015). Thus, 'maltreatment' covers 'physical abuse and sexual abuse' but also includes 'emotional abuse and neglect' . . . One of the reasons for making this distinction is that often, in the past, enquiries into child deaths and abuse have regularly made the point that professionals have not kept the focus on the child during investigations and assessments.

(Shemmings 2016b: 526)

Whatever the 'pathways to D', the root of the behaviour appears to be that the child cannot gain any comfort when experiencing high levels of fear or stress, which is generally accepted is not good for a child to experience for long periods of time. What is particularly encouraging and important to bear in mind is that disorganised attachment is responsive to targeted support, help and intervention (Granqvist et al. 2017).

Neuro-biochemical and genetic research into the effects of maltreatment

The design of neuro-biochemical and genetic research

Magnetic resonance imaging (MRI) scanners measure the structure and function of the brain by showing two- and three-dimensional 'slices'. Electroencephalography (EEG) 'nets' cover the head to measure electrical activity.

With any research on the brain using scans one needs to be mindful of what is colloquially known as the Dead Salmon problem! Bennett et al. (2010) report on a neuroscience team who put a dead salmon in an MRI scanner . . . and its brain registered some activity. This was thought to because there is fat in the brain which could have accounted for what happened and it is possible that there is 'noise in the machine'. The implication here is not to reject MRI scans. The results are a signal for researchers in this field to use what statisticians call 'multiple comparisons' and to raise automatically the criteria for the acceptance of significant results. (For another critical perspective on brain scanning, see Wastell and White 2017.)

Functional magnetic resonance imaging (fMRI) scans seek to measure the amount and location of blood in different areas of the brain to reveal precisely the areas that are active when an individual undertakes a task (such as looking at photos expressing different emotions). For example, McCrory et al. (2010) asked adolescents exposed to family violence, and controls, to look at pictures of male and female faces showing sad, calm or angry expressions. Worryingly, they found that children exposed to family violence show a similar pattern of brain activity to soldiers exposed to combat, specifically in the amygdala and anterior insula regions.

The HPA axis connects the hypothalamus, the pituitary gland and the adrenal glands, which regulate, among other things, cortisol levels produced when the body experiences fear and danger (the axis also helps to regulate temperature, digestion and the immune system, and plays a large part in the system controlling our reaction to stress, trauma and injury). Measuring cortisol levels is achieved by taking saliva samples. Too much or too little cortisol can cause problems. The under- or over-production of cortisol has been called 'toxic stress' (National Scientific Council on the Developing Child 2005) as the effects can be severe and lead to psychopathological conditions and psychiatric vulnerability in adulthood, as well as altering brain circuitry.

Genetic research usually needs large samples to overcome the problem of tracking single pathways from a specific genotype to something as complex as 'maltreatment', partly because the statistical power needed is large (Lyons-Ruth and Jacobvitz 2008). As a consequence:

Until recently, the preferred way to explore the effect of genetics was to compare monozygotic (identical) with dizygotic (non-identical) twins. Fortunately, complementary methods are now available to study the possibility of DA [disorganised attachment] being partly heritable. They involve analysing the structure of genes at the molecular level. This is achieved by taking 'buccal swabs' – a saliva sample taken from inside the cheek.

(Shemmings and Shemmings 2011: 93)

Most studies direct their attention at two neurotransmitters: oxytocin and dopamine. Oxytocin plays a significant role in the care of new-born infants, and low oxytocin levels are strongly related to emotional abuse (Heim et al. 2009). Dopamine regulates reward and attentional strategies and increases when we are under stress. At that point, the more logical and measured parts of the brain that delay gratification – especially the prefrontal cortex – disconnect and our sub-cortical, more impulsive, areas take over, resulting in increased impulsivity. The HPA axis controls the entire system when we are stressed. When a child has been maltreated, the HPA axis is often on 'red alert':

even though there may actually be no real threat, the body stays on permanent 'look-out' and remains in an almost permanent state of hypervigilance and anxiety. It is this state that can eventually impair or impede the structure, function and neural circuitry of the brain.

(Shemmings and Shemmings 2011: 90)

This is what Luyten refers to as a 'bio-behavioural switch' (Luyten et al. 2009). Chronic maltreatment in childhood leads to the switchover kicking in a lot earlier.

The most recent and comprehensive conceptualisation of these findings is, perhaps, Eamon McCrory's theory of latent vulnerability, which he explains as follows:

We review extant functional neuroimaging studies of children and adolescents exposed to early neglect and/or maltreatment, including physical, sexual and emotional abuse across four neurocognitive domains: threat processing, reward processing, emotion regulation and executive control. Findings are discussed in the context of 'latent vulnerability', where alterations in neurocognitive function are considered to carry adaptive value in early adverse caregiving environments but confer long-term risk.

(McCrory et al. 2017b: 338)

Bio-psychosocial research is beginning to reveal more precisely the mechanisms that produce the ambiguous and sometimes contradictory findings typical of this whole field; it helps in our understanding of why someone who is sexually abused, for example, might go on to abuse others, or develop mental illness, etc. whereas others do not. Until now, researchers have assumed that the differences would be the result of 'age of onset' or the 'duration of the abuse' but, as we have seen, two studies will reveal different results, even though the designs are similar. This research is expanding our understanding of the mediating processes between independent (for example, 'early child abuse') and dependent (for example, 'mental ill-health in adulthood') variables.

Specific findings: neurological and biochemical

McCrory et al. (2010, 2017a) offer the best summaries of these findings to date. In their detailed reviews they found, first, some evidence that abused or neglected children have smaller cranial and cerebral volume. Second, however, although there appears not to be any reduction in hippocampal volume – a sub-cortical area responsible for, among other things, long-term memory – in maltreated children, it *has* been noted in adults maltreated as children and who *also* exhibited PTSD or experienced chronic stress. Notice the need, again, to separate out stress as a confounding or mediating variable to understand the complexity of this finding – this is why it was built into the design. Third, maltreated children were noted to have a smaller corpus callosa – a key area of the brain responsible for arousal, emotion and higher cognitive abilities.

Genetic explanations

We now consider the growing field of genetic research and its connection to child maltreatment. Dopamine is a neurotransmitter involved in the regulation of reward. The dopamine D4 receptor (DRD4) gene crops up as having a mediating effect in children (Lakatos et al. 2000, 2002), as well as in adults who were abused as children. It also appeared at first to be related to attention-deficit hyperactivity disorder (ADHD) (Lasky-Su et al. 2008), but there are now doubts as a result of methodological problems similar to those that have bedevilled the field of research in the aetiology of child maltreatment (Turic et al. 2010).

Two subsequent papers (Bakermans-Kranenburg and Van IJzendoorn 2004; Spangler and Zimmermann 2007) contended that Lakatos et al. did not take account sufficiently of 'gene x environment' interactions. For example, 'children might inherit the tendency to be overweight, but if there is very little food around for them to eat, and they end up poorly nourished, they will be underweight for their age' (Shemmings and Shemmings 2011: 95).

Genes operate in complex, interactive ways. For example, certain 'polymorphisms' (small gene variants) provide resilience to maltreatment in one person while, in another, they will lead to vulnerability. To confuse matters further, the same genes can be connected to different outcomes. For example, the serotonin transporter 5-HTT gene has been linked to PTSD, depression *and* anti-social behaviour (Feder et al. 2009).

Applied to child protection, the fundamental idea behind 'gene–environment interaction' (G x E) is that some children are more susceptible to abusive parenting than others. It is referred to as 'differential susceptibility' (see, for example, Belsky 2005). Genetic explanations stress how and why different environmental features can produce different reactions and responses in different children.

Finally, in addition to the concept of G x E, some genes also interact with other genes. For example:

> there are now thought to be nine genes which help us 'pick up the baby' soon after its birth (and not do much else): if all goes well 'your ticket is punched when you hold your baby' . . . or, at least it is for most parents; for others, it can be a time of unbearable emotional pain, full of regular reminders of insensitive parenting provided during their own childhood.
>
> (Shemmings and Shemmings 2011: 95)

Bearing these points in mind, two other key genes so far identified (see McCrory et al. 2010) in maltreatment are monoamine oxidase-A (MAO-A), the so-called warrior gene as it is connected to aggression (Beach et al. 2010) and serotonin transporter (5-HTT), often referred to as the 'depression gene'. Combined with the dopamine neurotransmitter DRD4 7-repeat, which helps us deal with reward and impulse, we may have the ingredients of a genetic admixture in part responsible for stress reactivity and impulsivity (Maestripieri 2010) that, as we saw above, may be a key component in low mentalisation. The effect is that, in combination with caregiving, social support and other environmental features, G (x G) x E interactions can confer vulnerability or resilience (McCrory et al. 2010).

The growing appeal of the 'ACEs' movement

It was in the late 1990s, when Victor Felitti began to speak of the significance of a number of 'adverse childhood experiences' (ACEs) on the trajectories and sequelae of adults later in life. Put simply, childhood experiences such as physical abuse, sexual abuse, emotional abuse, physical neglect, emotional neglect, intimate partner violence, substance misuse within the household, household mental illness, parental separation or divorce and an incarcerated household member were all associated with a range of health and allied problems later in life (Felitti et al. 1998). Individual ACEs are tagged with indicative percentages identifying their predicted effect on a series of negative outcomes later on. More recently, research on the interactive effects of combining ACEs has been undertaken (Hughes 2017).

Since then, the 'ACEs too high movement' has begun to sweep across the world and now there is almost an industry of researchers, speakers and commentators extolling the virtues of ACE-analysis (usually in the top-rated journals for impact and prestige). At the level of epidemiology, this is unquestionably valuable as it enables politicians to harness resources and budgets to persuade their governments to institute social programmes at a time of competing demands.

There are, however, voices of dissent when the ACEs concept is used at an individual level to predict outcomes later on in life for a child who has been subjected to such experiences. These concerns will increase if courts' judicial processes were to instigate 'ACE tests' for individual children and families where alternative care arrangements are being considered for a child.

This idea – that what might work as a unit of analysis across an entire population might have severe consequences at the individual level – was debated at a recent UK Parliament Select Committee between, as 'protagonists', Professors Sue White and Ros Edwards and, as 'defenders', Mark Bellis and Eamon McCrory and can be found at http://parliamentlive.tv/Event/Index/730b9508-5ff6-4464-a7b8-2bbb6f709ef5.

Recommended reading

Allen, G. (2011) *Early Intervention: The Next Steps*. London: HM Government.

Beck, U. (2008) *World at Risk*. Cambridge: Polity.

Featherstone, B., Hooper, C.-A., Scourfield, J. and Taylor, J. (eds) (2010) *Gender and Child Welfare in Society*. Oxford: Wiley-Blackwell.

Lazenbatt, A. (2010) *The Impact of Abuse and Neglect on the Health and Mental Health of Children and Young People*. London: NSPCC.

Liebenberg, L. and Ungar, M. (eds) (2009) *Researching Resilience*. Toronto, ON: University of Toronto Press.

Out, D., Bakermans-Kranenburg, M. J. and Van IJzendoorn, M. H. (2009) The role of disconnected and extremely insensitive parenting in the development of disorganized attachment: the validation of a new measure, *Attachment & Human Development*, 11: 419–43.

White, S., Wastell, D. G., Broadhurst, K. and Hall, C. (2010) When policy o'erleaps itself: the 'tragic tale' of the Integrated Children's System, *Critical Social Policy*, 30(3): 405–29.

The evidence base for child protection practice

Key points in this chapter

- The evidence base for specific ways of working with child maltreatment, whether prevention or intervention, is improving, albeit from a low base.

> - There is a growing consensus that shared elements between different approaches and interventions are just as important, if not more so, than the differences between them.
> - Without a clearer understanding of – and agreement about – outcomes, it is difficult to undertake meaningful evaluative research.

Introduction

The aim of this chapter is to analyse what research tells us about the way in which health and welfare professionals respond to child abuse and neglect concerns and the effectiveness of this response.

Prior to the early 1990s, the amount of research into British child protection practice was limited. There were few studies of the work of mainstream statutory agencies (Dingwall et al. 1983; Corby 1987). Child protection public inquiry reports gave glimpses of practice, but as such inquiries were held when things appeared to have gone wrong, they formed a rather skewed sample. There were more, but still relatively few, accounts and evaluations of intervention into physical and sexual abuse cases by those working in voluntary agencies and hospital settings (Baher et al. 1976; Lynch and Roberts 1982; Dale et al. 1986; Bentovim et al. 1988) and a few accounts of action research projects (Smith and Rachman 1984; Browne and Saqi 1988). Overall, there were very few studies of the effectiveness of child protection interventions and only a small amount of research into the experiences and views of parents, let alone children and young people (Brown 1986; Corby 1987).

The picture changed considerably following the mid-1990s, with a relatively extensive body of research produced, largely sponsored by central government following events at Cleveland. There were two main branches to this: one summarised in *Child Protection: Messages from Research* (Department of Health 1995) and the other summarised in *The Children Act Now* (Department of Health 2001). The following key areas of child protection practice were included in the first branch: responding to referrals (Gibbons et al. 1995a), undertaking investigations (Cleaver and Freeman 1995; Farmer and Owen 1995), involving parents in the initial stages of intervention and at child protection conferences (Thoburn et al. 1995), inter-professional collaboration (Birchall with Hallett 1995) and responding to sexual abuse allegations (Sharland et al. 1996). In the second group of studies, there was a focus on responding to referrals of children in need in England and Wales (Aldgate and Tunstill 1995; Tunstill and Aldgate 2000), child protection interventions within a context of family support (Brandon et al. 1999; Thoburn et al. 2000), and the views of parents involved in child protection care proceedings (Freeman and Hunt 1998). These studies largely explored the way in which practice was conducted. They emphasised the extent of poverty and ill-health in most of the families referred for services. By and large, however, these studies did not attempt to examine the outcome of particular interventions. Rather, they sought the views of parents and children about being on the receiving end of state intervention and were particularly influential in the shaping and development of safeguarding children policy in the UK in the late 1990s and early part of the twenty-first century.

There were also other studies reported during this period, most of them smaller, more independent studies, into child protection investigations (Wellbourne 2002), child protection assessments (Holland 2000), parental participation at conferences and reviews (Corby et al. 1996; Horwath and Calder 1998; Marsh and Crowe 1998; Bell 1999; Shemmings 1999, 2000; Spratt and Callan 2004), and ongoing management and treatment of sexual abuse cases (Roberts and Taylor 1993; Corby 1998; Farmer and Pollock 2003). More recently, there has been a growth in studies looking in detail at the activities of child protection supervisors and social workers (Ferguson 2017; Forrester 2017; Wilkins et al. 2018), as well as a concerted effort, financed by central government, to understand more about 'what works' (and for whom, how and in what circumstances). Thus, the research scene in the UK is very active, although it has to be stressed that much of even this more recent work is focused on the process of how things work (or do not work), rather than their effectiveness in terms of successful outcomes. So, while we now have a clearer picture of how the British child protection system operates, we still lack a strong body of evidence about which preventive measures and which intervention strategies work (and for whom, how and in what circumstances) and which do not.

In the USA, child protection research is on a much larger scale, not least in terms of resources. The National Center on Child Abuse and Neglect was set up in the 1970s specifically to promote research initiatives into child protection issues. The emphasis of much North American research is on evaluating outcomes, but, even so, there remains much concern about the lack of knowledge about effectiveness (Melton and Flood 1994; Leventhal 2003).

The rest of this chapter will now consider a range of research findings under three broad headings: (1) preventing child maltreatment; (2) assessment and decision-making; and (3) the provision of help and support, before some concluding comments, including on the thorny topic of outcomes.

Prevention

Patterns

Prevention of child abuse appeared more on the agenda in both Britain (Tunstill and Aldgate 2000) and the USA (Leventhal 2001) after the mid-1990s. The way in which British child care policy developed during this period was to shift the emphasis from abuse incidents onto the more ongoing welfare needs of families (from child protection to safeguarding). Study after study showed that many of the families referred to children's services had multiple problems and difficulties. The *Children Act Now* report (Department of Health 2001) pointed to the following facts:

- high numbers of lone-parent families (between one-third and one-half in eight of the studies);
- high levels of partner changes in families;
- high levels of poverty (98 per cent in one study);
- high numbers living in poor standard rented accommodation;
- high levels of mobility;
- high levels of social isolation;
- high levels of disorganisation in neighbourhoods;
- high levels of chronic health problems (physical and mental) and inability to carry out parental functions as a result;
- high levels of acute illness;
- high levels of problem substance misuse;
- high levels of domestic violence and relationship problems with partners.

The wider picture

Not all families experienced all these problems all the time, but, particularly in the case of families whose children were the subject of care proceedings as a result of abuse or neglect, such problems were seen as 'multiple, long-standing and entrenched' (Department of Health 2001: 30). However, as we have pointed out on a number of occasions, of course not everyone in the above circumstances abused their children; and, to complicate matters, a number of carers were (and are) harmful to children who do not show any of the above 'risk factors'. Nevertheless, data such as these were rightly used to stress the need for a broad range of policies, services and practices that would support, meet the needs of and engage with parents in the process of preventing child abuse and at the same time address other behaviours damaging to the well-being of children (for example, absence from education or involvement in crime). From this point of view, the whole thrust of central government policy outlined in the Green Paper *Every Child Matters* (Department of Health 2003) was preventive. The key instruments in this process were the 250 Sure Start programmes for children under 5, and the Children's Fund initiative which aimed to bring agencies together to develop initiatives to encourage social inclusion of 5- to 12-year-olds in their communities. Initial evaluation of the Children's Fund projects was rather mixed, suggesting a degree of uncertainty about achieving broad preventive goals (Department for Education and Skills 2006). Other developments taking place at that time included the setting up of multi-purpose children's centres, and improved nursery, day-care and after-school provision. The aim of all these initiatives was to prevent social exclusion in a broad sense.

By and large, child protection concerns were not seen as best tackled by broader anti-poverty programmes. Thus, they might have what could be seen as a narrower conception of prevention in mind. For instance, Gough (1993) considered what sorts of preventive programmes were being implemented to raise awareness of child abuse and the means of tackling it. He found that, in this sense, there were three types of preventive strategy: (1) those aimed at the whole population, such as community education programmes; (2) those aimed at certain communities, usually those afflicted by poverty and deprivation; and (3) those aimed at certain groups of families in which children were considered to be at risk.

The first level of prevention

With regard to the first type of preventive strategy, Gough (1993) found little evidence of abuse awareness campaigns in Britain. The main exceptions to this were educational programmes in schools aimed at equipping children to protect themselves against sexual abuse. Gillham (1991: 48–63) provided a useful overview of such programmes and research related to them. He questioned their effectiveness, which has generally not been rigorously tested. Most programmes of this kind tended to focus on extra-familial abuse, and one study demonstrated that they have only limited impact (Kelly et al. 1991). In the USA, Finkelhor et al. (1995) found from a study of 2,000 children that 'victimisation prevention instruction', as they termed it, did increase knowledge among children and the likelihood of disclosure.

Much changed in this respect, however, from the mid-1990s. Voluntary agencies in the UK played an increasingly important role in highlighting and raising awareness of child abuse with a view to prompting preventive measures. The National Society for the Prevention of Cruelty to Children (NSPCC) led campaigns about child deaths and the psychological abuse of children. More recently, the NSPCC's 'Let's Talk Pants' campaign aimed to help children stay safe from sexual abuse by teaching them that 'pants are private, always remember your body belongs to you, no means no, and talk about secrets that upset you'.

Agencies such as Barnardo's and the Children's Society played a significant role in highlighting challenges in relation to children's involvement in sex work. Childline, which was set up in the late 1980s to provide direct confidential help and support to children, has campaigned to keep all forms of abuse, but particularly sexual abuse, of children in the public eye. However, while these kinds of campaigns are often very visible, we have little research evidence about the impact they have had on policy, practice or public perception.

The second level of prevention

The second strategy identified by Gough (1996) involves lay and professional people operating in community centres to provide general help and support with parenting for any family in a particular geographical area.

Such provision is open to whole communities; however, some facilities take (or assist) only families referred with child care problems. The former tend to be more family-oriented, i.e. designed to provide social support to families (Pithouse and Holland 1999). The latter are more child-focused and work more specifically on parental capacities. A key initiative of the Labour government (1997–2010) was the roll-out of a national network of children's centres, designed to bring together (preventative) services for children and families while also signposting families with more serious needs to specialist services.

Although there has been little evaluation of the effectiveness of such centres, a study by Ghate et al. (2000) found that very few men participate in their activities. However, as responsibility for these centres was 'devolved' to local authorities alongside significant funding cuts, the Sutton Trust estimated that by 2017, more than one-third of children's centres had closed. Those that remained were increasingly targeted at 'high need' families and concentrated in deprived areas, thus shifting their focus from being open-access to targeted support (Smith et al. 2018).

The broader-based family and community support approach is well used in European countries such as Belgium, the Netherlands and Germany. Thyen et al.'s (1995) study of the Child Protection Center in Lübeck, Germany, which worked on a supportive and volunteer basis with families where child maltreatment was a concern, demonstrates how an indirect approach can work well.

The third level of prevention

The third preventive strategy involves selecting certain types of parents who are considered to be potentially abusive to their children, or who might be said to have complex or high needs, in order to provide extra support from community health and welfare services. This type of approach was not a mainstream one in Britain until recently, although it was used in evaluative action research (Browne and Saqi 1988). In the USA, however, it formed the basis of what were termed 'Healthy Start' programmes which have been adopted in most states. These programmes consist of trained family workers or community nurses carrying out regular visits over several years to families whose children are identified at birth as at risk of abuse. The results of these initiatives have been mixed (Chaffin 2004). Olds et al. (1997) carried out a 15-year follow-up of a nurse home visitation programme and found a correlation between this intervention and reduced anti-social behaviour on the part of the children involved in it. Duggan et al. (2004), however, in an evaluation of a similar type of programme in Hawaii (though employing trained family aides rather than health professionals), found that home visiting had little impact on the reduction of abusive behaviour in the short term. They attributed this largely to the fact that the focus of support offered was not sufficiently directed towards abuse prevention.

In the UK, there are two recent examples that fit this third level of intervention. First, the Troubled Families programme and, second, the Family Nurse Partnership. The Troubled Families programme was launched in April 2012 with the aim of 'turning around' the lives of 120,000 'troubled families' in England. The stated aim of the programme was to shift services from a reactive mode to a proactive mode, intervening with families to address problems before they escalated or became acute. Thus, the programme stands as an example of 'early help' (see below). So-called troubled families were initially identified if they met five of the following seven criteria (these were used to estimate the figure of 120,000 mentioned above):

- No parent in the family in work.
- The family live in poor-quality or over-crowded housing.
- No parent had any qualifications.
- The mother had mental health problems.
- At least one parent had a long-standing limiting illness, disability or infirmity.
- The family had a low income (defined as below 60 per cent of the median).
- The family could not afford a number of items of food or clothing.

Funding was provided to local authorities to work with these families and a set of outcome criteria defined. A particular way of working was not specified, and so different authorities set up their services in different ways. For example, some created dedicated Troubled Families teams, with new staff, while others sought to change the way current staff were working. Whichever approach was taken, the idea was that each family would have a dedicated worker, who would offer practical support to the family, using a persistent and challenging approach, while considering the family as a whole and agreeing a common purpose with them and other professionals. Various outcomes were sought from these interventions, with the key ones relating to employment (adults moving into work), reduced contact with the criminal justice system, improved general health, reduced family conflict and improved school attendance.

In 2016, the Department for Communities and Local Government published an evaluation of the Troubled Families programme based on data from more than 15,000 adults and nearly 14,000 children. Families and individuals who entered the Troubled Families programme were compared with a matched sample of comparison families who did not. These data were drawn from 56 local authorities. While the report acknowledges the difficulties and complexities of comparing between such large numbers of families and based on data from different local authorities that in some instances were not directly comparable, nevertheless they concluded that '[there is] no consistent evidence that the Troubled Families Programme has led to any systemic or significant improvements in families' outcomes [and] our analysis found no impact on these outcomes attributable to the programme' (Day et al. 2016: 54). Despite these findings, continued funding for the Troubled

Families programme has been extended until 2020 and some authorities have reported they still believe it to be useful (Bracey 2018).

The Family Nurse Partnership (FNP) is another preventative programme that has also been extensively evaluated, both in the UK and in the USA. Interestingly, the programme was found to be more effective in the USA than in the UK, even though it was implemented reasonably consistently between the countries. The FNP programme involves specially trained family nurses working with parents aged 24 and under. The nurses visit the parents regularly from early pregnancy until the child is aged 2. The tools and number of visits are prescribed, with the aim of helping young parents develop a good relationship with their child and to give the child the best start in life. Specific outcomes include: fewer childhood injuries, fewer subsequent pregnancies, greater intervals between births, increased maternal employment and improved school readiness. According to the National Institute for Clinical Excellence in England, 'FNP has one of the best evidence bases for preventative early childhood programmes' and 'has been shown to result in significant economic savings to the government and to society more generally' (2012: 1). However, other evaluations in the UK have not found the same level of impact. For example, Robling et al. looked at the FNP in 18 local authority areas and concluded that

> *adding FNP to the usually provided health and social care provided no additional short-term benefit to primary outcomes. [As a result] programme continuation is not justified on the basis of available evidence, but could be reconsidered should supportive longer-term evidence emerge.*
>
> (2016: 146)

These different findings highlight the importance of context and the need for ongoing evaluation. As noted by the Early Intervention Foundation (2015, unpaginated), in response to the findings of this evaluation,

> *These results are part of the normal and healthy development of an early intervention programme, and the willingness of the FNP National Unit to look at how to adapt the programme in the light of these findings is to be commended. We should also remember that US studies of FNP tracked families for decades. FNP is still a relatively new intervention in England and ongoing evaluation will be important.*

Assessment and decision-making

There are two key assessment points in child protection work: the first is at the point of referral when there is a need for short-term decision-making; the second is when there is a need to decide on the action required to ensure the longer-term future protection and well-being of the child.

As with many other aspects of child protection work in Britain, there have been considerable changes in thinking about assessment work as a result of the 'refocusing' shift – away from a more reactive approach based on 'child protection' to a more preventive and collaborative 'family support' approach, which began in the mid-1990s. Prior to this, the effect of public inquiries into circumstances where professional intervention was seen to have failed to provide adequate child protection was to emphasise the need for speedy and decisive intervention wherever a child was thought to be at risk of being abused. Following the publication of the Cleveland report (Butler-Sloss 1988), which recommended more strategic forms of intervention in relation to sexual abuse concerns, and research findings that pointed to children who were persistently in need being overlooked because of over-concern with abuse (Gibbons et al. 1995a), health and welfare professionals were required to carry out more broad-based assessments which took into consideration both needs and risks. This culminated in the introduction of the *Framework for the Assessment of Children in Need and Their Families*, which was implemented in April 2001 (Department of Health 2000). However, since the time of Peter Connelly's death in 2007 – or, more accurately, since the lifting of reporting restrictions about his death in 2008 – in practice, if not in policy, child protection work has shifted away from assessments of need and supporting families and become very much more concerned again with risk, the avoidance of harm attributable to parental behaviour and the increasing use of public care placements (Family Rights Group 2018). The importance of context has been highlighted in the work of Benbenishty et al. (2015), who examined decision-making by child protection professionals in four different countries (Israel, the Netherlands, Northern Ireland and Spain). Altogether, 828 practitioners from the four countries were presented with a vignette of alleged child maltreatment and asked to determine the level and nature of risk to the child and recommend an intervention. Significant differences were found between professionals from the different countries, related to the different attitudes of the professionals. In other words, the context in which decisions were taken made a difference to judgements about maltreatment and forward planning. Thus, understanding how and why practitioners make their decisions must involve an exploration and analysis of context as much as individual factors.

However, the lack of detailed research into short-term assessment and decision-making in child protection cases made it hard to know how it was actually carried out. The process by which child abuse or neglect concerns become child protection cases is complex and still shrouded in mystery to some degree. The procedures to be followed are described in the *Working Together* guidelines (Department of Health 1999), the most recent of which was produced in 2018. All child protection concerns should be reported to social services department personnel who decide whether a case is of sufficient seriousness or complexity to warrant an assessment. This assessment might be under Section 47 of the Children Act 1989, if there are concerns that the child has been or could be significantly harmed or it might be under Section 17 of the Children Act 1989 if the child is thought to have additional needs but not to be at risk of significant harm. Gibbons et al.'s (1995a) research demonstrated how this system was operating in terms of numbers in the 1990s. In their study of 1,888 child concern referrals, they found that about a quarter were filtered out at the point of referral, and a further 50 per cent following closer assessment of the circumstances. Only a quarter of all child protection referrals resulted in a child protection conference being held. Finally, 17 per cent of the total number originally referred remained as cases being worked with by health and welfare professionals (15 per cent needing a child protection plan). More recent work by Bilson and colleagues has given us an updated picture, finding that one in five of all children born in a single year in England (2009/10) were referred to social services before the age of five (Bilson and Martin 2017). Of the 150,000 children referred from this birth cohort, 25 per cent were formally investigated in relation to child maltreatment, and 10 per cent became subject of a child protection plan. The vast majority of these referrals led to 'no further action'.

What neither of these studies can tell us is why these referrals were made and subsequent decisions taken. Attention to decision-making at the early stages of intervention has been relatively limited. Dingwall et al. (1983) and Buckley (2003) carried out ethnographic studies of child protection practice which gave some insight into how 'referrals' become 'cases'. Dingwall demonstrated how societal expectations and normative values influenced decision-making and argued that social workers operated by three general criteria: (1) those of natural love (belief that parental care for children is instinctual and therefore normal); (2) cultural relativity (belief that standards of care need to be seen in a context of cultural norms); and (3) the rule of optimism (belief in the potential for parental care to improve with support). These factors led social workers and others to filter child care cases out of the system where the concerns were not clear-cut, rather than draw them in. Buckley (2003) studied 72 child abuse referrals made to a social work health board in Ireland over a six-month period in the mid-1990s, at the end of which there were 14 open cases receiving attention from social workers and related professionals. She showed how social workers were as keen to eliminate potential cases from the system as they were to accept them, a state of affairs resulting from their need to realistically manage the amount of work coming to them. A range of devices are used to achieve this, some socially supported, such as those found by Dingwall et al. and others not, such as inter-agency buck-passing and avoidance of violent men. Earlier studies pointed out that social workers carrying out initial assessment do take into account factors such as the seriousness of the abuse, the cooperativeness of the parents and histories of previous abuse, but often do not make this explicit (Corby and Mills 1986).

More recently, Whittaker (2018) conducted an ethnographic study of one local authority and one court assessment service and found that practitioners used a mixture of rational and intuitive processes. More inexperienced practitioners were said to rely more on emotionally-driven intuition, while as practitioners became more experienced, they developed more sophisticated rational abilities. At the other end of the scale, the Behavioural Insights Team examined referrals for 49,000 children from three local authorities and considered the impact of a range of factors on decision-making (Tupper et al. 2016). For example, what might influence whether further action is taken in response to a referral compared with no further action. While their findings cannot tell us about causality, they did identify some interesting correlations, including referrals received at the weekend are less likely to proceed to further action than referrals received during the working week; in two of the three authorities, referrals received from family members were less likely to proceed to further action than referrals from professionals; referrals made via email or in writing were less likely to proceed to further action than referrals sent via other methods (for example, via the telephone or face-to-face) and referrals about children living in deprived areas were more likely to proceed to further action than those received about children living in more affluent areas.

Conferences and other inter-professional meetings

Child protection conferences and meetings are important for early deci-sion-making in child protection work and several studies exist that have examined these processes. Most of the findings from these studies sup-port the notion that there are many factors militating against reaching knowledge-informed decisions. Hallett and Stevenson (1980) made much of inter-professional defensiveness and dysfunctional group processes as impediments to good early assessment and decision-making. Dingwall et al. (1983) came to the conclusion that most assessments made at case con-ferences were, for a variety of structural reasons, including inter-professional conflict, likely to result in an underestimation of the degree of risk to a child. Dale et al. (1986) considered that there were grave dangers of profession-als becoming polarised over case conference decisions and exacerbating already existing difficulties. Corby (1987), while finding little inter-professional disagreement over cases of serious abuse, reported a good deal of confu-sion in more marginal cases about why some children were registered and others were not. Decisions did not seem to be reached on the basis of a rational assessment of the degrees of risk (see also Campbell 1991). Farmer and Owen (1995), in their study of child protection conferences, showed how one of their key functions is that of meeting the needs of professionals to demonstrate their accountability.

It is notable that little use is made of risk assessment models in screen-ing child protection referrals in Britain. Greater use has been made of such tools in the USA. However, Murphy-Beaman (1994) has pointed to the dan-gers of using risk assessment schedules as part of initial assessments:

Accurate predictions of violence are considerably more difficult to make for individuals who have not yet clearly behaviorally demonstrated harmful acts, but only show an apparent proneness for such acts. This would be the case with many parents who are suspected of being at risk for child abuse.

(Murphy-Beaman 1994: 194)

None of the tools we have reviewed would fulfill all of [the criteria for use]. However...the findings of the review suggest that the application of such tools [could] have the potential to improve assessment practice and, in particular, analysis and subsequent decision-making.

(Barlow et al. 2012: 12)

Providing help and support

It is important to understand clearly what we mean by the use of terms such as 'help' and 'support' in child protection work. While it is no doubt true that professionals always aim to be helpful and supportive, the experience of families may be quite different. Similarly, help and support may include specific therapeutic interventions, but it might just as easily encompass different forms of social support, only fuzzily related to the direct problem of child maltreatment. In general terms, the notion of providing specific forms of therapeutic help is less culturally encouraged in the UK than in the USA. Thus, if we look for therapeutic inputs (and outcomes) in the UK we find that they are fewer and further between than is the case in the USA. In this section, we will consider the provision of help and support more generally, as well as giving some consideration as to the effectiveness of the help provided by therapists and others, taking into account objective data and the views of parents and children on the receiving end.

The key challenge currently facing child protection workers in the UK is how to shift the focus onto providing more family-based support while at the same time maintaining awareness of the needs of children to be protected. As we have seen, government-sponsored research in the 1990s was critical of social work practice because of its concentration on abuse incidents to the neglect of other work (Department of Health 1995, 2001). Government-sponsored research more recently is critical of approaches which focus 'too heavily' on risk to children and thus result in more children coming into public care than thought necessary (with high associated levels of both human and financial cost). Families with considerable needs for support because of factors such as ill-health, domestic violence, financial problems and low standards of hygiene, are, according to the research findings, unlikely to receive ongoing help or support outside of a risk-based framework. We also find a picture of interventions that, to a large degree, alienate parents because they result in conflict and disputes over care standards and child safety but offer little in the way of supportive and practical help.

Research by Brandon et al. (1999) found that in the majority of cases referred, provision of supportive help without resort to the more formal aspects of the child protection system met needs without increasing risks to children. Indeed, there was a positive response to the provision of practical and supportive help. Statham and Holtermann (2004) found a similar appreciation of supportive services in a study in North Wales – a problem, however, was the lack of consistent ongoing support for a group of parents on the edge of family breakdown. These findings were echoed in a study by Tunstill and Aldgate (2000) which found that the most requested form of help by parents was social work support, including direct casework and advocacy. They were more likely, however, to receive a specific service to bolster a particular need such as referral for day-care or to a family centre. When families are provided with intensive family support services, even in situations of high-risk and complex need, they tend to find it helpful and to value it, particularly when the worker–parent relationship is well-established and experienced positively (Mason 2012). However, increasing trends towards 'modernisation' and public sector reform, combined with ever-increasing workloads, have in many places eroded the availability of professionals to engage in meaningful, face-to-face work with families.

Early help and intervention

If it is the case that preventative services can do more to reduce the incidence of child maltreatment than reactive services (Munro 2011b), then the case for providing families with 'early help' (as opposed to 'late help' or 'too late help') would seem unarguable. Services provided under the umbrella heading 'early help' therefore differ from earlier attempts to provide universal services in that they are, in policy at least, explicitly targeted at families living in 'difficult circumstances' (Ofsted 2015: 4). Various government-sponsored reviews have argued for the benefits and effectiveness of early help services (Field 2010; Allen 2011; Tickell 2011). The Early Intervention Foundation, set up to disseminate evidence on the effectiveness of specific early help programmes, defines this approach as 'working with children and families to help them', based on 'identifying children and families that may be at risk of running into difficulties'. Hence, early help and intervention are not a specific set of programmes or techniques, rather it is about *timing* and *targeting*. One of the most commonly cited benefits of early help, alongside improving the lives of children and their parents, is the amount of money that can be saved as a result. For example, Fitzsimons and Teager (2018) estimate that in Northern Ireland, it costs £536 million per year to fund services for children and families who otherwise could have been helped via earlier intervention.

While the logic of this argument may seem unassailable, Featherstone et al. (2014) argue instead that the language of 'intervention' is morally questionable and that what families want (and need) is for support to be universally available at a community level, rather than targeted. Similarly, Bilson et al. (2017: 318) suggest that the current policy of early help, especially in England, has led to a widening of the child protection net, with workers increasingly taking an 'investigative turn': 'It is possible that [the policy of early help] is contributing to the widening of the child protective net as agencies increasingly frame children in need of help as families needing to be investigated.'

A shift towards relationship-based practice

During the past few years, and certainly since the previous edition of this book, the focus has increased on the importance of supportive systems and relationship-based practice, as opposed to one of processes and procedures. Approaches have also become more explicitly outcome-focused (although, as we note below, this does not mean a consensus has been reached about which outcomes truly matter and how best to measure them, let alone how best to achieve them for most people):

> *A dominant theme in the criticisms of current practice is the skew in priorities that has developed between the demands of the management and inspection processes and professionals' ability to exercise their professional judgment and act in the best interests of the child. This has led to an over-standardised system that cannot respond adequately to the varied range of children's needs.*
>
> (Munro 2010: 5)

As one social worker in the report put it 'timescales can end up replacing professional judgment' (Munro 2010: 12). Furthermore,

> *The ones who lose out most are the very children the system is intended to protect. The reforms have driven compliance with regulation and rules over time, with social workers increasingly operating within an over-standardised framework that makes it difficult for them to prioritise time with children, to get to know them, and understand their feelings, wishes, and worries.*
>
> (Munro 2010: 7)

This thread runs through other reports written around the same time. Not surprisingly, in their review of safeguarding and child protection, Barlow and Scott (2011: 24) also report that:

> *a recent overview of the evidence about effective interventions for complex families where there were concerns about (or evidence of) a child suffering significant harm, showed the importance of providing 'a dependable professional relationship' for parents and children, in particular with those families who conceal or minimise their difficulties.*

Munro also found that professionals were often reluctant to form negative assessments about a family. This is problematic because while 'thinking the best' of families is an admirable quality, if uncritically applied, this mindset can become sentimental; moving too far in the opposite direction, however, can leave the professional acerbic – even aggressive and threatening. Other writers and researchers (for example, Forrester et al. 2008a; Ferguson 2011) have attempted to articulate alternative child protection practices, aimed at avoiding the extremes of naïve sanguinity and harsh confrontation when working with families, by returning professionals to their relational base (see also Ruch et al. 2018).

Children and young people are clear that they welcome workers who show empathy, who are reliable and respectful, but who can also take action and be decisive (Munro 2011a: 41). This attention to what social workers actually do and how they do it is welcome because, as Ferguson (2011) notes, there is 'a curious absence from a great deal of social work and child protection literature, policy and discussions about practice of any considered attention to the core dynamics, experience and methods of doing the work'.

In addition, much publicity has been devoted to the unnecessary complexity of some of the software systems designed to support the assessment procedures in operation across the UK, notably the *Common Assessment Framework* and the *Framework for the Assessment of Children in Need and Their Families* (Department of Health 2000). As Munro put it in her report 'computers have a lot to offer, but their use so far has been problematic' (2011a: 157). Other research, using a combination of quantitative and anthropological methods, has also been extremely critical (Bell et al. 2007; Shaw et al. 2009; White et al. 2009).

To change the prevailing system, the Munro report argues that the 'climate of fear, blame and mistrust that seems to be endemic within the child protection system' (Munro 2011a: 12) needs to be removed. We include below in full the principles and innovations her review considers essential in order to achieve this:

- the family is the best place for bringing up children and young people, but the child protection system faces difficult judgements in balancing the right of a child to be with their birth family with their right for protection from abuse and neglect;
- the child protection system is a multi-professional, multi-agency operation requiring all who work with children, young people and families to consider the effectiveness of their work;
- the child protection system should be child-centred, recognising children and young people as individuals with rights, including their right to participation in major decisions about them, in line with their evolving capacities;
- the child protection system understands its dual mandate to support families and help them provide adequate care and to intervene authoritatively when children and young people need protection;
- the general public and all who work with children, young people, families and carers have a responsibility for protecting children and young people;

- helping families involves working *with* them and therefore the quality of the relationship between the family and professionals directly impacts on the effectiveness of help given;
- children's needs and circumstances are varied and so the child protection system requires sufficient flexibility, with space for professional judgment to meet that variety of need;
- the complexity of the world means that uncertainty and risk are features of child protection work and that risk management cannot eliminate harm, only reduce its occurrence;
- a learning and adaptive system is characterised by regular questioning of how the system (locally and nationally) is functioning and whether children are receiving effective help;
- good professional practice is driven by knowledge of the latest theory and research.

(Munro 2011b: 19–20)

Given these principles, it is reasonable to ask now, more than seven years later, what changes have there been? Are social workers and other child protection professionals now freed up from the restraints of overly-prescriptive policies and procedures, do they work in learning organisations, driven by the latest theory and research, with families and children at the heart of practice systems? The short answer, applicable to most, if not all, areas, must be 'no'. There is much anecdotal evidence to support this conclusion, but one can also point to significant pieces of research, such as the recent *Care Crisis Review* (Family Rights Group 2018). However, there is also a growing recognition that relationship-based work is at the heart of good practice, even if this is easier to agree in principle than to implement consistently in practice. Yet this degree of consensus in the field is nonetheless relatively unusual. For example, Sebba et al. (2017a) reviewed 45 evaluations of different social care and social work interventions in England, funded via the Department for Education's innovation programme. Although many of these programmes differed from one another in not inconsiderable ways, Sebba et al. concluded that shared improvements, such as reduced numbers of children entering care, were attributable at least in part to the maximisation of contact between workers and families, and the use of family-focused and strengths-based approaches (2017a: 6–7). Ruch et al. summarised this position as follows:

> *Whatever intentions you have, whichever techniques you use, the medium in which matters are conducted is the relationship you have with the other, and the other has with you. The quality and character of these relationships therefore matter, they matter a great deal. Not surprisingly, outcomes have been shown to vary depending on the technique used or intervention chosen. However, more critically, outcomes have also been found to vary depending on the skill and quality of the relationship created*

by the practitioner as she engages with her client, no matter what tech-
nique or method she is using.

(2018: 7)

The overall effectiveness of child protection and the 'What works' agenda

There are two equally important ways of measuring effectiveness in child
protection work - in relation to outcomes (however defined) and in relation
to the views and experiences of those on 'the receiving end' (i.e. families,
parents, carers, children and others). Supportive intervention is, by and
large, well received by families, but most studies over time have shown
that the services available are not sufficient to meet their needs (Aldgate
and Tunstill 1995; Statham and Holtermann 2004). Studies seeking the
views of parents about the support they receive from social workers and
other professionals indicated that reliability, consistency, genuineness
and respect for them as individuals were the qualities they valued (Thoburn
et al. 1995; Corby and Millar 1997; Statham and Holtermann 2004) and
there is no real reason to suspect this will ever change. However, how
effective this kind of supportive work is in preventing child maltreatment is
extremely hard to measure (Ghate 2001).

In relation to more specific approaches, cognitive therapy carried out
with children and non-abusing parents can be particularly beneficial
(Deblinger et al. 1999). Children seem to cope with openness and candour
about the abuse they have experienced, particularly in relation to sexual
abuse (Roberts and Taylor 1993; Berliner and Conte 1995). It is also clear
that the views of children about how they wish to be treated are of key
importance in achieving effective help. In general terms, the same messages hold true for adults. Helping to change the behaviour of abusive
parents (for example, in relation to physical abuse) has not been well
researched in terms of its effectiveness or in eliciting the views of those at
the receiving end. There is evidence to suggest that family centre provision
has been well received, provided it is pitched to the level of more general
support (Pithouse and Holland 1999). What remains the case is the lack
of involvement of men in the various programmes and with social work
more generally (Maxwell et al. 2012).

With regard to sexual abuse, there is clearly more emphasis on males,
but much of the work is focused on extra-familial abusers. Most of the interventions have been cognitive-behavioural with a view to reducing the risks
of re-offending. As has been seen, the rates of re-offending remain high,
which is not an argument against this type of provision – but it is clearly
important. However, it is also important to ensure that such treatment has
a degree of flexibility and incorporates intra-familial abuse concerns as well.
Bentovim et al.'s work (1988) has been an exception in this respect.

At the serious end of the spectrum, it is evidently the case that at least
some children will always need to be protected via separation from their
parents (although not necessarily from their entire family), with some

studies also showing that with carefully planned help and support, many children can remain safely and happily with their parents (or other familiar adults).

In the early 1990s, in the UK, success rates, as measured by re-abuse over two years, were around the 70 per cent mark (Farmer and Owen 1995; Thoburn et al. 1995). Cohn and Daro (1987) in the USA found that 42 per cent of parents in federally funded programmes had reduced potential for neglect. They suggested that supportive interventions combined with individual work were more effective than working solely with individual families. Brandon et al. (1999) found that goals of intervention with families where there were child protection concerns could be just as well achieved by voluntary measures as by compulsory ones. Troncoso (2017) has looked again more recently at the question of re-referral rates in the UK, based on a study of 498,867 children from 145 local authorities. This study found that 54.5 per cent of eligible children had been re-referred at least once within five years. This could imply 'prolonged periods of unmet needs and recurrent episodes of abuse, neglect and maltreatment' (2017: 7). One possible factor cited in relation to this high rate of re-referral was the caseload of individual social workers in different authorities. Where the average caseload was high (more than ten 'child in need' cases), the probability of a child being re-referred rose significantly. These data suggest that, whatever the theoretical effectiveness of social work involvement in reducing need and risk, in practice, the reality for many workers is that they simply do not have the capacity to provide an effective service.

Increasingly, policy-makers have become interested in the notion of 'What Works?' because such a question appears, at first sight, to offer budget-holders a more rational basis for the allocation of resources. But in addition to asking what works, we need also to ask who does it work for, in what circumstances, how and why - and does it offer value for money? And perhaps even more importantly, we also need to ask not only does it work, for who, when, how and why - but is it the right thing to do? Consequently, a plethora of studies, using systematic reviews, meta-analyses and experimental designs have started to emerge (see, for example, MacMillan et al. 2009; Montgomery et al. 2009; Barlow and Schrader McMillan 2010; MacMillan 2010) and, albeit to a far lesser degree in the UK, experimental designs has now emerged. Other reviews and reports summarise the findings about specific interventions or participant groups and attempt to translate them into practice (see, for example, Littell et al. 2005; Utting et al. 2007; Hicks and Stein 2010).

One of the most comprehensive UK reviews of interventions in child protection was conducted by Davies and Ward in 2011 and the findings are summarised in the second stage of the Munro report (2011b: 46–7). We provide the full summary as it contains a series of key messages:

> *In deciding how to help children and families change, research also provides valuable evidence. A recent overview of the research listed the following as examples of programmes that have been proven to be*

effective in addressing the needs of maltreated children and their families in evaluative studies:

Programmes for parents

- *Parents Under Pressure* (PUP) and *Relational Psychotherapy* are effective interventions for substance misusing parents.
- The *Post-Shelter Advocacy Programme* is an effective intervention for women who have been exposed to domestic violence.
- The *Enhanced Triple P – Positive Parenting Programme* is effective in addressing adults' own experiences of poor parenting and the psychological consequences of abuse.
- *Cognitive Behavioural Therapy* (CBT) can be effective in reducing emotionally abusive parenting, particularly when individual sessions are combined with group based sessions.

Programmes for parents and children

- *Infant–Parent Psychotherapy* is effective in improving maternal and child representations where there is a known history of abuse in the family.
- *Interaction Guidance* may be an effective intervention in improving parent/child relationships in infants with faltering growth, but further evaluation would be valuable.
- *Parent–Child Interaction Therapy* is a cognitive behavioural model that has been shown to be effective in reducing physical abuse.
- Abuse-focused cognitive behavioural therapy can be more effective in reducing physical abuse and parent–child conflict than traditional family therapy.

Programmes for children

- *Therapeutic Pre-school* is an effective intervention for children aged 1–24 months who have been maltreated or are at risk of maltreatment. It has a significant and lasting impact on parenting and child behaviour.
- *Peer-led Social Skills training* is an effective intervention for 3–5 year olds with a history of maltreatment who are socially withdrawn.
- *Multi-treatment Foster Care for Pre-schoolers* is an effective intervention for maltreated infants who require permanent placements. Trials in the USA have produced promising results.

More recently, the Department for Education funded via an 'innovation programme' a series of local authority initiatives and evaluations of them. In total, 98 projects were supported by the programme. Although there was enormous variation between the projects, the aim of the programme as a whole was to obtain thematic knowledge about 'what worked' by collating evidence and information from across the projects, rather than treating each project as an individual case study. Five thematic reports have been produced to date, focusing on (1) good social work systems and practice; (2) services for adolescents; (3) child sexual exploitation and mental health; (4) systemic conditions for change; and (5) informing better decisions through use of data. These reports together aim to highlight the key findings that help make a difference for the successful implementation of specific programmes to address child maltreatment in various different forms. It is worth reading all of these reports in full, but we provide here a summary of the key points from each one:

1. What have we learned about good social work systems and practice? (McNeish et al. 2017):

   - Interventions are more likely to be successful when all key parts of the system have a set of shared aims.
   - Most models of good practice combine empathy and collaboration with purpose and authority.
   - There is good evidence for the value of multi-disciplinary working, combining adult specialists alongside children's practitioners in integrated teams.
   - Good practice requires good supervision, including group case discussions, access to clinical expertise and senior experienced colleagues.
   - Highly skilled administrative support can increase the amount of time for practitioners to focus on direct work.

2. Adolescent service change and edge of care (Rees et al. 2017):

   - Longitudinal studies are required to explore if more preventative interventions delay entry into care for young people or prevent it entirely.
   - Multi-professional co-location should be encouraged in order to facilitate genuine multi-disciplinary decision-making.
   - Short-term residential placements can be effective in helping services engage with young people.

3. Child sexual exploitation and mental health (Luke et al: 2017):

   - Interventions should aim to support young people and their families before a point of crisis is reached.
   - Multi-disciplinary teams enable the sharing of resources, experiences and expertise.
   - Approaches that work with whole families, rather than just individuals, can increase the likelihood of young people remaining in stable placements.
   - Relationships are the key mechanisms for change.

4. Systemic conditions for innovation in children's social care (Sebba et al. 2017a):

   - Strong consistent leadership is required, including the communication of a clear vision.

- In order to identify improvements due to specific interventions, it is necessary to draw on comparative data (preferably using control groups) from other areas or from other families not involved with the intervention.

5. Informing better decisions through use of data in children's social care (Sebba et al. 2017b):

- There is a lack of a common framework of indicators for measuring outcomes in children's social care services (see below).
- An appropriate set of national performance indicators should be developed to enable more meaningful evaluation and better comparison between different areas.

Outcomes

One crucial issue we have not considered so far is that of outcomes. What outcomes should we be aiming for and who gets to decide on them?. Evaluating the effectiveness of different approaches in the field of child protection and child maltreatment is made more difficult because of a lack of consensus about the nature of good outcomes (La Valle et al. 2016). If one thinks about the range of individuals, families and circumstances that professionals in this field might be expected to work with, the enormity of the challenge becomes apparent – from assessing the risk to an unborn child to working with a young adult with care experience finding it hard to engage with university; from families recently arrived in the country having fled their war-torn home countries to children experiencing mental health problems due to the excessively high educational aspirations of their parents; from babies being harmed and abused in their own homes by a family member to groups of adolescents being sexually exploited in the community. It is not easy to discern what outcomes might apply to all of these people in all of these situations beyond quite general ones such as 'to be safe'. While this is a wholly admirable outcome in practice, it is hard to measure and even harder to evidence how different interventions and approaches might lead to different levels or types or experiences of safety.

Within this debate, there arises the question of who can or should define the outcomes being sought. It is important first and foremost to understand what outcomes families, parents and young people want from the services they receive. For example, what goals do they have for themselves, if any, and what sort of help and resources do they have or need in order to achieve them? In practice, there is a great deal of merit in this approach. Yet for the purpose of evaluation, it can be problematic. One such problem is how to compare between different goals. However, using standardised measures is also challenging, not least because families and individuals may not agree that they have the problems ascribed to them by their worker.

In addition to these debates about outcomes, Forrester (2017) reminds us of the need to consider a number of other questions, including: What is the quality of service being offered? Are we working with the right families and children? And how helpful do parents and children find the help being offered? Forrester sets these questions alongside the more outcome-focused question: What difference are we making in relation to specific problems (2017:152)?

Conclusion

In many respects, the findings from social work research in the UK are a sad reflection of developments in child welfare and social care services generally: often poorly coordinated, overly bureaucratic, and procedure-led impersonal provision that seems to have lost sight of its core purpose – the care, protection and welfare *of the child and their family*. Although it is plainly evident there is much good practice going on 'out there' and many thousands of committed professionals, they continue to be let down by the problems outlined above. Ultimately, of course, it is families and children who are being let down. Child protection professionals are repeatedly advised, as they go about their daily working lives, to consider the question 'would this be good enough for my child?'. Irrespective of the individual qualities of individual workers, it is difficult when surveying the entire eco-system of services as currently organised to answer with a whole-hearted 'yes'. Yet there are also some grounds for optimism. The Children Act 1989 has 'stood the test of time, as has its underpinning principles' (Family Rights Group 2018: 5). In addition, in a recent paper by Esposti et al (2019), they report that over a very long period in England and Wales, child mortality by homicide or assault reduced by 90% between 1858 and 2016 and the incidence of people guilty of child cruelty or neglect reduced by 83% between 1893 and 2016. These data suggest, if nothing else, that much as child maltreatment remains a significant problem, equally we have as a society made much progress too.

There are also exciting developments on the horizon and already established, including the What Works Centre for Children's Social Care and the Family Drug and Alcohol Court (aimed at helping families to solve their problems, rather than providing a forum for adversarial contests between local authorities, parents and children). And there is, not least, the continuing commitment of professionals to practise in more humane ways, to work 'with' families (rather than 'doing to them') and from increasing numbers of children and parents an equally impressive commitment to co-produce with professionals a more helpful, more supportive and more responsive set of services.

Recommended reading

Barlow, J. and Scott, J. (2011) *Safeguarding in the 21st Century: Where to Now?* Totnes: Research in Practice.

Featherstone, B., Gupta, A., Morris, K. and White, S. (2018) *Protection Children: A Social Model.* Bristol: Policy Press.

Featherstone, B., White, S. and Morris, K. (2014) *Re-Imagining Child Protection: Towards Humane Social Work with Families.* Bristol: Policy Press.

Ferguson, H. (2011) *Child Protection Practice.* Basingstoke: Palgrave Macmillan.

Forrester, D. (2017) Outcomes in children's services, *Journal of Children's Services*, 12(2–3): 144–57.

Ruch, G., Turney, D. and Ward, A. (2018) *Relationship-Based Social Work: Getting to the Heart of Practice*, 2nd edn. London: Jessica Kingsley Publications.

Global challenges and cultural perspectives on child abuse

Key points in this chapter

- Contemporary research focuses significantly upon Western child protection concerns and associated responses: in examining the world picture, domestic challenges can be understood in a wider context.
- While countries with less developed child protection systems might consider adopting aspects of Western child protection systems, transposing them without understanding the local context may not realise the aspiration of the improved welfare and protection of their children.
- Awareness of our personal and professional conceptualisations of what constitutes child abuse and exploitation is important, if we are not to become inadvertent bystanders.

Introduction

In this chapter, attention will be focused on some of the key issues currently being debated by researchers and practitioners in the field of child protection in areas of the world beyond Britain and the USA. Consideration will be given to child abuse and neglect; the impact of war, and the dislocation, separation, loss and the possibility of hope associated with seeking asylum; child trafficking, non-familial exploitation and the wider abuse and neglect of children from a worldwide perspective, focusing upon a comparative study of two countries: China and Russia.

Examining the world picture helps to put some of our domestic concerns in a broader context of understanding. The aim is not to comfort ourselves that, compared with children's circumstances in other parts of the world, our children's problems are relatively slight. Rather, a worldwide perspective can be used to examine some of our assumptions about children and their rights and needs, and even to question the complexity of the systems that we have devised for dealing with child protection concerns (Freeman 2000). In Britain, we are not immune from the world's problems; children of asylum seekers and our responses to them are immediate pressing problems within our own society

It is worth reflecting that in many parts of the world, intra-familial child abuse and neglect remain low on the lists of priorities – for example, street children and children in substandard institutions dominate concerns in parts of South America. In many of the world's poorer countries, child sexual exploitation (previously referred to as 'child prostitution'), child labour, infanticide and the impact of AIDS and war on children are also major concerns. In such countries, rife with poverty and deprivation, as was true of Britain in the late nineteenth century, abuse or neglect of children by their parents has relatively low priority. It should be noted that these concerns are not confined to these countries; concerns about institutional abuse, runaway and homeless children, remained important issues in Britain and other rich countries at the end of the 1990s as well. However, the scale of these problems was quite different compared to that which faces poorer countries.

While richer countries can and should play a role in helping poorer countries tackle problems of child mistreatment, it is important to avoid assuming that 'our' ways of dealing with problems are the solutions that other less-advanced, often financially disadvantaged countries should follow. It is important to start where people are at, if one is to gain a full understanding of child care needs in poorer countries. Clearly for many such countries, the priority in relation to meeting the needs of their disadvantaged children is poverty reduction rather than the development of child protection systems. Analyses of the institutionalisation of children in Eastern European countries such as Romania point to poverty as the reason for so many children living in orphanages, rather than the death of one or both parents as UNICEF and global partners would define 'orphans' (UNICEF 2018). Many children are placed in such institutions simply because families cannot afford to care for them (Stephenson 1997; Ismayilova et al. 2014). These findings can surely inform how we view difficulties in other countries as well. While much good work is being done by foreign agencies to improve standards and develop more preventive measures, ultimately poverty is the key determinant of so many events (Herczog 2017).

We could, of course, turn this thinking back on ourselves. While the proportions of children in state care in Britain are much lower than in some other poorer countries, nevertheless all the indices about accommodated children and children subject to child protection plans point to their coming largely from very poor and disadvantaged families (Bebbington and Miles 1989: Sidebotham et al. 2016). Thus, the problems of two different countries, such as the UK and Romania, though different in form and degree, actually have many similarities. In such circumstances, great care needs to be taken in assuming that our responses to child abuse are more sophisticated and therefore superior to those of poorer countries. On the other hand, we have, through our experiences in tackling child abuse, neglect and exploitation, developed knowledge and skills that can be used to support and provide critical analyses on developments coming out of poorer countries. Clearly, however, it is a delicate business and there are no quick-fix transferable solutions across countries and cultures.

Child abuse and neglect: a worldwide perspective

The impact of war on children

The deleterious effects of war on children are myriad in scale, range and impact. Save the Children, the international, non-governmental organisation which promotes the rights of children, providing relief and support for children in developing countries, assesses an estimated 357 million children worldwide live in conflict zones; this equates to one in six children – representing an increase from the early 1990s of more than 75 per cent, when it was estimated to be around 200 million children. Countries identified as the most dangerous in 2016 for children (the most recent year in which comprehensive data were available) were Syria, Afghanistan and Somalia. The panoply of dangers faced by children include the increase in numbers of UN-verified cases of children being killed and maimed, representing an increase of nearly 300 per cent since 2010 (Kirollos et al. 2018). Concomitantly, there was estimated to be a 15-fold increase in the incidents of denial of humanitarian access. Save the Children further posit that despite improvements in international legal and normative standards of child protection, increasingly brutally harmful and, in some instances, lethal tactics are resulting in children not only becoming 'collateral damage' within the context of war – caught in the crossfire – but indeed being systematically targeted; methods include using children as suicide bombers, the deliberate targeting of schools and hospitals, and the widespread use of weapons such as cluster munitions, barrel bombs and improvised explosive devices (IEDs), which maim and kill. Further, children face being actively 'recruited' by armed groups in conflicts, forced to fight and kill – sometimes, their own family members. The numbers of children in this environment are assessed to total 13,000 children in South Sudan alone, changing their lives, and in many instances, life-chances, forever (Kirollos et al. 2018). As well as torture and forced work, the violence to children can be in the form of rape – the gendered, instrumental, systematic deployment of sexual violence, illustrated infamously by the case of the 276 girls abducted and kidnapped from the Government Secondary School, Chibok, Nigeria, in April 2014. Nigeria is not an exception, as other countries where sexual violence was recently used as an instrument of war include Bosnia, Uganda and Rwanda (Oriola 2016).

Considering the range of abuses to which children are subjected within the arena of war, it is not surprising that these adverse childhood experiences result in trauma, the impacts of which can, without support, continue to reverberate into adolescence and beyond. Research widely confirms that war-exposed children show significantly higher rates of psychopathology (Patel et al. 2017). Halevi et al. (2016) found in a prospective, longitudinal study of 232 children, 148 of whom were exposed to repeated wartime trauma, and 84 controls over a 10-year period, that war-exposed children showed significantly higher rates of psychopathology, with 81 per cent exhibiting pathology at some stage in their childhood. Children in the middle, 5–8 year range showed more post-traumatic stress disorders (PTSD), attention-deficit/hyperactivity disorders (ADHD), and anxiety disorders. In late childhood (between 9–11 years), conduct/oppositional defiant disorders and ADHD were more apparent. They assessed children exposed to war had more comorbid psychopathologies, the number of which increased with age, increasing the prevalence of chronic pathology 24-fold. With not only the destruction of the 'safe haven' of a family home, but in many cases, home country; for many children who become orphans, the loss of a 'secure base', war means dislocation, displacement, separation, and traumatic loss. A UNICEF report in 2016 found 1 in 45 children in the world to be on the move, totalling 50 million boys and girls migrating across borders or experiencing forced displacement in their own countries (Garin et al. 2016). Whether alone or with their families, many children leave their home countries, seeking protection and safety – and for many, asylum.

Asylum seekers

Asylum-seeking children and their families are defined as people who have left their country of origin and who have formally applied for asylum in another country, and whose application has yet to be concluded (Morgan and Bartlett 2017). Research would suggest asylum-seeking children and their families, if they remain together, are disadvantaged in a number of ways, including by the UK's asylum laws, which provide closely monitored and restricted access to reduced state benefits, pending the often drawn-out business of securing asylum (Cemlyn and Briskman 2003; Cunningham and Cunningham 2007). More recently, under Section 9 of the 2004 Asylum Act, children of 'failed' asylum seekers have been denied access to Section 17 resources under the Children Act 1989 (those relating to children in need). This means that if their parents do not return to their country of origin within the specified time limits, these children may well have to be accommodated by local authorities. In other words, children will be separated from their parents solely on the grounds of destitution. Cunningham and Tomlinson (2005) argue that this legislation is putting the politics of immigration before child welfare and will result in children being put at greater risk.

Thus, it can be seen that what is happening to children worldwide in terms of abuse and neglect is a challenge for child protection professionals in Britain. Clearly, we have a vested, as well as a moral, interest in using knowledge and experience to support poorer countries in developing policies and practices that meet the needs of disadvantaged children within their own boundaries. We also need to develop much more sensitive and supportive policies for dealing with the way in which the consequences for children of poverty and social upheaval worldwide impact here.

Trafficking and exploitation

There are a range of imperatives for children's movement within and across countries and continents. In reflecting further upon issues that impact directly on British and child protection services worldwide, another key area of international concern is the complex subject of child trafficking. An offence in its own right, trafficking is the often-associated 'facilitator' to a range of exploitative situations and contexts, through which children are moved and harmed (UNICEF 2017). The UN *Protocol to Prevent, Suppress and Punish Trafficking Persons, Especially Women and Children, Supplementing the UN Convention against Transnational Organized Crime* (commonly known as one of the 'Palermo protocols') defines person trafficking as:

> *The recruitment, transportation, transfer, harbouring or receipt of persons, by means of threat or use of force or other forms of coercion . . . for the purpose of exploitation. Exploitation shall include, at a minimum, the exploitation of the prostitution of others . . . forced labour or service, slavery . . . or the removal of organs.*

By virtue of the illegal, clandestine nature of human trafficking, its scale nationally, as well as internationally, is difficult to accurately assess. There is consensus, however, that the varying assessments of the scale of the problem are highly likely to represent an underestimate of the true figure (National Crime Agency 2014). This Palermo protocol states that children cannot give informed consent to being trafficked, so for this reason, 'threat or use of force or other forms of coercion' do not need to be proven for an offence of trafficking to have been committed, or experienced by children; evidence of movement and exploitation is sufficient. Stop the Traffik, a campaign coalition which aims to bring an end to the trafficking of humans worldwide, assesses that 40.3 million men, women and children from around the world are victims of human trafficking (Stop the Traffik 2018). Research suggests traffickers, wherever they are located, can variously comprise individuals or small groups who recruit small numbers of children from their local areas; medium-sized groups who recruit, move and exploit children on a small scale; or highly organised and financially profitable large-scale criminal networks operating internationally, trafficking large numbers of victims for substantial financial gain (NSPCC 2018). Trafficking involves children being taken away from their families by means of grooming, coercion, threat or deception for the purposes of exploitation. It is often assumed that the sole purpose of trafficking is sexual – i.e. children being groomed, coerced or threatened into contact exploitation which can also be live-streamed, increasing the number of indecent images in circulation. However, trafficking is also associated with the under-identified and under-reported provision of cheap labour, domestic service, illegal adoption, forced marriage, participation in armed conflict, benefit fraud, forced work in nail parlours and cannabis factories and organised begging – all forms of exploitation (Pearce et al. 2009). The International Labour Organisation (ILO) in 2014, estimated 21 million people internationally to be trapped in modern-day slavery, including sexual exploitation and state-imposed forced labour, of which 4.5 million (22 per cent) were assessed to be victims of sexual exploitation. By gender, the ILO assessed 45 per cent of trafficking victims to be men and boys, and 55 per cent to be women and girls (ILO 2014).

Contrary to popular understanding, trafficking can be the movement of children for the purpose of exploitation not only across countries and continents, potentially one country after another and, in some cases, over the course of a lifetime, it can be perpetrated within and between towns – even between streets — within the same country. 'Internal trafficking', as this is sometimes referred to, may involve as victims citizen children from the same country – illustrated and illuminated perhaps most powerfully in Professor Alexis Jay's report, where 1,400, mostly female, British children, were internally trafficked and sexually exploited over a 16-year period in the town of Rotherham in the north of England (Jay 2014). Trafficking therefore does not need to be perpetrated across borders or continents, although as the primary focus of this chapter, it often is.

The National Referral Mechanism (NRM), established in 2009 in the UK, is a framework for identifying victims of human trafficking, which aims to ensure victims receive appropriate protection and support. The NRM additionally comprises the mechanism through which the National Crime Agency (NCA) collates data about victims from the UK and around the world who have been trafficked within or to the UK. The number of trafficked children known to have entered Britain between 1998 and 2003 was relatively small – 250 in all. In 2011, the predecessor of the National Crime Agency in the UK, the Serious Organised Crime Agency, issued a report, *Making Every Child Matter . . . Everywhere* (2011). It stated that between January and September 2011, 202 children were identified as trafficked into or within the UK. Sixty-seven of these children were from Africa, 63 from Asia and 50 from Eastern Europe; the rest were from other parts of the world or their origin was unknown. Most of the children from Africa (48) and Eastern Europe (32) were female, whereas most from Asia (43) were male. Most were aged between 14 and 16, although the report acknowledges that it is more difficult to identify younger children as having been trafficked and, therefore, they are possibly under-represented in the figures. Most of the trafficked children were found to be victims of multiple types of exploitation; however, all the sexually exploited children were female, while most male victims had been found to be criminally exploited in the context of forced cannabis cultivation. In sharp comparison with the UK child trafficking statistics in 2011, for the whole of 2017, the number of children referred to the NRM by professionals as possible victims had jumped to 2,118 – an increase of 66 per cent from 2016 alone, when 1,278 children were referred. This is assessed to be due in part to the increase in numbers of primarily UK children being referred, owing to concerns they were being criminally exploited (the category being 'labour' exploitation) within the 'county lines' context where, characteristically, citizen children are targeted, groomed and exploited into possessing and supplying drugs, holding drug-related money and firearms for gangs or groups. Of the 85 confirmed countries reflected in the 2017 referrals by nationality, UK children comprised the majority of referrals, with a record 676 being made, followed by children from Vietnam (210), Albania (157), and Sudan (130). Overall, the primary exploitation type across nationalities affecting girls was sexual exploitation, while boys were assessed as more vulnerable to labour exploitation. These, along with the 'unknown' exploitation category and that of domestic servitude, all reflected an increase in the numbers experienced on the previous year (NCA 2018). Because of a complex combination of the clandestine nature of trafficking, the associated presence of silence-inducing grooming and initially, often trust and belief in their traffickers, thus, a combination of coercion, intimidation, threat to child and/or their family, a child's sense of being indebted, or being silenced as a result of trauma associated with experiencing actual physical and sexual violence, it is generally assumed that the overall figure of 1,278 children trafficked in this period is a considerable under-estimate. Further, research and practice would indicate that children can experience a range of exploitation, such as sexual and criminal exploitation within, for instance, the gang context. It is therefore likely that the officially published categories of exploitation inadvertently mask a more complex picture of multiple exploitative harms experienced by children within the trafficking and exploitation contexts.

When children arrive in the country and are identified as being unaccompanied (by an adult), often as a result of fleeing war or persecution, they immediately become the responsibility of the relevant local authority and should be accommodated under Section 20 of the Children Act 1989. The challenges for local authorities charged with safeguarding unaccompanied, often asylum-seeking children (and indeed, citizen children) from trafficking, and equally, for law enforcement agencies accountable for identifying, investigating and disrupting trafficking perpetrators. are legion in complexity and scale. Unaccompanied children continue to 'go missing' once accommodated by local authorities, and in so doing can disappear from professional view. It is likely that a significant proportion of these children are not just 'going missing' from care, but are actually re-trafficked, for the purpose of exploitation. A positive conclusive grounds decision by the NRM of a child having been trafficked is insufficient alone to safeguard that child; what is needed is a robust and coordinated multi-agency decision-making and safeguarding response. While for a variety of reasons, children may be assessed as vulnerable to sexual abuse, exploitation, and trafficking, they do not become victims on their own, without being targeted by perpetrators. Therefore, identifying the perpetrators – as well as the victims – of trafficking requires a multi-agency assessment of risk of re-trafficking and co-owned safety planning with access to specialist foster care and support. This must be the required, effective multi-agency safeguarding response (ecpat 2017). Engaging the nuanced knowledge of children from carers comprises a critical element of effective safeguarding and intelligence sharing. Carers, along with the wider professional group, have a key role to play in the unremitting, concurrent focus upon possible perpetrators of often associated trafficking, abuse and exploitation of children, if children are to be effectively and meaningfully safeguarded (Parents Against Child Exploitation 2016). Without this unrelenting, multi-agency, dual focus, children will continue to be vulnerable to further harm by perpetrators. More broadly, when considering the larger-scale organised crime networks which can operate in the trafficking of children both internationally and nationally, what is needed is an accurate, analysed, global triangulated understanding of these criminal networks, of local and global 'hotspots' or areas of concentrated crime, in order to address them (College of Policing 2013). Disentangling elevated public and professional awareness leading to increased reporting of children identified as victims of human trafficking, from actual increased incidence, remains an ongoing challenge (Stop the Traffik 2018). Recently, however, the NCA, in its 2017 national strategic assessment, stated it was likely that the scale of modern slavery, including trafficking, in terms of victim and offender numbers, as well as incidence rates, is likely to increase year on year, with this trend assessed as likely to continue (NCA 2017).

International figures for child abuse and neglect

Measuring and comparing prevalence rates for child abuse and neglect between different countries and areas of the globe is incredibly difficult. Different legal jurisdictions have different conceptions and thresholds of what constitutes child abuse or neglect and these legal differences are

often at least partly rooted in very different cultural or historical conceptions of what the role of parents should be; different ideas about parenting and caregiving; differing definitions of when children become adults
and the status of children in society more generally. Compounding these
challenges is the fact that different countries use different ways of gathering and interpreting data on child abuse and neglect; even where official records do exist, these remain open to question and interpretation.
It also needs to be borne in mind that as awareness and education
regarding child abuse and neglect increase, there is typically an increase
in the *reporting* of such problems (Creighton 2004). As Creighton, and
more recently, Dubowitz (2017) note, most academic studies of prevalence (and incidence) rates have been conducted in Western countries,
again making international comparisons outside Western nations more
difficult.

Even within the four countries that make up the UK, it is not straightforward to compare statistics. This is because the four countries collect different information, for example, England, Scotland and Northern Ireland all
collect data on the duration of child protection plans but Wales does not
(Munro et al. 2011b).

Figures for non-Western countries are typically, but not always, harder to
obtain. A meta-analysis by Stoltenborgh et al. (2015) of 244 publications
reporting on the prevalence of child sexual abuse from a wide range of
countries, in which 551 prevalence rates were reported for the various
categories of maltreatment, found the overall approximation of child maltreatment for estimated prevalence rates for self-report studies (usually
assessing maltreatment ever, during childhood) to be:

- 127 per 1,000 for sexual abuse (76 per 1,000 among boys and 180
  per 1,000 among girls);
- 226 per 1,000 for physical abuse;
- 363 per 1,000 for emotional abuse;
- 163 per 1,000 for physical neglect;
- 184 per 1,000 for emotional neglect.

The majority of the prevalence rates were provided for samples which originated from North America, followed by Europe – studies being concentrated
in countries with a Western culture. In contrast, the smallest numbers of
prevalence rates were provided for samples originating from South America and
Africa, effectively leaving billions of people significantly under-represented
in child maltreatment research. The main focus of self-report studies within
all continents was sexual abuse; the least number of self-report studies
focused on emotional abuse and neglect (Stoltenborgh et al. 2015). Consistent, however, was the substantial gap between the combined prevalence
rates of informant studies, and studies which used self-report measures of
child abuse. Although this meta-analysis confirms the global nature of child
sexual abuse as a phenomenon, it also points to the significant influence
of methodology on estimates of prevalence.

Our knowledge of other forms of abuse and neglect are far less developed than for child sexual abuse.

Child abuse and neglect in two specific countries

In this section we consider several questions related to child abuse and neglect in China and Russia. Clearly, there has been a large degree of arbitrary choice in including these particular countries and this decision has been taken purely at the authors' discretion. The intention is simply to give the reader a flavour of how two different but globally significant countries have addressed the issue of child protection.

China

We have selected China because of its growing economic and social importance, and because of distinctive policies in operation there, such as the 'one-child' policy, enacted from 1979 until 2015 when the restriction was relaxed due to China's rapidly ageing society, as well as demographic considerations such as having the world's largest population.

Based on the results of the most recent 2010 national government census, China has around 1.3 billion inhabitants, of which 16.6 per cent, or 222 million, are aged 0–14 years (the census groups people in age bands of 0–14, 15–59, and 60 and over; therefore, figures for the number of children aged 0–17 are not available). Much of the research regarding child abuse in China focuses on the issue of child sexual abuse, with far less attention being given to physical or emotional abuse. Neglect of children appears to be related at least in part to the impact of China's 37-year 'one-child' policy. When discussing child abuse and neglect in China, one must bear in mind, despite impressive economic growth, figures over the past 30 years show that marked poverty remains a daily reality for a significant minority of families and children (around 10 per cent of the population were living in poverty in 2004; Ravallion and Chen 2007). Taking a broader perspective on poverty, Wu and Qi (2016) analysed multidimensional child poverty status in China between 1989 and 2009, using the China Health and Nutritional survey data. Using the Alkire-Foster method to measure poverty, Wu and Qi calculated a multidimensional poverty index, separating this into seven dimensions of deprivation: nutrition, water, sanitation, health, education, shelter and information. The four key findings of the study were: (1) that the multidimensional child poverty rate in China declined gradually where the sanitation facility was the dimension most severely deprived; (2) the poverty gap between richer and poorer provinces remained over the duration; (3) the urban/rural disparity decreased in each of the seven dimensions; and (4) the poorest of the poor were able to leave the state of ultra-poverty, and became moderately poor, with some becoming non-poor.

In considering child abuse and neglect in China, a study of nearly 500 university students found that around half reported having been hit, kicked or slapped in childhood. Around one-third reported being hit with an object such as a stick (Hester et al. 2009). While there have been no national assessments of child maltreatment in China, with only a few comprehensive provincial studies having taken place, a more recent systematic review of previous community-based research on child maltreatment in China by Fang et al. (2015) estimated the prevalence of abuse and neglect for under 18-year-olds as follows: 26.6 per cent of Chinese children had suffered physical abuse, 19.6 per cent emotional abuse, 8.7 per cent sexual abuse and 26 per cent neglect.

Other sources of research also confirm the widespread nature of child abuse in China, although, as with studies of child abuse and neglect in Britain, there are quite marked differences in estimated prevalence levels. For example, Chen et al. (2004) surveyed 3,261 students in Hubei, Henan, Hebai and Beijing and found that the prevalence of unwanted sexual experiences before the age of 16 was 16.7 per cent for females and 10.5 per cent for males. One per cent of all respondents reported child rape, 8.9 per cent of females reported other forms of contact sexual abuse, while 5 per cent of males reported the same. As with other countries, the results of having been sexually abused were found to be significantly negative. Both males and females in China reported more depression, suicidal thoughts and increased use of alcohol following child sexual abuse. Females were also more likely to engage in anorexic or bulimic behaviour while males were more likely to engage in violence (a fairly clear example of a split between internalising and externalising responses to traumatic experiences) (Cui and Liu 2018). Another study by Chen et al. (2007) examined Chinese parents' knowledge and attitudes towards child sexual abuse and found that while 95 per cent of respondents agreed that schools should seek to educate children about the prevention of child sexual abuse, around half (46.8 per cent) expressed a concern that such programmes would lead to children knowing 'too much' about sex.

In terms of physical abuse, as noted above, studies of this phenomenon are less prevalent than studies of child sexual abuse, particularly studies of physical child abuse on mainland China. However, in their 2015 meta-analysis of child physical abuse prevalence, Ji and Finkelhor sought to estimate the prevalence of child physical abuse in China (Ji and Finkelhor 2015). They compared Chinese prevalence with international and Asian estimates and specifically sought to ascertain whether some differences in sample characteristics and methodological factors including time prevalence, regional or definitional differences, might explain variations in Chinese rates. They based their meta-analysis on 47 studies sourced from Chinese and English-language peer-reviewed journals which involved general populations of students or residents reporting child physical abuse prior to the age of 18. They found the lifetime prevalence of child physical abuse in China to be estimated at 36.6 per cent (95 per cent CI: 30.4–42.7), which was significantly higher than either the international or the Asian estimate in the Stoltenborgh et al. (2013a) study. Chinese prevalence was estimated at 43.1 per cent (95 per cent CI: 36.6–52.5) for minor physical abuse and

26.6 per cent (95 per cent CI: 21.4–31.8) for severe physical abuse, and 7.8 per cent (95 per cent CI: 5.0–10.5) for very severe physical abuse. Ji and Finkelhor found the prevalence of any and minor child physical abuse in mainland China was significantly higher than that in non-mainland China. They concluded the mainland and non-mainland difference was significant, even controlling for definitional and methodological factors as well as sample characteristics. They suggest the need to develop educational programmes to promote non-violent parenting of children, particularly in mainland China.

The effects of China's long-standing 'one-child' policy on the care of children are undoubtedly complex. Introduced in 1978 by Deng Xiaoping's administration, this policy restricted married, urban couples to having only one child, while exempting rural couples, ethnic minorities and parents without any siblings themselves. Foreigners living in China were also exempt from the policy. Although the one-child policy ceased at the end of 2015, in combination with a long-standing historical and cultural preference in many parts of the country for sons over daughters (in common with some other parts of the world), this has led to a skewed male:female sex ratio, reflected in their being 18 women to 20 men (Abrahamson 2016) in rural *and* urban areas (thus demonstrating it is not simply the 'one-child' policy that gave rise to such figures). Many studies found that girls were more likely to be abandoned by their families and many of these children lived in state-run orphanages, from which many were subsequently adopted internationally or nationally. In the 1990s, Human Rights Watch found evidence that the care that children received in these institutions was characterised by cruelty, neglect and abuse (Human Rights Watch 1996). Various bodies, including the US State Department, the British Parliament and Amnesty International, also found that China's policies on family planning contributed to an increase in infanticide.

The law in China regarding child abuse and neglect is clear, despite the difficulties discussed above. Since 2007, the Law on the Protection of Minors has banned family violence against children. However, there is no national system in place for actively detecting child abuse or neglect and much of the work of protecting children is conducted by non-governmental institutions, although many of these work at the policy rather than the practical level. Where practical efforts are made, families can refuse entry to non-governmental officials visiting them following concerns regarding potential violence in the family home (*China View* 2007). Official statistics in China do indicate that increasing knowledge and understanding of child abuse and neglect have led to an increase in reporting. Between 2005 and 2009, there was an increase in reported incidents of child abuse of 35 per cent (*The China Post* 2010). However, even with this increase, in 2009, only 13,400 cases of child abuse were officially recorded out of the total child population of more than 200 million; this indicates an officially recognised prevalence of only 0.006 per cent, far too low a figure to be considered accurate.

In summary, following China passing laws banning family violence against children, official statistics do indicate that reported cases of child abuse are increasing. However, self-report studies seem to indicate that far more children in China than is officially recognised are being abused, physically and sexually. Reasonable national estimates of children emotionally abused in China are not available and neither are figures for neglect. As we have seen, cultural preferences for boys and China's only recently ended 'one-child' policy may have exacerbated particularly the neglect of girls as well as encouraged families to abandon girl babies, some of whom were abused in state-run orphanages (or at least, they were in the 1990s – more up-to-date information is not available). As argued by Dunne et al. (2008), research which simply finds that Chinese children are maltreated is of limited value; we know that children in all societies in which studies have been undertaken are maltreated and therefore there is no real doubt that children in all societies are maltreated. The crucial question for researchers is whether there are different patterns in different societies, different prevalence rates for different types of abuse or neglect and, ultimately, what the causes of these are and how they can be addressed. Research in China is at a very early stage as far as these questions go.

Russia

We have selected Russia because of its dual role as both a European and an Asian country. It is also a developed and rich country with 142.9 million inhabitants, according the most recent 2010 Russian population census, making it the ninth most populated country in the world. However, compared with other 'European' countries, Russia's national system of child protection remains relatively undeveloped. In considering the prevalence of child abuse and neglect in Russia, definitional challenges make accurately assessing prevalence difficult. While definitions relating to child abuse and neglect are relatively clear in the USA and the UK promoting consistency of identification and assessment of children and their families, Rudnicki (2013) reflects the 1996 Russian Family Code is less specific, referring, for example, to 'chronic alcoholism', 'physical or psychological violence' and 'the commission of unthinkable crimes against the life or health of a child'. Without clarification and delineation in statute, policy and regulation, these broad definitions are likely to hamper the consistent identification, reporting and assessment of child maltreatment in practice. Notwithstanding these definitional difficulties, the number of children coming to the attention of the child protection system in Russia in 2009 was 703,000 children, or 2.7 per cent of the population, either as orphans or as children 'lacking parental care'. This percentage represented a decline of 3.3 per cent from 2006. It did, however, exceed the 0.7 per cent decline in total children aged 0–14 during the same period. Rudnicki further reflects upon wide regional variations in children coming to the attention of the Russian child protection system, ranging from 1.54 per cent of the total youth population of the Northern Caucasus region, to 4.09 per cent in the Far East of Russia. Understanding the meaning of these figures is a challenge, unless they are measured against the same standard, which as we have identified, is not explicit in existing child maltreatment Russian definitions. Prevalence can also be subject to the cultural context in which assessments are made. For instance, while corporal punishment is discouraged in many Western countries, Russia is a country in which physical punishment is still considered acceptable, despite efforts in some quarters to promote more diverse approaches to child-rearing. These definitional considerations will doubtless impact the reporting of possible instances of child abuse and neglect, which in turn will influence recorded prevalence in the country.

Possibly one of the more serious and enduring criticisms of the child welfare system in Russia, is its widely reported over-utilisation of orphanages, or 'institutions'. Russian official figures for 2011 identified 700,000 Russian children as 'orphans'. Of these, nearly two-thirds were 'social orphans' – children with one or two parents, but with whom it was not safe for them to live. Of the total number of 'orphans', approximately 370,000 lived in orphanages (Gatti 2014), with 45.8 per cent of these children (0–17 years of age) in 2010 being placed in orphanages by virtue of their having disabilities (United Nation's Children Fund 2010, cited in Johnson et al. 2014). Figures for 2009 reported that 2.5 per cent of Russia's children were in state care – double the number of children in state care compared to other developed countries. In addition to these numbers, research indicates that another category of 'orphans' – a further nearly 5 million Russian children – could be classified as 'street children', children assessed as either living on the streets with groups of similarly homeless children, or moving between the addresses of family and friends, with limited parental supervision (Kravchuk 2009). The environment of orphanages in Russia is frequently reported as diminishing for the children placed there, including accounts of children being severely environmentally, physically, emotionally and cognitively neglected and deprived, centrally, of a secure base – lacking social-emotional opportunities and the development of adult–child relationships with someone to love, empathise with them and establishing the conditions in which they can flourish into adulthood (Caprin et al. 2017). The transition into adulthood does not necessarily bring relief, and for many is fraught, with reports of nearly 40 per cent of children who have previously lived in an orphanage struggling with substance misuse (Gatti 2014). The Russian Children's Welfare Society estimates that approximately half the children who leave orphanages become involved in criminal activity, and one in ten children commit suicide (Boberiene and Yazykova 2014). According to the US Library of Congress, and a range of more recent research, children in Russia are increasingly becoming involved in criminal activity, and drug and alcohol misuse among the child population is increasing (Stickley et al. 2013). Russia also has a distinct problem with child trafficking and, according to Russian police statistics, between 30,000 and 60,000 women, most of whom are under the age of 18, are taken out of Russia each year and some may become sexually exploited (Roudik 2011).

The Russian health service estimates that 2.7 per cent (4 million) of Russia's 144 million teenagers are drug users and of those 1 million are

'hardened addicts'. Rates of drug use among teenagers in Russia are estimated to be 2.5 times as high as among Russian adults and 40 per cent
of Russian schoolchildren are thought to regularly consume alcohol. Various studies have considered why the rates of substance and alcohol misuse are so high in the Russian child population. Koposov et al. (2005)
found that dysfunctional family dynamics and parenting factors are significantly related to alcohol abuse, even after controlling for psychopathology
in the child.

The Russian Constitution of 1993 provides protection for children and
their rights and there are also well-developed child protection policies,
including the Civic Code, the Federal Law on State Support of Youth and
Children's Organisations and the Federal Law on Social Assistance. This
differentiates Russia from countries such as China, which have only more
recently introduced such laws. What this demonstrates clearly, if such
demonstration were required, is that laws themselves, even good laws,
are only a necessary condition of protecting children but they are far from
sufficient.

Conclusion

In this chapter, we have sought to demonstrate the difficulty in believing
that countries with less-developed systems of child protection need only to
copy the example of countries such as the UK or the USA in order to
improve the welfare of their child populations. As we saw perhaps most
clearly with China, local policies, such as the 'one-child' policy, had profound effects on children's welfare that are not translatable into any Western experience. We have also seen, as with Russia, that some countries
face difficulties and challenges with issues such as substance misuse
that would most likely overwhelm any Western system of child protection,
as currently arranged. For both these reasons, and others, the 'simple'
imposition of Western systems of child protection in non-Western countries would be deeply problematic.

We have also sought to show that global difficulties can have significant
local effects. The issue of the global trafficking of children both within and
from their country of origin to a country in which they are exploited in various ways is a clear example of this. The oft-found situation in which trafficked children are not seen primarily as children in need of protection, but
children with the potential either to be engaged in criminal behaviour or to
have links with criminals, continues to pose a conceptual and practical
challenge to child protection professionals in the West. A comparison can
be drawn between this and the state's response, in the UK, to children, as
we have seen, who are groomed into involvement with gang activity; in
both cases, the issue is seen primarily as one of the criminalisation of
children – as 'child prostitutes' once were – rather than viewing children
involved with gangs or those subjected to trafficking as primarily being
vulnerable and in need of protection.

Recommended reading

Serious Organised Crime Agency (2011) *Making Every Child Matter . . . Everywhere*. London: Child Exploitation and Online Protection Centre.

Tiurukanova, E. and the Institute for Urban Economics (2006) *Human Trafficking in the Russian Federation: Inventory and Analysis of the Current Situation and Responses*. Moscow: UNICEF/ILO/CIDA.

West, A. (2005) *Hubs and Centres for Developing Children's Participation and Child Protection in China*. Beijing: Save the Children.

10 Reflections for future child protection work

Key points in this chapter

- The differences between a bureaucratic and a social/relational model of child protection are considerable and require a great deal of thought, planning and support for practitioners.
- Relationship-based practice appears to be a core component when moving away from procedure-based models and methods of practice in child protection services.

Introduction

In this final chapter we offer an overview of how we see the challenges and possibilities within current child protection in the UK.

It is nearly 10 years since Professor Eileen Munro wrote her review of child protection in the UK and it is still having some effects on professional practice as well as on the management of the entire system of safeguarding and protection. Because professional *practice* has been neglected over the past 30 years in favour of systems, procedures, auditing and inspection, we unapologetically decided to focus on it, as we believe it is equally important.

In what follows we contrast a 'pre-Munro world' – the way practice has largely been operating in most areas of the UK – with a 'post-Munro world': a vision of child protection practice to which many professionals aspire. We aim no criticism at child protection professionals who, we believe, do an astonishing job under the most emotionally draining circumstances, and with workloads that virtually everyone now accepts are far too high. Furthermore, they are constantly being inspected, evaluated and reorganised, and may face dismissal, de-registration and even public humiliation if they are thought to have made a mistake. This is the case across all professions involved in child protection but the most vilified and blamed are social workers. We are concerned that the system itself, most often devised after knee-jerk reactions to high-profile cases, is the primary cause of the defensive practice we are about to describe. The Munro report, on the other hand, was written more 'in the cold light of day' and we believe it offers a unique opportunity to steer our gigantic procedural supertanker onto a different course before it hits the rocks (many believe it already has).

'Pre-Munro' child protection practice

The past 40 years of legislation and procedures in the UK arguably have produced practice with children and families based upon the sharing of concerns within written agreements aimed primarily at *protecting the practitioner* if things subsequently go wrong. So terrified are practitioners – as well as supervisors and managers – that the system is often geared to 'covering their backs' rather than helping families to keep their child safe. Managers often see the role of the worker as spelling out what a parent needs to do to protect the child and to minimise concerns; then it is the worker's job to monitor adherence and progress, often using the formal system of announced and unannounced visits, alongside child protection conferences and reviews. It is as if the worker is saying (for example): 'Your problems are concerned with substance misuse and mental ill-health and this results in poor parenting which, in turn, leads to your child being abused/neglected. What you have to do to get us out of your life is get off drugs, get help with your illness and improve your parenting. What we will do is get you on a parenting skills course, suggest a counsellor and insist that you attend and successfully complete a drugs rehabilitation programme. We will put this in writing and then monitor progress by visiting you.' Various veiled – and sometimes more transparent – threats are made about what will happen if the written 'agreement' is not implemented, most typically focusing on the removal of the child. This approach is basically saying, 'Get a grip, take responsibility, sort yourself out, because we are now keeping an eye on things and if they don't improve, you could lose your child/ren.'

This form of professional practice can be implemented 'firmly but fairly'; on the other hand, practitioners can become acerbic, even threatening and punitive. The latter kind of practice is well documented in Donald Forrester's innovative research in which he asked actors to role-play a parent alleged to be experiencing drug problems and in which case there are child protection concerns. It exposed bureaucratic and sometimes insensitive practice, including confrontational, aggressive and disrespectful communication (Forrester et al. 2008a; 2008b). Ironically, the social work profession has spent the past 20 odd years stressing such laudable values as 'user empowerment', 'respect for persons', 'valuing the individual', etc., yet there is reason to believe that professional practice in reality may operate at some distance from these values: 'research has also demonstrated that working relationships, professional relationships and attitudes toward service recipients are very often negative, judgmental, confrontational and aggressive' (Turnell 2009: 18).

One of us (DS) routinely asks practitioners on training events to 'write three words or very short phrases to describe how you think and feel about parents who abuse or neglect their children'. (As a focus for the exercise, they have watched the first 2 minutes of the BBC documentary, *Protecting Our Children* – episode 1 of 3 – first screened in 2012.) We have now asked 387 practitioners, during 15 different training and dissemination events, and the results are illuminating. (They were all experienced workers, most of whom were qualified.) Their words and phrases subdivide into three groups as follows (the relative proportions are shown in brackets):

Sympathetic (40 per cent), examples of which are:
- *Sad, frustrated, powerless, in need of help, unsupported, neglected, sympathy, stressed, personal problems, unloved, overwhelmed, desperate, curious about why, they need help and I want to help them*

Ambiguous (30 per cent), examples of which are:
- *Disturbed, frustration, pity, emotional deficit, damaged, uncontrolled, difficult to empathise with, angry, senseless, unrealistic, overwhelmed, shocked, disturbed, harsh/insensitive*

Judgemental (30 per cent), examples of which are:
- *Appalling, horrifying, dislike, disgusting, uneducated, need to be held accountable, irresponsible, cruel, evil, selfish, wicked, no capacity, no knowledge, inadequate, weak, 'What's wrong with you?', dangerous, put away and not let out, don't deserve children, should be locked up, thick*

Given that some of the *ambiguous* responses will contain negative and judgemental thoughts and feelings as well, it could be that nearly half of these, child protection practitioners harbour hostile, condemnatory and disapproving feelings about family members.

This, we argue, is likely to be a direct consequence of the present 'pre-Munro' system. It indicates a likelihood that there is inadequate supervision of the kind that is needed to address the highly emotional nature of child protection work. It is well known that professionals involved in child protection encounter on a daily basis some of the most distressing accusations and traumatic events.

Working in child protection services has considerable emotional costs. Without effective supervision and other forms of support to address and help regulate such emotion, practice suffers, as does the practitioner, who may progressively become anaesthetised and inured to the families they work with. Decision-making is also compromised when 'hot cognitions' – thinking imbued with powerful emotion – are involved. Research with surgeons, for example, has shown that they forget basic medical procedures when faced with an aggressive actor/patient during the latter stages of their training; but what is more astonishing is that they are rarely aware that they have done so (Kneebone 2009). When asked how they rated their performance on these basic medical procedures – for example, administering a drip, monitoring blood pressure and oxygen, sterilising the site for the insertion of a needle – they often self-reported competent performance, but when they watched themselves on film they were astounded to learn that they often did not perform *any of these procedures* if the actor/patient increased their aggressive behaviour.

There is a flip-side to the defensive practice described above which veers towards the other end of the spectrum. In this version of child protection practice, an excessive level of positive reinforcement and praise is shown to the parent or caregiver. An interchange might sound something like this:

Practitioner: How have things been for you?
Parent: Really good! I've decided to stop drinking after what you said.
Practitioner: Wow, I'm really pleased. I can tell too, as often when I've visited it seemed as though you *had* been drinking. Well done!

This visit may be written up in the record as indicative of 'positive change'. At one level, it could be dismissed as naïve practice, perhaps undertaken by an inexperienced or newly qualified worker. But we have seen and heard experienced practitioners working in this way. They explain their approach as that of trying to encourage the parent and as a way of developing trust with them. Our view is that such an approach relies too heavily on what the parent tells the worker is happening (as the worker is usually not in a position to verify the parent's assertions). We are not suggesting that practitioners should end up interrogating parents, or looking in dustbins for evidence of empty spirit bottles. Our argument is that a different kind of interaction is needed when exploring parents' intentions about changing lifestyles and addictions. Using the principles of *motivational interviewing* (Miller and Rollnick 2002), the aim is to try and explore what it was like for the parent when they *did* drink – 'What problems did it solve?', 'How did it achieve that?', 'How did drinking help matters?' The practitioner then encourages the parent to try and speak at some length. She or he listens, attends fully and empathises and then, from time to time, sensitively challenges the parent, perhaps by adding – at the appropriate time – something along the lines of, 'Hearing you talk like this is helping me get a better idea of how drinking helps you. So, perhaps what I'm now going to say might surprise you: I guess I don't really understand how or why you would have given up, because it strikes me that the same problems are still there for you.' The practitioner will need to gently and sensitively challenge a parent who responds by saying something such as, 'Well, I've decided to do it for my children', or 'I've just realised how stupid it all is and how stupid I've been', or 'I've decided to turn my life around'. Such interchanges build trust. But real, lasting trust cannot be developed and sustained by over-praising unverified assertions, no more than it impresses a student if a teacher tells them they have done really well when they know they have not!

Another problem with the pre-Munro paradigm is that, not surprisingly, with the emphasis on 'caseload throughput' (i.e. closing cases as quickly as possible in order to open new ones), practitioners routinely *ask parents about their parenting* rather than *seeing them do it*; yet, as we saw earlier, the evidence indicates that simply asking parents about their parenting capacity is partial and often highly unreliable. In 2010, in a systematic review of working with 'reluctant or resistant' families, submitted to the UK's Centre for Excellence in Outcomes for Children and Families (C4EO), the team pointed out that:

> There is an urgent need to review practitioners' tendency to rely almost exclusively on interviewing parents about their parenting skills to assess capacity. Practitioners need information from a variety of sources using a variety of techniques, of which observation is an important one. Attention needs to be paid to observing parent–child dynamics in order to assess caregivers actually parenting, as distinct from describing how they parent. The use of standardised questionnaires and assessments may be useful here as well. Convincing evidence exists to show that simulating sensitive parenting is very difficult to sustain. But to accomplish such a shift in emphasis it is likely that specific observational techniques ... will need to be acquired by practitioners.
>
> (Fauth et al. 2010: 8–9)

An additional problem with current practice is that it can lead to a lack of focus on the child. The practitioners we have spoken to regularly tell us that they sometimes have to interpret the requirement to 'see the child' as literally that: 'I *saw* the child in the garden/in the classroom . . . but I didn't actually speak to them.' Others who *do* talk to the child tell us that it often amounts to little more than saying to the child 'How are you?', 'How's it going?', 'How are you doing?', 'How did your football match/contact visit/maths test, etc. go last week?' But such an approach rarely reveals much about the child's world or their wishes and feelings; it is yet another procedurally based approach. Again, we are not reporting these points in order to criticise practitioners: quite the reverse, we are doing so in order that the context of their work is appreciated more fully.

Talking to practitioners we also get the distinct impression that some families are subjected to an indefinite amount of assessment, conducted by a range of professionals. On the other hand, the professionals themselves often tell us that, at the end of such investigative processes, they may well end up feeling none the wiser about the precise mechanisms leading to alleged abuse or neglect. Other than composing a written agreement spelling out in detail what is wrong and what needs to change, they remain at a loss to know how to help.

Finally, despite child protection practice being procedurally based and somewhat adversarially driven, high court judges, magistrates and local authority lawyers will all give examples of social workers and others losing cases because their evidence is not well argued (see Dickens 1993), critically analysed or guided by research and theory (this point also applies to recording and report-writing generally). We are not suggesting that there were halcyon days when these problems were not present; consequently, we agree again with Andrew Turnell when he contends that:

> Anyone who was influenced by the open, almost-anything-goes field that was social work in the 1970s, knows that while there was extraordinarily good child protection work happening at that time, there was also correspondingly appalling work happening at the other end of the practice continuum.

(Turnell 2009: 4)

'Post-Munro' child protection practice: a realistic vision for the future

The subtitle of this book is 'An evidence base for confident practice'. We conclude, therefore, with some indications of what such practice needs to comprise. The problem is that 'a significant difficulty is that little attention is given within the literature of social work and the broader helping professions about how to build constructive helping relationships when the professional also has a strong coercive role' (Turnell 2009: 18). We return to this at the end of this section but now we identify two gaps in practice identified by Munro and numerous serious case reviews over the years.

First, the Munro report, as well as many serious case reviews, comment unfavourably on the level of analysis in child protection reports and records. Visits, observations and conversations are described but they lack either a theoretical or an evidence base; even an argument threaded with sound 'practice wisdom' is often missing. Considerable amounts of information are gathered but it is often not assessed; it is not evaluated in the sense of different viewpoints being weighed and balanced against each other. Part of the problem seems to lie in a legacy over the years whereby social work in particular has developed a mistrust of 'expertise' and as a consequence has become ambivalent, disinterested and even hostile towards theory and research.

Second, and as we saw above, also missing is a 'child's-eye' view within assessments. The entire second report in the Munro review is entitled *The Child's Journey*; indeed, the *Framework for the Assessment of Children in Need and Their Families* (Department of Health 2000) was subtitled *The*

Child's World. So when, in the Victoria Climbié report, Lord Laming used the phrase 'the child is "missing" from the files', he was among many to express concerns about the invisibility of *children* in child protection practice (Laming 2003). We now offer two examples which we believe offer a 'child's-eye view'. They include theoretical insights and draw heavily on research; notice how, in each, they do not read as 'academic assignments' as they are written in plain language and without references.

Example A

Specific indications of how Ricky experiences chronic lack of parental affection emerge when he is asked to complete a story involving mild conflict between two PlayPeople. In the story, one of them says, 'You've lost my keys'; the other replies, 'I haven't lost your keys.' The child is asked, 'Can you show and tell me what happens next?' Even quite *insecure* children will develop an *organised* way of finishing the story – there might be an argument, more shouting and the keys may never be found, but eventually there emerges an organised way to complete the task. Not so for Ricky; he is more than 'merely' insecure; his story ends very abruptly. The two PlayPeople immediately 'die' which Ricky confirms by saying, 'They can't get up.' This sudden and unexpected catastrophising after only mild disagreement is potentially of some concern and I will follow this up during the next visit.

Example B

During this visit Ms X gave Y his dinner. She made him a chocolate spread sandwich and gave him some crisps. She gave him a bottle of fizzy drink. Ms X did not encourage Y to sit at the table and consequently Y dropped part of his sandwich onto the floor, and he started to play with it and move it across the carpet.

Ms X became annoyed by this. She told him to stop it but he continued. Ms X then bent down near to him and said in an aggressive tone, 'Give that to me.' When Y did not respond she repeated herself and pointed to the crust on the floor. Y did not respond and Ms X removed the crust herself and said to Y in an aggressive tone 'You're *disgusting*.'

I was surprised by this reaction. Ms X had given Y his sandwich while he was sat on the floor. The likelihood of a 2-year-old managing this without spilling some on the carpet is remote. Yet Ms X was unable to reflect on this and instead directed her anger and verbal abuse at Y.

'Disgusting' was used to describe Y on other occasions. The most worrying incident occurred when Ms X removed Y's nappy after I had informed her that it was leaking, as there were wet patches on his trousers. Ms X then dressed Y in the wet trousers, but did not put another nappy on him. While myself and Ms X were talking in the living room, Y went into the hallway, removed his trousers and 'pooed' onto the carpet. When Ms X discovered this she shouted, 'Urgh – that is *disgusting.*'

This was an understandable response, but she then took hold of Y and held him against her with one arm (facing the poo). She said to him in an aggressive tone 'I am *not* happy. *What* do you say?' When he did not respond she repeated this in a louder tone of voice. Y remained still, with his eyes looking downwards. She then repeatedly said to him in an increasingly loud and aggressive tone, '*What* is it, tell me *what* it is?' When Y did not respond she removed her arm from around him and said, 'You're disgusting – *you're a disgusting child.*' Y then walked into the living room and repeated this, saying 'Disgusting child.' Ms X removed the faeces, but did not wipe his bottom.

The need for good relationship skills

The need for good communication skills is also highlighted in the Munro review. There is growing evidence that the experience of 'epistemic trust' increases mentalising capacity (McCrory et al. 2017a), thereby reducing some of the mis-synchronised interactions observed in maltreating parents (see, for example, Shemmings et al. 2012). Fonagy and Allison (2014) capture the notion of *epistemic trust* as an experience whereby an individual feels – and believes – that an actual or potentially 'significant other' is trying to understand them, fathom them – 'get them'. The need, however, is for practitioners with counselling skills, but not skilled counsellors. Practitioners need to be able to discuss gaps in parenting in an open, honest and respectful way, but it is also important to be able to help a parent with the daily minute-to-minute interactions with their child. There is an impressive and developing body of research claiming that showing short, filmed vignettes of parent–child interactions, selected by the practitioner to highlight synchronised parenting and/or the child demonstrating their need and affection for the parent, re-sensitises caregivers with low capacity for mentalisation in ways which more didactic approaches are unable to achieve. Video-based interaction for positive parenting (VIPP; Juffer et al. 2008) is a manualised intervention run over four to six one-hour sessions but many of the principles can be used by busy child protection professionals, sometimes to help assessment accuracy. The following examples show how this can be achieved.

The following practice refers to a 60-minute contact session between a young father and his 3-month-old daughter.

Despite being advised by the regular contact supervisor that the father's interaction with his baby was very positive, a few exploratory questions with him . . . *'Why do you think she did that?'*, *'Does she know how you feel about it?'*, *'So is she being sick on your shoulder on purpose?'* . . . identified that he had persecutory beliefs about his daughter and was placing negative attributions on age-appropriate behaviour: 'She's never been sick on her mum, and she knows I'm wearing a new shirt today!'

Teams are beginning to advise contact supervisors to assess low mentalisation and emotional attunement. This guidance includes prompts like:

> *For infants, does the parent help interpret the child's presumed internal state using exaggerated expressions and tones? Does the parent show a willingness to understand their child? Is the parent able to speculate on their child's feeling states?*

By maintaining curiosity about what psychological traffic is passing between the parent and child, the worker needs to be prepared to ask specific, clarifying questions to the parent rather than maintaining a strictly passive, observational stance. We also try to assess low mentalisation and parental sensitivity by filming approximately 10–15 minutes of parent–child interaction, during a *guided parenting task*, and later inviting the parent to undertake a 'speaking for the child' exercise. This involves playing the footage back to the parent and stopping at frequent intervals to ask questions such as: *'So, what might your child be thinking/feeling here?'*, *'What do you think that cry means?'*, *'Is she upset about something in particular, do you think?'*, *'What's in her mind here?'*

A *guided parenting task* (see Juffer et al. 2008) comprises five stages, two of which involve short but mildly challenging components for the child: the 'don't touch' task and the 'clear up' task. Even though they have to learn not to touch grandma's precious vase, or the electric plug, most children usually struggle when asked not to touch a particular toy. Equally, when they are having fun with a new toy, they want to carry on doing so. The purpose of the guided parenting task is to observe parenting directly, rather than simply ask the parent to comment on their 'parenting capacity' because of the obvious problems of relying heavily on the accuracy of their account. The practitioner also gently asks questions aimed at exploring the parent's mentalising capacity, in the way we saw above, such as, 'What do you think is in his mind when he's getting cross?', 'Why do you think he doesn't want to clear up?'

A guided parenting task

1. Child plays on their own with an unfamiliar toy (2 mins) – parent is asked to 'be with' their child but not to join in.
2. Parent joins in (5 mins) – parent has to tell the child they can't touch one of the toys yet.
3. Parent and child read a story, or make lunch, or sing a song – the aim is for them to do it together.
4. Parent and child play with paints, felt-tips, crayons, etc. (5 mins).
5. Parent and child clear up.

Problems with the current method of predicting child abuse and neglect: inadvertently 'looking in the wrong place for the wrong things'

The promise of predicting abuse and neglect is an attractive one because of its preventive potential. It also has financial appeal because it raises the possibility of targeting limited resources at those areas where they are most needed and most likely to be effective. Predicting child abuse by observing caregiver responses to new-born babies and collecting other available data are still an important part of child protection policy and practice in the USA. There is a relatively long history of prediction studies, starting with Kempe and Kempe (1978), who claimed a 79 per cent successful prediction rate for their method of assessment. Montgomery (1982) criticised this study for its use of a very broad definition of child abuse. Judged by the rate of substantiated child abuse, Kempe's predictions were 16 per cent accurate rather than 79 per cent. In addition, even if the 79 per cent rate were accepted, this still means that 21 per cent were wrongly 'diagnosed'.

In Britain, where prediction of this kind is not part of mainstream policy, studies that have been conducted have not come up with encouraging results. Lealman et al. (1983), using maternity records to predict the likelihood of child abuse, forecast that 500 from a sample of 2,802 children were likely to be abused. In fact, 28 children were registered for abuse, 17 of whom were predicted. The remaining 483 were wrongly predicted (false negatives).

Browne and Saqi (1988) reported on a series of predictive studies carried out with health professionals in the Surrey area. Using a 12-item checklist at birth and after one month on a population of 14,238 families, they identified 949 of these as high risk. However, the results after two years were disappointing in terms of successful prediction – only 1 in 17 (6 per cent) had abused their children (using child protection conferences as an indicator).

A more recent study by Peters and Barlow (2003) conducted a systematic review of 220 published articles on the subject of predicted maltreatment around the time of birth. They found eight studies that met the criteria of using evaluated standard instruments (of which the Browne and Saqi study was one). However, none of these studies had a positive prediction value of over 50 per cent and only two approximated acceptable standards of accuracy.

In summary, therefore, the various studies considered here demonstrate that it is extremely difficult to predict future abuse. In this process, at least 20 per cent of any sample will be wrongly predicted of being likely to abuse or neglect their children, but if one uses a narrower definition of child abuse, such as that of child protection registration, then the rate of false prediction can rise to a much higher level. Therefore, it can be concluded that these studies fail in their aims of accurately targeting those families who might benefit from specialist help. In addition, the programmes to which parents are assigned following these predictions have not been proven to be consistently effective (Duggan et al. 2004).

It is not only the effectiveness of the predictive approach that is in question. There are also major questions about the ethics of this kind of activity. Is it, for instance, ethical to make an assessment of potential parental care without informing parents of what is happening? Is it ethical not to inform parents about concerns resulting from this assessment? The only justification for this lack of openness can be that secrecy is essential in order to ensure the well-being of the child. There is, however, no evidence that lack of candour is likely to improve the safety of the child. Working with parents on the basis of shared concerns may be a more effective strategy in achieving this goal.

The problem with current prediction methods is that they are circumscribed by what Munro (2008) called the 'base rate problem'. We illustrate this by referring to what Marian Brandon calls the toxic trio of 'risk factors': mental ill-health, substance misuse and domestic violence. As experienced practitioners will quickly attest, one or more of these factors is usually present when maltreatment occurs; but retrospective associations and correlations are very different from prospective prediction: many people have a 'mental health' problem or diagnosis – estimates are that around 25 per cent of us will have a 'mental health' problem during our lifetimes and, at any given point in time, the figure is about 1 in 6 of us – but this doesn't mean we are a risk to children.

But there is another problem with existing 'risk factors': even if they contained more predictive validity, almost all of them are extremely difficult to change. How does a parent easily and quickly become drug- or alcohol-free? How do they overcome mental illness? We can help families with rehousing and even help alleviate chronic levels of poverty, but experienced practitioners know only too well that, while such social actions are essential in terms of social justice and equality, they may have little effect in the short, or even medium, term on child abuse and neglect.

So, the problem may be expressed as follows: *some* parents who are mentally ill later go on to abuse their own children . . . *but others do not; some* drug users abuse their own children . . . *yet others do not.* In fact, the majority – around 75 per cent (see Crittenden 2008) – of parents who were abused themselves as children do *not* go on to abuse their own children. Another way of appreciating this is by considering that, although the majority of children who are sexually abused are girls, by far the greater proportion of sexual abusers are men, so clearly other mechanisms operate in the pathway from caregiver characteristics to child maltreatment.

What we feel is needed is a re-focusing of attention by child protection professionals. It requires an interest, awareness and genuine curiosity about the mental states of parents and children, as well as the environment they are living in. This shift in perspective stresses not what happened to people in the past, but the sense they make of it all *now*; the emphasis is not about people's current lifestyles in isolation but how they understand and make sense of close relationships. Above all, the key to understanding maltreatment crystallises when practitioners develop curiosity and skill in understanding whether parents can accurately make sense of their child's mental states.

In the relatively short space of time between this and the last edition in 2012 we have witnessed many changes in the field of child abuse and maltreatment. No doubt there will be more over the next 5–10 years. It would be a brave person who would try to predict what they will be; we are not planning to be so foolhardy as we conclude this edition.

What we feel more comfortable in predicting is that there will continue to be thousands of child protection professionals who will carry on working diligently to support families and protect children. In some parts of the world – and unfortunately here in the UK – when they get it wrong or make a mistake, they will more than likely continue to be pilloried in some parts of the media. In other areas in the world, particularly Scandinavian countries, there appears to be more of a shared responsibility between the state, local communities and individual practitioners.

Our wish for the immediate future is for an easing in some of the dichotomous, binary arguments that, regrettably, we hear again and again. Arguably, we need 'both-and' inclusive logic to permeate discussions in child protection practice, not 'either-or' positioning. We shouldn't be arguing about whether there should be 'support services to families and social action to strengthen communities' *or* 'money for child protective services': surely we must do both, albeit by paying attention to relative priorities in times of austerity? Similarly, we need to resist the urge to talk about 'family preservation policies at all costs' versus 'putting the needs of the child first': again, we have to maintain both policies in parallel. Maintaining 'both-and' indeterminate logic isn't easy because we sometimes opt for the seductive cadence of the promise of a 'right answer'. The reality, as we've seen throughout this book, is that 'child abuse' is too complex a phenomenon to permit simple, linear explanations or solutions.

So, can we end with a realistic message of hope and optimism for practitioners reading this edition? We believe we can, and it centres on their potential to be 'one caring adult' for children and families (see https:// joshshipp.com/). We need to give professionals the time and emotional space to do more of this kind of work; away from computers, meetings, forms, 'tick boxes' and the rest of the paraphernalia of bureaucratic, defensive practice.

Recommended reading

Allen, J. G., Fonagy, P. and Bateman, A. W. (2008) *Mentalising in Clinical Practice*. Arlington, VA: APP.

Cohen, J. A., Mannarino, A. P. and Deblinger, E. (2006) *Treating Trauma and Traumatic Grief in Children and Adolescents*. New York: Guilford Press.

Forrester, D., Kershaw, S., Moss, H. and Hughes, L. (2008) Communication skills in child protection: how do social workers talk to parents?, *Child and Family Social Work,* 13(1): 41–51.

Juffer, F., Bakermans-Kranenburg, M. J. and van IJzendoorn, M. H. (eds) (2008) *Promoting Positive Parenting: An Attachment-based Intervention*. New York: Lawrence Erlbaum/Taylor & Francis.

Miller, W. R. and Rollnick, S. (2002) *Motivational Interviewing: Preparing People to Change*, 2nd edn. New York: Guilford Press.

Shemmings, D. and Shemmings, Y. (2011) *Understanding Disorganised Attachment: Theory and Practice for Working with Children and Adults*. London: Jessica Kingsley Publications.

Notes

Introduction

1. It is important to distinguish between the terms 'prevalence' and 'incidence'. Prevalence studies measure how many people in a given sample have experienced a particular phenomenon at least once over a particular period of time. Incidence studies measure the number of occurrences of a particular phenomenon in a given sample of people over a particular period of time. Thus, if a sample of 100 people were asked if they had been sexually abused at least once before the age of 15, and 20 said that they had, the prevalence rate of abuse of such children would be 20 per cent. If these 100 people were asked how often they had been sexually abused before the age of 15, the answer would probably be higher. They might report abuse on 60 occasions. The incidence rate of abuse would then be 60 per 100 people over the first 15 years of their lives. La Fontaine (1990: Chapter 2) gives a fuller, very useful account of these and other issues relating to prevalence and incidence studies.

Chapter 1 Childhood, child abuse and history

1. This day a quarter past two in the afternoone my Mary fell asleepe in the Lord, her soule past into that rest where the body of Jesus, and the soules of the saints are, shee was: 8 yeares and 45 dayes old when shee dyed, my soule had aboundant cause to blesse god for her, who was our first fruites, and those god would have offered to him, and this I freely resigned up to him[,] it was a pretious child, a bundle of myrrhe, a bundle of sweetnes, shee was a child of ten thousand, full of wisedome, woman-like gravity, knowledge, sweet expressions of god, apt in her learning, tender hearted and loving, an obedient child [to us.] it was free from [the rudenesse of] litle children, it was to us as a boxe of sweet ointment, which now its broken smells more deliciously than it did before, Lord I rejoyce I had such a present for thee, it was patient in the sicknesse, thankefull to admiracion; it lived desired and dyed lamented, thy memory is and wille bee sweete unto mee. [26 May 1650]
(Macfarlane 1970: 203)

2. It should be noted that Boswell (1990) has been criticised by some historians for being over-optimistic about the fate of abandoned children (see Tilly et al. 1992).
3. This statement, while demonstrating public concern about child sexual abuse, also shows that there was probably a hierarchy of concerns. No mention is made of female children and those of non-citizen status.
4. La Fontaine (1990: 210), drawing on anthropological work, lends some support to such a view with regard to sexual abuse.

Chapter 2 A history of child abuse and neglect: 1870 to the present day

1. It would be wrong, however, to suggest that there was no relevant legislation at all. The Poor Law Amendment Act 1868 made wilful neglect by a parent of a child under 14 that threatened or resulted in serious injury an offence. The weakness of this law was that only Poor Law officials were empowered to bring cases of this kind to court and they very rarely did so. The Offences Against the Person Act 1861 could also be used to prosecute parents for assaults on their children, but no particular agency was mandated to report or seek out such abuse.

2. This may seem counter-intuitive but despite the Great Depression of the 1930s, from a long-enough perspective, as taken by Stevenson and Cook, by the late 1930s and early 1940s, the economy in the UK had grown substantially when compared with the 1910s. Unemployment dropped substantially from 1930 onwards and gross domestic product (GDP) was also higher in 1940 than it had been between 1900 and 1920 (see Hicks and Allen 1999).

3. The major legislative change of this period was the 1933 Children and Young Persons Act, which followed in the tradition of previous legislation by extending the range of prosecutable offences against children. It also blurred distinctions between neglected children and young offenders by such measures as the creation of approved schools for all who came into these two categories (before this, they had attended separate institutions). By 1946, when the Curtis Committee reported, this type of thinking was well established: 'According to the evidence of the Home Office, it is often an accident whether a child is before the court for an offence or as a neglected child, and it is accordingly appropriate that the same methods of treatment be equally available' (Curtis 1946: 14, para. 38).

4. See Housden (1955: 209–10), which provides an extract of an NSPCC inspector's discovery of and response to a child sexual abuse case. The case is undated, but as the children involved were committed to industrial schools, it must have been before the implementation of the Children and Young Persons Act 1933. The case involved a 12-year-old girl, her 11-year-old sister and her 9-year-old brother. Their mother was dead and they were living with their father and a 46-year-old male lodger. It was revealed that the two girls slept in the same bed as the lodger. The inspector's records described the children as being dirty and neglected. A medical examination was arranged by the inspector. 'This proved that the girl aged 12 had been interfered with.' The father and the lodger were prosecuted. The father, a first-time offender, received a light sentence and the lodger 18 months' hard labour. The children, as mentioned above, were committed to industrial schools. The tenor of the report is very factual. The response to this case comes across as insensitive by our standards but unequivocally child-protective.

5. See Cleveland inquiry report (Butler-Sloss 1988: 64, para. 4.80). A 10-year-old girl and her two siblings were examined with their mother's consent by Dr Higgs in the hospital. Their father removed them. They were subsequently brought into police custody under place of safety orders and examined by a police surgeon, Dr Beeby. His diagnosis conflicted with that of Dr Higgs, who re-examined the children. The following day they were re-examined by Dr Irvine, another police surgeon. The report adds that the children 'were later examined by three more doctors'.

6. La Fontaine (1998: 9–12) provided some useful information about the different terminologies used to describe this form of abuse. The term 'satanic' implies that children are being abused as part of devil-worship ceremonies. It is a term used usually by extreme fundamentalists who are committed to wiping out such forms of worship. The term 'satanist' is used by those who attribute the abuse to devil worship, but do not believe in the devil; their concerns are more objectively focused on child abuse issues. 'Ritual abuse' is a term used to describe any form of child abuse taking place within a ritual setting (including devil worship).

7. The accounts of the interviews with the child, MT, are a very good example of this (see Clyde 1992: paras 11.91–6). MT is described in the report as an 'articulate and able child who rarely showed visible signs of emotion. She appeared very grown up' (para. 11.91). In the following paragraphs she gives a clear and detailed account of taking part in a ritual where children were hurt 'in the wrong places'.

Chapter 4 Defining child abuse

1. The Female Circumcision Act was replaced in 2004 by the Female Genital Mutilation Act 2003. This was introduced to prevent children being taken abroad to have circumcision operations, thus

blocking a loophole in the previous legislation. The Department of Education and Skills estimated that there were 7,000 girls under the age of 16 who were at risk of female genital mutilation (Department for Education and Skills 2004b).

2. The social worker in this case made assumptions about Caribbean culture that placed heavy expectations on Tyra's grandmother to provide care and protection for her. West Indian grandmothers were stereotypically considered to be the linch-pins of the family. As far as Beatrice Henry was concerned, nothing could have been further from the truth. She had experienced the death of her husband and the severe mistreatment of her grandson. She was a lone parent dealing with the problems of her own three children, was inadequately housed and had multiple debts. As events proved, she was completely unable to protect Tyra.

3. At her second referral to hospital, Victoria presented with scald marks on her head and face which, according to her great-aunt, resulted from her pouring boiling water on herself to stop the itching being caused by scabies. This was a highly implausible account, and the fact that there had been several hours between the incident happening and Victoria being brought to hospital should have aroused much more suspicion than it actually did. Instead, there was a good deal of circumspection on all parts and eventually after a short stay in hospital Victoria was discharged home without any agreed follow-up arrangements (see Laming 2003: Chapter 10, North Middlesex Hospital).

4. The following two vignettes, with consequences in parentheses, are taken from Giovannoni and Becerra's (1979: 116) study and give a flavour of the general approach used: 'The parents regularly left their child alone outside the house during the day until almost dark (neighbours have spotted the child wandering five blocks from home).' 'The parents banged the child against the wall while shaking him by the shoulders (the child suffered a concussion)' (Giovannoni and Becerra 1979: 113).

5. Political factors may also play a part in this relative lack of attention to neglect. Wolock and Horowitz (1984) argued that neglect of children is far more common than physical abuse in the USA, but receives far less attention. This 'neglect of neglect', as they termed it, results from the fact that closer inspection of many children's lives would reveal the extent to which poverty contributes to neglect and this would create political embarrassment for governments.

6. The Jasmine Beckford report (Brent 1985: 69–74) provides useful detailed material on the failure-to-thrive syndrome. At birth, Jasmine weighed 2.58kg. By four months, she had reached an average weight for a child of her age and, therefore, would have been expected to maintain this average growth throughout her early childhood. After 10 months, Jasmine had slipped back and her weight was well below the average. It was below the third centile (that is, Jasmine was among the 3 per cent most poorly developed of all children). At age 15 months Jasmine weighed 8.33kg, even further down in the third centile. At 20 months, when she experienced her first serious injury, she was still well down in the third centile. At the age of 27 months, after she had been in foster care for seven months, Jasmine had grown considerably and weighed 11.48kg (on the 25th centile). At this point she was returned to her mother and step-father. She was not weighed again until her death 27 months later. She weighed 10.43kg.

Chapter 5 Perpetrators of child abuse

1. The views put forward on this subject in the Cleveland report are of interest. The term 'collusive mother' is not explicitly used. However, the implications are clear from the following extract:

> Again quoting Professor Sir Martin Roth, 'In many cases mothers play a role in the genesis of the sexual abuse of their daughters. They may be too physically ill or inadequate in personality to provide proper care and protection for their children. In other cases mothers elect the eldest or one of the oldest daughters to the role of "child mother". The girl in her early teens or even earlier is expected to take the responsibility for the caring of the younger children whose mothering role

is allowed to slide into a sexual relationship with the father. This is tolerated with little or no protest. I refer to lack of protest of [*sic*] the part of the mother for a variety of reasons and the mother may in such cases deny what is happening. She conceals the truth from herself as well as others; the relationship continues and when the situation is brought to light it may be insisted by the mother that it had been unknown to her.'

(Butler-Sloss 1988: 8, para. 29)

2. A survey conducted in 2000/1 found that Pakistani/Bangladeshi and black families were three to four times more dependent on social security benefits than other families in Britain. Only 36 per cent of Pakistani/Bangladeshi families were able to obtain income from earnings compared with 60 per cent for the rest of the population (Department for Work and Pensions 2002).
3. This is another difficult issue to untangle. Abel et al. (1987) report that 44 per cent of convicted sex offenders had committed sexual crimes within and outside the family.
4. Christine Mason, the mother of Doreen Aston, was known to have been depressed in October 1985, seven months before Doreen was born. In January 1985, her 10-week-old son, Karl, had died in suspicious circumstances. Nine months later Christine was said to be continuing 'to give cause for concern as she was carrying the ashes of her dead child around with her' (Lambeth, Lewisham and Southwark 1989: 9, para. 15). There is no further reference to depression or grief reaction in the report. Beatrice Henry, Tyra Henry's grandmother, on whom great reliance was placed by Lambeth Social Services Department for her protection, had experienced the death of her husband and the maiming and loss of her grandson in 1982 (she had also previously suffered the death of her own son). The inquiry report points out that there was 'not a line in the contemporary records and not a line in the evidence given to us which recognises that by the time of Tyra's birth, Beatrice Henry was struggling with private grief along with the difficulties of her daily life' (Lambeth 1987: 112). The inquiry panel recommended that social workers receive training in this area and be directed to devote attention to such matters in future. The Koseda inquiry noted that the cohabitation of Heidi Koseda's mother, Rosemary, with Nicholas Price 'seems to have been the start of a marked deterioration in her mental state and way of life, which culminated in serious mental illness after the discovery of Heidi's body early in 1985' (Hillingdon 1986: para. 1.1).

Bibliography

Abrahamson, P. (2016) End of an era? China's one-child policy and its unintended consequences, *Asian Social Work and Policy Review*, 10(3): 326–38.

Adler, N. and Schutz, J. (1995) Sibling incest offenders, *Child Abuse & Neglect*, 19: 811–19.

Aldgate, J. and Tunstill, J. (1995) *Making Sense of Section 17: Implementing Services for Children in Need Within the 1989 Children Act*. London: HMSO.

Allen, A. and Morton, A. (1961) *This Is Your Child: The Story of the NSPCC*. London: Routledge & Kegan Paul.

Allen, G. (2011) *Early Intervention: The Next Steps*. London: HM Government.

Allen, J. G., Fonagy, P. and Bateman, A. W. (2008) *Mentalising in Clinical Practice*. Arlington, VA: APP.

Allen, R. E. and Oliver, J. M. (1982) The effects of child maltreatment on language development, *Child Abuse & Neglect*, 6(3): 299–305.

Allen, S. and Daly, K. (2007) The effects of father involvement: an updated research summary of the evidence. Available at: https://www.fira.ca/cms/documents/29/Effects_of_Father_Involvement.pdf (accessed June 2018).

Angelides, S. (2004) Feminism, child sexual abuse, and the erasure of child sexuality, *GLQ: A Journal of Lesbian and Gay Studies*, 10(2): 141–77.

Angelou, M. (1983) *I Know Why the Caged Bird Sings*. London: Virago.

Archard, D. (2004) *Children: Rights and Childhood*, 2nd edn. London: Routledge.

Ariès, P. (1962) *Centuries of Childhood*. Harmondsworth: Penguin.

Armstrong, L. (1978) *Kiss Daddy Goodnight*. New York: Dell.

Asen, K., George, E., Piper, R. and Stevens, A. (1989) A systems approach to child abuse: management and treatment issues, *Child Abuse & Neglect*, 13: 45–57.

Audit Commission (1994) *Seen But Not Heard: Coordinating Community Child Health and Social Services for Children in Need*. London: HMSO.

Australian Bureau of Statistics (2005) *Personal Safety*. Available at: http://www.abs.gov.au/ausstats/abs@.nsf/mf/4906.0.

Baher, E., Hyman, C., Jones, C., Kerr, A. and Mitchell, R. (1976) *At Risk: An Account of the Battered Child Research Department*. London: Routledge & Kegan Paul.

Bailey, T., Alvarez-Jimenez, M., Garcia-Sanchez, A. M. et al. (2018) Childhood trauma is associated with severity of hallucinations and delusions in psychotic disorders: a systematic review and meta-analysis, *Schizophrenia Bulletin*, 44(5): 1111–22.

Baker, A. and Duncan, S. (1985) Child sexual abuse: a study of prevalence in Great Britain, *Child Abuse & Neglect*, 9: 457–67.

Bakermans-Kranenburg, M. and Van IJzendoorn, M. H. (1997) Intergenerational transmission of attachment: a move to the contextual level, in L. Atkinson and K. Zucker (eds) *Attachment and Psychopathology*. New York: Guilford Press, pp. 135–70.

Bakermans-Kranenburg, M. and Van IJzendoorn, M. H. (2004) No association of the dopamine D4 receptor (DRD4) and -521 C/T promoter polymorphisms with infant attachment disorganization, *Attachment & Human Development*, 6: 211–18.

Bandura, A. (1965) *Principles of Behaviour Modification*. New York: Holt, Rinehart & Winston.

Barash, D. (1981) *Sociobiology: The Whisperings Within*. London: Fontana.

Baril, K., Tourigny, M., Paille, P. and Pauze. R. (2016) 'Characteristics of sexually abused children and their nonoffending mothers' followed by 'child welfare services: the role of maternal history of child sexual abuse', *Journal of Child Sexual Abuse*, 255(5): 504–23.

Barlow, J., Fisher, J. D. and Jones, D. (2012) *Systematic Review of Models of Analysing Significant Harm*. London: The Stationery Office.

Barlow, J. and Schrader McMillan, A. (2010) *Safeguarding Children from Emotional Maltreatment: What Works?* Available at: www.education.gov.uk/research.

Barlow, J. and Scott, J. (2011) *Safeguarding in the 21st Century: Where to Now?* Totnes: Research in Practice.

Baron-Cohen, S. (2011) *Zero Degrees of Empathy: A New Theory of Human Cruelty*. London: Allen Lane.

Barratt, A., Trepper, T. and Fish, L. (1990) Feminist informed family therapy for the treatment of intra-familial child sexual abuse, *Journal of Family Psychology*, 4: 151–66.

Baumrind, D. (1973) The development of instrumental competence through socialization, in D. Pick (ed.) *Minnesota Symposia on Child Psychology*, vol. 7. Minneapolis, MN: University of Minnesota Press, pp. 3–46.

Beach, S. R., Brody, G. H., Gunter, T. D. et al. (2010) Child maltreatment moderates the association of MAOA with symptoms of depression and antisocial personality disorder, *Journal of Family Psychology*, 1: 12–20.

Bebbington, A. and Miles, J. (1989) The background of children who enter local authority care, *British Journal of Social Work*, 19: 349–68.

Beck, U. (1992) *Risk Society: Towards a New Modernity*. London: Sage.

Beck, U. (2008) *World at Risk*. Cambridge: Polity Press.

Becker, J. and Quinsey, V. (1993) Assessing suspected child molesters, *Child Abuse & Neglect*, 17: 169–74.

Beckett, C. (2005) The Swedish myth: the corporal punishment ban and child death statistics, *British Journal of Social Work*, 35: 125–38.

Behlmer, G. (1982) *Child Abuse and Moral Reform in England, 1870–1908*. Stanford, CA: Stanford University Press.

Beitchman, J., Zucker, K., Hood, J., Da Costa, G. and Akman, D. (1991) A review of the short-term effects of child sexual abuse, *Child Abuse & Neglect*, 15: 537–56.

Beitchman, J., Zucker, K., Hood, J. et al. (1992) A review of the long-term effects of child sexual abuse, *Child Abuse & Neglect*, 16: 101–18.

Bell, M. (1999) Working in partnership in child protection, *British Journal of Social Work*, 29: 437–55.

Bell, M., Shaw, I., Sinclair, I., Sloper, P. and Rafferty, J. (2007) *The Integrated Children's System: An Evaluation of the Practice, Process and Consequences of the ICS in Councils with Social Services Responsibilities*. York: SPRU.

Belsky, J. (1980) Child maltreatment: an ecological integration, *American Psychologist*, 35: 320–35.

Belsky, J. (2005) Differential susceptibility to rearing influence: an evolutionary hypothesis and some evidence, in B. J. Ellis and D. F. Bjorklund (eds) *Origins of the Social Mind: Evolutionary Psychology and Child Development*. New York: Guilford Press.

Belsky, J., Bakermans-Kranenburg, M. and Van IJzendoorn, M. (2007) For better *and* for worse: differential susceptibility to environmental influences, *Current Directions in Psychological Science*, 16(6): 300–4.

Belsky, J. and Jaffee, S. R. (2006) The multiple determinants of parenting, in D. Cicchetti and D. Cohen (eds) *Developmental Psychopathology: Risk, Disorder and Adaptation*. New York: Wiley, pp. 38–85.

Belsky, J. and Vondra, J. (1989) Lessons from child abuse: the determinants of parenting, in D. Cicchetti and V. Carlson (eds) *Child Maltreatment: Theory and Research on the Causes and Consequences of Child Abuse and Neglect*. Cambridge: Cambridge University Press.

Benard, B. (1995) Fostering resilience in children. Available at: http://eric.ed.gov/PDFS/ED386327.pdf.

Benbenishty, R., Davidson-Arad, B., Lopez, M. et al. (2015) Decision making in child protection: an international comparative study on maltreatment substantiation, risk assessment and interventions recommendations, and the role of professionals' child welfare attitudes, *Child Abuse and Neglect*, 49: 63–75.

Bennett, C. M., Baird, A. A., Miller, M. B. and Wolford, G. L. (2010) Neural correlates of interspecies perspective taking in the post-mortem Atlantic salmon: an argument for proper multiple comparisons correction, *Journal of Serendipitous and Unexpected Results*, 1: 1–5.

Bentley, H., O'Hagan, O., Brown, A. et al. (2017) *How Safe Are Our Children? The Most Comprehensive Overview of Child Protection in the UK*. London. NSPCC.

Bentovim, A. and Boston, P. (1988) Sexual abuse – basic issues: characteristics of children and families, in A. Bentovim, A. Elton, J. Hildebrand, M. Tranter and E. Vizard (eds) *Child Sexual Abuse Within the Family: Assessment and Treatment*. London: Butterworth, pp. 1–15.

Bentovim, A., Elton, A., Hildebrand, J., Tranter, M. and Vizard, E. (eds) (1988) *Child Sexual Abuse Within the Family: Assessment and Treatment*. London: Wright.

Berger, L., Carlson, M., Bzostek, S. and Osborne, C. (2008) Parenting practices of resident fathers: the role of marital and biological ties, *Journal of Marriage and Family*, 70: 625–39.

Berliner, L. and Conte, R. (1995) The effects of disclosure and intervention on sexually abused children, *Child Abuse & Neglect*, 19: 371–84.

Bernard, C. (1999) Child sexual abuse and the black disabled child, *Disability and Society*, 14(3): 325–39.

Bichard, Sir M. (2004) *The Bichard Inquiry Report*, HC653. London: The Stationery Office.

Biehal, N., Clayden, J., Stein, M. and Wade, J. (1995) *Moving On: Young People and Leaving Care Schemes*. London: HMSO.

Bijur, P. E., Kurzon, M., Overpeck, M. D. and Scheidt, P. C. (1992) Parental alcohol use, problem drinking and child injuries, *Journal of the American Medical Association*, 23: 3166–71.

Bilson, A. and Martin, K. (2017) Referrals and child protection in England: one in five children referred to children's services and one in nineteen investigated before the age of five, *British Journal of Social Work*, 47(3): 793–811.

Birchall, E. with Hallett, C. (1995) *Working Together in Child Protection*. London: HMSO.

Boberiene, L. V. and Yazykova, E. (2014) Children with disabilities in Russian institutions: can the West help protect the most vulnerable?, *American Journal of Orthopsychiatry*, 84(3): 266–72.

Bolen, R. (2001) *Child Sexual Abuse: Its Scope and Our Failure*. New York: Kluwer Academic Press.

Bolger, K., Patterson, C. and Kupersmidt, J. (1998) Peer relationships and self-esteem among children who have been maltreated, *Child Development*, 69: 1171–97.

Booth, T. and Booth, W. (1993) Parenting with learning difficulties: lessons for practitioners, *British Journal of Social Work*, 23: 459–90.

Booth, T. and Booth, W. (1998) *Growing Up with Parents Who Have Learning Difficulties*. London: Routledge.

Booth, T., Booth, W. and McConnell, D. (2005) The prevalence and outcomes of care proceedings involving parents with learning difficulties in the family courts, *Journal of Intellectual Disability Research*, 18: 7–17.

Bornstein, B., Kaplan, D. and Perry, A. (2007) Child abuse in the eyes of the beholder: lay perceptions of child sexual and physical abuse, *Child Abuse & Neglect*, 31: 375–91.

Boswell, J. (1990) *The Kindness of Strangers: The Abandonment of Children in Western Europe from Late Antiquity to the Renaissance*. New York: Vintage.

Bourke, M. and Hernandez, A. (2009) The 'Butner Study' redux: a report of the incidence of hands-on child victimization by child pornography offenders, *Journal of Family Violence*, 24: 183–91.

Bovarnick, S., Scott, S. and Pearce, J. (2017) Direct work with sexually exploited or at risk children and young people: a rapid evidence assessment. Available at: www.beds.ac.uk/__data/assets/pdf_file/0006/540492/FINAL-REA-3.pdf (accessed June 2018).

Bowlby, J. (1951) *Maternal Care and Mental Health: A Report Prepared on Behalf of the World Health Organization as a Contribution to the United Nations Programme for the Welfare of Homeless Children*. Geneva: World Health Organization.

Bowlby, J. (1971) *Attachment and Loss:* vol. 1, *Attachment*. Harmondsworth: Penguin.

Bowlby, J., Fry, S. and Ainsworth, M. (1965) *Child Care and the Growth of Love.* Harmondsworth: Penguin.

Boyer, D. and Fine, D. (1992) Sexual abuse as a factor in adolescent pregnancy and child maltreatment, *Family Planning Perspectives*, 24: 4–11, 19.

Bracey, M. (2018) Funding for troubled families is vital, *The Guardian*. Available at: https://www.theguardian.com/social-care-network/social-life-blog/2018/feb/14/troubled-families-funding-vital-childrens-services (accessed June 2018).

Brady, K. (1979) *Father's Days: A True Story of Incest.* New York: Dell.

Brandon, M., Bailey, S. and Belderson, P. (2010) *Building on the Learning from Serious Case Reviews: A Two-year Analysis of Child Protection Database Notifications 2007-2009.* London: The Stationery Office.

Brandon, M., Bailey, S., Belderson, P. et al. (2009) *Understanding Serious Case Reviews and their Impact: A Biennial Analysis of Serious Case Reviews, 2005-2007.* London: DCSF.

Brandon, M., Belderson, P., Warren, C. et al. (2008) *Analysing Child Deaths and Serious Injury Through Abuse and Neglect: What Can We Learn? A Biennial Analysis of Serious Case Reviews, 2003-2005.* London: DCSF.

Brandon, M., Thoburn, J., Lewis, A. and Way, A. (1999) *Safeguarding Children with the Children Act 1989.* London: The Stationery Office.

Brent (London Borough of) (1985) *A Child in Trust: The Report of the Panel of Inquiry into the Circumstances Surrounding the Death of Jasmine Beckford.* London: London Borough of Brent.

Brewsaugh, K. and Strozier, A. (2016) Fathers in child welfare: what do social work textbooks teach our students?, *Children and Youth Services Review*, 60: 34–41.

Brewster, A., Nelson, J., Hymel, K. et al. (1998) Victim, perpetrator, family and incident characteristics of 32 infant maltreatment deaths in the United States Air Force, *Child Abuse & Neglect*, 22: 91–101.

Bridge (Child Care Consultancy Service) (1997) *Report on the Professional Judgements and Accountability in Relation to Work with the Neave Family (on Behalf of Cambridgeshire Area Child Protection Committee).* London: The Bridge.

Bridge (Child Care Consultancy Service) (1998) *Neglect and Developmental Delay: Part 8 Case Review. Overview Report re: Case 1/99 in Caerphilly (on behalf of Caerphilly Area Child Protection Committee).* London: The Bridge.

Bright, M. A., Huq, M. S., Spencer, T., Applebaum, J. W. and Hardt, N. (2018) Animal cruelty as an indicator of family trauma: using adverse childhood experiences to look beyond child abuse and domestic violence, *Child Abuse and Neglect*, 76: 287–96.

Brilleslijper-Kater, S., Friedrich, W. and Corwin, D. (2004) Sexual knowledge and emotional reaction as indicators of sexual abuse in young children: theory and research challenges, *Child Abuse & Neglect*, 28: 1007–17.

Bronfenbrenner, U. (1979) *The Ecology of Human Development: Experiments by Nature and Design.* Cambridge, MA: Harvard University Press.

Brown, C. (1986) Child abuse parents speaking: parents' impressions of social workers and the social work process, Working Paper. Bristol: Bristol School of Applied and Urban Studies.

Brown, T. and Waters, J. (1985) *Parental Participation at Case Conferences.* Rochdale: British Association for the Prevention of Cruelty and Neglect.

Browne, A. and Finkelhor, D. (1986) Initial and long-term effects: a review of the research, in D. Finkelhor et al. (eds) *A Sourcebook on Child Sexual Abuse.* Beverly Hills, CA: Sage.

Browne, K. and Saqi, S. (1988) Approaches to screening for child abuse and neglect, in K. Browne, C. Davies and P. Stratton (eds) *Early Prediction and Prevention of Child Abuse.* Chichester: Wiley.

Bryson, B. (2011) *At Home: A Short History of Private Life.* New York: Doubleday.

Buckley, H. (2003) *Child Protection Work: Beyond the Rhetoric.* London: Jessica Kingsley Publications.

Burgess-Proctor, A., Comartin, E. B. and Kubiak, S. P. (2017) Comparing female- and male-perpetrated child sexual abuse: a mixed-methods analysis, *Journal of Child Sexual Abuse*, 26(6): 657–76.

Burke, J., Chandy, J., Dannerbeck, A. and Watt, J. (1998) The parental environment cluster model of child neglect: an integrative conceptual model, *Child Welfare*, 77: 389–406.

Burnett, B. (1993) The psychological abuse of latency age children: a survey, *Child Abuse & Neglect*, 17: 441–54.

Burns, B. J., Mustillo, S. A., Farmer, E. M. Z. et al. (2009) Caregiver depression, mental health service use, and child outcomes, in M. B. Webb, K. Dowd, B. J. Harden, J. Landsverk and M. Testa (eds) *Child Welfare and Child Well-being: New Perspectives from the National Survey of Child and Adolescent Well-being*. New York: Oxford University Press, pp. 351–79.

Butler-Sloss, Lord Justice E. (1988) *Report of the Inquiry into Child Abuse in Cleveland 1987*, Cmnd 412. London: HMSO.

Bywaters, P., Brady, G., Bunting, L. et al. (2018) Inequalities in English child protection practice under austerity: a universal challenge?, *Child & Family Social Work*, 23(1): 53–61.

Bywaters, P., Brady, G., Sparks, T. and Bos, E. (2016) Inequalities in child welfare intervention rates: the intersection of deprivation and identity, *Child & Family Social Work*, 21(4): 452–63.

Bywaters, P., Kwhali, J., Brady, G., Sparks, T. and Bos, E. (2017) Out of sight, out of mind: ethnic inequalities in child protection and out-of-home care intervention rates, *British Journal of Social Work*, 47(7): 1884–902.

Calam, R. and Franchi, C. (1987) *Child Abuse and its Consequences*. Cambridge: Cambridge University Press.

Calam, R., Horn, L., Glasgow, D. and Cox, A. (1998) Psychological disturbance and child sexual abuse: a follow-up study, *Child Abuse & Neglect*, 22: 901–13.

Calheiros, M., Monteiro, M., Patricio, J. and Carmona, M. (2016) Defining child maltreatment among lay people and community professionals: exploring consensus in ratings of severity, *Journal of Child and Family Studies*, 25(7): 2292–305.

Campbell, B. (1988) *Unofficial Secrets*. London: Virago.

Campbell, M. (1991) Children at risk: how different are children on child abuse registers?, *British Journal of Social Work*, 21: 259–75.

Camras, L. and Rappaport, S. (1993) Conflict behaviors of maltreated and non-maltreated children, *Child Abuse & Neglect*, 17: 455–64.

Caprin, C., Benedan, L., Ballarin, L. and Gallace, A. (2017) Social competence in Russian post-institutionalized children: a comparison of adopted and non-adopted children, *Children and Youth Services Review*, 75: 61–88.

Carmen, E., Rieker, P. and Mills, T. (1984) Victims of violence and psychiatric illness, *American Journal of Psychiatry*, 141: 378–83.

Carr, A. (2009) The effectiveness of family therapy and systemic interventions for adult-focused problems, *Journal of Family Therapy*, 31: 46–74.

Cassidy, J. and Shaver, P. R. (2008) *Handbook of Attachment: Theory, Research and Clinical Applications*, 2nd edn. New York: Guilford Press.

Cawson, P., Wattam, C., Brooker, S. and Kelly, G. (2000) *Child Maltreatment in the United Kingdom*. London: NSPCC.

Ceci, S. J. and Bruck, M. (1995) *Jeopardy in the Courtroom: A Scientific Analysis of Children's Testimony*. Washington, DC: American Psychological Association.

Cemlyn, S. and Briskman, L. (2003) Asylum, children's rights and social work, *Child & Family Social Work*, 8: 163–78.

Centre for Social Justice (2009) Dying to belong: an in-depth review of street gangs in Britain. Available at: https://www.centreforsocialjustice.org.uk/library/dying-belong-depth-review-street-gangs-britain.

Chaffin, M. (2004) Is it time to re-think Healthy Start/Healthy Families?, *Child Abuse & Neglect*, 28: 589–95.

Chen, J., Dunne, M. P. and Han, P. (2004) Child sexual abuse in China: a study of adolescents in four provinces, *Child Abuse & Neglect*, 28: 1171–86.

Chen, J., Dunne, M. P. and Han, P. (2007) Prevention of child sexual abuse in China: knowledge, attitudes, and communication practices of parents of elementary school children, *Child Abuse & Neglect*, 31: 747–55.

Chesin, M., Jeglic, E., Moster, A. and Wnuk, D. (2010) Cognitive-behavioral therapy in the treatment and management of sex offenders, *Journal of Cognitive Psychotherapy*, 24: 92–103.

Chester, D. L., Jose, R. M., Aldlyami, E., King, H. and Moiemen, N. S. (2006) Non-accidental burns in children – are we neglecting neglect?, *Burns*, 32: 222–8.

Children's Commissioner (2017) Children's voices: A review of evidence on the subjective well-being of children involved in gangs in England. Available at: https://www.childrenscommissioner.gov.uk/wp-content/uploads/2017/11/Childrens-Voices-A-review-of-evidence-on-the-subjective-wellbeing-of-children-involved-in-gangs-in-England-2.pdf (accessed June 2018).

China View (2007) China working to prevent child abuse. Available at: http://news.xinhuanet.com/english/2007-10/11/content_6862247.htm.

Choi, N. G., DiNitto, D. M., Marti, C. N. and Choi, B. Y. (2016) Association of adverse childhood experiences with lifetime mental and substance use disorders among men and women aged 50+ years, *International Psychogeriatric Association*, 29(3): 359–72.

Cleaver, H. and Freeman, P. (1995) *Parental Perspectives in Cases of Suspected Child Abuse*. London: HMSO.

Clements, H., Dawson, D. L. and das Nair, R. (2014) Female perpetrators of sexual abuse: a review of victims and professional perspectives, *Journal of Sexual Aggression*, 20(2): 197–215.

Clyde, Lord (1992) *Report of the Inquiry into the Removal of Children from Orkney in February 1991*, HC 195. London: HMSO.

Coates, D. (2010) Impact of childhood abuse: biopsychosocial pathways through which adult mental health is compromised, *Australian Social Work*, 63(4): 391–403.

Cohn, A. and Daro, D. (1987) Is treatment too late? What ten years of evaluative research tell us, *Child Abuse & Neglect*, 11: 433–42.

College of Policing (2013) *The Effects of Hot-Spot Policing on Crime: What Works Briefing*. Coventry: College of Policing.

Colman, R. and Widom, C. (2004) Childhood abuse and neglect and adult intimate relationships: a prospective study, *Child Abuse & Neglect*, 28: 1133–51.

Colton, M. and Vanstone, M. (1996) *Betrayal of Trust: Sexual Abuse by Men who Work with Children – In Their Own Words*. London: Free Association Books.

Conway, E. E. (1998) Non-accidental head injury in infants: the shaken baby syndrome revisited, *Paediatric Annals*, 27(10): 677–90.

Conway, E. E., Alexander, R. C. and Smith, W. L. (1998) Shaken baby syndrome, *Infants and Young Children*, 10(3): 1–9.

Coohey, C. (1996) Child maltreatment: testing the social isolation hypothesis, *Child Abuse & Neglect*, 20: 241–54.

Coohey, C. and Braun, N. (1997) Toward an integrated framework for understanding child physical abuse, *Child Abuse & Neglect*, 21: 1081–94.

Cooper, A. (2018) The use of self in social work practice, in M. Bower and R. Solomon (eds) *What Social Workers Need to Know: A Psychoanalytic Approach*. London: Routledge, pp. 109–23.

Corby, B. (1987) *Working with Child Abuse*. Buckingham: Open University Press.

Corby, B. (1998) *Managing Child Sexual Abuse Cases*. London: Jessica Kingsley Publications.

Corby, B. (2003) Supporting families and protecting children – assisting child care professionals in initial decision-making and review of cases, *Journal of Social Work*, 3: 195–210.

Corby, B., Doig, A. and Roberts, V. (2001) *Public Inquiries into the Abuse of Children in Residential Care*. London: Jessica Kingsley Publications.

Corby, B. and Millar, M. (1997) A parents' view of partnership, in J. Bates, R. Pugh and N. Thompson (eds) *Protecting Children: Challenges and Change*. Aldershot: Avebury Press.

Corby, B., Millar, M. and Young, L. (1996) Parental participation in child protection work: rethinking the rhetoric, *British Journal of Social Work*, 26: 475–92.

Corby, B. and Mills, C. (1986) Child abuse: risks and resources, *British Journal of Social Work*, 16: 531–42.

Cox, P., Kershaw, S. and Trotter, J. (eds) (2001) *Child Sexual Assault: Feminist Perspectives*. Basingstoke: Palgrave.

Crawford, C. and Krebs, D. (2008) *Foundations of Evolutionary Psychology*. New York: Lawrence Erlbaum Associates.

Crawford, M. (2003) *The Little Princesses: The Story of the Queen's Childhood by Her Nanny*. London: Orion.

Cree, V. (2003) Worries and problems of young carers: issues for mental health, *Child & Family Social Work*, 8: 301–9.

Creighton, S. (2004) *Prevalence and Incidence of Child Abuse*. London: NSPCC.

Creighton, S. and Noyes, P. (1989) *Child Abuse Trends in England and Wales 1983–1987*. London: NSPCC.

Crittenden, P. M. (2008) *Raising Parents: Attachment, Parenting and Child Safety*. Portland, OR: Willan.

Crittenden, P. and Ainsworth, M. (1989) Child maltreatment and attachment theory, in D. Cicchetti and V. Carlson (eds) *Child Maltreatment: Theory and Research into the Causes and Consequences of Child Abuse and Neglect*. Cambridge: Cambridge University Press.

Crown Prosecution Service (2016) *Violence Against Women and Girls Crime Report 2015/16*. London: CPS.

Cui, N. and Liu, J. (2018) Physical abuse, emotional abuse, and neglect and childhood behaviour problems: a meta-analysis of studies in mainland China, *Trauma, Violence and Abuse*, published online 13 Feb. 2018.

Cunningham, H. (1991) *Children of the Poor*. Oxford: Blackwell.

Cunningham, J. and Cunningham, S. (2007) 'No choice at all': Destitution or deportation? A commentary on the implementation of Section 9 of the Asylum and Immigration (Treatment of Claimants, etc.) Act 2004, *Critical Social Policy: A Journal of Theory and Practice in Social Welfare*, 27(2): 277–98.

Cunningham, S. and Tomlinson, J. (2005) 'Starve them out': does every child really matter? A commentary on Section 9 of the Asylum and Immigration (Treatment of Claimants, etc.) Act, 2004, *Critical Social Policy*, 25: 253–75.

Curtis, Dame M. (1946) *Report of the Care of Children Committee*. London: HMSO.

Curtis, P. and McCullough, C. (1993) The impact of alcohol and other drugs on the child welfare system, *Child Welfare*, 72: 533–42.

Cyr, C., Euser, E. M., Bakermans-Kranenburg, M. J. and Van IJzendoorn, M. H. (2010) Attachment security and disorganization in maltreating and high-risk families: a series of meta-analyses, *Development and Psychopathology*, 22(1): 87–108.

Dale, P., Davies, M., Morrison, T. and Waters, J. (1986) *Dangerous Families: Assessment and Treatment of Child Abuse*. London: Tavistock.

Dale, P., Morrison,T., Davies, M., Noyes, P. and Roberts, W. (1983) A family therapy approach to child abuse: countering resistance, *Journal of Family Therapy*, 5: 117–43.

Dallos, R. and Draper, R. (2005) *Introduction to Systemic Family Therapy*, 2nd edn. Maidenhead: Open University Press.

Daly, M. and Wilson, M. (2005) The 'Cinderella effect' is no fairy tale, *Trends in Cognitive Sciences*, 9: 507–8.

Daniel, B. and Taylor, J. (2006) Gender and child neglect: theory, research and policy, *Critical Social Policy*, 26: 426–39.

Daniels, H. and Livingstone, M. (2014) *Hackney Child*. London: Simon & Schuster.

Davies, C. and Ward, H. (2011) Safeguarding children across services: messages from research on identifying and responding to child maltreatment. Available at: http://www. mars.stir.ac.uk/resources/2011/05/davies-c-ward-h-2011-safeguarding-children-across-services-messages-from-research-on-identifying-and-responding-to-child-maltreatment/.

Davin, A. (1990) The precocity of poverty, in *The Proceedings of the Conference on Historical Perspectives on Childhood*. Trondheim: University of Trondheim.

Day, L., Bryson, C., White, C. et al. (2016) *National Evaluation of the Troubled Families Programme: Final Synthesis Report*. London: Department for Communities and Local Government.

Deacon, L. and Gocke, B. (1999) *Understanding Perpetrators, Protecting Children: A Practitioner's Guide to Working Effectively with Child Sexual Abusers*. London: Whiting & Birch.

Dearden, C. and Becker, S. (2001) Young carers: needs, rights and assessments, in J. Horwath (ed.) *The Child's World: Assessing Children in Need*. London: Jessica Kingsley Publications.

Deblinger, E., McLeer, S., Atkins, M., Ralphe, M. and Foa, E. (1989) Posttraumatic stress in sexually abused, physically abused and non-abused children, *Child Abuse & Neglect*, 13: 403–8.

Deblinger, E., Steer, R. and Lippmann, J. (1999) Two-year follow-up of cognitive-behavioral therapy for sexually abused children suffering post-traumatic stress symptoms, *Child Abuse & Neglect*, 23: 1371–8.

de Mause, L. (ed.) (1976) *The History of Childhood*. London: Souvenir Press.

Demos, J. (1986) *Past, Present and Personal*. Oxford: Oxford University Press.

Department for Children, Schools and Families (2009) *Safeguarding Children and Young People from Sexual Exploitation*. London: DCSF.

Department for Children, Schools and Families/Home Office (2010) *Safeguarding Children and Young People Who May Have Been Affected by Gang Activity*. London: The Stationery Office.

Department for Education (2017a) *Characteristics of Children in Need: 2016 to 2017 England*, SFR 61/2017, 2 November 2017. London: Department for Education.

Department for Education (2017b) *Children Looked After in England (including adoption), year ending 31 March 2017*, SFR 50/2017, 28 September 2017. London: Department for Education.

Department for Education (2017c) *Child Sexual Exploitation: Definition and a Guide for Practitioners, Local Leaders and Decision Makers Working to Protect Children from Child Sexual Exploitation*. London: Department for Education. Available at: https://assets.publishing.service.gov.uk/government/uploads/system/uploads/attachment_data/file/591903/CSE_Guidance_Core_Document_13.02.2017.pdf.

Department for Education and the Home Office (2011) *Safeguarding Children Who May Have Been Trafficked: Practice Guidance*. London: DfE and Home Office. Available at: https://assets.publishing.service.gov.uk/government/uploads/system/uploads/attachment_data/file/177033/DFE-00084-2011.pdf.

Department for Education and Skills (2006) *Referrals, Assessments and Children and Young People on Child Protection Registers, England – Year Ending 31 March 2004, 2005 and 2006*. London: DfES.

Department for Education and Skills (2007) *Every Parent Matters*. London: DfES.

Department of Health (1988) *Protecting Children: A Guide for Social Workers Undertaking a Comprehensive Assessment*. London: HMSO.

Department of Health (1989, 1990, 1991c, 1992, 1993, 1996, 2000b, 2003a) *Survey of Children and Young Persons on Child Protection Registers, Year Ending 31 March 1988, 1989, 1990, 1991, 1992, 1995, 1999, 2000, 2002, England*. London: HMSO.

Department of Health (1991a) *Child Abuse: A Study of Inquiry Reports, 1980–1989*. London: HMSO.

Department of Health (1991b) *Working Together under the Children Act 1989: A Guide to Arrangements for Inter-agency Cooperation for the Protection of Children from Abuse*. London: HMSO.

Department of Health (1995) *Child Protection: Messages from Research*. London: HMSO.

Department of Health (1998) *The Quality Protects Programme: Transforming Children's Services*, LAC(98)26. London: Department of Health.

Department of Health (1999) *Working Together to Safeguard Children: A Guide to Inter-agency Working to Safeguard and Promote the Welfare of Children*. London: HMSO.

Department of Health (2000a) *Framework for the Assessment of Children in Need and Their Families: The Child's World*. London: The Stationery Office.

Department of Health (2001) *The Children Act Now: Messages from Research – Studies in Evaluating the Children Act 1989*. London: The Stationery Office.

Department of Health (2003b) *Every Child Matters*, Cm 5860. London: The Stationery Office.

Department of Health/Department for Children, Schools and Families/Department for Business, Innovation and Skills (2010) *Building a Safe and Confident Future: Implementing the Recommendations of the Social Work Task Force*. London: HMSO.

Department of Health/Department for Education and Skills (2007) *Good Practice Guidance on Working with Parents with a Learning Disability*. London: HM Government.

Department of Health/Home Office/Department of Education and Employment/National Assembly for Wales (2000) *Safeguarding Children Involved in Prostitution: Supplementary Guidance to Working Together to Safeguard Children*. London: The Stationery Office.

Department of Health/NHS Executive (2000) *The Protection of Children Act 1999: A Practical Guide to the Act for all Organizations Working with Children*. London: DH.

Department of Health and Social Security (1974) *Report of the Committee of Inquiry into the Care and Supervision Provided in Relation to Maria Colwell*. London: HMSO.

Department of Health and Social Security (1975) *Report of the Committee of Inquiry into the Provision of Services to the Family of John George Auckland*. London: HMSO.

Department of Health and Social Security (1980) *Child Abuse: Central Register Systems*, LASSL (80)4. London: HMSO.

Department of Health and Social Security (1982) *Child Abuse: A Study of Inquiry Reports, 1973–1981*. London: HMSO.

Department of Health and Social Security (1985a) *Social Work Decisions in Child Care: Recent Research Findings and Their Implications*. London: HMSO.

Department of Health and Social Security (1985b) *Review of Child Care Law: Report to Ministers of an Interdepartmental Working Party*. London: HMSO.

Department of Health and Social Security (1986) *Child Abuse – Working Together: A Draft Guide to Arrangements for Inter-agency Cooperation for the Protection of Children*. London: HMSO.

Department of Health and Social Security (1988) *Working Together: A Guide to Inter-agency Cooperation for the Protection of Children from Abuse*. London: HMSO.

de Shazer, S. (2005) *More than Miracles: The State of the Art of Solution-focused Therapy*. Binghamton, NY: Haworth Press.

Devaney, J. (2009) Chronic child abuse: the characteristics and careers of children caught in the child protection system, *British Journal of Social Work*, 39: 24–45.

DeViney, E., Dicert, J. and Lockwood, R. (1983) The care of pets within child abusing families, *International Journal for the Study of Animal Problems*, 4: 321–9.

Dibble, J. and Straus, M. (1980) Some structural determinants of inconsistency between attitudes and behavior: the case of family violence, *Journal of Marriage and the Family*, 42: 71–82.

Dickens, J. (1993) Assessment and control of social work: an analysis of the reasons for the non-use of the child assessment order, *Journal of Social Welfare and Family Law*, 15: 88–100.

di Giacomo, E. and Clerici, M. (2013) Physical and sexual violence as risk factors for those who commit acts of rape and pedophilia, *European Psychiatry*, 28: 1.

Diggins, M. (2011) *Think Child, Think Parent, Think Family: A Guide to Parental Mental Health and Child Welfare. Parental Mental Health and Child Welfare: A Guide for Adult and Children's Health and Social Care Services*. London: SCIE. Available at: http://www.scie.org.uk/ publications/guides/guide30/.

Dingwall, R., Eekelaar, J. and Murray, T. (1983) *The Protection of Children: State Intervention and Family Life*. Oxford: Blackwell.

Dingwall, R., Eekelaar, J. and Murray, T. (1984) Childhood as a social problem: a survey of the history of legal regulation, *Journal of Law and Society*, 11: 207–32.

Dobash, R. and Dobash, R. (1992) *Women, Violence and Social Change*. London: Routledge.

Doidge, J. C., Higgins, D. J., Delfabbro, P. et al. (2017) Economic predictors of child maltreatment in an Australian population-based birth cohort, *Child and Youth Services Review*, 71: 14–25.

Dominelli, L. (1986) Father-daughter incest: patriarchy's shameful secret, *Critical Social Policy*, 16: 8–22.

Dore, M., Doris, J. and Wright, P. (1995) Identifying substance abuse in maltreating families: a child welfare challenge, *Child Abuse & Neglect*, 19: 531–43.

Dozier, M., Chase Stovall-McClough, K. and Albus, K. E. (2008) Attachment and psychopathy in adulthood, in J. Cassidy and P. R. Shaver (eds) *Handbook of Attachment*. New York: Guilford Press.

Driver, E. and Droisen, A. (eds) (1989) *Child Sexual Abuse: Feminist Perspectives*. London: Macmillan.

Dubanoski, R., Evans, I. and Higuchi, A. (1978) Analysis and treatment of child abuse: a set of behavioral propositions, *Child Abuse & Neglect*, 2: 153–72.

Dubowitz, H. (2017) Child sexual abuse and exploitation: a global glimpse, *Child Abuse & Neglect*, 66: 2–8.

Dufour, S., Lavergne, C., Larrivee, M. and Trocme, N. (2008) Who are these parents involved in child neglect? A differential analysis of parent gender and family structure, *Children and Youth Services Review*, 30: 141–56.

Duggan, A., Macfarlane, E., Fuddy, L. et al. (2004) Randomized trial of a statewide home visiting program: impact in preventing child abuse and neglect, *Child Abuse & Neglect*, 28: 597–622.

Dunne, M. P., Chen, J. Q. and Choo, W. Y. (2008) The evolving evidence base for child protection in Chinese societies, *Asia-Pacific Journal of Public Health*, 20(4): 267–76.

Durrant, J. (1999) Evaluating the success of Sweden's corporal punishment ban, *Child Abuse & Neglect*, 23: 435–48.

Duschinsky, R. (2015) The emergence of the disorganized/disoriented (D) attachment classification, 1979–1982, *History of Psychology*, 18(1): 32–46.

Duschinsky, R. and Solomon, J. (2017) Infant disorganized attachment: clarifying levels of analysis, *Clinical Child Psychology and Psychiatry*, 22(4): 524–38.

Early Intervention Foundation (2015) EIF responds to evaluation of family nurse partnership. Available at: http://www.eif.org.uk/eif-responds-to-evaluation-of-family-nurse-partnership/ (accessed June 2018).

Early Intervention Foundation and the Home Office (2015) What works to prevent gang involvement, youth violence and crime. A rapid review of interventions delivered in the UK and abroad. Available at: https://www.eif.org.uk/files/pdf/preventing-gang-and-youth-violence-rapid-review.pdf.

Edleson, L. (1999) The overlap between child maltreatment and woman battering, *Violence Against Women*, 5: 134–54.

Egeland, B., Sroufe, L. and Erickson, M. (1983) Developmental consequences of different patterns of maltreatment, *Child Abuse & Neglect*, 7: 459–69.

Elliot, M. (2002) *Bullying: A Practical Guide to Coping for Schools*. Harlow: Pearson Education.

Elmer, E. (1977) *Fragile Families, Troubled Children*. Pittsburgh, PA: University of Pittsburgh Press.

Elwell, M. and Ephloss, P. (1987) Initial reactions of sexually abused children, *Social Casework*, 68: 109–16.

End Child Prostitution and Trafficking (2017). *Time to Transform: Results of a Survey of Frontline Professionals on the National Referral Mechanism for Child Victims of Trafficking and Modern Slavery*. London: ecpat.

English, D., Thompson, R., Graham, J. and Briggs, E. (2005) Towards a definition of neglect in young children, *Child Abuse & Neglect*, 29: 19–29.

Ennew, J. (1986) *The Sexual Exploitation of Children*. Cambridge: Polity Press.

Erickson, M. and Egeland, B. (1996) Child neglect, in J. Briere, L. Berliner, J. Bulkley, C. Jenny and T. Reid (eds) *The APSAC Handbook on Child Maltreatment*. Thousand Oaks, CA: Sage.

Erickson, M., Egeland, B. and Pianta, R. (1989) Effects of maltreatment on the development of young children, in D. Cicchetti and V. Carlson (eds) *Child Maltreatment: Theory and Research on the Causes and Consequences of Child Abuse and Neglect*. Cambridge: Cambridge University Press.

Esposti, M., Humphreys, D., Jenkins, B., Gasparrini, A., Pooley, S., Eisner, M. and Bowes, L. (2019) Long-term trends in child maltreatment in England and Wales, 1858-2016: an observational, time-series analysis. *The Lancet*, doi.org/10.1016/S2468-2667(19)30002-7.

Europol (2011) *Knowledge Product: Trafficking in Human Beings in the European Union*. The Hague: Europol.

Euser, S., Alink, L., Tharner, A. et al. (2015) The prevalence of child sexual abuse in out-of-home care: increased risk for children with a mild intellectual disability, *Journal of Applied Research in Intellectual Disabilities*, 29(1): 83–92.

Evans, S., Davies, C. and DeLillo, D. (2008) Exposure to domestic violence: a meta-analysis of child and adolescent outcomes, *Aggression and Violent Behavior*, 13: 131–40.

Faller, K. (1989) Why sexual abuse? An exploration of the intergenerational hypothesis, *Child Abuse & Neglect*, 13: 543–8.

Family Rights Group (2018) *Care Crisis Review, Options for Change*. Available at: https://www.frg.org.uk/images/Care_Crisis/CCR-FINAL.pdf.

Fang, X., Fry. D. A., Finkelhor, D. et al. (2015) The burden of child maltreatment in China: a systematic review, *Bulletin of the World Health Organization*, 93: 176–85.

Farmer, E. and Owen, M. (1995) *Child Protection Practice: Private Risks and Public Remedies – A Study of Decision-making, Intervention and Outcome in Child Protection Work*. London: HMSO.

Farmer, E. and Pollock, S. (2003) Managing sexually abused and/or abusing children in substitute care, *Child & Family Social Work*, 8: 101–12.

Fauth, R., Jelicic, H., Hart, D. et al. (2010) *Effective Practice to Protect Children Living in 'Highly Resistant' Families*. London: Centre for Excellence and Outcomes in Children and Young People's Services.

Fearon, R. P., Bakermans-Kranenburg, M. J., van IJzendoorn, M. H., Lapsley, A. M. and Roisman, G. I. (2010) The significance of insecure attachment and disorganization in the development of children's externalizing behavior: a meta-analytic study, *Child Development*, 81(2): 435–56.

Featherstone, B. (1997) What has gender got to do with it? Exploring physically abusive behaviour towards children, *British Journal of Social Work*, 27: 419–33.

Featherstone, B. (2007) What difference does outreach make to family support?, in P. Avis et al. (eds) *Supporting Children and Families: Lessons from Sure Start*. London: Jessica Kingsley Publications.

Featherstone, B., Gupta, A., Morris, K., Warner, J. and White, S. (2015) Child protection must not be used for dealing with the symptoms of increased poverty, *Community Care*, 30 June.

Featherstone, B., Gupta, A., Morris, K. and White, S. (2018) *Protecting Children: A Social Model*. Bristol: Policy Press.

Featherstone, B., Hooper, C. A., Scourfield, J. and Taylor, J. (eds) (2010) *Gender and Child Welfare in Society*. Oxford: Wiley-Blackwell.

Featherstone, B. and Lancaster, E. (1997) Contemplating the unthinkable: men who sexually abuse children, *Critical Social Policy*, 17: 51–68.

Featherstone, B., Morris, K., Bywaters, P. et al. (2017) Poverty, inequality, child abuse and neglect: changing the conversation across the UK in child protection? *Child and Youth Services Review*.

Featherstone, B. and Trinder, L. (1997) Familiar subjects? Domestic violence and child welfare, *Child & Family Social Work*, 2: 147–59.

Featherstone, B., White, S. and Morris, K. (2014) *Re-imagining Child Protection: Towards Humane Social Work with Families*. Bristol: Policy Press.

Feder, A., Alonso, A., Tang, M. et al. (2009) Children of low-income depressed mothers: psychiatric disorders and social adjustment, *Depression and Anxiety*, 26(6): 513–20.

Fehrenbach, P., Smith, W., Monastersky, C. and Deister, R. (1986) Adolescent sex offenders: offender and offense characteristics, *American Journal of Orthopsychiatry*, 56: 225–33.

Felitti, V. J., Anda, R. F. and Nordenberg, D. et al. (1998) Relationship of childhood abuse and household dysfunction to many of the leading causes of death in adults. The Adverse Childhood Experiences (ACE) study, *American Journal of Preventive Medicine*, 14: 245–58.

Ferguson, H. (1990) Rethinking child protection practices: a case for history, in The Violence Against Children Study Group, *Taking Child Abuse Seriously*. London: Unwin Hyman.

Ferguson, H. (2004) *Protecting Children in Time: Child Abuse, Child Protection and the Consequences of Modernity*. Basingstoke: Palgrave Macmillan.

Ferguson, H. (2011) *Child Protection Practice*. Basingstoke: Palgrave Macmillan.

Ferguson, H. (2017) How children become invisible in child protection work: findings from research into day-to-day social work practice, *British Journal of Social Work*, 47(4): 1007–23.

Ferguson, H. and Gates, P. (2015) Early intervention and holistic, relationship-based practice with fathers: evidence from the work of the Family Nurse Partnership, *Child & Family Social Work*, 20(1): 96–105.

Field, F. (2010) *The Foundation Years: Preventing Poor Children Becoming Poor Adults*. London: HM Government.

Finkelhor, D. (1993) Epidemiological factors in the clinical identification of child sexual abuse, *Child Abuse & Neglect*, 17(1): 67–70.

Finkelhor, D. (1994) Current information on the scope and nature of child sexual abuse, *The Future of Children*, 4(2): 31, 46–8.

Finkelhor, D. (2008) *Child Victimization: Violence, Crime, and Abuse in the Lives of Young People*. New York: Oxford University Press.

Finkelhor, D. with Araji, S. et al. (eds) (1986) *A Sourcebook on Child Sexual Abuse*. Newbury Park, CA: Sage.

Finkelhor, D., Asdigan, N. and Dziuba-Leatherman, J. (1995) The effectiveness of victimization prevention instruction: an evaluation of children's responses to actual threats and assaults, *Child Abuse & Neglect*, 19: 141–53.

Finkelhor, D. and Baron, L. (1986) High risk children, in D. Finkelhor et al. (eds) *A Sourcebook on Child Sexual Abuse*. Newbury Park, CA: Sage.

Finkelhor, D., Hotaling, G., Lewis, I. and Smith, C. (1990) Sexual abuse in a national survey of adult men and women: prevalence characteristics and risk factors, *Child Abuse & Neglect*, 14: 19–28.

Finkelhor, D. and Korbin, J. (1988) Child abuse as an international issue, *Child Abuse & Neglect*, 12: 3–23.

Finkelhor, D. and Tucker, C. J. (2015) A holistic approach to child maltreatment, *The Lancet*, 2(6): 480–1.

Firmin, C. (2017) *Contextual Safeguarding. An Overview of the Operational, Strategic and Conceptual Framework*. Luton: University of Bedfordshire.

Fitzsimons, P. and Teager, W. (2018) The cost of late intervention in Northern Ireland. Early Intervention Foundation. Available at: https://www.eif.org.uk/files/pdf/cost-late-intervention-northern-ireland.pdf.

Fonagy, P. and Allison, E. (2014) The role of mentalizing and epistemic trust in the therapeutic relationship, *Psychotherapy*, 51(3): 372–80.

Fonagy, P. and Target, M. (2005) Bridging the transmission gap: an end to an important mystery of attachment research?, *Attachment & Human Development*, 7: 333–43.

Fook, J. (2002) *Social Work: Critical Theory and Practice*. London: Sage.

Forrester, D. (2017) Outcomes in children's services, *Journal of Children's Services*, 12 (2–3): 144–57.

Forrester, D., Kershaw, S., Moss, H. and Hughes, L. (2008a) Communication skills in child protection: how do social workers talk to parents?, *Child & Family Social Work*, 13(1): 41–51.

Forrester, D., McCambridge, J., Waissbein, C. and Rollnick, S. (2008b) How do child and family social workers talk to parents about child welfare concerns?, *Child Abuse Review*, 17(1): 23–35.

Freeman, M. (1983) *The Rights and Wrongs of Children*. London: Pinter.

Freeman, M. (ed.) (2000) *Overcoming Child Abuse: A Window on a World Problem*. Dartmouth: Ashgate.

Freeman, P. and Hunt, J. (1998) *Parental Perspectives on Care Proceedings*. London: The Stationery Office.

Frost, N. and Stein, M. (1989) *The Politics of Child Welfare: Inequality, Power and Change*. Hemel Hempstead: Harvester Wheatsheaf.

Fuller-Thompson, E., Roane, J. L. and Brennenstuhl, S. (2016) Three types of adverse childhood experiences, and alcohol and drug dependence among adults: an investigation using population-based data, *Substance Use and Misuse*, 51(11): 1451–61.

Furniss, T. (1991) *The Multi-professional Handbook of Child Sexual Abuse: Integrated Management, Therapy and Legal Intervention*. London: Routledge.

Gagnon, J. and Parker, R. (1995) *Conceiving Sexuality: Approaches to Sex Research in the Modern World*. London: Routledge.

Galbally, M. and Lewis, A. J. (2017) Depression and parenting: the need for improved intervention models, *Current Opinion in Psychology*, 15: 61–5.

Garbarino, J. (1977) The human ecology of child maltreatment: a conceptual model for research, *Journal of Marriage and the Family*, 39: 721–35.

Garbarino, J. (1982) *Children and Families in Their Social Environment*. New York: Aldine.

Garbarino, J. and Vondra, J. (1987) Psychological maltreatment: issues and perspectives, in M. Brassard, R. Germain and S. Hart (eds) *Psychological Maltreatment of Children and Youth*. Oxford: Pergamon Press.

Garin, E., Belse, J., Hug, L., You, D. and Mukerjee, A. (2016) *Uprooted: The Growing Crisis for Refugee and Migrant Children*. London: UNICEF.

Gatti, S. (2014) After Artyom: how efforts to reform U.S.–Russia adoption failed, and what Russia must do now to ensure the welfare of her orphans, *Case Western Reserve Journal of International Law*, 46(3): 589–625.

Gaughan, K. and Kalyniak, S. (2011) The centrality of relationships, in S. Goodman and I. Trowler (eds) *Reclaiming Social Work*. London: Jessica Kingsley Publications.

Gazmararian, J., Petersen, R., Spitz, A. et al. (2000) Violence and reproductive health: current knowledge and future research directions, *Maternal and Child Health Journal*, 4: 79–84.

Gedaly, L. R. and Leerkes, E. M. (2016) The role of sociodemographic risk and maternal behavior in the prediction of infant attachment disorganization, *Attachment & Human Development*, 18(6): 554–69.

Gelles, R. (1982) Towards better research on child abuse and neglect: a response to Besharov, *Child Abuse & Neglect*, 6: 495–6.

Ghate, D. (2001) Community-based evaluations in the UK: scientific concerns and practical constraints, *Children & Society*, 15: 23–32.

Ghate, D., Shaw, C. and Hazel, N. (2000) *Fathers and Family Centres: Engaging Fathers in Preventive Strategies*. York: Joseph Rowntree Foundation.

Giaretto, H., Giaretto, A. and Sgroi, S. (1978) Co-ordinated community treatment of incest, in A. Burgess, A. Groth, L. Holmstrom and S. Sgroi (eds) *Sexual Assault of Children and Adolescents*. Lexington, MA: Lexington Books.

Gibbons, J., Conroy, S. and Bell, C. (1995a) *Operating the Child Protection System: A Study of Child Protection Practices in English Local Authorities*. London: HMSO.

Gibbons, J., Gallagher, B., Bell, C. and Gordon, D. (1995b) *Development after Physical Abuse in Early Childhood: A Follow-up Study of Children on Child Protection Registers*. London: HMSO.

Gil, D. (1970) *Violence Against Children*. Cambridge, MA: Harvard University Press.

Gil, D. (1975) Unravelling child abuse, *American Journal of Orthopsychiatry*, 45: 346–56.

Gil, D. (1978) Societal violence and violence in families, in J. Eekelaar and S. Katz (eds) *Family Violence*. Toronto: Butterworth.

Gillham, B. (1991) *The Facts about Sexual Abuse*. London: Cassell.

Giovannoni, J. and Becerra, R. (1979) *Defining Child Abuse*. New York: Free Press.

Gladman, A. and Heal, A. (2017) *Child Exploitation After Rotherham*. London: Jessica Kingsley Publications.

Glaser, D. (2000) Child abuse and neglect and the brain: a review, *Journal of Child Psychology and Psychiatry*, 41: 97–116.

Glaser, D. (2002) Emotional abuse and neglect (psychological maltreatment): a conceptual framework, *Child Abuse & Neglect*, 26: 697–714.

Glaser, D. and Frosh, S. (1988) *Child Sexual Abuse*. London: Macmillan.

Gomes-Schwartz, B., Horowitz, J. and Cardarelli, A. (1990) *Child Sexual Abuse: The Initial Effects*. Beverly Hills, CA: Sage.

Goodman, S. and Brumley, H. E. (1990) Schizophrenic and depressed mothers: relational deficits in parenting, *Developmental Psychology*, 26: 31–9.

Gordon, D., Parker, R. and Loughran, F. (2000) *Disabled Children in Britain: A Re-analysis of the OPCS Disability Surveys*. London: TSO.

Gordon, L. (1989) *Heroes of Their Own Lives: The Politics and History of Family Violence, Boston, 1880–1960*. London: Virago.

Gough, D. (1993) *Child Abuse Interventions: A Review of the Research Literature*. London: HMSO.

Gough, D. (1996) Defining the problem, *Child Abuse & Neglect*, 20: 993–1002.

Graham-Bermann, S. A., Cutler, S. E., Litzenberger, B. W. and Schwartz, W. E. (1994) Perceived sibling violence and emotional adjustment during childhood and adolescence, *Journal of Family Psychology*, 8: 85–97.

Granqvist, P., Sroufe, L. A., Dozier, M. et al. (2017) Disorganized attachment in infancy: a review of the phenomenon and its implications for clinicians and policy-makers, *Attachment & Human Development*, 19: 534–58.

Greenland, C. (1958) Incest, *British Journal of Delinquency*, 9: 62–5.

Greenland, C. (1987) *Preventing CAN Deaths: An International Study of Deaths Due to Child Abuse and Neglect*. London: Tavistock.

Greenwich (London Borough of) (1987) *A Child in Mind: The Protection of Children in a Responsible Society – Report of the Commission of Inquiry into the Circumstances Surrounding the Death of Kimberley Carlile*. London: London Borough of Greenwich.

Griffiths, D. and Moynihan, F. (1963) Multiple epiphyseal injuries in babies ('battered baby syndrome'), *British Medical Journal*, 5372: 1558–61.

Gunby, C. and Woodhams, J. (2010) Sexually deviant juveniles: comparisons between the offender and offence characteristics of 'child abusers' and 'peer abusers', *Psychology, Crime and Law*, 16: 47–64.

Halevi, G., Djalovski, A., Vengrober, A. and Feldman, R. (2016) Risk and resilience trajectories in war-exposed children across the first decade of life, *Journal of Child Psychology and Psychiatry*, 57(100): 1183–93.

Hallett, C. and Stevenson, O. (1980) *Child Abuse: Aspects of Inter-professional Cooperation*. London: Allen & Unwin.

Halston, A. and Richards, D. (1982) Behind closed doors, *Social Work Today*, 14: 7–11.

Hanawalt, B. (1977) Childrearing among the lower classes of late medieval England, *Journal of Interdisciplinary History*, 8: 1–22.

Hanawalt, B. (1995) *Growing Up in Medieval London*. New York: Oxford University Press.

Hanson, R. and Morton-Bourgon, K. (2005) The characteristics of persistent sexual offenders: a meta-analysis of recidivism studies, *Journal of Consulting and Clinical Psychology*, 73: 1154–63.

Haringey (London Borough of) (2008) *Haringey Local Safeguarding Children Board Serious Case Review 'Child A'*. London: Department for Education.

Harper, C. A. and Perkins, C. (2017) Reporting child sexual abuse within religious settings: challenges and future directions, *Child Abuse Review*, 27(1): 30–41.

Harris, J. (1995) Where is the child's environment? A group socialization theory of development, *Psychological Review*, 102: 458–89.

Harrow (Area Child Protection Committee) (1999) *Part 8 Summary Report*. Harrow: Harrow ACPC.

Hartley-Parkinson, R. (2017) Nobody has come forward for 'Baby Harry' who was abandoned in a park, *Metro*. Available at: http://metro.co.uk/2017/12/21/nobody-come-forward-baby-harry-abandoned-park-7176745/ (accessed January 2018).

Hassan, M. A., Gary, F., Killion, C., Lewin, L. and Totten, V. (2015) Patterns of sexual abuse among children: victims' and perpetrators' characteristics, *Journal of Aggression, Maltreatment and Trauma*, 44(4): 400–18.

Hearn, J. (1990) Child abuse and men's violence, in The Violence against Children Study Group, *Taking Child Abuse Seriously*. London: Unwin Hyman.

Heim, C., Young, L. J., Newport, D. J. et al. (2009) Lower CSF oxytocin concentrations in women with a history of childhood abuse, *Molecular Psychiatry*, 14(10): 954–8.

Heller, S. S., Larrieu, J. A., D'Imperiod, R. and Boris, N. W. (1999) Research on resilience to child maltreatment: empirical considerations, *Child Abuse & Neglect*, 23(4): 321–38.

Henderson, B. B., Hensley, C. and Tallichet, S. E. (2011) Childhood animal cruelty methods and their link to adult interpersonal violence, *Journal of Interpersonal Violence*, 26(11): 2211–27.

Hendrick, H. (1994) *Child Welfare: England, 1872–1989*. London: Routledge.

Herczog, M. (2017) Investing in children: the best way to prevent separation from parents and families, *Child Abuse and Neglect*, 70: 402–5.

Herman, J. (1981) *Father-Daughter Incest*. Cambridge, MA: Harvard University Press.

Hester, M., He, J. and Tian, L. (2009) Girls' and boys' experiences and perceptions of parental discipline and punishment while growing up in China and England, *Child Abuse Review*, 18: 401–13.

Heywood, C. (2001) *A History of Childhood: Children and Childhood in the West from Medieval to Modern Times*. Cambridge: Polity Press.

Hicks, J. and Allen, G. (1999) *A Century of Change: Trends in UK Statistics since 1900*. London: House of Commons Library.

Hicks, L. and Stein, M. (2010) *Neglect Matters: A Multiagency Guide for Professionals Working Together on Behalf of Teenagers*. London: The Stationery Office.

Hildyard, K. and Wolfe, D. (2002) Child neglect: developmental issues and outcomes, *Child Abuse & Neglect*, 26: 679–95.

Hillingdon (London Borough of) (1986) *Report of the Review Panel into the Death of Heidi Koseda*. London: London Borough of Hillingdon.

Hingley-Jones, H. and Mandin, P. (2007) Getting to the root of problems: the role of systems ideas in helping social work students to develop relationship-based practice, *Journal of Social Work Practice*, 21(2): 177–91.

Hinsliff, G. (2016) The world is becoming more violent but we shouldn't be afraid to explore it, *The Guardian*. Available at: https://www.theguardian.com/commentisfree/2016/mar/18/isis-shut-down-tourism (accessed January 2018).

HM Government (2015) *Working Together to Safeguard Children: A Guide to Inter-agency Working to Safeguard and Promote the Welfare of Children*. London: The Stationery office.

HM Government (2018) *Working Together to Safeguard Children: A Guide to Inter-Agency Working to Safeguard and Promote the Welfare of Children*. Available at: https://assets.publishing.service.gov.uk/government/uploads/system/uploads/attachment_data/file/729914/Working_Together_to_Safeguard_Children-2018.pdf.

Hobbs, C. and Wynne, J. (1986) Buggery in childhood: a common syndrome of child abuse, *The Lancet*, 2(8510): 792–6.

Holland, S. (2000) The assessment relationship: interactions between social workers and parents in child protection assessments, *British Journal of Social Work*, 30: 149–63.

Holmes, L., Munro, E. and Soper, J. (2010) *Calculating the Cost and Capacity Implications for Local Authorities Implementing the Laming (2009) Recommendations*. Report to the Local Government Association. Loughborough: Centre for Child and Family Research, Loughborough University.

Holt, J. (1974) *Escape from Childhood*. Harmondsworth: Penguin.

Home Office (1923) *Report of the Work of the Children's Branch*. London: HMSO.

Home Office (1945) *Report by Sir Walter Monckton on the Circumstances which led to the Boarding-out of Dennis and Terence O'Neill at Bank Farm, Minsterley and the Steps Taken to Supervise their Welfare*, Cmd 6636. London: HMSO.

Home Office (1950) *Children Neglected or Ill-treated in their Own Homes*. Joint Circular with the Ministry of Health and Ministry of Education. London: HMSO.

Home Office (2014) The right to choose: multi-agency statutory guidance for dealing with forced marriage. Available at: https://assets.publishing.service.gov.uk/government/uploads/system/uploads/attachment_data/file/322310/HMG_Statutory_Guidance_publication_180614_Final.pdf (accessed June 2018).

Home Office (2015) *Controlling or Coercive Behaviour in an Intimate or Family Relationship: Statutory Guidance Framework*. London: Home Office.

Home Office/Department of Health (1992) *Memorandum of Good Practice on Video-recorded Interviews with Child Witnesses for Criminal Proceedings*. London: HMSO.

Horwath, J. and Calder, M. (1998) Working together to protect children on the child protection register: myth or reality, *British Journal of Social Work*, 28: 879–95.

Hotaling, G. T., Straus, M. A. and Lincoln, A. J. (1990) Intrafamily violence and crime and violence outside the family, in M. A. Straus and R. J. Gelles (eds) *Physical Violence in American Families*. New Brunswick, NJ: Transaction Books, pp. 431–70.

Housden, L. (1955) *The Prevention of Cruelty to Children*. London: Cape.

House of Commons (1984) *Children in Care*, vol. 1, *Second Report from the Social Services Committee: Session 1983–4*. London: HMSO.

Howe, D. (1991) Knowledge, power and the shape of social work practice, in M. Davies (ed.) *The Sociology of Social Work*. London: Routledge.

Howe, D. (2005) *Child Abuse and Neglect: Attachment, Development and Intervention*. Basingstoke: Palgrave Macmillan.

Howe, D. (2011) *Attachment Across the Lifecourse*. Basingstoke: Palgrave Macmillan.

Hrdy, S. (1977) *The Langurs of Abu*. Cambridge, MA: Harvard University Press.

Hrdy, S. B. (2009) *Mothers and Others: The Evolutionary Origins of Mutual Understanding*. Cambridge, MA: Harvard University Press.

Huber, J. and Stanig, P. (2009) *Individual Income and Voting for Redistribution Across Democracies*. Available at: http://www.columbia.edu/~jdh39/Site/Research_files/huber_stanig_voting.pdf.

Hughes, K., Bellis, M., Hardcastle, K. A. et al. (2017) The effect of multiple adverse childhood experiences on health: a systematic review and meta-analysis, *Lancet Public Health*, 2(8): e356–e366.

Human Rights Watch (1996) *Death by Default: A Policy of Fatal Neglect in China's State Orphanages*, 1 January 1996, 1-56432-163-0. Available at: http://www.unhcr.org/refworld/docid/3ae6a85a0. html (accessed 28 May 2012).

Humphreys, C. (2006) *Research and Practice Briefings: Domestic Violence and Child Abuse*. Available at: http://www.uea.ac.uk/menu/acad_depts/swk/MRC_web/public_html/files/qpb14.pdf.

Humphreys, C. and Stanley, N. (2006) *Domestic Violence and Child Protection: Directions for Good Practice*. London: Jessica Kingsley Publications.

Hunt, P. (1994) *Report of the Independent Inquiry into Multiple Abuse in Nursery Classes in Newcastle-upon-Tyne*. Newcastle upon Tyne: City Council of Newcastle upon Tyne.

Hunter, R. and Kilstrom, N. (1979) Breaking the cycle in abusive families, *American Journal of Psychiatry*, 136: 1320–2.

Ingleby, Viscount (1960) *Report of the Committee on Children and Young Persons*, Cmnd 1191. London: HMSO.

International Labour Office (2014) *Profits and Poverty: The Economics of Forced Labour*. Geneva: International Labour Office.

Irfan, S. and Cowburn, M. (2004) Disciplining, chastisement and physical abuse: perceptions and attitudes of the British Pakistani community, *Journal of Muslim Minority Affairs*, 24: 89–98.

Ismayilova, L., Ssewamala, F. and Huseynli, A. (2014) Reforming child institutional care in the post-Soviet bloc: the potential role of family-based empowerment strategies, *Children and Youth Services Review*, 47(2): 136–48.

Itzin, C. (1997) Pornography and the organisation of intrafamilial and extrafamilial child sexual abuse: developing a conceptual model, *Child Abuse Review*, 6: 94–106.

Iwaniec, D., Herbert, M. and McNeish, A. (1985) Social work with failure to thrive children and their families, Part II: behavioural social work intervention, *British Journal of Social Work*, 15: 375–89.

Iwaniec, D. and Sneddon, H. (2001) Attachment style in adults who failed to thrive as children: outcomes of a 20-year follow-up study of factors influencing maintenance or change in attachment style, *British Journal of Social Work*, 31: 179–95.

Jack, G. (2000) Ecological influences on parenting and child development, *British Journal of Social Work*, 30: 703–20.

Jackson, S. (1996) Educational success for looked-after children: the social worker's responsibility, *Practice*, 10: 47–56.

Jaffe, A. (2011) Failure to thrive: current clinical concepts, *Pediatrics in Review*, 32: 100–8.

Jaffee, S. R. and Maikovich-Fong, A. K. (2011) Effects of chronic maltreatment and maltreatment timing on children's behavior and cognitive abilities, *Journal of Child Psychology and Psychiatry*, 52(2): 184–94.

Jaser, S. S., Langrock, A. M., Keller, G. et al. (2005) Coping with the stress of parental depression II: adolescent and parent reports of coping and adjustment, *Journal of Child and Adolescent Psychology*, 34: 193–205.

Jaudes, P. and Morris, M. (1990) Child sexual abuse: who goes home?, *Child Abuse & Neglect*, 14: 61–8.

Jay, A. (2014) *Independent Inquiry into Child Sexual Exploitation in Rotherham 1997–2013*. Available at: https://www.rotherham.gov.uk/downloads/file/1407/independent_inquiry_cse_in_rotherham (accessed June 2018).

Jenkins, H. and Asen, K. (1992) Family therapy without the family: a framework for systemic practice, *Journal of Family Therapy*, 14: 1–14.

Ji, K. and Finkelhor, D. (2015) A meta-analysis of child physical abuse prevalence in China, *Child Abuse & Neglect*, 43: 61–72.

Johnson, D. E., Dovbnya, S. V., Morozova, T. U., Richards, M. A. and Bogdanova, J. G. (2014) From institutional care to family support; development of an effective early intervention network in Nizhny Novgorod region, Russian Federation, to support family care for children at risk for institutionalization, *Infant Mental Health Journal*, 35(2): 172–84.

Johnson, T. (1989) Female child perpetrators: children who molest other children, *Child Abuse & Neglect*, 13: 571–86.

Jones, D., Gonzalez, M., Ward, D. et al. (2013) Should child obesity be an issue for child protective services? A call for more research on this critical public health issue, *Trauma, Violence and Abuse*, 15(2): 113–25.

Jones, N. (2013) Good enough parents? Exploring attitudes of family centre workers supporting and assessing parents with learning difficultie, *Social Work in Action*, 25(3): 169–90.

Jones, R. (2014) *The Story of Baby P*. Bristol: Policy Press.

Jordanova, L. (1989) Children in history: concepts of nature and society, in G. Scarre (ed.) *Children, Parents and Politics*. Cambridge: Cambridge University Press.

Joseph, Sir K. (1972) The next ten years, *New Society*, 5 October, pp. 8–9.

Juffer, F., Bakermans-Kranenburg, M. J. and Van IJzendoorn, M. H. (eds) (2008) *Promoting Positive Parenting: An Attachment-based Intervention*. New York: Lawrence Erlbaum/Taylor & Francis.

Kadushin, A. and Martin, J. (1981) *Child Abuse: An Interactional Event*. New York: Columbia University Press.

Kahn, M. (2002) *Basic Freud*. Basic Books, New York: NY.

Kajese, T., Nguyen, L., Pham, G. et al. (2011) Characteristics of child abuse homicides in the state of Kansas from 1994 to 2007, *Child Abuse & Neglect*, 35: 147–54.

Kaplan, S. J., Labruna, V., Pecovitz, D. and Salzinger, S. (1999) Physically abused adolescents: behavior problems, functional impairment, and comparison of informants, *Pediatrics*, 104(1): 43–9.

Katz, E. (2016) Beyond the physical incident model: how children living with domestic violence are harmed by and resist regimes of coercive control, *Child Abuse Review*, 25: 46–59.

Kaufman, D. and Widom, C. (1999) Childhood victimisation, running away and delinquency, *Journal of Research in Delinquency and Crime*, 36: 347–70.

Kaufman, J. and Zigler, E. (1989) The intergenerational transmission of child abuse, in D. Cicchetti and V. Carlson (eds) *Child Maltreatment: Theory and Research on the Causes and Consequences of Child Abuse and Neglect*. Cambridge: Cambridge University Press.

Kearney, P., Levin, E., Rosen, G. and Sainsbury, M. (2003) *Families that Have Alcohol and Mental Health Problems: A Template for Partnership Working*. London: SCIE. Available at: http://www.scie.org.uk/publications/guides/guide02/index.asp.

Keen, J. and Alison, L. (2001) Drug misusing parents: key points for health professionals, *Archives of Disease in Childhood*, 85: 296–9.

Kelly, L., Regan, L. and Burton, S. (1991) *An Exploratory Study of the Prevalence of Sexual Abuse in a Sample of 16–21 Year Olds*. London: Child Abuse Studies Unit, University of North London.

Kelly, P. and Koh, J. (2006) Sexually transmitted infections in alleged sexual abuse of children and adolescents, *Journal of Paediatrics and Child Health*, 42(7–8): 434–40.

Kempe, C., Silverman, P., Steele, B., Droegemueller, W. and Silver, H. (1962) The battered child syndrome, *Journal of the American Medical Association*, 181: 17–24.

Kempe, R. and Kempe, C. (1978) *Child Abuse*. London: Fontana.

Kendall-Tackett, R., Lyon, T., Taliaferro, G. and Little, L. (2005) Why child maltreatment researchers should include children's disability status in their maltreatment studies, *Child Abuse & Neglect*, 29: 147–51.

Kilgallon, W. (1995) *Report of the Independent Review into Allegations of Abuse at Meadowdale Children's Home and Related Matters*. Morpeth: Northumberland County Council.

Kim, M. J. and Cicchetti, D. (2010) Longitudinal pathways linking child maltreatment, emotion regulation, peer relations, and psychopathology, *Journal of Child Psychology and Psychiatry*, 51(6): 706–16.

Kim, M. J., Tajima, E. A., Herrenkohl, T. I. and Huang, B. (2009) Early child maltreatment, runaway youths, and risk of delinquency and victimization in adolescence: a mediational model, *Social Work Research*, 33(1): 19–28.

Kinard, E. (1998) Methodological issues in assessing resilience in maltreated children, *Child Abuse & Neglect*, 22: 669–80.

Kirollos, M., Anning, C., Fylkes, G. K. and Denselow, J. (2018) *The War on Children: Time to End Grave Violations Against Children in Conflict*. London: Save the Children International.

Kneebone, R. L. (2009) Practice, rehearsal, and performance: an approach for simulation-based surgical and procedure training, *Journal of the American Medical Association*, 302: 1336–8.

Knight, K. E., Ellis, C. and Simmonds, S. B. (2014) Parental predictors of children's animal abuse: findings from a national and intergenerational sample, *Journal of Interpersonal Violence*, 29(16): 3014–34.

Knutson, J. F. and Schartz, H. A. (1997) Physical abuse and neglect of children, in T. A. Widiger, A. J. Frances, H. A. Pincus et al. (eds) *DSM-IV Sourcebook*, vol. 3. Washington, DC: American Psychiatric Association, pp. 713–803.

Koposov, R. A., Ruchkin, V. V., Eisemann, M. and Sidorov, P. I. (2005) Alcohol abuse in Russian delinquent adolescents: associations with comorbid psychopathology, personality and parenting, *European Child & Adolescent Psychiatry*, 14(5): 254–61.

Korbin, J. (ed.) (1981) *Child Abuse and Neglect: Cross-Cultural Perspectives*. Berkeley, CA: University of California Press.

Korbin, J., Coulton, C., Lindstrom-Ufuti, H. and Spilsbury, J. (2000) Neighborhood views on the definition and etiology of child maltreatment, *Child Abuse & Neglect*, 24: 1509–27.

Korkman, J., Pekka, J. and Sandnabba, K. (2006) Dynamics of verbal interaction between interviewer and child in interviews with alleged victims of child sexual abuse, *Scandinavian Journal of Psychology*, 47: 109–19.

Krähenbühl, S. J. and Blades, M. (2006) The effect of question repetition within interviews on young children's eyewitness recall, *Journal of Experimental Child Psychology*, 94: 57–67.

Kravchuk, N. (2009) Children in post-communist Russia: some aspects of the child's right to protection, *International Journal of Children's Rights*. 17: 611–14.

Kroll, B. (2004) Living with an elephant: growing up with parental substance misuse, *Child & Family Social Work*, 9: 129–44.

Kroll, B. and Taylor, A. (2003) *Parental Substance Misuse and Child Welfare*. London: Jessica Kingsley Publications.

Kroll, J. and Bachrach, B. (1986) Child care and child abuse in Early Medieval Europe, *Child and Adolescent Psychiatry*, 25(4): 562–8.

Krug, R. (1989) Adult male report of childhood sexual abuse by mothers: case descriptions, motivations and long-term consequences, *Child Abuse & Neglect*, 13: 111–19.

Kumar, V. (1993) *Poverty and Inequality in the UK: The Effects on Children*. London: National Children's Bureau.

La Fontaine, J. (1990) *Child Sexual Abuse*. Cambridge: Polity Press.

La Fontaine, J. (1994) *The Extent and Nature of Organised and Ritual Abuse: Research Findings*. London: HMSO.

La Fontaine, J. (1998) *Speak of the Devil: Tales of Satanic Abuse in Contemporary England*. Cambridge: Cambridge University Press.

Lakatos, K., Nemoda, Z., Toth, I. et al. (2002) Further evidence for the role of the dopamine D4 receptor (DRD4) gene in attachment disorganization: interaction of the exon III 48-bp repeat and the 521 C/T promoter polymorphisms, *Molecular Psychiatry*, 7: 27–31.

Lakatos, K., Toth, I., Nemoda, Z. et al. (2000) Dopamine D4 receptor (DRD4) gene polymorphism is associated with attachment disorganization in infants, *Molecular Psychiatry*, 5: 633–7.

LaLiberte, T., Piescher, K., Mickelson, N. and Lee, M. (2017) Child protection services and parents with intellectual and developmental disabilities, *Journal of Applied Research in Intellectual Disabilities*, 30: 521–32.

Lambeth (London Borough of) (1987) *Whose Child? The Report of the Public Inquiry into the Death of Tyra Henry*. London: London Borough of Lambeth.

Lambeth, Lewisham and Southwark (London Boroughs of) (1989) *The Doreen Aston Report*. London: Lambeth, Lewisham and Southwark Area Review Committee.

Laming, Lord (2003) *The Victoria Climbié Inquiry: Report of an Inquiry by Lord Laming*, Cm 5730. London: The Stationery Office.

Laming, Lord (2009) *The Protection of Children in England: A Progress Report*. London: The Stationery Office.

Lamont, A. (2011) Child abuse and neglect statistics, Australian Institute of Family Studies. Available at: http://www.aifs.gov.au/nch/pubs/sheets/rs1/rs1.html.

Langer, W. (1974) Infanticide: a historical survey, *History of Childhood Quarterly*, 1: 353–65.

Larrance, D. and Twentyman, C. (1983) Maternal attribution and child abuse, *Journal of Abnormal Psychology*, 92: 449–57.

Lasky-Su, J., Lange, C., Biederman, J. et al. (2008) Family-based association analysis of a statistically derived quantitative traits for ADHD reveal an association in DRD4 with inattentive symptoms in ADHD individuals, *American Journal of Medical Genetics Part B: Neuropsychiatric Genetics*, 147B(1): 100–6.

La Valle, I., Holmes, L., Gill, C. et al.. (2016) *Improving Children's Social Care Services: Results of a Feasibility Study*. London: CAMHS Press.

Lazenbatt, A. (2010) *The Impact of Abuse and Neglect on the Health and Mental Health of Children and Young People*. London: NSPCC.

Leach, P. (1999) *The Physical Punishment of Children: Some Input from Recent Research*. London: NSPCC.

Lealman, C., Haigh, D., Phillips, J., Stone, J. and Ord-Smith, C. (1983) Prediction and prevention of child abuse – an empty hope?, *The Lancet*, 1(8339): 1423–4.

Lee, M. and O'Brien, R. (1995) *The Game's Up: Redefining Child Prostitution*. London: The Children's Society.

Letourneau, C. (1981) Empathy and stress: how they affect parental aggression, *Social Work*, 26: 383–90.

Leventhal, J. (2001) The prevention of child abuse and neglect: successfully out of the blocks, *Child Abuse & Neglect*, 25: 431–9.

Leventhal, J. (2003) The field of child maltreatment enters its fifth decade, *Child Abuse & Neglect*, 27: 1–4.

Levitt, L., Hoffer, T. A. and Loper, A. B. (2016) Criminal histories of a subsample of animal cruelty offenders, *Aggression and Violent Behaviour*, 30: 48–58.

Lewisham (London Borough of) (1985) *The Leeways Inquiry Report*. London: London Borough of Lewisham.

Liebenberg, L. and Ungar, M. (eds) (2009) *Researching Resilience*. Toronto: University of Toronto Press.

Littell, J. H., Popa, M. and Forsythe, B. (2005) *Multisystemic Therapy for Social, Emotional, and Behavioural Problems in Youth aged 10–17*, Cochrane Database of Systematic Reviews, Issue 4.

Loftus, E. and Ketcham, K. (1994) *The Myth of Repressed Memory: False Memories and Allegations of Sexual Abuse*. New York: St Martin's Press.

Lovell, E. (2001) *Megan's Law: Does it Protect Children? A Review of Evidence on the Impact of Community Notification as Legislated for through Megan's Law in the United States – Recommendations for Policy Makers in the United Kingdom*. London: NSPCC.

Lowe, N. (1989) The role of wardship in child care cases, *Family Law*, 19: 38–45.

Lownsbrough, H. and O'Leary, D. (2005) *The Leadership Imperative: Reforming Children's Services from the Ground Up*. London: Demos.

Luke, N., Sebba, J., Rees, A. and McNeish, D. (2017) *Child Sexual Exploitation and Mental Health*. London: Department for Education.

Luyten, P., Kempke, S. and Van Houdenhove, B. (2009) Stressonderzoek in de psychiatrie: een complex verhaal [Stress research in psychiatry: a complex story], *Tijdschrift voor Psychiatrie*, 51: 611–18.

Lynch, M. and Roberts, J. (1982) *The Consequences of Child Abuse*. London: Academic Press.

Lyon, C. (1989) Legal developments following the Cleveland report in England: a consideration of some aspects of the Children Bill, *Journal of Social Welfare Law*, 11: 200–6.

Lyon, C. (2003) *Child Abuse*, 3rd edn. Bristol: Jordan Publishing.

Lyons, J. S., Anderson, R. L. and Larson, D. B. (1993) The use and effects of physical punishment in the home: a systematic review. Paper presented at the meeting of the American Academy of Pediatrics, Washington, DC.

Lyons-Ruth, K. and Jacobvitz, D. (2008) Attachment disorganisation: genetic factors, parenting contexts, and developmental transformation from infancy to adulthood, in J. Cassidy and P. R. Shaver (eds) *Handbook of Attachment: Theory, Research and Clinical Applications*, 2nd edn. New York: Guilford Press, pp. 666–97.

Lyons-Ruth, K., Lyubchik, A., Wolfe, R. and Bronfman, E. (2002) Parental depression and child attachment: hostile and helpless profiles of parent and child behavior among families at risk, in S. H. Goodman and I. H. Gotlib (eds) *Children of Depressed Parents: Mechanisms of Risk and Implications for Treatment*, Washington, DC: American Psychological Association, pp. 89–120.

Macfarlane, A. (1970) *The Family Life of Ralph Josselin*. Cambridge: Cambridge University Press.

Macfarlane, A. (1979) Review of 'The family, sex and marriage in England 1500–1800' by Lawrence Stone, *History and Theory*, 18: 103–26.

Macfarlane, K. and Waterman, J. (1986) *The Sexual Abuse of Young Children*. New York: Holt, Rinehart & Winston.

Macleod, M. and Saraga, E. (1988) Challenging the orthodoxy: towards a feminist theory and practice, *Feminist Review*, 28: 15–55.

MacMillan, H. L. (2010) *Interventions to Prevent Child Maltreatment*. PreVAiL: Preventing Violence Across the Lifespan Research Network. Available at: www.uwo.ca/fims/prevail/docs.

MacMillan, H. L., Wathen, C. N., Barlow, J. et al. (2009) Interventions to prevent child maltreatment and associated impairment, *The Lancet*, 373(9659): 250–66.

Madigan, S., Bakermans-Kranenburg, M. J., Van IJzendoorn, M. H. et al. (2006) Unresolved states of mind, anomalous parenting behaviour, and disorganized attachment: a review and meta-analysis of a transmission gap, *Attachment & Human Development*, 8: 89–111.

Maestripieri, D. (2010) Neurobiology of social behavior, in M. Platt and A. Ghazanfar (eds) *Primate Neuroethology*. Oxford: Oxford University Press.

Maestripieri, D., Wallen, K. and Carroll, K. (1997) Infant abuse runs in families of group-living pigtail macaques, *Child Abuse & Neglect*, 21: 465–71.

Maguire-Jack, K., Lanier, P., Johnson-Motoyama, M., Welch, H. and Dineen, M. (2015) Geographic variation in racial disparities in child maltreatment: the influence of country poverty and population density, *Child Abuse and Neglect*, 47: 1–13.

Main, M., Hesse, S. and Hesse, S. (2011) Attachment theory and research: overview with suggested applications to child custody, *Family Court Review*, 49(3): 426–63.

Manion, K. (2002) Trafficking in women and children for sexual purposes: a growing threat in Europe, *Social Work in Europe*, 9: 14–22.

Margolin, L. (1992) Sexual abuse by grandparents, *Child Abuse & Neglect*, 16: 735–41.

Margolin, L. (1994) Child sexual abuse by uncles: a risk assessment, *Child Abuse & Neglect*, 18: 215–24.

Marsh, P. and Crowe, G. (1998) *Family Group Conferences in Child Welfare*. Oxford: Blackwell.

Martin, G., Bergen, H., Richardson, A., Roeger, L. and Allison, S. (2004) Sexual abuse and suicidality: gender differences in a large community sample of adolescents, *Child Abuse & Neglect*, 28: 491–503.

Mason, C. (2012) Social work, the 'art of relationship': parents' perspectives on an intensive family support project, *Child & Family Social Work*, 17(3): 368–77.

Mason, W. and Bywaters, P. (2016) Poverty, child abuse and neglect: patterns of cost and spending, *Families, Relationships and Societies*, 5(1): 155–61.

Masson, H., Hackett, S., Phillips, J. and Balfe, M. (2015) Developmental markers of risk or vulnerability? Young females who sexually abuse – characteristics, backgrounds, behaviours and outcomes, *Child & Family Social Work*, 20(1): 19–29.

Masson, H. and O'Byrne, P. (1990) The family system approach: a help or hindrance?, in The Violence against Children Study Group, *Taking Child Abuse Seriously*. London: Unwin Hyman.

Masson, J. (1984) *Freud: The Assault on Truth*. London: Faber & Faber.

Masson, J., Pearce, J. and Bader, O. (2008) *Care Profiling Study*. London: Ministry of Justice.

Masten, A., Best, K. and Garmezy, N. (1990) Resilience and development: contributions from the study of children who overcome adversity, *Development and Psychopathology*, 2: 425–44.

Matias, C., O'Connor, T. G., Futh, A. and Scott, S. (2014) Observational attachment theory-based measures predict children's attachment narratives independently from social learning theory-based measures, *Attachment & Human Development*, 16(1): 77–92.

Maxwell, N., Scourfield, J., Featherstone, B., Holland, S. and Tolman, R. (2012) Engaging fathers in child welfare services: a narrative review of recent evidence, *Child & Family Social Work*, 17(2): 160–9.

May-Chahal, C. and Cawson, P. (2005) Measuring child maltreatment in the United Kingdom: a study of the prevalence of child abuse and neglect, *Child Abuse & Neglect*, 29(9): 969–84.

McCafferty, S. (2011) Behavioural-based interventions: social learning theory, in S. Goodman and I. Trowler (eds) *Social Work Reclaimed*. London: Jessica Kingsley Publications.

McCloskey, K. and Raphael, D. (2005) Adult perpetrator gender asymmetries in child sexual assault victim selection: results from the 2000 National Incident-Based Reporting System, *Journal of Child Sexual Abuse*, 14: 1–24.

McClure, R. (1981) *Coram's Children: The London Foundling Hospital in the Eighteenth Century*. New Haven, CT: Yale University Press.

McCluskey, U. (2005) *To Be Met as a Person: The Dynamics of Attachment in Professional Encounters*. London: Karnac.

McConnell, D. and Llewellyn, G. (2000) Disability and discrimination in statutory child protection proceedings, *Disability and Society*, 15: 883–95.

McCracken, K., Priest, S., Fitzsimons, A. et al. (2017) *Evaluation of Pause*. London: Department for Education.

McCrory, E., De Brito, S. A. and Viding, E. (2010) Research review: the neurobiology and genetics of maltreatment and adversity, *Journal of Child Psychology and Psychiatry*, 51(10): 1079–95.

McCrory, E. J., Gerin, M. I. and Viding, E. (2017) Annual Research Review: childhood maltreatment, latent vulnerability and the shift to preventative psychiatry – the contribution of functional brain damage, *Journal of Child Psychology and Psychiatry*, 58: 338–57.

McCrory, E., Palmer. A. and Puetz. V. B. L. (2017) The neurobiology and genetics of childhood maltreatment, in *The Wiley Handbook of What Works in Child Protection; An Evidence-based Approach to Assessment and Intervention in Child Protection*. Chichester: Wiley Blackwell.

McDonald, S. E., Collins, E. A., Nicotera, N. and Graham-Bermann, S. A. (2015) Children's experience of companion animal maltreatment in households characterized by intimate partner violence, *Child Abuse & Neglect*, 50: 116–27.

McEwen, F., Moffitt, T. E. and Arseneault, L. (2014) Is childhood cruelty to animals a marker for physical maltreatment in a prospective cohort of children?, *Child Abuse & Neglect*, 38(3): 533–43.

McLaren, H. J. (2013) Un-blaming mothers whose partners sexually abuse children: in view of heteronormative myths, pressures and authorities, *Child & Family Social Work*, 18(4): 439–48.

McNeish, D., Sebba, J., Luke, N. and Rees, A. (2017) *What Have We Learned About Good Social Work Systems and Practice?* London: Department for Education.

McRedmond, P. (2010) Defining organised crime in the context of human trafficking, in G. Wylie and P. McRedmond (eds) *Human Trafficking in Europe: Character, Causes and Consequences*. Basingstoke: Palgrave Macmillan, pp. 181–97.

Meadow, R. (1977) Munchausen syndrome by proxy: the hinterland of child abuse, *The Lancet*, 2(8033): 343–5.

Meadow, R. (1997) *The ABC of Child Abuse*. London: British Medical Association.

Meiselman, K. (1978) *Incest*. San Francisco, CA: Jossey-Bass.

Melton, G. and Flood, M. (1994) Research policy and child maltreatment: developing the scientific foundation for effective protection of children, *Child Abuse & Neglect*, 18 (suppl. 1): 1–28.

Mennen, F. E., Kim, K., Sang, J. and Trickett, P. K. (2010) Child neglect: definition and identification of youth's experiences in official reports of maltreatment, *Child Abuse & Neglect*, 34: 647–58.

Messing, J. (2011) The social control of family violence, *Journal of Women and Social Work*, 26: 154–68.

Meyers, A. (2015) Lifting the veil: the lived experience of sibling abuse, *Qualitative Social Work*, 16(3): 333–50.

Michenbaum, D. (1977) *Cognitive Behavior Modification: An Integrative Approach*. New York: Plenum Press.

Mikton, C. R., Butchar, A., Dahlberg, L. L. and Krug, E. G. (2014) Global status report on violence prevention 2014, *American Journal of Preventative Medicine*, 50(5): 652–9.

Millar, M. and Corby, B. (2006) The framework for assessing the needs of children and their families: a basis for a 'therapeutic' encounter?, *British Journal of Social Work*, 36(6): 887–99.

Miller, A. (1985) *Thou Shalt Not Be Aware*. London: Pluto Press.

Miller, D. (2002) *Disabled Children and Abuse*. Available at: http://www.nspcc.org.uk/inform/ research/ briefings/disabledchildrenandabuse_wda48224.html.

Miller, W. R. and Rollnick, S. (2002) *Motivational Interviewing: Preparing People to Change*, 2nd edn. New York: Guilford Press.

Ministry of Justice (2011) *Achieving Best Evidence in Criminal Proceedings: Guidance on Interviewing Victims and Witnesses, and Guidance on Using Special Measures*. London: Ministry of Justice.

Minuchin, S. (1974) *Families and Family Therapy*. Cambridge, MA: Harvard University Press.

Mitchell, J. (1974) *Psychoanalysis and Feminism*. London: Allen Lane.

Montgomery, P., Gardner, F., Bjornstad, G. and Ramchandani, P. (2009) *Systematic Reviews of Interventions Following Physical Abuse: Helping Practitioners and Expert Witnesses Improve the Outcomes of Child Abuse*, Research Brief DCSF-RBX-09-08A. Available at: www.education.gov.uk/research.

Montgomery, S. (1982) Problems in the perinatal prediction of child abuse, *British Journal of Social Work*, 12: 189–96.

Moran-Ellis, J. (2010) Reflections on the sociology of childhood in the UK, *Current Sociology*, 58(2): 186–205.

Morgan, C. and Bartlett, E. (2017) *Making Homelessness Applications for Refugees in England. A Guide for Anyone Supporting Newly Recognized Single Refugees.* Stratford: Refugee Council.

Morton, N. and Browne, K. (1998) Theory and observation of attachment and its relation to child maltreatment: a review, *Child Abuse & Neglect*, 22: 1093–104.

Mrazek, P. and Mrazek, D. (1987) Resilience in child maltreatment victims: a conceptual exploration, *Child Abuse & Neglect*, 11: 357–66.

Mulderrig, J. (2016) Fat-shaming: Change4Life's anti-obesity 'nudge' campaign glosses over social inequalities. Available at: http://eprints.lse.ac.uk/80510/1/democraticaudit.com-Fat-shaming%20 Change4Lifes%20anti-obesity%20nudge%20campaign%20glosses%20over%20social%20 inequalities.pdf (accessed June 2018).

Mullender, A. and Morley, R. (1994) *Children Living with Domestic Violence: Putting Men's Abuse of Women on the Child Care Agenda.* London: Whiting & Birch.

Munir, A. and Yasin, S. (1997) Commercial sexual exploitation, *Child Abuse Review*, 6: 147–53.

Munro, E. (2002) *Effective Child Protection.* London: Sage.

Munro, E. (2008) *Effective Child Protection*, 2nd edn. London: Sage.

Munro, E. (2010) *The Munro Review of Child Protection – Part One: A Systems Analysis.* London: The Stationery Office.

Munro, E. (2011a) *The Munro Review of Child Protection – Interim Report: The Child's Journey.* London: The Stationery Office.

Munro, E. (2011b) *The Munro Review of Child Protection: Final Report. A Child-Centred System.* London: The Stationery Office.

Munro, E. R., Brown, R. and Manful, E. (2011a) *Safeguarding Children Statistics: The Availability and Comparability of Data in the UK.* London: Childhood Wellbeing Research Centre.

Munro, E. R., Brown, R., Sempick, J., Ward, H. and Owen, C. (2011b) *Scoping Review to Draw Together Data on Child Injury and Safeguarding and to Compare the Position of England with that in Other Countries.* London: Childhood Wellbeing Research Centre.

Murphy-Beaman, V. (1994) A conceptual framework for thinking about risk assessment and case management in child protective services, *Child Abuse & Neglect*, 18: 193–201.

Mustillo, S., Dorsey, S., Conover, K. and Burns, B. (2011) Parental depression and child outcomes: the mediating effects of abuse and neglect, *Journal of Marriage and Family*, 73: 164–80.

National Crime Agency (2014) *NCA Strategic Assessment. The Nature and Scale of Human Trafficking in 2014.* London: National Crime Agency.

National Crime Agency (2017) *National Crime Agency: 2017 Analysis of Serious and Organized Crime Threats.* London: National Crime Agency.

National Crime Agency (2018) *National Referral Mechanism Statistics – End of Year Summary 2017.* London: National Crime Agency.

National Institute for Clinical Excellence (2012) *The Evidence Base for Family Nurse Partnership.* Available at: https://www.nice.org.uk/guidance/ph40/documents/social-and-emotional-wellbeing-early-years-expert-report-42 (accessed June 2018).

National Institute of Alcohol Abuse and Alcoholism (1993) *Eighth Special Report to U.S. Congress on Alcohol and Health.* Washington, DC: US Government Printing Office.

National Research Council and Institute of Medicine (2009) *Depression in Parents, Parenting, and Children: Opportunities to Improve Identification, Treatment, and Prevention.* Washington, DC: National Academies Press.

National Scientific Council on the Developing Child (2005) Excessive stress disrupts the architecture of the developing brain, Working Paper no. 3. Cambridge, MA: Center on the Developing Child, Harvard University. Available at: http://developingchild.harvard.edu/ library/reports_and_working_ papers/wp3/ (accessed 4 December 2009).

National Society for the Prevention of Cruelty to Children (2005) *Understanding the Links Between Child Abuse, Animal Abuse and Domestic Violence: Information for Professionals.* London: NSPCC.

National Society for the Prevention of Cruelty to Children (2018) *Child Trafficking: What Is Child Trafficking?* London: NSPCC.

Nelson, B. (1984) *Making an Issue of Child Abuse: Political Agenda Setting for Social Problems*. Chicago, IL: University of Chicago Press.

Nelson, S. (1987) *Incest: Fact and Myth*. Edinburgh: Strathmullion.

Neursten, L., Goldering, J. and Carpenter, S. (1984) Non-sexual transmission of sexually transmitted diseases: an infrequent occurrence, *Pediatrics*, 74: 67–76.

Newberger, C. and White, K. (1989) Cognitive foundations for parental care, in D. Cicchetti and V. Carlson (eds) *Child Maltreatment: Theory and Research on the Causes and Consequences of Child Abuse and Neglect*. Cambridge: Cambridge University Press.

Newberry, M. (2017) Pets in danger: exploring the link between domestic violence and animal abuse, *Aggression and Violent Behaviour*, 34: 273–81.

Nilsson, T., Carlstedt, A., Baudin, C. et al. (2014) Intra- and extra-familial child sexual abusers and recidivism in Sweden: a 10- to 15-year follow-up study, *Journal of Forensic Psychiatry & Psychology*, 25(3): 341–61.

Observer (2010) Female circumcision growing in Britain despite being illegal, 25 July.

Office for National Statistics (2001) *Census 2001*. Cardiff: ONS.

Office for National Statistics (2016) *Divorces in England and Wales: 2016*. London: Office for National Statistics.

Office for National Statistics (2017) *Domestic Abuse in England and Wales*. London: Office for National Statistics.

Ofsted (2015) Early help: whose responsibility? Available at: https://assets.publishing.service.gov.uk/government/uploads/system/uploads/attachment_data/file/410378/Early_help_whose_responsibility.pdf (accessed June 2018).

Olds, D. L., Eckenrode, J., Henderson, C. R., Jr. et al. (1997) Long-term effects of home visitation on maternal life course and child abuse and neglect: fifteen-year follow-up of a randomized trial, *Journal of the American Medical Association*, 278: 637–43.

Oliver, J. (1985) Successive generations of child maltreatment, *British Journal of Psychiatry*, 147: 484–90.

Ong, B. (1985) The paradox of 'wonderful children': the case of child abuse, *Early Child Development and Care*, 21: 91–106.

Oriola, T. B. (2016) 'Unwilling cocoons': Boko Haram's war against women, *Studies in Conflict and Terrorism*, 40(2): 99–121.

Osborn, A. (2005) Russia's youth faces worst crisis of homelessness and substance misuse since Second World War, *British Medical Journal*, 330(1348): 3.

Out, D., Bakermans-Kranenburg, M. J. and Van IJzendoorn, M. H. (2009) The role of disconnected and extremely insensitive parenting in the development of disorganized attachment: the validation of a new measure, *Attachment & Human Development*, 11: 419–43.

Owen, R. and Sweeting, A. (2007) *Hoodie or Goodie? The Link Between Violent Victimisation and Offending in Young People: A Research Report*. London: British Market Research Bureau.

Packman, J. (1975) *The Child's Generation: Child Care Policy from Curtis to Houghton*. Oxford: Blackwell.

Packman, J. (1986) *Who Needs Care?* Oxford: Blackwell.

Panter-Brick, C. (2002) Street children, human rights and public health: a critique and future directions, *Annual Review of Anthropology*, 31: 147–71.

Parents Against Child Exploitation (PACE) (2016) 'Parents speak out: crucial partners in tackling child sexual exploitation'. Parents Against Child Exploitation. Available at: paceuk.info/wp-content/uploads/Parents-Speak-Out-final.pdf.

Parton, N. (1979) The natural history of child abuse: a study in social problem definition, *British Journal of Social Work*, 9: 431–51.

Parton, N. (1981) Child abuse, social anxiety and welfare, *British Journal of Social Work*, 11: 391–414.

Parton, N. (1985) *The Politics of Child Abuse*. London: Macmillan.

Parton, N. (1991) *Governing the Family: Child Care, Child Protection and the State*. London: Macmillan.

Parton, N. (2005) *Safeguarding Childhood: Early Intervention and Surveillance in Late Modern Society*. London: Palgrave Macmillan.

Parton, N. (2007) Safeguarding children: a socio-historical analysis, in K. Wilson and A. James (eds) *The Child Protection Handbook*. Oxford: Baillière Tindall.

Parton, N. and O'Byrne, P. (2000) *Constructive Social Work: Towards a New Practice*. Basingstoke: Macmillan.

Patel, S. G., Staudenmeyer, A. H., Wickham, R. et al. (2017) War-exposed newcomer adolescent immigrants facing daily life stressors in the United States, *International Journal of Intercultural Relations*, 60: 128–31.

Patterson, G. R. (1982) *Coercive Family Process*. Eugene, OR: Castalia Press.

Pavlov, I. (1927) *Conditioned Reflexes: An Investigation of the Physiological Activity of the Cerebral Cortex*. Oxford: Oxford University Press.

Pearce, J. J., Hynes, P. and Bovarnick, S. (2009) *Breaking the Wall of Silence: Practitioners' Responses to Trafficked Children and Young People*. London: NSPCC.

Pelton, L. (1978) Child abuse and neglect: the myth of classlessness, *American Journal of Orthopsychiatry*, 48: 608–17.

Perrin, S., Smith, P. and Yule, W. (1999) Practitioner review: the assessment and treatment of post-traumatic stress disorder in children and adolescents, *Journal of Child Psychology and Psychiatry*, 41: 277–89.

Perry, B. (2002) Childhood experience and the expression of genetic potential: what childhood neglect tells us about nature and nurture, *Brain and Mind*, 3: 79–100.

Peters, R. and Barlow, J. (2003) Systematic review of instruments designed to predict child maltreatment during the antenatal and postnatal periods, *Child Abuse Review*, 12: 416–39.

Pfohl, S. (1977) The 'discovery' of child abuse, *Social Problems*, 24: 310–23.

Pincus, A. and Minahan, A. (1973) *Social Work Practice: Models and Methods*. Itasca, IL: Peacock.

Pinker, S. (2012) *The Better Angels of Our Nature. A History of Violence and Humanity*. London: Penguin Books.

Pithouse, A. and Holland, S. (1999) Open access family centres and their users: positive results, some doubts and new departures, *Children & Society*, 13: 167–78.

Platt, D. (2001) Refocusing children's services: evaluation of an initial assessment process, *Child & Family Social Work*, 6: 139–48.

Polansky, N., Chalmers, M., Buttenweiser, E. and Williams, D. (1985) *Damaged Parents: An Anatomy of Child Neglect*. Chicago, IL: University of Chicago Press.

Pollock, L. (1983) *Forgotten Children: Parent–Child Relations from 1500 to 1900*. Cambridge: Cambridge University Press.

Porter, C., Lawson, J. and Bigler, E. (2005) Child neuropsychology, *Neuropsychology, Development and Cognition: Section C*, 11(2): 203–20.

Porter, R. (ed.) (1984) *Child Sexual Abuse within the Family*. London: Tavistock.

Prevent Child Abuse America (2005) *Fact Sheet: Emotional Child Abuse*. Chicago, IL: Prevent Child Abuse America.

Pritchard, C. (2004) *The Child Abusers: Research and Controversy*. Maidenhead: Open University Press.

Radford, L., Corral, S., Bradley, C. et al. (2011) *Child Abuse and Neglect in the UK Today*. London: NSPCC.

Ravallion, M. and Chen, S. (2007) China's (uneven) progress against poverty, *Journal of Development Economics*, 82(1): 1–42.

Read, J. (1998) Child abuse and severity of disturbance among adult psychiatric patients, *Child Abuse & Neglect*, 22: 359–68.

Reavley, W. and Gilbert, M. (1979) The analysis and treatment of child abuse by behavioural psychotherapy, *Child Abuse & Neglect*, 3: 509–14.

Reder, P. and Duncan, S. (1998) A proposed system for reviewing child deaths, *Child Abuse Review*, 7: 280–6.

Reder, P., Duncan, S. and Gray, M. (1993) *Beyond Blame: Child Abuse Tragedies Revisited*. London: Routledge.

Rees, A., Luke, N., Sebba, J. and McNeish, D. (2017) *Adolescent Service Change and the Edge of Care*. London: Department for Education.

Rees, G. (1993) *Hidden Truths: Young People's Experiences of Running Away*. London: The Children's Society.

Rees, G. and Smeaton, M. (2001) *Child Runaways: Under 11s Running Away in the UK*. London: The Children's Society.

Reijman, S., Foster, S. and Duschinsky, R. (2018) The infant disorganised attachment classification: patterning within the disturbance of coherence, *Social Science and Medicine*, 200: 52–8.

Reisz, S., Duschinsky, R. and Siegel, D. J. (2017) Disorganized attachment and defense: exploring John Bowlby's unpublished reflections, *Attachment & Human Development*, 20(2): 107–34.

Roberts, J., Lynch, M. and Golding, J. (1980) Postneonatal mortality in children from abusing families, *British Medical Journal*, 281: 102–4.

Roberts, J. and Taylor, C. (1993) Sexually abused children and young people speak out, in L. Waterhouse (ed.) *Child Abuse and Child Abusers: Protection and Prevention*. London: Jessica Kingsley Publications.

Robling, M., Bekkers, M., Bell, K. et al. (2016) Effectiveness of a nurse-led intensive home-visitation programme for first-time mothers (Building Blocks): a pragmatic randomised controlled trial, *The Lancet*, 387(10014): 146–55.

Rose, L. (1986) *The Massacre of the Innocents*. London: Routledge & Kegan Paul.

Rose, L. (1991) *The Erosion of Childhood: Child Oppression in Britain 1860–1918*. London: Routledge.

Roudik, P. (2011) Children's rights: Russian Federation. Available at: http://www.loc.gov/law/help/child-rights/russia.php.

Rowe, J. and Lambert, L. (1973) *Children Who Wait*. London: Association of British Agencies for Fostering and Adoption.

Royal College of Paediatrics and Child Health (2009) *Fabricated or Induced Illness by Carers (FII): A Practical Guide for Paediatricians*. Available at: http://www.rcpch.ac.uk/sites/default/files/Fabricated%20or%20Induced%20Illness%20by%20Carers%20A%20Practical%20Guide%20for%20Paediatricians%202009.pdf.

Ruch, G., Turney, D. and Ward, A. (2010) *Relationship-based Social Work: Getting to the Heart of Practice*. London: Jessica Kingsley Publications.

Ruch, G., Turney, D. and Ward, A. (2018) *Relationship-based Social Work: Getting to the Heart of Practice*, 2nd edn. London: Jessica Kingsley Publications.

Rudnicki, A. A. (2013) The development of Russia's child protection and welfare system, *Demokratizatsiya*. 21(1): 29–44.

Rush, F. (1980) *The Best Kept Secret*. Englewood Cliffs, NJ: Prentice Hall.

Rutter, M. (1978) *Maternal Deprivation Reassessed*. Harmondsworth: Penguin.

Sack, W., Mason, R. and Higgins, J. (1985) The single-parent family and abusive child punishment, *American Journal of Orthopsychiatry*, 55: 253–9.

Samayam, P., Chander, R. and Reddy, S. (2011) An unusual case of failure to thrive in a child, *The National Medical Journal of India*, 24: 86–7.

Scarre, G. (1980) Children and paternalism, *Philosophy*, 55: 117–24.

Schore, A. N. (2000) Attachment and the regulation of the right brain, *Attachment & Human Development*, 2(1): 23–47.

Schore, A. N. (2001) Effects of a secure attachment relationship on right brain development, affect regulation and infant mental health, *Journal of Infant Mental Health*, 22: 7–66.

Schwartz, M., O'Leary, S. G. and Kendziora, K. T. (1997) Dating aggression among high school students, *Journal of Violence and Victims*, 12: 295–305.

Scott, M. (1989) *A Cognitive-behavioural Approach to Clients' Problems*. London: Tavistock.

Scourfield, J. (2001) Constructing women in child protection work, *Child & Family Social Work*, 6: 77–87.

Scourfield, J. (2003) *Gender and Child Protection*. Basingstoke: Palgrave Macmillan.

Scourfield, J. (2014) Improving work with fathers to prevent child maltreatment, *Child Abuse & Neglect* 38(6): 974–81.

Scourfield, J., Roen, K. and McDermott, E. (2011) The non-display of authentic distress: public–private dualism in young people's discursive construction of self-harm, *Sociology of Health and Illness*, 33(5): 777–91.

Seagull, E. (1987) Social support and child maltreatment: a review of the evidence, *Child Abuse & Neglect*, 11: 41–52.

Sebba, J., Luke, N., McNeish, D. and Rees, A. (2017) *Children's Social Care Innovation Programme, Final Evaluation Report*. London: Department for Education.

Sebba, J., Luke, N., Rees, A. and McNeish, D. (2017a) *Systemic Conditions for Innovation in Children's Social Care*. London: Department for Education.

Sebba, J., Luke, N., Rees, A. and McNeish, D. (2017b) *Informing Better Decisions Through Use of Data in Children's Social Care*. London: Department for Education.

Searing, H. (2003) The continuing relevance of casework ideas to long-term child protection work, *Child & Family Social Work*, 8: 311–20.

Sedlak, A. J. and Broadhurst, D. (1996) *Executive Summary of the Third National Incidence Study of Child Abuse and Neglect (NIS-3)*. Washington, DC: US Department of Health and Human Services, US Government Printing Office.

Sedlak, A. J., Mettenburg, J., Basena, M. et al. (2010) *Fourth National Incidence Study of Child Abuse and Neglect (NIS-4): Report to Congress, Executive Summary*. Washington, DC: US Department of Health and Human Services, Administration for Children and Families.

Seebohm, F. (1968) *Report of the Committee on Local Authority and Allied Personal Social Services*, Cmnd 3703. London: HMSO.

Seng, J. S., Low, L. K., Sperlich, M., Ronis, D. L. and Liberzon, I. (2011) Post-traumatic stress disorder, child abuse history, birthweight and gestational age: a prospective cohort study, *BJOG: An International Journal of Obstetrics and Gynaecology*, 118(11): 1329–39.

Serious Organised Crime Agency (2011) *Making Every Child Matter . . . Everywhere*. London: Child Exploitation and Online Protection Centre.

Shahar, S. (1990) *Childhood in the Middle Ages*. London: Routledge.

Shapiro, F. (2014) The role of eye movement desensitization and reprocessing (EMDR) therapy in medicine: addressing the psychological and physical symptoms stemming from adverse life experiences, *The Permanente Journal*, 18(1): 71–7.

Sharland, E., Seal, H., Croucher, M., Aldgate, J. and Jones, D. (1996) *Professional Intervention in Child Sexual Abuse*. London: HMSO.

Sharpe, J. (1984) *Crime in Early Modern England, 1550–1750*. London: Longman.

Shaw, I., Bell, M., Sinclair, I. et al. (2009) An exemplary scheme? An evaluation of the Integrated Children's System, *British Journal of Social Work*, 39(4): 613–26.

Shemmings, D. (ed.) (1999) *Involving Children in Family Support and Child Protection*. London: The Stationery Office.

Shemmings, D. (2000) Professionals' attitudes to children's participation in decision-making: dichotomous positions and doctrinal contests, *Child & Family Social Work*, 5(3): 235–44.

Shemmings, D. (2016a) Disorganised attachment in pre-school children, Special Edition of the *International Journal of Birth and Parent Nursing*, 4(1): 21–6.

Shemmings, D. (2016b) Letter to the journal *Attachment & Human Development*, 18(6): 526–8.

Shemmings, D. and Shemmings, Y. (2011) *Understanding Disorganised Attachment: Theory and Practice for Working with Children and Adults*. London: Jessica Kingsley Publications.

Shemmings, D. and Shemmings. Y. (forthcoming, 2018a) Contemporary attachment theory: how can it inform social workers?, in the *Routledge Handbook of Social Work*. Abingdon: Routledge.

Shemmings, D. and Shemmings, Y. (forthcoming, 2018b) Emotional and behavioural development: the importance of attachment, in J. Howarth and D. Platt (eds) *The Child's World*. London: Jessica Kingsley Publications.

Shemmings, D., Shemmings, Y. and Cook, A. (2012) Gaining the trust of 'highly resistant' families: insights from attachment theory and research, *Child & Family Social Work*, 17(2): 130–7.

Sheppard, M. (2003) The significance of past abuse to current intervention strategies with depressed mothers in child and family care, *British Journal of Social Work*, 33: 769–86.

Sherr, L., Mueller, J. and Fox, Z. (2009) Abandoned babies in the UK: a review utilizing media reports, *Childcare, Health and Development*, 35(3): 419–30.

Shin, S. H., Edwards, E. M. and Heeren, T. (2009) Child abuse and neglect: relations to adolescent binge drinking in the National Longitudinal Study of Adolescent Health (AddHealth) Study, *Addictive Behaviors*, 34: 277–80.

Shin, S. H., Lee, S., Jeon, S.-M. and Wills, T. A. (2015) Childhood emotional abuse, negative emotion-driven impulsivity, and alcohol use in young adulthood, *Child Abuse & Neglect*, 50: 94–103.

Shorter, E. (1976) *The Making of the Modern Family*. London: Collins.

Sidebotham, P., Brandon, M., Bailey, S. et al. (2016) *Pathways to Harm, Pathways to Protection: A Triennial Analysis of Serious Case Reviews 2011 to 2014. Final Report*. London: Department for Education.

Sidebotham, P. and Heron, J. (2006) Child maltreatment in the 'Children of the Nineties': a cohort study of risk factors, *Child Abuse & Neglect*, 30: 497–522.

Silva, R. R., Alpert, M., Munoz, D. M. and Singh, S. (2000) Stress and vulnerability to posttraumatic stress disorder in children and adolescents, *American Journal of Psychiatry*, 157(8): 1229–35.

Silverstein, L. (1996) Fathering is a feminist issue, *Psychology of Women Quarterly*, 20(1): 3–37.

Silverstein, M., Augustyn, M., Young, R. and Zuckerman, B. (2009) The relationship between maternal depression, in-home violence and use of physical punishment: what is the role of child behaviour?, *Archives of Disease in Childhood*, 94: 138–43.

Simmel, C. and Shpiegel, S. (2013) Describing the context and nature of emotional maltreatment reports in children, *Children and Youth Services Review*, 35: 626–33.

Simone, T.R., Shattuck, A., Kacha-Ochana, A. et al. (2018) Injuries from physical abuse: national survey of children's exposure to violence I–II, *American Journal of Preventative Medicine*, 54(1): 129–32.

Simons, D., Wurtele, S. and Durham, R. (2008) Developmental experiences of child sexual abusers and rapists, *Child Abuse & Neglect*, 32: 549–60.

Sinclair, I. and Gibbs, I. (1998) *Children's Homes: A Study in Diversity*. Chichester: Wiley.

Skinner, A. (1992) *Another Kind of Home: A Review of Residential Child Care*. Edinburgh: HMSO.

Skinner, B. (1953) *Science and Human Behaviour*. Basingstoke: Collier Macmillan.

Slack, K., Berger, L., DuMont, K. et al. (2011) Risk and protective factors for child neglect during early childhood: a cross-study comparison, *Children and Youth Services Review*, 33: 1354–63.

Slayter, E. (2016) Youth with disabilities in the United States Child Welfare System, *Children and Youth Services Review*, 64: 155–65.

Smart, S., Neale, B. and Wade, A. (2001) *The Changing Experience of Childhood: Families and Divorce*. Cambridge: Polity Press.

Smith, G., Sylva, K., Smith, T., Sammons, P. and Omonigho, A. (2018) Stop, start: survival, decline or closure? Children's Centres in England, 2018. Available at: https://www.suttontrust.com/wp-content/uploads/2018/04/StopStart-FINAL.pdf.

Smith, J. and Rachman, S. (1984) Non-accidental injury to children II: a controlled evaluation of a behavioural management programme, *Behaviour Research and Therapy*, 22: 349–66.

Smith, M. and Prader, L. (1980) *Michelle Remembers*. New York: Congdon & Lattes.

Social Services Inspectorate (1999) *Inspection of Services to Support Disabled Adults in their Parenting Role*. Bristol: Department of Health.

Social Services Inspectorate, Wales, and Social Information Systems (1991) *Accommodating Children: A Review of Children's Homes in Wales*. Cardiff: Welsh Office.

Social Work Task Force (2009) *Building a Safe, Confident Future*. London: DH/DCSF.

Social Work Task Force (2010) *Building a Safe and Confident Future: One Year On – Detailed Proposals from the Social Work Reform Board*. London: DfE.

Sommerville, J. (1982) *The Rise and Fall of Childhood*. Beverly Hills, CA: Sage.

Spangler, G. and Zimmermann, P. (2007) Genetic contribution to attachment and temperament, paper presented at the biennial meeting of the Society for Research in Child Development, Boston, MA, 29 March–1 April.

Sparks, J. and Duncan, B. (2004) The ethics and science of medicating children, *Ethical Human Psychology and Psychiatry*, 6: 25–39.

Spencer, J. (1989) *Suffer the Child*. New York: Simon & Schuster.

Spratt, T. (2001) The influence of child protection orientation on child welfare practice, *British Journal of Social Work*, 31: 933–54.

Spratt, T. and Callan, J. (2004) Parents' views on social work interventions in child welfare cases, *British Journal of Social Work*, 34: 199–224.

Sroufe, L. A., Egeland, B., Carlson, W. and Collins, A. (2009) *The Development of the Person: The Minnesota Study of Risk and Adaptation from Birth to Adulthood*. New York: Guilford Press.

Staffordshire County Council (1991) *The Pindown Experience and the Protection of Children: The Report of the Staffordshire Child Care Inquiry 1990*. Stafford: Staffordshire County Council.

Stalker, K., Taylor, J., Fry, D. and Stewart, A. (2015) A study of disabled children and child protection in Scotland – A hidden group?, *Children and Youth Services Review*, 56: 126–34.

Stanley, N., Miller, P., Richardson Foster, H. and Thomson, G. (2010) *Children and Families Experiencing Domestic Violence: Police and Children's Social Service's Response*. London: NSPCC.

Stanley, N., Penhale, B., Riordan, D., Barbour, S. and Holden, S. (2003) *Child Protection and Mental Health Services: Inter-professional Responses to the Needs of Mothers*. Bristol: Polity Press.

Stark, E. (2007) *Coercive Control: The Entrapment of Women in Personal Life*. New York: Oxford University Press.

Stark, E. (2009) *Coercive Control: How Men Entrap Women in Personal Life*. Oxford: Oxford University Press.

Statham, J. and Holtermann, S. (2004) Families on the brink: the effectiveness of family support services, *Child & Family Social Work*, 9: 153–66.

Steele, B. (1986) Notes on the lasting effects of early child abuse throughout the life cycle, *Child Abuse & Neglect*, 10: 283–91.

Steele, B. and Pollock, C. (1974) A psychiatric study of parents who abuse infants and small children, in R. Heifer and C. Kempe (eds) *The Battered Child*, 2nd edn. Chicago, IL: University of Chicago Press.

Steen, K. and Hunskaar, S. (2004) Gender and physical violence, *Social Science and Medicine*, 59: 567–71.

Stephenson, P. (1997) *The Causes of Institutionalisation in Romania*. Bucharest: UNICEF.

Stevenson, J. and Cook, C. (1977) *The Slump: Society and Politics During the Depression*. London: Jonathan Cape.

Stevenson, O. (1998) *Neglected Children: Issues and Dilemmas*. Oxford: Blackwell.

Stevenson, O. (2007) *Neglected Children and Their Families*. Oxford: Blackwell.

Stickley, A., Koyanagi, A., Koposov, R., Razvodovsky, Y. and Ruchkin, V. (2013) Adolescent binge drinking and risky health behaviours: findings from northern Russia, *Drug and Alcohol Dependence*, 133(3): 838–44.

Stith, S., Ting Liu, L., Davies, C. et al. (2009) Risk factors in child maltreatment: a meta-analytic review of the literature, *Aggression and Violent Behaviour*, 14: 13–29.

Stoltenborgh, M., Bakermans-Kranenburg, M., Lenneke, R. A. A., van Ijzendoom, M. H. and Alink, L. R. A. (2013a) Cultural-geographical differences in the occurrence of child physical abuse? A meta-analysis of global prevalence, *International Journal of Psychology*, 48(2): 81–94.

Stoltenborgh, M., Bakermans-Kranenburg, M., Lenneke, R. A. A. and van Ijzendoom, M. H. (2015) The prevalence of child maltreatment across the globe: review of a series of meta-analyses, *Child Abuse Review*, 24: 37–50.

Stoltenborgh, M., Bakermans-Kranenburg, M. J. and van Ijzendoorn, M. H. (2013b) The neglect of child neglect: a meta-analytic review of the prevalence of neglect, *Social Psychiatry and Psychiatric Epidemiology*, 48(3): 345–55.

Stone, L. (1977) *The Family, Sex and Marriage in England, 1500–1800*. London: Weidenfeld & Nicolson.

Stop It Now (2007) *Do Children Sexually Abuse Other Children? Preventing Sexual Abuse Among Children and Youth*. Brandon, VT: Safer Society Press.

Stop the Traffik (2018) Available at: www.stopthetraffik.org.

Straus, M. (1979) Family patterns and child abuse in a nationally representative sample, *Child Abuse & Neglect*, 3: 213–25.

Straus, M. (1994) *Beating the Devil Out of Them: Corporal Punishment in American Families*. New York: Lexington Books.

Straus, M. and Gelles, R. (1986) Societal change and change in family violence from 1975 to 1985 as revealed by two national surveys, *Journal of Marriage and the Family*, 48: 465–79.

Straus, M. and Kantor, G. (2005) Definition and measurement of neglectful behavior: some principles and guidelines, *Child Abuse & Neglect*, 29: 19–29.

Sullivan, J., Beech, A., Craig, L. and Gannon, T. (2011) Comparing intra-familial and extra-familial child sexual abusers with professionals who have sexually abused children with whom they work, *International Journal of Offender Therapy and Comparative Criminology*, 55: 56–74.

Sullivan, P. and Knutson, J. (2000a) Maltreatment and disabilities: a population-based epidemiological study, *Child Abuse & Neglect*, 23: 1257–73.

Sullivan, P. and Knutson, J. (2000b) The prevalence of disabilities and maltreatment among runaway children, *Child Abuse & Neglect*, 23: 1275–88.

Swann, S. (1998) *Whose Daughter Next?* Essex: Barnardo's.

Swanston, H., Plunkett, A., O'Toole, B. et al. (2003) Nine years after child sexual abuse, *Child Abuse & Neglect*, 27: 967–84.

Tajima, E. A., Herrenkohl, T. I., Moylan, C. A. and Derr, A. S. (2011) Moderating the effects of childhood exposure to intimate partner violence: the roles of parenting characteristics and adolescent peer support, *Journal of Research on Adolescence*, 21(2): 376–94.

Testa, M., Hoffman, J. and Livingston, J. (2011) Intergenerational transmission of sexual victimization vulnerability as medicated via parenting, *Child Abuse & Neglect*, 35: 363–71.

The China Post (2010) Reports of child abuse increasing significantly. Available at: http://www.chinapost.com.tw/taiwan/national/national-news/2010/04/03/250970/Reports-of.htm.

Thoburn, J., Lewis, A. and Shemmings, D. (1995) *Paternalism or Partnership? Family Involvement in the Child Protection Process*. London: HMSO.

Thoburn, J., Wilding, J. and Watson, J. (2000) *Family Support in Cases of Emotional Maltreatment and Neglect*. London: The Stationery Office.

Thyen, U., Thiessen, R. and Heisohn-Krug, M. (1995) Secondary prevention: serving families at risk, *Child Abuse & Neglect*, 19: 1337–47.

Tickell, C. (2011) *The Early Years: Foundations for Life, Health and Learning*. Available at: http://www.education.gov.uk/tickellreview.

Tisdall, E. K. M. and Plumtree, A. (1997) The Children Act 1989 and the Children (Scotland) Act 1995: a comparative look, *Adoption and Fostering*, 21(3): 14–22.

Tiurukanova, E. and the Institute for Urban Economics (2006) *Human Trafficking in the Russian Federation: Inventory and Analysis of the Current Situation and Responses*. Moscow: UNICEF/ILO/CIDA.

Tomak, S., Weschler, F., Ghahramanlou-Holloway, M., Virden, T. and Nademin, M. (2009) An empirical study of the personality characteristics of internet sex offenders, *Journal of Sexual Aggression*, 15: 139–48.

Tooley, G. A., Karakis, M., Stokes, M. and Ozannesmith, J. (2006) Generalising the Cinderella effect to unintentional childhood fatalities, *Evolution and Human Behavior*, 27: 224–30.

Toth, S., Cicchetti, D., Macfie, J. and Emde, R. (1997) Representations of self and other in the narratives of neglected, physically abused and sexually abused pre-schoolers, *Development and Psychopathology*, 9(4): 781–96.

Trickey, D. and Black, D. (2009) Child trauma, in M. Gelder, N. Andreasen, J. Lopez-Ibor, Jr. and J. R. Geddes (eds) *New Oxford Textbook of Psychiatry*, 2nd edn. Oxford: Oxford University Press.

Troncoso, P. (2017) *Analysing Repeated Referrals to Children's Services in England*. London: Department for Education.

Tunstill, J. and Aldgate, J. (2000) *Services for Children in Need: From Policy to Practice*. London: The Stationery Office.

Tupper, A. et al. (2016) Decision-making in children's social care: quantitative data analysis. Available at: http://38r8om2xjhhl25mw24492dir-wpengine.netdna-ssl.com/wp-content/uploads/2016/07/Social_Worker_Decision_Making__BIT.pdf.

Turic, D., Swanson, J. and Sonuga-Barke, E. (2010) DRD4 and DAT1 in ADHD: functional neurobiology to pharmacogenetics, *Pharmacogenomics and Personalized Medicine*, 3: 61–78.

Turnell, A. (2009) *Of Houses, Wizards and Fairies: Involving Children in Child Protection Casework*. Perth: Resolutions Consultancy.

UNICEF (2008) *Handbook on Legislative Reform: Realising Children's Rights*. New York: UNICEF.

UNICEF (2011) *The State of the World's Children*. New York: UNICEF.

UNICEF (2017) *Identify. Protect. Repeat*. London: UNICEF.

UNICEF (2018) *Facts about War and Conflict*. London: UNICEF.

United Nations (2000) *Protocol to Prevent, Suppress and Punish Trafficking Persons, Especially Women and Children, Supplementing the UN Convention Against Transnational Organisational Crime*. New York: Office of the United Nations High Commissioner for Human Rights.

US Department of Health and Human Services, Administration on Children, Youth and Families (2007a, 2008, 2009) *Child Maltreatment 2005, 2006, 2007*. Washington, DC: US Government Printing Office.

US Department of Health and Human Services, Administration on Children, Youth and Families (2007b) *National Child Abuse and Neglect Data System*. Washington, DC: US Government Printing Office.

US Department of Health and Human Services (2017) *Child Maltreatment 2016*. Washington, DC: Department of Health and Human Services.

Utting, D., Monteiro, H. and Ghate, D. (2007) *Interventions for Children at Risk of Developing Antisocial Personality Disorder*. London: PRB/Department of Health/Cabinet Office.

Utting, Sir W. (1991) *Children in the Public Care: A Review of Residential Child Care*. London: HMSO.

Utting, Sir W. (1997) *People Like Us: The Report of the Review of the Safeguards for Children Living Away from Home*. London: HMSO.

Veltman, M. W. and Browne, K. D. (2001) Three decades of child maltreatment research: implications for the school years, *Trauma, Violence, and Abuse*, 2(3): 215–39.

Verduyn, C. and Calam, R. (1999) Cognitive behavioral interventions with maltreated children and adolescents, *Child Abuse & Neglect*, 23: 197–207.

Vinchon, M., Defoort-Dhellemmes, S., Desurmont, M. and Dhellemmes, P. (2005) Accidental and non-accidental head injuries in infants: a prospective study, *Journal of Neurosurgery*, 102: 380–4.

Viner, R. M., Roche, E., Maguire, S. A. and Nicholls, D. A. (2010) Childhood protection and obesity: framework for practice, *British Medical Journal*, 341, DOI: https://doi.org/10.1136/bmj.c3074.

Wald, M. (1982) State intervention on behalf of endangered children: a proposed legal response, *Child Abuse & Neglect*, 6: 3–45.

Wardhaugh, J. and Wilding, P. (1993) Towards an explanation of the corruption of care, *Critical Social Policy*, 37: 4–31.

Warner, J. (2012) *The Emotional Politics of Social Work and Child Protection*. Bristol: Policy Press.

Warner, N. (1992) *Choosing with Care: The Report of the Committee of Inquiry into the Selection, Development and Management of Staff in Children's Homes*. London: HMSO.

Wastell, D., Peckover, S., White, S. et al. (2011) Work in the laboratory: using microworlds for practice research, *British Journal of Social Work*, 41: 744–60.

Wastell, D. and White, S. (2017) *Blinded by Science: The Social Implications of Epigenetics and Neuroscience*. Bristol: Policy Press.

Waterhouse, Sir R. (2000) *Lost in Care: The Report of the Tribunal of Inquiry into the Abuse of Children in Care in the Former County Council Areas of Gwynedd and Clwyd since 1974*, HC 201. London: The Stationery Office.

Webb, E., Maddocks, A. and Bongilli, J. (2002) Effectively protecting black and minority children from harm: overcoming barriers to the child protection process, *Child Abuse Review*, 11: 394–410.

Webster-Stratton, C. and Reid, J. M. (2005) *Adapting the Incredible Years Child Dinosaur: Social, Emotional, and Problem-solving Intervention to Address Co-morbid Diagnoses and Family Risk Factors*. Seattle, WA: University of Washington.

Wellbourne, P. (2002) Videotaped evidence of children: application and implications of the *Memorandum of Good Practice*, *British Journal of Social Work*, 32: 553–71.

West, A. (2005) *Hubs and Centres for Developing Children's Participation and Child Protection in China*. Beijing: Save the Children.

Westcott, H. and Kynan, S. (2006) Interviewer practice in investigative interviews for suspected child sexual abuse, *Psychology, Crime and Law*, 12: 367–82.

Westcott, H., Kynan, S. and Few, C. (2006) Improving the quality of investigative interviews for suspected child abuse: a case study, *Psychology, Crime and Law*, 12: 77–96.

Westcott, H. and Page, M. (2002) Cross-examination, sexual abuse and child witness identity, *Child Abuse Review*, 11: 137–52.

Whitaker, D., Le, B., Hanson, K. et al. (2008) Risk factors for the perpetration of child sexual abuse: a review and meta-analysis, *Child Abuse & Neglect*, 32: 529–48.

White, I. and Hart, K. (1995) *Report of the Management of Child Care in the London Borough of Islington*. London: London Borough of Islington.

White, S. (1997) Beyond retroduction? Hermeneutics, reflexivity and social work practice, *British Journal of Social Work*, 27(5): 739–53.

White, S., Hall, C. and Peckover, S. (2009) The descriptive tyranny of the Common Assessment Framework: technologies of categorisation and professional practice in child welfare, *British Journal of Social Work*, 39(7): 1197–217.

White, S., Wastell, D. G., Broadhurst, K. and Hall, C. (2010) When policy o'erleaps itself: the tragic tale of the Integrated Children's System, *Critical Social Policy*, 30(3): 405–29.

Whitmore, E., Kramer, J. and Knutson, J. (1993) The association between punitive childhood experiences and hyperactivity, *Child Abuse & Neglect*, 17: 357–66.

Whittaker, A. (2018) How do child protection practitioners make decisions in real-life situations? Lessons from the psychology of decision making, *British Journal of Social Work*, 48(7): 1967–84.

Widom, C. (2000) Childhood victimization: early adversity, later psychopathology, *National Institute of Justice Journal*. Available at: www.communitycare.co.uk/Articles/2007/10/31/106309/research-children-with-antisocial-personality-disorders.htm.

Widom, C., Raphael, K. and Dumont, K. (2004) The case for prospective longitudinal studies in child maltreatment research: commentary on Dube, Williamson, Thompson, Felitti and Anda (2004), *Child Abuse & Neglect*, 28: 715–22.

Wiedemann, T. (1989) *Adults and Children in the Roman Empire*. London: Routledge.

Wiehe, V. (1989) Child abuse: an ecological perspective, *Early Child Development and Care*, 42: 141–5.

Wiehe, V. (1991) *Perilous Rivalry: When Siblings Become Abusive*. San Francisco, CA: Lexington Books.

Wilkins, D., Lynch, A. and Antonopoulou, V. (2018) A golden thread? The relationship between supervision, practice and family engagement in child and family social work, *Child & Family Social Work*, 23(3): 494–503.

Wilkinson, R. and Pickett, K. (2010) *The Spirit Level*. London: Penguin.

Wilhoit, L. F., Scott, D. A. and Simecka, B. A. (2017) Fetal alcohol spectrum disorders: characteristics, complications, and treatment, *Community Mental Health Journal*, 53(6): 711–71.

Wilson, S. (1984) The myth of motherhood: the historical view of European child rearing, *Social History*, 9: 181–98.

Wohl, A. (1978) Sex and the single room: incest among the Victorian working classes, in A. Wohl (ed.) *The Victorian Family*. London: Croom Helm.

Wolak, J., Finkelhor, D., Mitchell, D. and Jones, L. (2011) Arrests for child pornography production: data at two time points from a national sample of US law enforcement agencies, *Child Maltreatment*, 16: 184–95.

Wolfe, D. (1985) Child-abusive parents: an empirical review and analysis, *Psychological Bulletin*, 97: 462–82.

Wolock, L. and Horowitz, B. (1984) Child maltreatment as a social problem: the neglect of neglect, *American Journal of Orthopsychiatry*, 54: 530–43.

Woodhead, M. and Montgomery, H. (2003) *Understanding Childhood: An Interdisciplinary Approach.* Chichester: Wiley.

Wu, Y. and Qi, D. (2016) The breadth and depth of multidimensional child poverty in China, *International Journal of Social Welfare*, 25: 373–87.

Yelloly, M. (1980) *Social Work Theory and Psychoanalysis.* New York: Van Nostrand Reinhold.

Zagrodney, J. L. and Cummings, J. A. (2017) Qualitatively understanding mother fault after childhood sexual abuse, *Journal of Interpersonal Violence*, 25(8): 827–45.

Zanoni, L., Warburton, W., Bussey, K. and McMaugh, A. (2014) Are all fathers in child protection families uncommitted, uninvolved and unable to change?, *Children and Youth Services Review*, 41: 83–94.

Index